Transdisciplinary
Play-Based
Assessment

TPBA | *Play-Based* | TPBI

TPBC

Other products available in the [TPBA] [Play-Based] [TPBI] / [TPBC] system include:

• *Transdisciplinary Play-Based Intervention: Guidelines for Developing a Meaningful Curriculum for Young Children,* by Toni W. Linder, Ed.D.

• *Transdisciplinary Play-Based Assessment and Intervention: Child and Program Summary Forms,* by Toni W. Linder, Ed.D.
shrink-wrapped package of 5 complete pads, each including all key forms of the *TPBA* and *TPBI* manuals:

> • Instructions to All Forms and Child/Family Identification Sheet (1 page)
> • Cognitive Observation Worksheet (8 pages) and Summary Sheet (2 pages)
> • Social-Emotional Observation Worksheet (8 pages) and Summary Sheet (2 pages)
> • Communication and Language Observation Worksheet (10 pages) and Summary Sheet (2 pages)
> • Sensorimotor Observation Worksheet (8 pages) and Summary Sheet (2 pages)
> • Cumulative Summary Sheet (1 page)
> • Team Ideas for Play (TIP)/Team Assessment of Play (TAP) Sheet (4 pages)
> • Play-Based Curriculum Planning Sheet: Infant/Toddler (1 page)
> • Play-Based Curriculum Planning Sheet: Preschool/Kindergarten (2 pages)

• *And You Thought They Were Just Playing: Transdisciplinary Play-Based Assessment* (videotape), produced and written by Toni W. Linder, Ed.D.
65-minute VHS videocassette

• *Observing Kassandra: A Transdisciplinary Play-Based Assessment of a Child with Severe Disabilities* (videotape), produced and written by Toni W. Linder, Ed.D.
50-minute VHS videocassette accompanied by companion workbook and one tablet of *Child and Program Summary Forms*

• *Read, Play, and Learn!: Storybook Activities for Young Children*
by Toni W. Linder, Ed.D., with invited contributors
a transdisciplinary play-based curriculum that includes a *Teacher's Guide* and individual manuals of lesson plans based on popular children's storybooks, packaged in modules of 8 as *Collection 1* and *Collection 2*

Collection 1 modules based on the following stories: *The Kissing Hand,* by Audrey Penn; *Somebody and the Three Blairs,* by Marilyn Tolhurst; *Picking Apples & Pumpkins,* by Amy and Richard Hutchings; *The Little Old Lady Who Was Not Afraid of Anything,* by Linda Williams; *The Knight and the Dragon,* by Tomie dePaola; *Abiyoyo,* by Pete Seeger; *Night Tree,* by Eve Bunting; *The Snowy Day,* by Ezra Jack Keats.

Collection 2 modules based on the following stories: *A Porcupine Named Fluffy,* by Helen Lester; *First Flight,* by David McPhail; *Friends,* by Helme Heine; *The Three Billy Goats Gruff,* by Janet Stevens; *The Three Little Javelinas,* by Susan Lowell; *Franklin Has a Sleepover,* by Paulette Bourgeois & Brenda Clark; *The Rainbow Fish,* by Marcus Pfister.

Visit www.readplaylearn.com for excerpts, sample materials, and more information about *Read, Play, and Learn*!

To order, contact Brookes Publishing Co.:
  by phone: 800-638-3775
            410-337-9580 (outside the U.S.A.)
  by fax: 410-337-9585
  by web: www.brookespublishing.com
  by mail: P.O. Box 10624, Baltimore, MD 21285-0624, U.S.A.

Transdisciplinary
Play-Based
Assessment

A Functional Approach to Working with Young Children

·REVISED EDITION·

by

Toni W. Linder, Ed.D.
Professor
School of Education
University of Denver
Denver, Colorado

with invited contributors

·P A U L ·H·
BROOKES
PUBLISHING C⁰

Baltimore • London • Toronto • Sydney

Paul H. Brookes Publishing Co.
P.O. Box 10624
Baltimore, Maryland 21285-0624

www.brookespublishing.com

Typeset by Brushwood Graphics, Inc., Baltimore, Maryland.
Manufactured in the United States of America by
Sheridan Books, Chelsea, Michigan

The photograph on the back cover of the author and her son was
taken by J. Fred Katzman.

Second printing, November 1994.
Third printing, August 1996.
Fourth printing, October 1997.
Fifth printing, January 1999.
Sixth printing, August 2001.

For companion products to *Transdisciplinary Play-Based
Assessment*, including *Transdisciplinary Play-Based Intervention*
and *Read, Play, and Learn!* (the *Transdisciplinary Play-Based
Curriculum*), see p. ii. Visit www.brookespublishing.com and
www.readplaylearn.com for more information.

Library of Congress Cataloging-in-Publication Data

Linder, Toni W., 1946–
  Transdisciplinary play-based assessment : a functional approach to working with young chil-
dren / Toni W. Linder ; with invited contributors.—Rev. ed.
      p.   cm.
  Previously pub. : Baltimore : P.H. Brookes, 1990.
  Includes bibliographical references and index.
  ISBN 1-55766-162-6
  1. Transdisciplinary Play-Based Assessment.   I. Title.
RJ51.T73L56   1993
618.92′0075—dc20   93-28981
                                                                    CIP

British Library Cataloguing-in-Publication data are available from the British Library.

Contents

About the Author

Toni W. Linder, Ed.D., is Professor and Graduate Coordinator for the College of Education at the University of Denver, Colorado. Dr. Linder also directs the Early Childhood Special Education and the Child and Family Studies programs at the University. Her background includes teaching and administration of programs for children with disabilities and children who are at risk for developmental concerns. She is the author of numerous articles and two other books, *Early Childhood Special Education: Program Development and Administration* (Paul H. Brookes Publishing Co., 1983) and *Transdisciplinary Play-Based Intervention: Guidelines for Developing a Meaningful Curriculum for Young Children* (Paul H. Brookes Publishing Co., 1993). Dr. Linder consults nationally on issues relating to young children and their families.

Also contributing to this volume:

Kim Dickson, M.A., C.C.C., speech-language pathologist, has worked with infants and preschool children with disabilities for over 10 years. She is also endorsed to teach early childhood special education classes. Ms. Dickson is currently teaching in San Francisco, California.

Susan Hall, M.A., P.T., has served as the Program Director at the United Cerebral Palsy Association in Denver, Colorado. She is currently in private practice and is an adjunct instructor in the Early Childhood Special Education Program at the University of Denver, Colorado.

Paula Hudson, Ph.D., C.C.C., is Assistant Research Professor at the University of Colorado at Denver. She is directing a federal grant entitled "Teacher I: Family Focus in Special Education." In addition, she manages the Special Services Budget for the Colorado Department of Health: Handicapped Children's Program.

The transdisciplinary play-based assessment Observation Guidelines contained in this volume were developed by Toni W. Linder, Susan Hall, Kim Dickson, and Paula Hudson.

Foreword

All parents lament the time their child failed to demonstrate a new or desired behavior: silence at the pediatrician's office when asked if the child talks yet, noncompliance when the new song was to be sung for company visiting the home, tears and tantrums when the psychologist asked the child to "come play a game with these toys." This frustration is shared by the professional whose job is to screen or assess a youngster. While the child's failure to comply and perform may be perfectly understandable in a new and unfamiliar situation, often few opportunities are available for a comprehensive assessment of the child's development. The professional's inability to get an adequate or accurate view of the child's behavior will seriously limit the assessment process and subsequent planning.

The transdisciplinary play-based assessment (TPBA) model may go a long way toward reducing these difficulties, because it capitalizes on what children like to do and do best—play. Children are observed engaged in tasks and activities that are more meaningful and enjoyable to them than is the case under more traditional testing situations. Furthermore, the TPBA model places emphasis on a team approach to assessment. This approach actively involves the child's parent(s) and includes all relevant members of the assessment team working together in a collaborative effort.

A number of advantages are likely for all the participants in the assessment process. For the child, the situation is likely to be less threatening and more engaging. Therefore, the child will be more likely to demonstrate the full range of behaviors in his or her repertoire. For the parent, the assessment procedure is likely to be more meaningful and less frustrating. The child is observed in activities that more closely parallel those activities that occur daily in home and play situations, and the parent can actively participate. For the professional team members, this process is an opportunity to look at the child together and share information and observations. Such planned, collaborative efforts not only contribute to team building, but also expand the range and type of information that can be gathered. When team members have the opportunity to try different approaches to gleaning information, discuss observations, and examine the child jointly, more meaningful assessment and instructional plans are likely to emerge from the process.

The transdisciplinary play-based assessment model shows great promise for use in early intervention/early childhood special education settings, where parents are actively involved and professionals from a wide range of disciplines work together. The process enables both individualization for each child and a comprehensive look at the "whole child" through the collective observation. These issues are critical to the assessment of young children with special needs. As the author indicates, like the weavers in the parable, the transdisciplinary team, by sharing knowledge and interweaving skills, can create an image of the child that contains "sumptuous colors, luxurious texture, lavish detail, and a story" (p. *x*) that is meaningful to all.

Marci J. Hanson, Ph.D.
Professor, Department of Special Education
San Francisco State University

Preface
to the Revised Edition

In the 3 years since this book was originally published, the author has had the opportunity to present the transdisciplinary play-based assessment model around the United States and to interact with thousands of teachers, therapists, and parents. The author has learned much from these dialogues about what is needed in the field of early intervention. She has been gratified by the tremendous support for the shift in paradigm that has led to widespread adoption of a play-based approach to working with young children. Throughout the country, support for the TPBA model has consistently been followed by a request for a transdisciplinary play-based intervention model.

The companion to *Transdisciplinary Play-Based Assessment* was written in response to this request. *Transdisciplinary Play-Based Intervention: Guidelines for Developing a Meaningful Curriculum for Young Children* (Paul H. Brookes Publishing Co., 1993) allows persons to make the link from assessment to intervention using results obtained from a TPBA session. A model was developed that can be used with infants, toddlers, preschoolers, and kindergartners in a variety of types of programs. The TPBI model allows practitioners to conduct ongoing transdisciplinary play-based assessment updates in the home and school, thus ensuring the most current and relevant program for the child and family. Contributors to *Transdisciplinary Play-Based Intervention* include Anita C. Bundy, Sc.D., O.T.R., a nationally recognized expert in using play in motor intervention; Sandy Patrick, M.S., CCC-SLP, a speech-language pathologist with extensive experience with children who are at risk and children who have disabilities; Carol Lay, Ed.D., a private therapist with expertise in working with young children with emotional issues; Jane C. O'Brien, M.S.O.T., O.T.R., a professional who has extensive clinical experience working with children who have motor delays and deficits.

The development of TPBI in conjunction with input from those who have used TPBA led to the modification of certain aspects of *Transdisciplinary Play-Based Assesssment*. These modifications are reflected here in this revised edition published in conjunction with the release of *Transdisciplinary Play-Based Intervention*. Terminology (e.g., the word *disability* replaces *handicap, things I'm ready for* replaces *need*) has been updated, and forms have been modified to respond to users' requests for clarification of Observation Worksheets and Summary Sheets. The worksheets are now more detailed to enable quicker, more comprehensive note-taking. A separate packet of forms, *Transdisciplinary Play-Based Assessment and Intervention: Child and Program Summary Forms* (Paul H. Brookes Publishing Co.,1993a), for both assessment and intervention is also now available to supplement the texts. (See p. *ii* for ordering information.) This revised edition also now reflects the connection to the transdisciplinary play-based intervention process where appropriate. In addition, revisions were made in this edition to reflect changes from PL 99-457 (the Education of the Handicapped Act Amendments of 1986) to PL 102-119 (the Individuals with Disabilities Education Act Amendments of 1991); however, no attempt has been made to include citations from the literature since 1990 although there has certainly been much exciting new work in the past 3 years.

Toni W. Linder
1993

Preface

The transdisciplinary play-based assessment (TPBA) process is a natural, functional approach to assessment. Developed to enable a team to create an accurate, intricate, dynamic portrait of a child, TPBA allows cross-disciplinary analysis of development level, learning style, interaction patterns, and other relevant behaviors. The assessment process is implemented in order to determine the eligibility of a child for services, ascertain developmental functioning, and define appropriate intervention or curriculum strategies.

The transdisciplinary play-based assessment model evolved through many encounters with children, families, and colleagues. These experiences elucidated the importance of a developmental, functional, integrated approach to assessing children. Concurrently, two parallel tracks were developing in the literature. First, separate professional disciplines were adding to the knowledge base related to child development; and second, the research on the importance of play in children's development was building. In the early 1980s, various play scales also began to appear in the literature.

The excursion that has culminated in this book began many years ago. In 1984, the author visited John and Elizabeth Newson at the University of Nottingham in England. Their use of play observations with children who had disabilities resulted in practical, meaningful descriptions of children. Upon returning to the United States, the author organized a team of interested graduate students, and work on transdisciplinary play-based assessment began. The original assessment guidelines (Linder, Hall, & Dickson, 1985) have been modified over the years. As the guidelines have evolved, the team has come to embrace the concept of TPBA with the sincere conviction that the model provides an accurate, functional, and worthwhile appraisal of the child's skills and learning processes.

Most powerful, however, were the author's observations of the reactions of children and their parents to the process as it was implemented. Children who were previously deemed untestable played and interacted comfortably in the play-based assessment. Parents who had been unhappy with a long string of previous assessments lavished praise on the team conducting the assessment. During training sessions in front of up to a hundred people, children were so engrossed in their play interactions, they were oblivious to the people watching them.

Children and their parents were not the only persons intrigued by the process. After initial hesitation concerning role release, colleagues have also responded positively to the model. Many have been amazed at the amount of information that can be obtained about a child's abilities and learning style. As the team worked with the model and received feedback from others who used the model, they became convinced that the transdisciplinary model is an exceedingly powerful method for looking at children's development.

For the author, who watched and was involved in these transformations, a sense of maturation and insight has occurred. Prior to involvement in the development of the play-based model, the author had achieved a level of comfort with the knowledge base and intervention approaches available to children with disabilities and their families. Feedback from these same children and families, however, led to a growing awareness that much was lacking in both professional knowledge and skill.

At first, when testing was unsuccessful or strategies for intervention resulted in less-than-anticipated results, reasons were easily identified. The child was untestable. The family would not follow through on suggestions. The child's behavior prohibited the use of specific techniques. The family was too dysfunctional. The child was too dysfunctional. The list of justifications was endless.

From a range of disciplines, assessment of the child had been looked at from distinct points of view. All of these vantage points are valid, but a child is a complex organism, and often our separate views have resulted in fragmented representation of a child that only slightly resembles the complicated, intriguing person known to the family.

A Parable

Many years ago, there existed four excellent weavers who, each in their own artist's studio, had developed a unique approach to weaving. Starting with different colors of thread, distinct styles of weaving, disparate subject matter, and varying degrees of detail, each thought the art of the other weavers was lacking something. One thought the colors used by the others were too dull. Another thought the style of the other artists was dated. A third thought the subject matter of the other tapestries was pedestrian. The fourth thought the needlework of the others lacked detail. But a patron saw the work of the four and thought each was wonderful. He commissioned the artists and offered them fame and fortune, under one condition—that they find a way to combine the unique aspects of their art into a unified whole. The artists, wanting fame and needing fortune, agreed. They spent many long days arguing about the virtues of their various approaches to their art. Each effort started with an artist in a separate corner of the tapestry working toward the middle. The end result, with four different corners, always looked disastrous. One day they fell to the ground in exhaustion and lay there surveying their work. Finally, the first weaver asked, "How *do* you get those colors?" The second told him, and they all listened and learned. The second weaver queried of the first, "How do you get such depth and texture?" The first weaver told him, and they all listened and learned. The third weaver questioned the fourth, and as the fourth told them, they all listened and learned. The fourth weaver inquired of the third, "What method do you use to instill such detail?" The third weaver told them and they all listened and learned. With renewed enthusiasm the four began anew. The synergistic effect achieved by intermingling their talents and skills in a cooperative, noncompetitive effort was marvelous. The sumptuous colors, the luxurious texture, the lavish detail, and the imaginative story told by the tapestry immediately won the praise of all who beheld it. The four became a medieval sensation whose work was celebrated far and wide.

Just as the weavers could not create the whole fabric alone, small cracks appeared in this author's professional armor, as individual children and families demonstrated the necessity for a different approach. A mother of a child with autism had been labeled by previous staff as "pushy," "overbearing," "unrealistic," and "unreliable." She claimed that her nonverbal child, who did nothing in school all day but wander, was able to put together a 50-piece puzzle, sign 200 words, and sequence letters in the alphabet. The team was skeptical, but went to her home and videotaped her working with her child. Her child did indeed do everything she said he did—in his own home.

A child with motor impairments who had been deemed mentally retarded on a standardized intelligence test was found in a play session to be able to direct the facilitator's play through a sequence of dramatic play events using her eyes and vocalizations. Her conceptualization of dramatic play was found to be at age level. The significance of the play approach was underscored for the family and the team.

Transdisciplinary play-based sessions provided information on the child's developmental skills and learning style, and not only translated into objectives for the child, but also elucidated intervention strategies for the teams that worked with the child. The child-centered approach to assessment provided a direct link to child-centered approaches to intervention. Writing functional objectives became an easier task. As a result of the families' involvement in the assessment, they felt less intimidated by the program planning process, their verbal contribution was greater, and the plans that were developed integrated home and school. The partnership between parents and the intervention team was initiated on a solid basis of equal contribution and commitment.

We, as parents and professionals serving young children, have been the weavers. As a model for TPBA evolved, the author found it necessary to learn as much as possible about all the various disciplines involved with children and families. This has become an ongoing task, one that will not end with the publication of this book. This personal transformation reflects a larger trend that is evident in early childhood special education. Much can be learned from reading cross-disciplinary research and observing colleagues.

Evolution is an unending process. The transdisciplinary play-based assessment model will continue to evolve. The team who has developed the model, and others who adopt it will undoubtedly adapt, expand, delete, and in many other ways modify the present model. That is as it should be. Models should be adapted to conform to needs. As presented, the TPBA results in a detailed, meaningful description of a child that can be used to generate an IEP or an IFSP and provides guidance related to appropriate intervention techniques.

Toni W. Linder
1990

REFERENCES

Linder, T.W. (1993a). *Transdisciplinary play-based assessment and intervention: Child and program summary forms.* Baltimore: Paul H. Brookes Publishing Co.

Linder, T.W. (1993b). *Transdisciplinary play-based intervention: Guidelines for developing a meaningful curriculum for young children.* Baltimore: Paul H. Brookes Publishing Co.

Linder, T.W., Hall, S., & Dickson, K. (1985). *Transdisciplinary play-based assessment.* Unpublished document. Denver, CO: University of Denver.

Acknowledgments

Transdisciplinary Play-Based Assessment* has evolved over the course of several years and, consequently, has involved the assistance of many people. My gratitude goes to graduate students Susan Hadlock, Karen Riley, Kim Dickson, and Susan Hall who became excited about the process and volunteered many hours in conceptualizing, researching, and field testing the original model.

I must extend special thanks to Susan Hall, who has continued to work on the development of the sensorimotor guidelines, has directed field work, and has conducted training and research. She has remained a mainstay of the changing transdisciplinary team. Kim Dickson and Paula Hudson co-authored the language and communication guidelines and chapter, and deserve credit for their enthusiastic support and contribution to the final model.

Nancy Graham, Philippa Campbell, and especially Gordon Williamson provided valuable input on the sensorimotor guidelines and chapter. Their contribution has strengthened the book.

I would also like to thank Kari Shanks, Catherine Kelly, Heather Scott, and Denise Carrico for their research and editing assistance. Special thanks to my friends Carol Bliss, Carol Lay, and Michael Abramovitz who spent many hours reviewing and editing sections of the manuscript, and to my stepdaughter Lisa, for her typing assistance in the final phase of editing.

My husband Fred provided continuous love and support. He assumed far more parenting responsibility for our infant son Adam than he had anticipated, and I thank him for grumbling infrequently.

Of course, the development of the TPBA model would not have been possible without the cooperation of the many children and families who have been involved in the process over the years. We have learned from each family and recognize the importance of their contribution to the transdisciplinary play-based assessment process. They are valuable members of the team.

I would also like to acknowledge the teams at Sewell Rehabilitation Center, Laradon Hall, the United Cerebral Palsy Association, and Hope Center for their assistance. I would like to thank the staff, parents, and children at the United Cerebral Palsy Association for enabling us to photograph the transdisciplinary play-based assessment process. Special credit goes to Dave Brown for his photographic expertise.

Those of us who have worked on the development of the TPBA process are hopeful that these efforts will result in a more functional, responsive, humane approach to assessment of young children. This book serves as one step toward making services to children and families more child- and family-focused.

To Dad,
who has always been there for me,
to Fred,
who makes sure I laugh every day,
and
to Adam,
whose birth delayed the completion
of this book, but whose presence
brought life to these pages.

Transdisciplinary
Play-Based
Assessment

TPBA	*Play-Based*	TPBI
	TPBC	

1

Introduction

Transdisciplinary play-based assessment (TPBA) involves the child in structured and unstructured play situations with, at varying times, a facilitating adult, the parent(s), and another child or children. Designed for children functioning between infancy and 6 years of age, TPBA provides an opportunity for developmental observations of cognitive, social-emotional, communication and language, and sensorimotor domains.

WHAT IS TRANSDISCIPLINARY PLAY-BASED ASSESSMENT?

The TPBA model is developmental, transciplinary, holistic, and dynamic. Flexibility in the structure allows content, participants, and sequences of events to be changed, depending on the needs of the individual child being evaluated. The model examines the child's developmental skills and, equally important, underlying developmental processes, learning style, and interaction patterns.

TPBA is implemented by a team. The team, consisting of the parents and representatives of disciplines who are knowledgeable about all areas of development, observes the child for an hour to an hour and a half during play activities with a play facilitator, the parents, and a peer. Developmental level, learning style, interaction patterns, and other relevant behaviors are analyzed based on the TPBA guidelines. Communication between the parents and other team members, prior to and during the assessment, is the key to ongoing dialogue that will continue throughout the child's involvement in an intervention program.

The content of assessment, the team members involved, the structure of the play session, and the questions asked and answered will vary depending on the individual child being evaluated. TPBA will be unique for every child. The process is dynamic and ongoing, changing in response to the needs of the participants—the child, family, and professionals. The results, in the form of a report and program plan for the child and family, are also individualized. The total process, or certain aspects of the process, may be repeated as necessary to update the child's program plan.

WHY USE TPBA?

Transciplinary play-based assessment is a natural, functional approach to assessment and intervention. Parents are actively involved throughout the process. The model is less stressful for the child, less intimidating to the family, and results in meaningful information that

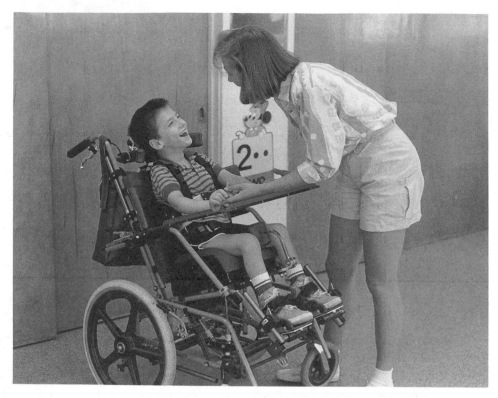

Transdisciplinary play-based assessment is a dynamic process that can be adapted to meet the needs of the individual child.

readily translates into objectives and strategies for intervention. Programs that do not require norm-based assessment instruments for placement may instead use TPBA to document that the child is not functioning at age level or needs intervention to improve quality of
performance.

   As a multidimensional approach to assessing young children, TPBA also meets legislative and professional requirements while addressing the diverse needs of children and their
families (Brooks-Gunn & Lewis, 1981; Fewell, 1983; Neisworth & Bagnato, 1988; Simeonsson, 1986). TPBA can be used as the basis for IEP or IFSP development (see Chapters 5 &
11). However, the TPBA model is not intended to respond to all assessment requirements.
Depending on state requirements, agency policy, and child and family needs, the process
serves multiple purposes. Combined with other child and family assessment techniques,
TPBA functions as the infrastructure for the total assessment process.

To Identify Service Needs

Summary information from TPBA can help identify areas of concern in the domains of
cognitive, social-emotional, communication and language, and sensorimotor development.
Specific guidelines are provided for each of these areas. Problems or limitations are recognized through the use of age ranges (that accompany the guidelines) on skill items and
professional judgment on traits and subjective behaviors. Examination of the child's performance in categories of each domain can assist the team in ascertaining the type and amount
of services needed.

To Develop Intervention Plans

In TPBA, detailed information is obtained about the child's functioning in several different situations, with several different people. The team also has data on skill level, learning style, interaction patterns, underlying processes, and other specific behaviors. This information is used to develop individualized family service plans (IFSPs) or individualized education programs (IEPs) that are developmental, process-oriented, functional, and meaningful to both parents and the intervention team.

To Evaluate Progress

The TPBA process may be incorporated into both formative (ongoing) and summative (year-end) evaluations. Federal legislation mandates yearly reviews for IEPs and semiannual reviews for IFSPs. Individual programs may require more frequent updates. The child will be involved in play sessions throughout the year. These sessions, conducted within the intervention program, will allow the team to record progress and modify the child's individual objectives. The team may repeat the TPBA process at the end of the year for pre- or post-evaluation.

WHO CAN BE ASSESSED?

The process can be used with all children who are developmentally functioning between infancy and 6 years of age. The approach can be used with children who do not have disabilities, are at-risk, or have disabilities to obtain developmental information for the generation of educational or therapeutic programs.

WHO CAN CONDUCT A TPBA?

The assessment process can be used by any number and combination of professionals in conjunction with parents. Parents, of course, are an integral part of TPBA. Because the TPBA guidelines address cognitive, social-emotional, speech-language, and motor development, the involvement of professionals or paraprofessionals with expertise in these areas is important, but anyone with knowledge of child development can participate. TPBA allows for a nontechnical approach so that nonspecialized personnel and parents can understand and utilize the information.

Functioning as a team, parents and professionals are able to share information and broaden their knowledge base concerning developmental issues.

HOW ARE PARENTS INVOLVED?

Parents are involved in the TPBA process prior to, during, and after the play session. Before the session, parents complete developmental checklists that identify their child's level of performance at home. During the session, parents observe and participate in the play. After the play sessions, parents are involved in the discussion of their child's performance and in planning an appropriate program for their child and family.

WHERE IS THE TPBA CONDUCTED?

TPBA can be conducted in any creative play environment. Usually a preschool or infant intervention room is used, as these settings are already arranged with materials to encourage play. All areas of development are observed, so the environment needs to include toys and materials to facilitate exploratory, manipulative, and problem-solving behaviors, emotional expression, and language skills. The child's home can also be the site for the TPBA. Toys and materials within the home may be supplemented by others brought in by the team.

WHAT DOES THE TPBA PROCESS INVOLVE?

TPBA is both an assessment and an intervention process. The approach is initiated by gathering information from the parents concerning the developmental status of the child. This information is then used to plan a play session, the content and sequence of which are structured to provide observation of the child across developmental domains (see Chapter 4). Toys and materials that are appropriate to the child's level are arranged to entice the child to play using various play strategies and developmental skills. One team member facilitates the child's play to encourage the expression of optimal abilities.

TPBA is divided into phases that may be shifted as required to meet the developmental, emotional, or behavioral needs of the child. The parents enter the session with the child and stay with him or her until he or she is comfortable with the play facilitator. A parent facilitator then observes and discusses the session with the parents. The play facilitator begins Phase I with unstructured facilitation, during which the child leads the play and the play facilitator imitates, models, and expands the child's play. Structured facilitation, during Phase II, is provided to incorporate aspects of play that the child did not spontaneously initiate. A peer is introduced in Phase III to enable observation of child–child interaction. During Phase IV, the parents are observed playing with the child in unstructured and structured play. The parents are also asked to leave the room to permit the team to observe separation and reunion behaviors. Phase V includes unstructured and structured motor play. The final Phase (VI) of the TPBA is a snack, which allows the team to screen for oral motor difficulties and conduct other developmental observations.

Videotaping the play session is strongly recommended. Videotape analysis and comparison of summary data will allow documentation of progress over the course of the year. Videotapes also serves as a graphic illustration of the child's progress for parents and staff.

The TPBA guidelines provide a structure for observation of cognitive, social-emotional, communication and language, and sensorimotor development. The guidelines are divided into categories and are primarily stated in the form of questions. Questions encourage the team members to address qualitative aspects of "how" the child performs, not just "if" the child performs a task. Each set of guidelines is accompanied by worksheets and age ranges for that particular domain. The sample worksheets provided in the text are designed to assist team members in noting specific behaviors associated with categories listed in the guidelines while observing the play session. They also serve as a means of organizing the observational data for later analysis. Full-size worksheets are included in a separate packet of assessment and intervention forms available from Paul H. Brookes Publishing Co. (Linder, 1993a). The age ranges within each chapter permit team members to document developmental skill levels for specific milestones. TPBA thus produces quantitative data on ability levels as well as qualitative descriptive information about the child's performance.

After the play session, seven steps are followed (see Chapter 5) to take the team from the observations gathered from the TPBA guidelines to a program plan for the child. Following a post-session meeting (Step 1), videotape analysis (Step 2), and a guideline review (Step 3), the child's strengths, rating of abilities and justification for the rating, and corresponding areas of program readiness are organized on Summary Sheets (Step 4). Interdisciplinary recommendations can then be developed (Step 5) and a program planning meeting can be convened (Step 6), where an IEP or IFSP is developed with the parents. Program planning will then lead to a formal report (Step 7), and other measures such as an IEP or IFSP, as appropriate. New forms discussed in *Transdisciplinary Play-Based Intervention* (Linder, 1993b) enable the team to generate Team Ideas for Play (TIP) Sheets that will link program objectives to home intervention and the classroom curriculum. TPBA's design is in accord with the requirements of PL 102-119, and can serve as the basis for ongoing review and evaluation of the success of intervention.

Helping the teacher and other team members then plan further for a transdisciplinary play-based classroom curriculum is *Read, Play, and Learn! Storybook Activities for Young Children* (Linder, 1999a, 1999b, 1999c). This third component of the transdisciplinary play-based system extends the individualized planning of TPBA and TPBI into group settings with a storybook-based curriculum that supports cognitive, sensorimotor, communication and language, social-emotional, and literacy skill development.

DO DATA SUPPORT TPBA AS RELIABLE AND VALID?

TPBA is a promising method for assessing the developmental competencies of young children. It has received growing recognition across the United States as an alternative assessment technique to traditional standardized testing. In light of this, it has become increasingly important that information about TPBA's reliability and validity be available. Such information about these psychometric properties is critical to support the use of TPBA in making program and curriculum decisions for young children.

Recently, preliminary data have been presented as part of the ongoing research on TPBA (Friedli, 1994). This initial study, summarized here, was conducted to examine TPBA's quantitative and qualitative properties. Specifically, this study looked at the validity of TPBA in terms of content and concurrent validity. Reliability was tested in both test–retest and interrater conditions. This study sets the foundation for the methodology and provides preliminary results in support of the reliability and validity of TPBA for a holistic assessment of young children's development.

The content validity of TPBA, specifically addressing the developmental guidelines and procedures, was supported by the professional judgments of early childhood experts, including school psychologists, educators, and speech-language and motor therapists. These experts rated the developmental domains and subcategories for relevance, clarity, and comprehensiveness. All of the developmental domains were judged favorably by both users and nonusers. Some suggestions were offered to improve the comprehensiveness and ease of interpretation for a few subcategories. Many of these have been addressed by the expanded Observation Worksheets provided in this revised edition.

The concurrent validity of TPBA was measured by comparing the outcomes of play-based assessment to traditional standardized and norm-referenced testing for children with and without disabilities. TPBA was found to be as accurate as traditional testing in identifying and determining whether a child was eligible for special services.

Reliability is a critical component of an assessment procedure. It ensures that the procedure provides stable results across time and raters. TPBA was well supported in both test–retest and interrater conditions. In this study, a group of children was assessed with TPBA at two separate points in time (up to 6 weeks apart). At both times, the TPBA profiles for the children revealed similar outcomes. This result indicates that TPBA can be used to assess the underlying developmental competencies of young children, despite differences in their play performance and specific setting during the assessments.

The interrater reliability of TPBA was also well supported. In this study, videotaped TPBA sessions were viewed and rated by several independent raters. The results revealed that the reliability for the language, motor, and combined domains met the strictest criteria for tests used to make service eligibility decisions. The cognitive and social-emotional domains met the reliability criteria for tests used to make decisions about individual education program decisions. The agreement on these two domains was slightly less on several subcategories. This appeared to be an artifact of the research methods, which relied on videotaped observations. Of special interest was the finding that professionals across disciplines were as accurate in rating the developmental competence of the children as experts in their own fields.

In conclusion, the study described above provided much needed support and information on the reliability and validity of TPBA. This is critical in making important decisions about children's educational and therapeutic goals. Both the reliability and validity of TPBA, when used as described in this volume, meet the highest criteria needed for tests used to make service eligibility decisions. These preliminary data revealed that TPBA can be as accurate, and in some cases is more sensitive, in identifying children with developmental delays and in specifying significant areas for intervention, than traditional testing procedures. Moreover, this study supports the use of professional judgment when using the TPBA guidelines as an accurate basis for assessing children's development. Furthermore, it was found that professionals can make judgments across developmental domains, which is the basis of the transdisciplinary model.

REFERENCES

Brooks-Gunn, J., & Lewis, M. (1981). Assessing young handicapped children: Issues and solutions. *Journal of the Division of Early Childhood, 2,* 84–85.

Fewell, R.R. (1983). New directions in the assessment of young handicapped children. In C.R. Reynolds & J.H. Clark (Eds.), *Assessment and programming for young children with low incidence handicaps* (pp. 1–41). New York: Plenum.

Friedli, C. (1994). *Transdisciplinary play-based assessment: A study of reliability and validity.* Unpublished doctoral dissertation, University of Colorado at Boulder.

Linder, T.W. (1993a). *Transdisciplinary play-based assessment and intervention: Child and program summary forms.* Baltimore: Paul H. Brookes Publishing Co.

Linder, T.W. (1993b). *Transdisciplinary play-based intervention: Guidelines for developing a meaningful curriculum for young children.* Baltimore: Paul H. Brookes Publishing Co.

Linder, T.W. (1999a). *Read, Play, and Learn!: Storybook activities for young children. Collection 1.* Baltimore: Paul H. Brookes Publishing Co.

Linder, T.W. (1999b). *Read, Play, and Learn!: Storybook activities for young children. Collection 2.* Baltimore: Paul H. Brookes Publishing Co.

Linder, T.W. (1999c). *Read, Play, and Learn!: Storybook activities for young children. Teacher's guide.* Baltimore: Paul H. Brookes Publishing Co.

Neisworth, J.T., & Bagnato, S.J. (1988). Assessment in early childhood special education: A typology of dependent measures. In S.L. Odom & M.B. Karnes (Eds.), *Early intervention for infants and children with handicaps* (pp. 23–49). Baltimore: Paul H. Brookes Publishing Co.

Simeonsson, R.J. (1986). *Psychology and developmental assessment of special children.* Boston: Allyn & Bacon.

I

Rationale for TPBA

The transdisciplinary play-based assessment process is enjoyable for the parent and child.

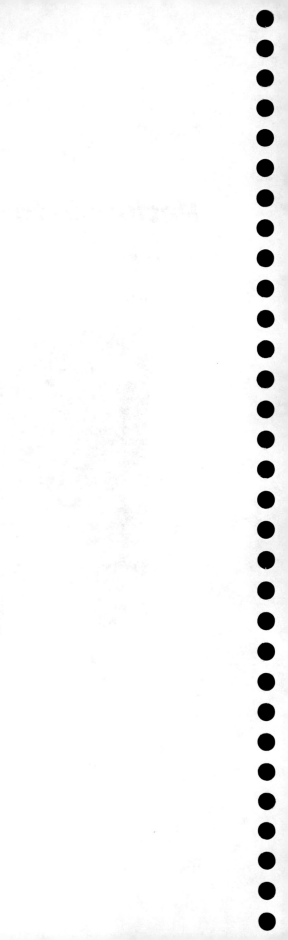

2

Traditional Assessment and Transdisciplinary Play-Based Assessment

A Comparison

$\mathbf{T}$he unique contributions of transdisciplinary play-based assessment are perhaps best understood when compared to traditional assessment procedures.

TRADITIONAL ASSESSMENT

Imagine yourself as a 3-year-old child who has been referred to a developmental center for evaluation because of suspected developmental delays. Both your mother and father have come with you to a place called "the Center."

When you walk in the door, a woman meets you and takes you to her office. You sit on your mom's lap while the woman behind the desk asks your mom and dad questions about your birth and your first 3 years of life. Your mom and dad sound worried and your mom even cries when she talks about you. You feel sad and think that something about you must be making her cry.

After a while, another woman comes to take you to "play some games." Your mom and dad tell you to go with the "nice lady" and it will be fun. The nice lady takes your hand. You walk with her down a hall to a small room with a table and two wooden chairs and some pictures on the wall. You don't see any games anywhere. Then the lady pulls out a suitcase and starts to put things like blocks and puzzles in front of you. She then asks you to do certain things with them. At first this is fun, but after a while the lady asks you to do some things that are not so much fun. It's hard. You tell her this, but she just keeps putting things that are not fun in front of you. She also asks you questions that you can't answer. You want to go back to your mommy and daddy, but the lady keeps saying that you'll be finished soon. "Soon" is a long time. Finally, the lady says that you're all done playing games. You feel relieved! This lady doesn't know much about how to have fun!

After a necessary potty break and a few tears, the lady lets you see your mommy and daddy. But not for long. Here comes another lady to take you to another little room with another table and chairs and different pictures on the wall. This lady doesn't talk much. She just keeps putting pictures in front of you and asking you what they are. Many of the pictures are things that you have seen, but you just don't know what to call them. So you look down at the floor and up at the pictures on the wall. You pull on your shirt and wiggle a lot. You wish this lady would quit with the pictures. You've seen more than enough pictures. Then the lady gets out another suitcase, only it's a different color. She pulls out a couple of toys at a time and tells you what she wants you to do with them. Some of these are neat toys and you'd really like to play with them. Every time you start to do something other than what the lady told you to do, however, she takes the toys away. This lady sure is stingy. You are getting tired, so you put your head down on the table. The lady makes you sit up. Finally, she is through. She takes you back to your mommy and daddy and tells them that you were "somewhat resistant."

Mom and Dad look worried, so when they ask, you tell them you had fun playing games with the ladies. That was a mistake. In the car they tell you that you are coming back tomorrow to play some more games. When you tell them you don't want to go back, you didn't like the ladies, they say that tomorrow you will play with a different nice lady.

Wrong. The next day a man comes out to meet you. He says you are going to play some more fun games. You are not convinced. This time you go to a big room with many stairs and boards that wobble and boards that don't wobble and hanging nets and balls and all kinds of neat stuff. You think that maybe this will be fun! You run and jump and climb the stairs and are generally having a great time. Then the man puts you up on a big ball and tries to make you fall off. At least that's how it feels, though the man keeps saying he won't let you fall. You don't trust him. You want your mommy and daddy, so you cry. Then the man makes your arms and legs go different directions and bounces you around some. This doesn't seem fun anymore. The man is nice enough, he just doesn't know when to stop! You cry louder, and finally the man says, "We've had enough for today." He's right about that.

You go back to your mommy and daddy who are still sitting with that worried look on their faces. They tell you that they will take you to get a hamburger for being so good. You don't tell them that you really weren't that good. They don't need to know everything.

Disadvantages of Traditional Assessment

The previous scenario may seem a bit exaggerated, but in reality much of what professionals do in assessing young children, particularly young children with disabilities, is not pleasant. The child's optimal performance is not promoted. In many cases, the information gathered may lead to inaccurate conclusions concerning the child's abilities and overall developmental level. The traditional assessment process may not give the best picture of the child for a variety of reasons.

Unnatural Environment   The traditional environment in which the child has been commonly tested is an office. In most cases, this is an unfamiliar sterile environment that is not appealing to a child. This environment has been used because it is important for standardized testing to be conducted in a nondistracting environment. The child must focus on the test materials, since only the standardized items on the test are scored; if the child is distracted by more interesting materials, test results may be influenced. And when the child is tested in a stimulating environment full of toys, the child is usually restricted to playing with these materials only at established times. The child may play with the toys in the room before testing, to establish "rapport," or after testing, as a reward for good behavior, but for a greater part of the time the child must interact with prescribed test materials.

Unfamiliar Examiner   Traditionally, adults who are unfamiliar to the child have often conducted the assessment. Although they attempt to establish rapport with the child through informal play, they must then direct the child through structured activities. The child is placed in a continual response mode; in other words, the child never initiates, only responds to the questions and demands of the examiner. Behaviors observed under these circumstances may be very different from those behaviors that the child initiates. Language, for example, may be more restricted in a testing situation than in a natural situation where children are initiating and talking about their interests.

Biased Tests   Many tests are biased against the child who is unable to demonstrate what he or she knows due to physical, emotional, sensory, or other impairments (Brooks-Gunn & Lewis, 1981; Garwood, 1982; Zelazo, 1982). Results from such tests may inaccurately demonstrate the child's level of functioning.

For example, most psychological tests for young children include items that call for the child to manipulate objects. Children are asked to stack blocks, place pieces in a form board, and put together puzzles. A child with motor impairments is often unable to accurately perform these tasks. However, whether this inability means that the child is unable to comprehend the task, does not have the visual/spatial abilities needed to complete the task, or does not have the cognitive abilities to see the relational or part-to-whole concepts is not indicated by traditional testing. As most psychological tests, however, claim to measure intellectual functioning, the child's inability to perform these tasks is viewed as a cognitive deficit. This is a particular problem for children with subtle motor problems; a test with more appropriate performance expectations would be administered to the child with severe motor impairments. For the child whose motor difficulties may not be obvious to the untrained eye, the motor impairment may affect the total score, erroneously indicating a cognitive deficit.

Many tests are biased against the largest group of children referred for evaluation: those with language delays or impairments. As with the child with motor impairment, the child with a language deficit may seem to have a cognitive deficit when assessed by traditional measures. Most tests for young children are heavily weighted with items requiring comprehension and/or oral expression of language. The child who is not expressive or is unintelligible is therefore penalized in the cognitive evaluation as well.

Because developmental domains are interrelated (Linder, 1983; Neisworth & Bagnato, 1988), a perceived deficit in one area may mask a deficit in another area. Many tests are designed to evaluate one area of development, and results can be easily misinterpreted by the specialist who is unfamiliar with the child's abilities in other areas of development. For example, a child with emotional problems may exhibit noncompliant behavior during the structured testing, and language patterns may appear bizarre or severely delayed. The scores derived from traditional assessment often distort the child's abilities.

Structure of Instruments   Most assessment instruments for young children presume an invariable sequence of development, and deviations due to disabling conditions are not taken into account (Johnson, 1982; Sheehan, 1982). The child with disabilities may not acquire skills in the same sequence as the child who does not have disabilities. In addition, many norm-referenced instruments, or instruments where the child's performance is compared to the performance of the norming sample, are additive in nature. Each item is equally weighted toward the child's total score, creating a situation that is unfavorable for a child with disabilities, who may have deficits that make some items invalid in that child's assessment. As each item is weighted equally, the overall performance score may not reflect his or her individual strengths and weaknesses (Sheehan, 1982).

Criterion-referenced instruments are tests containing lists of skills that the child may be expected to perform at different ages. Criterion-referenced tests, unlike norm-referenced tests, compare the child's performance to a criterion for passing an item. The child's performance is not compared to others. Items commonly derived from various norm-referenced instruments and a review of the literature are frequently used to determine the child's individual objectives. Many of these items are of questionable importance to the program of a child with disabilities (Garwood, 1982). For example, the item "stands on one foot for 10 seconds" does not assess the motor components necessary to perform this skill and, therefore, may be an inappropriate objective.

Both norm-referenced and criterion-referenced instruments may have large age increments between items. For children with developmental problems, widely spaced items may not allow for identification of their specific ability levels. Professionals working with the children then find it difficult to select appropriate intervention targets. Posttesting after intervention using the same instruments may also be problematic, as children may show negligible change on such scales (Bricker, 1986; Garwood, 1982).

Lack of Process Information   Most traditional procedures result in information about specific skills that are present or lacking. They also provide numbers relating the child's performance to other children of his or her age. For example, the numbers may give the child's score or ranking, plus or minus a standard error of measurement. The score may reveal how many standard deviations above or below the mean the child is functioning, and there may be a profile of strengths and weaknesses on individual subtests.

However, information is lacking about the child's learning style or strengths and weaknesses in underlying developmental processes that lead to the development of various skills (Zelazo, 1982). For example, children acquire much of their information about the world through imitation, trial and error problem-solving, and organizing and structuring their world. Most tests provide little or no information about the child's ability to use such underlying processes in the acquisition and expression of his or her skills.

Returning to the previous example, a child may be unable to stand on one foot for 10 seconds. Nothing is known, however, about the child's muscle tone, stability, protective reactions, equilibrium responses, righting reactions, or weight shifting—all developmental processes that are necessary for a child to stand on one foot for any length of time. Intervention that focuses on the skill without addressing the underlying process is working on an isolated objective. Intervention time is better spent developing processes that enable the child not only to stand on one foot for 10 seconds, but also to complete other motor skills involving balance.

Lack of Functional Assessment   Many tests also do not address the issue of greatest significance to parents, the child's ability to perform functional skills. "Stacking five blocks" is important as a motor and cognitive milestone, but the skill is not particularly useful in the parents' life with the child at home. More relevant to the parents and the child is the "generic" goal of functional use of objects (McLean, Snyder-McLean, Jacobs, & Rowland, 1981; Vincent, Laten, Salisbury, Brown, & Baumgart, 1980). Combing hair or using a spoon and a cup, for example, are more functional skills. As a child acquires an understanding of the relations of objects (spoons can go in cups), he or she will also acquire the more conventional assessment targets (blocks can be stacked). *Functional assessment,* assessment of skills the child needs on a regular basis, is more meaningful to parents and ultimately to the child's intervention program (Bailey & Wolery, 1984; Guess et al., 1978).

Lack of Other Information   Traditional assessment instruments provide little information on other areas that seem to be related to child success. Three areas that have been shown to hold promise for future assessment are characteristics of temperament, mastery motivation, and interaction patterns.

Characteristics of Temperament

Temperament has been shown to affect interrelationships (Kagan, 1988; Keogh, 1982b), teacher expectations (Keogh, 1982a; Pullis & Cadwell, 1985; Thomas & Chess, 1977; Thomas, Chess, & Birch, 1968), and behavior (Kagan, 1988; Keogh, 1982b, Keogh & Burstein, 1988). Temperament scales are available (Carey & McDevitt, 1977; Fullard, McDevitt, & Carey, 1978; McDevitt & Carey, 1975), but these are infrequently incorporated into traditional assessments. Temperament characteristics are obtained by interviewing parents or observing the child. Information gained about temperament characteristics may help staff to anticipate different aspects of the child's behavior, and staff may then plan to handle difficult situations before they arise. Temperament scales may also provide a means for looking at strengths that will support learning.

Mastery Motivation   Mastery motivation (Emde, Gaensbauer, & Harmon, 1981; Harter, 1978; Morgan & Harmon, 1984; White, 1959) has also gained attention in the literature. The child's drive to master or understand his or her environment appears to be a critical factor in developmental growth. The desire to understand and control the environment leads the child to experiment, problem-solve, and ultimately to integrate new knowledge into his or her existing knowledge base. Traditional assessments do not examine this aspect of the child's cognitive and emotional system.

Interaction Patterns   Interaction patterns have come under scrutiny as well. Studies on the success and problems of adults with disabilities (Wilcox & Bellamy, 1982; Wolfensberger, 1972), as well as studies on parent–child interaction (Hanson, 1984; Rosenberg & Robinson, 1988) and peer interaction (Strain & Kohler, 1988), have led researchers to place more importance on the child's interaction patterns. Children capable of initiating and maintaining positive interactions with parents, peers, and others are more likely to grow into adults who have rewarding social interactions. Social skills appear to be a crucial factor in the successful integration of an individual with disabilities into society (Certo, Haring, & York, 1984; Guralnick, 1976; Rule et al., 1987). Typically, the traditional assessment process does not address the strengths and weaknesses of the interaction patterns of the child.

Inappropriate Tests   Children with severe disabilities are often labeled "untestable" when norm-referenced tests are used, meaning that the child was unable to perform the tasks on the test due to behavior problems or a disabling condition. Children with severe emotional disturbances, children with autism, and children with multiple disabilities are frequently termed "untestable." In truth, the examiners failed to determine more appropriate ways to identify the child's developmental abilities.

A related problem arises when the child has severe developmental delays and the norms for a particular test do not allow the examiner to determine an appropriate basal level (lower limit) or ceiling (upper limit). In such a case, the norms tables do not cover an age span wide enough to encompass the child's skill level. On the McCarthy Scales of Children's Abilities (McCarthy, 1972), for example, a 4-year-old child who is developmentally below the age of 2½ years will not receive a specific score. The child may be given the Bayley Scales of Infant Development instead. However, the norms tables for this test do not extend to 4 years of age. The examiner must extrapolate the age equivalent of the child's score, which is not a recommended procedure. The validity of the results on either test, therefore, is questionable.

The child who is functioning between 2 and 3½ years of age may also fall in the gap between tests designed to assess infants and those designed to assess preschool-age children. Infant tests may not have an adequate ceiling while preschool tests may not have a low enough "basal." The child's developmental level, therefore, may preclude an accurate assessment using standardized measures.

Time and Cost of Assessment   The traditional assessment process usually involves the child seeing a succession of professionals. Each professional may see the child for at least an hour, depending on the testing being conducted. Interviews with the parents and observations of the child in the home or in a classroom may require more time. After each professional sees the child, separate reports are generated. A staffing, including all team members and the parents, follows. This process is time-consuming and may require the family to bring the child to the center several times over the course of a week or more. The process is also costly.

TRANSDISCIPLINARY PLAY-BASED ASSESSMENT

You are still the same 3-year-old child who has been referred for evaluation due to suspected developmental delays. As you enter the Center, you are greeted by the same woman. This time, however, she takes you to a large room containing many different toys. A playhouse is in one corner, an area with blocks and cars is in another, a table with puzzles and little toys is in another, and a water table with toys is in another.

Hey! This place is neat! Mommy is holding your hand, but you let go and run to the dollhouse area. It has a sink, refrigerator, and stove just like at home, only smaller. And it has dolls and beds and dishes and telephones. You look in the refrigerator. Suddenly you notice another lady next to you. She is telling you about what's in the refrigerator. She doesn't seem to mind that you just helped yourself to all these toys. In fact, when you pick up a doll and start to feed it, she does the same thing. She says her doll is hungry. You tell her yours is hungry too. Well, actually, all you say is "ungy," but she seems to understand. She pours more "milk" in your baby's cup. You and the lady play together in the dollhouse. Sometimes she does what you do, and sometimes you look at her and do what she does. You think she is a nice lady.

All of a sudden you remember your mommy and daddy. You look around and see them sitting there watching you. They are talking to the other lady. A man is also watching you and he has a videocamera. You say "hi" to Mommy and Daddy. The lady hands you a telephone and tells you Mommy and Daddy are on the phone. You talk to Mommy and Daddy and they say "hi" to you. Then you talk to the lady who's playing with you. The two of you have lots of fun dressing the dolls for bed, brushing their teeth, combing their hair, and putting them to bed. Every once in a while, you check to see if Mommy and Daddy are still there. They are.

A little boy comes into the dollhouse. You don't know who invited him, but he wants to play with the toys, too. The play lady says he wants to play with you. As long as he doesn't take your doll, it's okay with you. He plays with the dishes and cooks. He pours juice and gives you some. You take it, but go back to putting your doll to bed. The play lady gives the boy some dishes and he puts them on the table. He says that dinner is ready, so you go to the table with your baby. You feed your baby. The boy talks to you, but you don't answer. You just don't feel like talking to him. After a while he wanders off to play somewhere else. That's okay with you.

Then the play lady goes over to the water table with her doll and starts to wash her doll. That looks like fun, so you go too. You wash the doll for a while, then you play with the water wheel, boats, funnels, and other fun stuff. When you get tired of this, you go over to see what's in the block area. This is fun, too. You and the play lady build bridges, drive cars over a road, put gas in your cars, have a car crash, and get the cars fixed. This place sure has neat toys.

Your mommy and daddy tell you they are leaving for a few minutes. You watch them go and are a little worried, but you don't mind staying here with the play lady. After a few minutes Mommy and Daddy come back, and Daddy comes over to play with you. You drive cars and crash them off bridges and laugh. Then Mommy comes over and takes you to the table. The two of you put puzzles together. Some of them are hard and Mommy helps you.

Mommy is a good helper. Then you and Mommy and the play lady draw pictures and count and look at pictures. It's fun to have Mommy and Daddy playing, too.

When you're all done with your pictures and puzzles, the play lady takes all of you to another room with stairs, boards that wobble, boards that don't wobble, hanging nets, balls, and tricycles. You run and jump and climb up and down the stairs. The play lady throws the ball to you and your daddy and mommy. You get the play lady to follow you up and over and through things. This play lady sure is a good sport! When she looks all worn out, you give her a rest. You try to ride the tricycle but it's too hard. The play lady and your daddy toss you around in the air. She puts you on the big ball and plays a game with you about not falling off. You are scared and want to get down, but the play lady says she won't let you fall. She's been nice so far, so you trust her. Besides, Mommy and Daddy are right there, and you know they wouldn't let anyone hurt you.

After everyone is all worn out, including you, all of you go back to the playroom. There is a snack of crackers and juice in the middle of the table, and the little boy is there. The play lady lets you pour the juice and put peanut butter on the crackers. You give some to the boy and take some for yourself. You try to give some to Mommy and Daddy, but they don't seem too interested. The play lady talks to you and the boy. You ask the boy if he wants more. He seems to be a pretty nice boy after all.

After you're all done eating and drinking, the play lady says it's time to go. You are tired, but you'd still like to play with those cars some more. The play lady says maybe another day. That sounds good to you. How about tomorrow?

Advantages of Transdisciplinary Play-Based Assessment

As you can see, there are numerous differences between the first and second scenarios. The following discussion addresses some of the characteristics and major advantages of transdisciplinary play-based assessment (TPBA).

Natural Environment   TPBA is conducted in an environment that is conducive to eliciting the child's highest skill level. A natural environment, in which the child feels comfortable, is best (Neisworth & Bagnato, 1988). The TPBA team has a better opportunity to hear a child's typical language usage in his or her natural environment. Traditional testing environments tend to dampen language. Language may be elicited, but it may not be qualitatively the same as language used in functional environments with familiar people.

An environment containing elements that are familiar to the child is also helpful. In the second scenario, the child was brought into a preschool classroom. The room contained toys and materials that most 3- or 4-year-olds have seen, particularly if enrolled in a child care center or preschool. Children from low socioeconomic backgrounds may not be familiar with such a setting, but will find this environment inviting. (Knowledge of the child's previous experiential background is important for interpretation of observations.) TPBA can also be conducted in the parents' home, which is appropriate for infants and toddlers. The team should bring novel toys and materials to supplement the toys found in the home, to ensure that exploratory, manipulative, and problem-solving behaviors can be elicited.

Rapport with Examiner   Although the examiners in both scenarios are unfamiliar to the child, critical differences are evident. In the first (traditional) situation, several different examiners, including a psychologist, a speech-language therapist, and a physical therapist, interact directly with the child. Each has a unique personality and way of relating to the child. Each tries to establish rapport in his or her own way, some more successfully than others. A child's lack of rapport with a professional may influence results from a particular discipline, and could influence the child's subsequent interactions with other professionals.

TPBA is conducted in a natural environment, where play encourages rapport with the examiner and spontaneous demonstration of a child's highest abilities.

However, in the scenario of the TPBA play session, there is only one facilitator (examiner) with whom the child has to relate. Other team members are present and observing, but the child, for the most part, is oblivious to their presence. It is evident that interaction with fewer professionals will be less stressful for the child.

Another difference in the two assessment examples involves the role assumed by the examiner. In the traditional model, the examiner plays the leading role. He or she presents materials to the child and requests a response, either verbal or physical. For example, the examiner might request that the child build a house with the blocks or draw a circle. The traditional examiner's role is, therefore, a directive one. The child is a follower. In the TPBA model, the facilitator follows the child's lead, and the child is in the directive role. The facilitator imitates, models, suggests, and only rarely requests. For example, if the child chooses to play in the house area first, then that is where the play begins. If the child chooses to dump and fill with a toy truck, the facilitator does the same. The facilitator might then introduce a spoon to see if the child will imitate another means of filling. More structured or directed tasks are saved until the child has established a level of trust and comfort with the examiner.

Flexibility in Testing   Unlike standardized tests that follow a prescribed set of tasks in a standardized manner, TPBA allows different sets of materials, varying conditions, variations in language, and alteration of sequence and content—depending on the child. It can be adapted to the needs of different children and to different disabling conditions.

For children with physical disabilities, for example, toys with switches can be incorporated, and puzzles and materials with adaptive handles for stability can be used. Therapeutic positioning techniques may be tried in order to facilitate stability and movement. For children with visual impairments, additional visual cues may be added, such as flashlights or bright contrasting colors; in addition, tactile modifications, such as using books and puzzles with diverse textures on them, can be included.

Variations in the sequence can also be made to fit the interests and pace of the child. For a child who is having difficulty separating from his or her parents, the sequence may be varied to allow the parent to participate in the beginning of the play session. An advantage of TPBA is that all team members are involved at all times (although not directly with the child), so that changing the sequence of activities does not depend on any one member's schedule and availability.

The language used in traditional testing is also standardized. In TPBA, the opposite is true. The facilitator adapts his or her language to the level of the child. Verbalizations, gestures, signs, and eye-pointing are all accepted as meaningful communication. The facilitator can use whatever means are most successful for maintaining communication with the child.

Holistic Assessment   In TPBA, all team members observe the same behaviors at the same time. The traditional assessment process has each team member evaluating separate aspects of the child at different times, which results in a fragmented, and sometimes contradictory, view of the child's abilities and disabilities.

For example, the psychologist engaged in traditional assessment tests a 4-year-old girl and finds that she is functioning in the low average range for her age. He determines through analysis of her block building, puzzle solving, and drawing that she is delayed in spatial reasoning, body concept awareness, and manipulative skills. In traditional assessment, the speech-language therapist discovers poor syntactic and grammatical abilities, a 2-word mean length of utterance (MLU), and slightly below average receptive language understanding; the physical therapist identifies hypotonia, poor shoulder stability, and weak grasp. However, these individuals cannot report on how her cognitive, language, and motor skills are functionally interacting.

In TPBA, working as a team, these professionals might have discovered that although the child understands many concepts and can label and describe them with short utterances, she is not communicating. She is responding to questions and imitating adults' phrases, but not initiating language. They might have established a relationship between the hypotonia, poor shoulder stability, weak grasp, and inability to carry out fine motor tasks (e.g., puzzle solving and drawing). In addition, they might have seen that the child's concept of body parts, as reflected in her play, was age-appropriate. And they might have identified a lack of interactional skill with adults, parents, and peers as a major problem influencing her development in all areas.

TPBA gives the team of professionals and parents an opportunity to view the child at the same time, and then to discuss how the deficits they observed may be interrelated. Team discussion is critical, and having the same frame of reference gives everyone the same foundation and improves team communication. The jargon of other disciplines is also easier to interpret when comparisons can be made with reference to the same behaviors; in fact, jargon tends to be reduced in this team context. Reports that evolve from the TPBA reflect this transdisciplinary interpretation of how the child functionally uses his or her skills.

Involvement of the Parents   As the example demonstrated, parents both observe and participate in TPBA. This involvement can have positive benefits for the child and for the parents. The child is more secure in the new situation and can visually or verbally "check in" when he or she feels the need. (If the parents' presence is having a deleterious effect on the child's performance, the parents can be asked to wait outside or can watch through a one-way window, if available.) Benefits to the parents are also important; as part of the team, they observe and contribute to the assessment process. In addition, they participate in the play session, so they have a better understanding of specific skills that are being addressed.

In the traditional assessment process, the parents may have no idea about how their child was tested until the follow-up conference. They must wait outside the testing room until the testing is completed, or until they are interviewed in a separate room. At the conference, the parents are surrounded by professionals who report data relating to their child. Traditional assessment reports are full of jargon and numbers that supposedly describe the child's functioning. These data are meaningful to other professional team members, but are rarely meaningful to parents, who often feel intimidated by such a process (Vincent et al., 1980).

In contrast, after TPBA, parents have firsthand knowledge of what occurred during the assessment. Shared information can be framed in reference to specific behaviors the team (which includes the parents) has observed. Recommendations from a functional assessment are also more relevant to parents. The team, however, must still work to make sure that jargon does not interfere with parents' understanding of the process.

Process Information   TPBA provides information concerning the child's skills in cognitive, social-emotional, communication and language, and sensorimotor development. It also addresses the child's learning style, temperament characteristics, mastery motivation, and interaction patterns. In addition, TPBA looks at qualitative information, such as the underlying processes related to the development of skills in each area. Processes include: imitation and problem-solving in language and cognition; muscle tone, stability, and equilibrium responses in the motor domain; and initiation and turn-taking in the social-emotional area. In all areas, qualitative aspects such as frequency and response mode are also examined.

Every Child Is Testable   With the transdisciplinary play-based assessment model, all children are testable. Assessment proceeds from whatever the child is capable of doing within the play setting. As long as the child relates to objects and/or people, the team can obtain valuable information.

Helpful To Plan Intervention   As previously discussed, traditional assessment does not always result in useful recommendations for intervention. One of the most useful aspects of TPBA, however, is that it complements a functional play-based intervention approach. The information derived from TPBA is functional, process-based, and skill-oriented, and relates to the classroom and home.

An evaluation determined that Melody enjoyed and initated dramatic play. She was capable of putting together a 3-step sequence of activities with objects in relation to a doll. She poured "milk" in a cup, fed the doll, and burped it. The evaluation also found that Melody had difficulty taking turns with adults and peers. Her language was intelligible about half the time and was limited to 2-word approximations ("a o," for "want more"). Melody was able to label familiar objects, but did not attempt to imitate new words.

Program recommendations for Melody should include:

1. *Encouraging Melody's dramatic play and modeling 3-step sequences in new behaviors with the doll, in order to promote generalization (washing the doll's hair, drying it, and combing it)*
2. *Expanding her existing 3-step schemes by adding one more step (after burping the doll, putting it to bed)*
3. *Helping Melody to generalize her vocabulary by presenting variations of common objects (different shaped and colored combs, brushes, socks, etc.) every day. Also, adding one common object not presently in her expressive vocabulary each week was recommended (deciding with the parents which common objects are most relevant in her life)*

Transdisciplinary Training   This transdisciplinary staffing pattern, in which professionals from different disciplines support each other in working with the child in a holistic approach, has gained wide acceptance in recent years (Woodruff & McGonigel, 1988) and has had a philosophical impact on service delivery systems. However, most persons in early childhood special education were not trained in transdisciplinary knowledge and intervention techniques. The transition to transdisciplinary staffing patterns has frequently been accomplished without the prerequisite knowledge, understanding, and desire on the part of various team members. The result is often a team that calls itself transdisciplinary, but does not function in that capacity (Garland & Linder, 1988).

The transdisciplinary play-based assessment guidelines presented in this text offer a method for on-the-job training in all of the areas of development. The TPBA guidelines offer team members a format for exchanging knowledge and expertise. In addition, play facilitators learn how to structure situations in order to elicit desired behaviors for all developmental domains. Team discussions of observations and conclusions, using actual child data, provide another learning opportunity. And the translation of data into functional program objectives lends itself to transdisciplinary intervention planning. Thus, the TPBA model provides in-service training, secondary to its child assessment purpose.

Limitations of TPBA

Depending on the child and the needs he or she presents, TPBA may be either a partial or total evaluation. Some states require standardized testing that provides psychometric data comparing the child to other children of the same age. These data serve as documentation of a delay or confirmation of a disability such as mental retardation (which is partially defined by a range of I.Q. scores for varying levels of severity). This is to ensure that children with identifiable disabilities are served. In other states, requirements are not as rigid. Many states are even identifying the "at-risk" population (those children who are biologically or environmentally "at-risk" for developing a disability).

Where state guidelines mandate standardized testing, the transdisciplinary play-based assessment may still be part of a total evaluation. TPBA can provide information on processes and functional use of skills, involve parents in the assessment process, and provide the forum for transdisciplinary collaboration. The summary forms at the end of each set of guidelines will enable the team to identify areas of concern or those in need of further evaluation. In other states, the documentation obtained from the TPBA will be sufficient for determination of need for services.

Even if TPBA becomes the primary means of assessment, additional testing may be needed to obtain information not derived from the play session. Receptive language, for example, is difficult to ascertain in a play-based session, unless the facilitator asks the child a great number of direct questions. This technique puts the facilitator in the examiner role, which is in philosophical opposition to the TPBA approach. The integrity of the play interactions should not be challenged. Receptive language testing may be conducted at another time.

Many physical and occupational therapists like to spend additional time with a child who has motor problems to get a better "feel" for the child's muscle tone, range of motion, and so forth. If the physical or occupational therapist is also the facilitator, these aspects may be assessed during the TPBA, but further evaluation may be needed. Sensory integration is another area in which it is difficult to obtain an adequate evaluation within the TPBA format. Here, too, additional testing may be warranted.

The play-based assessment provides a brief look at parent–child interaction. The observations of informal interactions and structured interactions offer an opportunity to identify some strengths and difficulties within the parent–child dyad. If concerns are evident, further observation and assessment are warranted.

Many situations will arise in which a particular team member may want to conduct further evaluation of a child to obtain specific information. With advanced planning (and enough preliminary information about the child), however, materials may be added, or activities devised so that this specific information can be obtained within the TPBA.

The use of transdisciplinary play-based assessment within a program may vary, depending on the type of children assessed, the information needed, and the requirements of the state. It may be modified to incorporate individual team members' assessment styles.

At the time of this writing, another limitation of the TPBA model is the lack of reliability and validity data. Studies are currently underway that will address both of these issues. Until these studies are complete, persons using the model may feel comfortable that their clinical observations and professional judgment will provide valuable input into the development of intervention plans for children.

REFERENCES

Bailey, D.B., & Wolery, M. (1984). *Infants and preschoolers with handicaps.* Columbus, OH: Charles E. Merrill.

Bricker, D.D. (1986). *Early education of at-risk and handicapped infants, toddlers, and preschool children.* Glenview, IL: Scott, Foresman.

Brooks-Gunn, J., & Lewis, M. (1981). Assessing young handicapped children: Issues and solutions. *Journal of the Division of Early Childhood. 2,* 84–85.

Carey, W.B., & McDevitt, S.C. (1977). *Infant temperament questionnaire (ITQ).* Media, PA: Carey Associates.

Certo, N., Haring, N., & York, R. (Eds.). (1984). *Public school integration of severely handicapped students: Rational issues and progressive alternatives.* Baltimore: Paul H. Brookes Publishing Co.

Emde, R.N., Gaensbauer, T.J., & Harmon, R.J. (1981). Using our emotions: Some principles for appraising emotional development and intervention. In M. Lewis & L. Taft (Eds.), *Developmental disabilities in preschool children* (pp. 409–424). New York: S.P. Medical and Scientific Books.

Fullard, W., McDevitt, S., & Carey, W. (1978). *Toddler temperament scale.* Media, PA: Carey Associates.

Garland, C.W., & Linder, T.W. (1988). Administrative challenges in early intervention. In J.B. Jordon, J.J. Gallagher, P.L. Hutinger, & M.B. Karnes (Eds.), *Early childhood special education: Birth to three.* Reston, VA: Council for Exceptional Children.

Garwood, S.G. (1982). (Mis)Use of developmental scales in program evaluation. *Topics in Early Childhood Special Education, 1*(4), 61–69.

Guess, D., Horner, R., Utley, B., Holvoet, J., Maxon, D., Tucker, D., & Warren, S. (1978). A functional curriculum sequencing model for teaching severely handicapped. *AAESPH/Review, 3,* 202–215.

Guralnick, M. (1976). The value of integrating handicapped and non-handicapped preschool children. *American Journal of Orthopsychiatry, 46*(2), 236–245.

Hanson, M.J. (1984). Parent–infant interaction. In M.J. Hanson (Ed.), *Atypical infant development* (pp. 179–206). Baltimore: University Park Press.

Harter, S. (1978). Effectance motivation reconsidered: Toward a developmental model. *Human Development, 21,* 34–64.

Johnson, N.M. (1982). Assessment paradigms and atypical infants: An intervention perspective. In D.D. Bricker (Ed.), *Intervention with at-risk and handicapped infants* (pp. 129–138). Baltimore: University Park Press.

Kagan, J. (1988, August). *Temperamental contributions to social behavior.* Paper presented as a distinguished scientific award address to the American Psychological Association. Atlanta, Georgia.

Keogh, B.K. (1982a). Temperament: An individual difference of importance in intervention programs. *Topics in Early Childhood Special Education, 2*(2), 25–30.

Keogh, B.K. (1982b). Individual differences in temperament: A contributor to the personal-social and educational competence of learning disabled children. In J.D. McKinney & L. Feagens (Eds.), *Current topics in learning disabilities.* Norwood, NJ: Ablex Publishing Corp.

Keogh, B.K., & Burstein, N.D. (1988). Relationship of temperament to preschoolers' interactions with peers and teachers. *Exceptional Children, 54*(5), 456–461.

Linder, T.W. (1983). *Early childhood special education: Program development and administration.* Baltimore: Paul H. Brookes Publishing Co.

McCarthy, D. (1972). *McCarthy scales of children's ability: Manual.* Cleveland, OH: Psychological Corporation.

McDevitt, S., & Carey, W. (1975). *Behavioral style questionnaire.* Media, PA: Carey Associates.

McLean, J.E., Snyder-McLean, L., Jacobs, P., & Rowland, C.M. (1981). *Process-oriented educational programs for the severely/profoundly handicapped adolescent.* Parsons: Parsons Research Center, University of Kansas, Bureau of Child Research.

Morgan, G.A., & Harmon, R.J. (1984). Developmental transformations in mastery motivation. In R.N. Emde & R.J. Harmon (Eds.), *Continuities and discontinuities in development.* New York: Plenum.

Neisworth, J.T., & Bagnato, S.J. (1988). Assessment in early childhood special education: A typology of dependent measures. In S.L. Odom & M.B. Karnes (Eds.), *Early intervention for infants and children with handicaps: An empirical base* (pp. 23–49). Baltimore: Paul H. Brookes Publishing Co.

Pullis, M., & Cadwell, J. (1985). Temperament as a factor in the assessment of children educationally at risk. *Journal of Special Education. 19*(1), 91–102.

Rosenberg, S.A., & Robinson, C.C. (1988). Interaction of parents with their young handicapped children. In S.L. Odom & M.B. Karnes (Eds.), *Early intervention for infants and children with handicaps: An empirical base* (pp. 159–177). Baltimore: Paul H. Brookes Publishing Co.

Rule, S., Stowitschek, J.J., Innocenti, M., Striefel, S., Killoran, V., Swezey, K., & Boswell, C. (1987). The social integration program: An analysis of the effects of mainstreaming handicapped children into day care centers. *Education and Treatment of Children, 10*(2), 175–192.

Sheehan, R. (1982). Infant assessment: A review and identification of emergent trends. In D.D. Bricker (Ed.), *Intervention with at-risk and handicapped infants.* Baltimore: University Park Press.

Strain, P.S., & Kohler, F.W. (1988). Social skill intervention with young children with handicaps: Some new conceptualizations and directions. In S.L. Odom & M.B. Karnes (Eds.), *Early intervention for infants and children with handicaps: An empirical base* (pp. 129–143). Baltimore: Paul H. Brookes Publishing Co.

Thomas, A., & Chess, S. (1977). *Temperament and development.* New York: Brunner/Mazel.

Thomas, A., Chess, S., & Birch, H.G. (1968). *Temperament and behavior disorders in children.* New York: New York University Press.

Vincent, L., Laten, S., Salisbury, C., Brown, P., & Baumgart, D. (1980). Family involvement in the educational process of severely handicapped students: State of the art and directions for the future. In B. Wilcox & R. York (Eds.), *Quality education for the severely handicapped? The federal investment.* Washington, DC: U.S. Department of Education.

White, R. (1959). Motivation reconsidered: The concept of competence. *Psychological Review, 66,* 297–333.

Wilcox, B., & Bellamy, G.T. (1982). *Design of high school programs for severely handicapped students.* Baltimore: Paul H. Brookes Publishing Co.

Wolfensberger, W. (1972). *The principles of normalization in human services.* Toronto: National Institute on Mental Retardation.

Woodruff, G., & McGonigel, M.J. (1988). Early intervention team approaches: The transdisciplinary model. In J.B. Jordon, J.J. Gallagher, P.L. Hutinger, & M.B. Karnes (Eds.), *Early childhood special education: Birth to three.* Reston, VA: Council for Exceptional Children.

Zelazo, P.R. (1982). Alternative assessment procedures for handicapped infants and toddlers: Theoretical and practical issues. In D.D. Bricker (Ed.), *Intervention with at-risk and handicapped infants* (pp. 107–128). Baltimore: University Park Press.

3

Play, Assessment, and Transdisciplinary Process

Why Each Is Important

Transdisciplinary play-based assessment has not been developed in isolation from the theories and practices in the numerous fields involved in child development and early intervention. Indeed, the TPBA model draws on previous work on play assessment by Belsky and Most (1981), Calhoun and Newson (1984), Fewell (1984), McCune-Nicholich (1980), Nicholich (1977), Parten (1932), Rogers (1986a), and Westby (1980). While TPBA differs from suggestions in these writings for total number of domains and range of observations to be addressed, it does derive its philosophical basis and some of its content from these earlier works.

Research on play, assessment, and transdisciplinary approaches all lend support to the validity of the TPBA model. The TPBA model is also consistent with developments in early childhood special education since the passage of PL 94-142 (now known as IDEA, the Individuals with Disabilities Education Act, since its reauthorization in 1990 as PL 101-476).

PLAY

> Because there can be no Recreation without Delight, which depends not always on Reason, but oftener on Fancy, it must be permitted Children not only to divert themselves, but to do it after their own fashion. (John Locke)

Many of a person's most pleasant childhood memories are affiliated with youthful play. Memories of building stilts that enabled the wearer to tower over peers like a spindly giant; dressing up in fanciful costumes at Halloween; and playing cowboys and Indians with ropes, toy guns, make-believe horses, and a fort built of scraps of wood and cardboard can still bring smiles to adult faces. Memorable times for others might be dressing up in Daddy's coal miner's hat and taking his lunch pail to "work;" playing emergency to save workers; or singing songs on the back porch, accompanied by homemade instruments. Outdoor activities may be fond memories for others; opening up the fire hydrant on a hot day, playing kick-the-can in the street, and pretending to be cops and robbers. These memories are powerful. They are a record of initial cultural and psychological achievements, and the child's first mastery of thoughts and feelings.

Play, although on the surface an uncomplicated word, has profound implications for a child's optimal development. Investigation of the definitions of play reveals many aspects of meaning. Garvey (1977) and Bronfenbrenner (1979) identify several critical characteristics of play. Play is pleasurable, is valued by the participants, is spontaneous and voluntary, and requires the active engagement of involved players. The motivation for play is intrinsic and has no extrinsic goals. As Bettelheim (1987) states, "Play refers to the young child's activities characterized by freedom from all but personally imposed rules (which are changed at will), by free-wheeling fantasy involvement, and by the absence of any goals outside the activity itself" (p. 37). Play is also systematically related to areas of learning and development, as is discussed throughout this book.

These learning and development characteristics of play hold significant ramifications for assessment and intervention with children. As can be seen by examining the importance of play, the key elements of play need to be retained in order to nurture the child's development.

Importance of Play

Many theorists and researchers have investigated play and its relationship to various facets of development. In fact, play has been said to lead development (Fromberg, 1987). When children are engaging in play, they are functioning close to their optimal developmental level (Vygotsky, 1967). A brief overview of the pivotal nature of play in the child's early years follows. Specific information on the sequences of developmental change will be found in individual chapters related to developmental domains.

Play Influences Cognitive Understanding   Play and cognitive development interact in a reciprocal manner, with play leading to more complex, sophisticated cognitive behavior, which in turn affects the content of play (Athey, 1984; Piaget, 1962). During play, the child is involved in cognitive tasks that require making choices and directing activity (Hohmann, Banet, & Weikart, 1979). The child has control over both the content and process of play. He or she can decide whether to engage in exploration of the familiar or to extend behaviors into activities that are physically or cognitively novel (Almy, Monighan, Scales, & Van Hoorn, 1984).

Because manipulation of objects is often involved, play provides an optimal arena for problem-solving (Sharp, 1970). As challenges arise, the child confronts them and unravels solutions through physical and mental trial and error. Play with numerous materials leads to a greater ability to discriminate between information that is relevant or irrelevant to a given purpose (Athey, 1984). Mastery motivation, or persistence in problem-solving, is acquired through determined acquisition and enthusiastic practice of a new skill until it can easily be accomplished (Morgan & Harmon, 1984). Perseverance is most easily learned in enjoyable activities. As Bettelheim (1987) indicated, if perseverance has not become a habit in the satisfying activities of play, it is not likely to develop in endeavors such as schoolwork. In play, the child develops the capacity to derive pleasure from completing a task and solving a problem posed by play materials, independent of adult praise and approval (Freud, 1970). Play activity also broadens a child's experience, and thus increases the number of responses available for solving the next problem (Herron & Sutton-Smith, 1971). As problem-solving skills develop, the child establishes relationships between objects, words, and ideas, and can apply them to novel situations (Cass, 1973; Dansky & Silverman, 1975; Pellegrini, 1984; Pellegrini & Greene, 1980). Feitelson and Ross (1973) also found that play increases creative thinking.

Pellegrini (1980, 1987) found achievement to be related to higher levels of play. Classification skills and spatial understanding have also been found to correlate with higher levels of play (Rubin & Maioni, 1975). Symbolic play also appears to increase recognition of numbers and understanding of set theory (Yawkey, Jones, & Hrncir, 1979), as well as sequential memory performance (Saltz & Johnson, 1974). As pretend play evolves, the child's ability to conceive of objects and situations as representing other objects and situations contributes to later skill in planning, hypothetical reasoning, and the understanding of abstract symbols and logical transformations (Almy et al., 1984). Play leads to the internal mental processes of association, logical memory, and abstract thinking that are necessary for the transition from preschool to elementary school (Vygotsky, 1967). Play is a powerful medium for learning because it is self-initiated, pleasurable, active, and implies learning through discovery in situations that are personally meaningful.

Play Influences Social-Emotional Development   Play is the practice ground for the social skills needed in adult life (Piaget, 1962). Children develop social understanding through having to take into account the role of others (Mead, 1975); thus, play is a vehicle for broadening empathy for others and lessening egocentrism (Curry & Arnaud, 1984). As the child explores fantasy in an emotionally safe environment, feelings can be freely expressed. Children use play to work through and master the perplexing psychological complications of past and present. Much of representational play is motivated by inner processes, desires, issues, and anxieties (Bettelheim, 1987). As such, play is a means of self-realization (Arnaud, 1971). The dramatization of fears and anxieties enables children to understand themselves, and gives them a source of control over the obstacles and dilemmas within their lives (Axline, 1969; Freud, 1970; Gould, 1972; Isaacs, 1972). The child also learns through play that to enjoy continuous interactions with others, aggression must be controlled and various intrinsic rules must be followed. Symbolic play with peers provides an opportunity for others to respond to the child's behaviors. Peer pressure appears to increase control over impulsivity (Saltz, Dixon, & Johnson 1977). Therefore, play serves as the initial informal stage for learning the system of roles and social rules, and for practicing for sanctioned mores of the culture and society (Erickson, 1951).

Play Influences Language Usage   As Garvey (1977) has pointed out:

> Almost all levels of organization of language (phonology, grammar, meaning) and most phenomena of speech and talking, such as expressive noises, variation in timing and intensity,

Play is the practice ground for social skills needed in adult life.

the distribution of talk between participants, the objectives of speech (what we try to accomplish by speaking) are potential resources for play. (p. 59)

The child from 2 to 6 years of age is fascinated by language and can freely experiment within play with the various nuances of language. As the child learns to represent objects, actions, and feelings in symbolic play, a corresponding ability to represent them through language also develops (Nicholich, 1977, 1981). In the same way that the child masters cognitive problems through experimentation, the child can master the phonological, syntactic, and semantic rules of language through the medium of play (Athey, 1984). Social play with language allows the child to practice sounds, intonations, spontaneous rhyming, and word play; play with fantasy and nonsense; and play with speech acts and discourse (Garvey, 1977). Smilansky (1968) found that training in sociodramatic play led to: 1) a greater number of words spoken, 2) longer sentence length, 3) play-related speech, and 4) a larger vocabulary. A positive relationship also exists between play with language and subsequent metalinguistic awareness or cognitive understanding of various aspects of language (e.g., "boy begins with the letter "b") (Cazden, 1974; Pellegrini, 1980, 1981). The child also becomes aware of the effects that distinct or unconventional language patterns produce in interaction, thus enabling the child to establish and practice the social conventions of language.

Play Influences Physical and Motor Development   The exploratory and play behaviors of the early years contribute to the growth and control of the sensory and muscular systems. "It appears that repetition of movements, or sequences of movements, has the effect of establishing neural pathways that facilitate performance and make these sequences readily available for future use" (Athey, 1984, p. 12). Practice of motor responses in play activities results in motor skills that are swift, fluid, and accurate. During play, the child learns about the influence and control that his or her own body can exert on the world. In gross motor play, the child gains mastery over larger and more mobile objects and tools as well as an understanding of how the body moves through space, while fine motor skills and eye-hand coordination are developed through play with smaller objects (Athey, 1984). Aspects of self-confidence also derive from the child's perception of his or her body image and physical abilities (Harter, 1981).

Characteristics of the Play of Children with Disabilities

A much less extensive body of research exists on the play of children with disabilities. In part this may be due to the heterogeneous nature of the population, but is also a result of an emphasis on non-play assessment and intervention approaches (Fewell & Kaminski, 1988; Rogers, 1986b). Quinn and Rubin (1984) report that much of the research on the play of children with disabilities is of poor quality and shows inconsistent results.

Based on current literature, it does appear that the play of children with disabilities is dissimilar from that of children who do not have disabilities, in both quantity and quality. A brief review of the characteristics of the play of children with various types of disabilities is presented in this chapter. More extensive reviews can be found in Fewell and Kaminski (1988), Quinn and Rubin (1984), and Rogers (1982).

Play of Children with Developmental Delays   Children with developmental delays appear to progress through the same sequences of development as children who do not have developmental delays (Hill & McCune-Nicholich, 1981; Mahoney, Glover, & Finger, 1981; Motti, Cichetti, & Sroufe, 1983; Rogers, 1977; Sigman & Ungerer, 1984); however, several areas of deficiency are evident in this population. For instance, in a review of the literature, Li (1981) notes that the play of children with mental retardation is characterized by a restricted repertoire of play skills, including reduced language during play, less sophisticated representational play, and a limited selection of play materials.

Vocal imitation in infants with Down syndrome is decreased (Mahoney et al., 1981), and the verbal child demonstrates diminished frequency of speech and shorter mean length of utterance (Hulme & Lunzer, 1966). Differences in attention span also affect the play of children with developmental delays. These children appear to monitor the environment and engage their mothers in social play less often than children without disabilities, and spend more time in unoccupied behavior than children without disabilities (Krakow & Kopp, 1983). The presence of stereotyped behaviors in children with severe and profound delays also mitigates their play (Rogers, 1982; Thompson & Berkson, 1985).

Play of Children with Physical Disabilities   The child who has physical disabilities is restricted in very obvious ways. Poor head control affects the child's ability to look at, track, and anticipate object appearance; judge distances; and identify objects within the environment. Inability to move affects the capacity to explore, to find objects to combine, or to ask someone in another room to help accomplish a difficult task. Poor motor control of limbs affects the accuracy of reaching, grasping, and releasing objects (Newson & Head, 1979). Difficulty in accomplishing simple tasks can also affect mastery motivation, as the child is dependent on others and can become increasingly passive in play and in using self-help skills (Greenberg & Field, 1982: Heffernan, Black, & Poche, 1982; Jennings, Connors, Stegman, Sankaranarayan, & Medolsohn, 1985). The child's emotional development may also be affected by the inability to seek social interaction with others (Newson & Head, 1979; Mogford, 1977). Those children with physical disabilities who are capable of moving about the environment have been found to be less involved in their play, to spend more time wandering aimlessly, and to engage in more solitary play and less social play with peers (Jennings et al., 1985).

Play of Children with Autism   The literature on autism is confounded by varying labels that have been applied to these children, as well as compound diagnoses. Studies of children with autism and autistic-like behavior have also found it necessary to discuss mental retardation, psychosis, language delays, and behavior problems. As noted by Quinn and Rubin (1984), the fundamental difference between children with autistic behaviors who are mentally retarded and those who are labeled psychotic is that children with mental retardation show delays in development, whereas children who are psychotic demonstrate distortions in the timing, rate, and sequence of most psychological functions. As with some children with severe mental retardation, children with autism may demonstrate behaviors that are antithetical to play. Rocking movements, head banging or shaking, finger flicking, hand flapping, and the flicking or spinning of objects close to the face are some of the behaviors seen in the child with autism (Newson & Head, 1979), although not universally (Weiner, Ottinger, & Tilton, 1969). These behaviors have the effect of precluding the child from engaging in meaningful play with objects and from making social contacts with others.

Children with autism demonstrate specific sensorimotor deficits in imitation skills, especially those requiring symbolic substitution of objects (Curcio & Piserchia, 1978; Hammes & Langdell, 1981; Sigman & Ungerer, 1984). Qualitatively, the play of the child with autism exhibits fewer play sequences, less diversity, less time in advanced play skills, and less symbolic play related to dolls or people (Ricks & Wing, 1975; Sigman & Ungerer, 1984). The level of the child's language abilities seems related to his or her symbolic play skills (Curcio & Piserchia, 1978).

Play of Children with Visual Impairments   The developing baby is usually spurred into action by what he or she sees. However, babies with visual impairments may be unaware of wanting nearby objects or the possibility of going after an object. Because children who are blind cannot see the toys in front of them, they have no incentive to reach out or move to attain objects (Campos, Svejda, Campos, & Bertenthal, 1982). In turn, once toys are placed in their hands, they will not want to let go of them, as they may not be able to retrieve them. Their means of exploration involves keeping the objects close to the body by biting, licking, or rubbing the objects against their face or eyes (Fraiberg & Adelson, 1977; Newson & Head, 1979). As with children with autism, this stereotyped behavior can also negatively affect social interaction.

As a result of these characteristics, the play of the child with visual impairments is affected in several ways. They appear to be delayed in exploration of toys and the environment (Fewell, 1983; Fraiberg & Adelson, 1977; Sandler & Wills, 1965). They do not engage in complex social play routines (Sandler & Wills, 1965), and imitation of actions and role-playing is delayed (Mogford, 1977; Rogers & Puchalski, 1984) and sometimes absent (Sandler & Wills, 1965). Blindness or severe visual impairment results in an inability to observe others in play, increased solitary play, and fewer exchanges in play with others (Fewell & Kaminski, 1988). As a result, the cognitive, social-emotional, communication and language, and motor skills acquired and practiced in play are also negatively affected.

Play of Children with Language Delays and Hearing Impairments   Children with language delays have also been found to engage in symbolic play less and solitary play more often, to make fewer social contacts, and to have less organized play than their age peers who do not have language delays (Lovell, Hoyle, & Siddall, 1968; Williams, 1980).

Unlike language delays, lack of hearing does not appear to affect play during the sensorimotor period. During this period, children who are deaf or have hearing impairments observe, explore, and imitate others. After two years of age, when symbolic use of words appears, the child with hearing impairments begins to show delays in representational play (Gregory, 1976); social interactions decrease, with the child engaging in more solitary and parallel play (McKirdy, 1972).

Summary of Play Characteristics   Although the research on the play of young children with disabilities is limited, and more is needed, a growing body of evidence exists that demonstrates qualitative and quantitative differences between the play of children who have disabilities and those who do not. The areas of symbolic play and social interaction appear to be significantly affected in children with disabilities. Because play is the means through which children grow and develop, a careful examination of play skills should be a major aspect of the assessment of the young child.

Facilitating Play

The earlier discussion of the importance of play to the lives of young children highlights the necessity of including play as an integral part of the curriculum for those children. Research has documented that development is enhanced through improving play skills. To ensure that play becomes a focus of programs for young children, several factors must be incorporated into programs. First, play skills must be addressed as curriculum content. Second, the environment must foster play. And, third, processes for facilitating play need to be developed into natural and spontaneous techniques used by all staff members working with children.

Curricula   Although play is frequently a part of curricula for children without disabilities, its relevance for the child with disabilities has not been sanctioned until recently. Education of children with disabilities has emphasized learning theory, direct teaching, and individualized therapy approaches. Individualized education programs (IEPs) seldom include or reflect play objectives (Fewell & Kaminski, 1988). Renewed attention to the importance of play for children without disabilities has also focused attention on the relationship between play and the development of children with disabilities (Bailey & Wolery, 1984; Fewell &

Kaminski, 1988; Quinn & Rubin, 1984). Play must have a central role in the curriculum. Developmental sequences and therapeutic objectives can be addressed within a child-centered, highly individualized, play-based curriculum (Linder, 1999; Musselwhite, 1986).

Environment   Play is facilitated by an environment where toys and materials are visible and accessible to children. Play areas that are clearly defined and have toys arranged in an orderly fashion help children to structure their play (Curry & Arnaud, 1984; Hohmann et al., 1979). Toys that lend themselves to diverse types of play (e.g., that encourage manipulation, construction, dramatic, and creative play) are important. Props that promote symbolic play, such as models of things found in adult activities (e.g., telephones, cars, tools) and models or replicas of emotionally meaningful entities (e.g., babies, wild animals, miniature dolls, adult apparel) should be present. Duplicate materials should be available to encourage sharing and turn-taking. Unstructured materials lend themselves to creative uses. Sand and water, blocks, clay, paper, and paint are examples of materials with which the child can improvize.

Processes   Competent facilitation of play can result in dramatic gains in the quality and quantity of play skills (Curry & Arnaud, 1984). Facilitation involves not only structuring the environment and addressing the developmental and cultural content of the child's play, but also continuously adjusting the mode of interaction with the child. Providing attention to the child's interests, commenting on the child's play, and elaborating on the child's verbalizations or actions demonstrates to the child that someone cares about what he or she thinks and does. The facilitator also becomes a central figure through modeling for the child, selectively reinforcing the child's responses, and channeling energy into self-motivating play. By entering into the child's play, the teacher or staff member helps the child to clarify roles and interrelationships, extend play into higher levels, and solve cognitive and social problems. The person who facilitates play can also assist the child in confronting feelings and establishing a sense of confidence in his or her abilities (Curry & Arnaud, 1984; Fromberg, 1987; McCune-Nicholich & Fenson, 1984; Tizard, 1977).

Imitation is a fundamental means by which the child learns. McCune-Nicholich and Fenson (1984) note that the child's imitation of a teacher generally enhances play. "It appears that young children typically imitate only those actions that are meaningful to them, rather than mimic a model's actions in a rote manner without comprehension . . . Elicitation techniques elevate performances at all ages . . . " (p. 98). Fromberg (1987) suggests that teachers need to model behavior that stimulates development by challenging the child's abilities. In addition, the effective facilitator provides the child more than one option, for which there can be more than one possible outcome. In other words, the creative play facilitator can structure the play in such a way as to inspire problem-solving on the part of the child.

The process of facilitation also includes the selective use of language. Use of such techniques as mirroring (reflecting the child's nonverbal expression), self-talk (commenting on one's own actions), parallel talk (talking about the child's actions), imitation (repeating the child's comments), elaborating (introducing new information to build on the child's words), corroborating (repeating correctly what the child has said in error), expanding (responding with corrected and expanded version of the child's words), and modeling (conversing without using the child's words) are effective in improving language and social interaction (Weiss, 1981).

Although play is spontaneous on the part of the child, the adult who facilitates play must plan scenarios and use toys, materials, props, and space for isolated and group play. The innovative adult will infuse enthusiasm, novelty, variety, challenge, and curiosity into play activities. The process of facilitating play is not as easy as it might seem; however, the ability to effectively interact with, stimulate, and extend a child's play is essential in both assessment and intervention.

ASSESSMENT

No one would dispute the importance of assessment. However, its multifaceted nature is sometimes overlooked. Neisworth and Bagnato (1988) have reviewed the various assessment approaches available to teams along a multidimensional continuum. A brief examination of these provides a framework for discussion of the related aspects of the TPBA model. Indeed, many of these approaches are reflected in the TPBA model.

Curriculum-based assessment is defined by Neisworth and Bagnato as tracing "a child's achievement along a continuum of objectives, especially within a developmentally sequenced curriculum" (1988, p. 27). The transdisciplinary play-based assessment process is not a checklist of developmental skills that translate directly into objectives. However, developmental skill sequences are included in each chapter containing observational guidelines; objectives may be derived from those identified skill areas with which the child has difficulty. TPBA is intended to be used for identifying individual treatment objectives, including those related to specific skill deficits, and for tracking the child's progress regarding these objectives. TPBA contains aspects of a curriculum-based approach.

Adaptive-to-disability assessment, according to Neisworth and Bagnato, "include[s] or permit[s] the use of alternative sensory or response modes to minimize false item failure" (1988, p. 30). This refers to the use of instruments that are designed for, or can be modified for, children with sensory impairments. In the TPBA play session, the structure, materials, or interaction style and response modes may be altered, depending on the needs of the child. It is, therefore, an adaptive-to-disability approach.

Process assessment is another model presented by Neisworth and Bagnato (1988):

> Process assessment examines changes in child reactions (e.g., smiling, vocalizing, heart rate, surprise, glee) as a function of changes in stimulus events, to produce, by inference, an indication of the child's level of cognitive abilities, or a qualitative advance in cognitive stage. (p. 32)

Much of TPBA is process assessment. Piagetian processes of problem-solving through behavioral manipulation, imitation, means/end, and cause-and-effect are represented in TPBA, along with the examination of affective and behavioral changes in response to diverse stimuli. TPBA is meant to identify such underlying processes, which influence the child's learning.

Another approach reviewed by Neisworth and Bagnato (1988), but not part of TPBA, is norm-based assessment. "Norm-based assessment compares a child's developmental skills and characteristics to those of a referent (normative) group that is comparable in child and demographic dimensions" (p. 33). TPBA is not a standardized, norm-based instrument.

Judgment-based assessment, as defined by Neisworth and Bagnato, "collects, structures, and usually quantifies the impressions of professionals and caregivers about child development characteristics" (1988, p. 36). Judgment-based assessment can be based on the judgments of a broad range of parents, professionals, and others acquainted with the child; their impressions and value judgments of a more subjective but still valuable nature are shared. Judgment-based measures often tap more ambiguous traits that cannot be assessed in other instruments. Temperament, motivation, muscle tone, play style, and impulse control are some of the traits or behaviors that are evaluated through professional judgment during TPBA. The data summary system of TPBA, as discussed in Chapter 5, is also judgment-based.

Ecological assessment is also addressed by Neisworth and Bagnato. "Ecological assessment refers to the examination and recording of the physical, social, and psychological features of the child's developmental context" (p. 39). Features of ecological assessment that have been incorporated into TPBA include: 1) the extent and type of peer interaction; 2) parent interaction patterns; and 3) the child's response to various stimuli, contingencies, and consequences. Ecological assessment is built on the interactive model, the foundation of transdisciplinary play-based assessment.

Interactive assessment is viewed as a component of ecological assessment by Neisworth and Bagnato, examining "the social capabilities of the infant and caregiver and the content and extent of synchrony between them" (p. 41). TPBA screens parent–child interactions. Facilitator–child, child–peer, and child–group interactions are also observed.

The last type of assessment discussed by Neisworth and Bagnato is systematic observation. This refers to "structured procedures for collecting objective and quantifiable data on ongoing behavior" (1988, p. 43). Observation takes place in naturalistic settings, in simulated settings, or in role play. Frequency/rate, duration, latency, intensity, topography, and locus are aspects of behavior that can be systematically measured. Data are collected using either continuous or sampling techniques. Although the TPBA model incorporates these elements, sampling or continuous data notation is not strictly used. When desired, however, the videotape enables systematic observation and counting of behaviors.

If play is vital to development, and facilitation of play is a critical aspect of programs for young children, it would seem likely that assessment of the child's play skills has been commonly practiced. Not so. Although a variety of tools exist for investigating children's play (Table 3.1), many were developed as part of research investigations, and few were developed to assess play as it relates directly to intervention. Moreover, none of the existing scales addresses all areas of the child's development through play. Nevertheless, there are valuable components to these instruments, and many have contributed in some way to the development of the transdisciplinary play-based assessment (TPBA) guidelines (see Part III of this book).

As Quinn and Rubin (1984) state:

> The study of play may prove, ultimately, to be very important in the diagnosis, assessment, and treatment of exceptional children. Because many of these children possess handicaps that make standardized testing nearly impossible, systematic observation of their play could provide a useful, unobtrusive diagnostic device. Moreover, play could be used as a non-threatening and enjoyable medium for therapeutic intervention, training and skill building. (pp. 76–77)

As reviewed earlier, research has proliferated on types of play, components of play, play sequences, and differences in play among different age groups and among children with and without disabilities. Play is now viewed as a medium for assessment and intervention.

TRANSDISCIPLINARY PROCESS

An important aspect of the philosophy of TPBA is the transdisciplinary approach to assessment. The transdisciplinary approach was developed by the United Cerebral Palsy Collaborative Infant Project (1976) and was defined as "of or relating to a transfer of information, knowledge, or skills across disciplinary boundaries" (p. 1).

Table 3.1.   Play assessment instruments

Assessment instrument or resource	Description
From Exploration to Play: A Cross-Sectional Study of Infant Free Play Behavior. (1981). Belsky, J., & Most, R.K. *Developmental Psychology, 17*(5), 630–639.	A twelve-step sequence of developmental exploration and play that begins with infant explorations and concludes with pretend substitutions. A set of toys is specified.
Play Assessment Checklist for Infants. (1981). Bromwich, R.M., Fust, S., Khokha, E., & Walden, M.H. Unpublished document. Northridge: California State University, Northridge.	An observation instrument to be used in free play situations. A checklist is used in conjunction with a specified toy set.
Play Assessment Scale. (1984). Fewell, R.R., & Vadasy, P.F. (4th Ed.). Unpublished document. Seattle: University of Washington.	Children interact with specified toy sets. The scale looks at sequences of play behaviors and produces a play age.
Levels of Child Object Play. (1984). Gowen, J.W., & Schoen, D. Unpublished coding scheme manuscript. Chapel Hill, NC: Carolina Institute for Research on Early Education of the Handicapped, Frank Porter Graham Child Development Center.	Observational study of play using content, signifiers, and modes of representational analysis. The child is evaluated in an unstructured free play situation.
Developmental Progression in Play Behavior of Children Between Nine and Thirty Months. (1979). Largo, R.H., & Howard, J.A. *Developmental Medicine and Child Neurology, 21,* 299–310.	Using a specified toy set, the tool assesses play behavior in the categories of exploratory, functional, spatial, and nonspecific play behavior.
A Scale of the Organization of Behavior for Use in the Study of Play. (1958). Lunzer, E.A. *Educational Review, 11,* 205–217.	An abstract instrument that provides a 9-point developmental scale of the complexity of play, emphasizing adaptiveness and the use of materials and integration of materials.
The Symbolic Play Test. (1976). Lowe, M., & Costello, A.J. Berkshire, England: NFER-Nelson Publishing Co. Ltd.	An evaluation of children's spontaneous, nonverbal play activities with four specified sets of miniature objects.
A Manual for Analyzing Free Play. (1980). McCune-Nicholich. New Brunswick: Douglas College, Rutgers University.	An organized format for analyzing children's symbolic play according to Piagetian stages. A specified toy set is used.
Play Observation Scale. (1986). Rogers, S.J. Denver: University of Colorado Health Sciences Center.	Assesses sensorimotor and symbolic stages of play and includes a set of items on social/communicative behavior.
Play Observation Scale. Rubin, K.H. (1984). (Revised). Waterloo, Ontario, Canada: University of Waterloo.	Assesses play and non-play categories in an unstructured environment.
Symbolic Play Checklist. (1980). Westby, C.E. Assessment of cognitive and language abilities through play. *Language, Speech and Hearing Services in the School, 11,* 154–168.	Integrates language, cognitive and social aspects of play in a 10-step hierarchy. Includes ages 9 months through 5 years.

Programs serving young children with disabilities have evolved through several different staffing patterns (Garland & Linder, 1988; Linder, 1983; Woodruff & McGonigel, 1988). In the *unidisciplinary* approach, the child is seen in therapy by the individual therapist who is most closely related to the child's disability. In a *multidisciplinary* staffing pattern, several therapists see the child, but separately. The *interdisciplinary* staffing pattern is used when several professionals from different disciplines see the child, but the team discusses and collaborates on the child's program. In the *transdisciplinary* approach, professionals from various disciplines again see the child, but each team member is knowledgeable about the other disciplines. As discussed in Chapter 2, the TPBA model serves as means for providing in-service training in the transdisciplinary approach. A fundamental approach of transdisciplinary services is role release (Woodruff & McGonigel, 1988). Role release includes five dimensions.

The first facet of role release is *role extension*. As reviewed by Woodruff and McGonigel (1988), role extension involves the acquisition of knowledge and skills in relation to other disciplines. The TPBA team acquires knowledge and skills related to each of the domains of development. Team members need to be familiar with all of the guidelines to be able to compare their observations with alternative interpretations from each discipline. The teacher, for example, will need to understand terminology related to the language and motor guidelines. Gaining this information through readings is important. Understanding the principles and theoretical underpinnings of each discipline develops through each team member actively integrating the others' knowledge base into their own conceptualization of development.

Role enrichment, directly related to role extension, is the active process of sharing information about basic practices (Woodruff & McGonigel, 1988). During the TPBA process, this occurs in team planning prior to assessment and in team discussions following assessment. Each team member explains his or her perceptions regarding the observations of the child and the implications for intervention. The speech-language therapist, for instance, may describe the pragmatic aspects he or she observed in the play session. The motor therapist might relate how the child's lack of motor skills affects use of gestures as an intent to communicate.

Role expansion involves continuing the sharing process by exchanging ideas across disciplines. This occurs in discussions around programmatic implications. The speech-language therapist, for example, may give the teacher ideas for increasing social interaction in cognitive activities. The team works together to develop integrated approaches to intervention, with each discipline contributing to the others.

Role exchange occurs when team members implement techniques from disciplines other than their own (Woodruff & McGonigel, 1988). This does not mean that team members from any of the disciplines are dispensable; members of all disciplines are required for ongoing input and expertise. In the TPBA, exchange takes place when any one member of the team becomes the play facilitator or the parent facilitator. The play facilitator, for example, must know what information each discipline needs and be able to facilitate the expression of those behaviors in the child's play. In addition, the parent facilitator needs to know what information to obtain from the parent.

Role support provides the necessary back-up to team members as they assume the roles of other disciplines or when their discipline is needed in direct service. For example, within the TPBA process one team member may cue the play facilitator to include an activity that will assist the team in observing specific behaviors. A team member may also decide to see the child separately if the TPBA does not furnish adequate information to make professional judgments about the child's level of ability. The same may be true to team members who need more information from the parent. The TPBA process reduces the number of professionals with whom the child and parent must relate, but no hard-and-fast rule prohibits team members from interacting with other team members when necessary. The transdisciplinary process should not constrain the evaluation, but make it more effective and efficient. Transdisciplinary play-based assessment is a systematic process that will provide the bridge from functional assessment to individualized play intervention.

SUMMARY

Play is vital to and reflective of the child's development. Cognitive understanding, emotional development, social skills, language usage, and physical and motor development are influenced by the child's play experiences. Delays, defects, or deviations in development can also be reflected in the child's play. Use of a stimulating environment and facilitative techniques enable a transdisciplinary team to conduct a play-based assessment that can be adapted to disabling conditions, is process-oriented, takes into consideration ecological and interactive variables, and provides relevant information for intervention.

REFERENCES

Almy, M., Monighan, P., Scales, B., & VanHoorn, J. (1984). Recent research play: The teacher's perspective. In L.G. Katz (Ed.), *Current topics in early childhood education, 5*, 1–25. Norwood, NJ: Ablex.

Arnaud, S. (1971). Introduction: Polish for play's tarnished reputation. *Play: The child strives toward self realization.* Washington, DC: National Association for the Education of Young Children.

Athey, I. (1984). Contributions of play to development. In T.D. Yawkey & A.D. Pellegrini (Eds.), *Child's play: Developmental and applied* (pp. 9–28). Hillsdale, NJ: Lawrence Erlbaum Associates.

Axline, V. (1969). *Play therapy.* New York: Ballantine.

Bailey, D.B., Jr., & Wolery, M. (1984). *Teaching infants and preschoolers with handicaps.* Columbus, OH: Charles E. Merrill.

Belsky, J., & Most, R.K. (1981). From exploration to play: A cross-sectional study of infant free play behavior. *Developmental Psychology, 17*(5), 630–639.

Bettelheim, B. (1987). The importance of play. *Atlantic Monthly*, March, 35–46.

Bronfenbrenner, U. (1979). Toward an experimental exology of human development. *American Psychologist, 32*, 513–531.

Calhoun, M.L., & Newson, E. (1984). Parents as experts: An assessment approach for hard-to-test children. *Diagnostique, 9*(4), 239–244.

Campos, J.J., Svejda, M.J., Campos, R.G., & Bertenthal, B. (1982). The emergence of self-produced locomotion: Its importance for psychological development in infancy. In D.D. Bricker (Ed.), *Intervention with at-risk and handicapped infants: From research to application.* Baltimore: University Park Press.

Cass, J. (1973). *Helping children grow through play.* New York: Schocken Books.

Cazden, C. (1974). Play with language and metalinguistic awareness: One dimension of language experience. *The Urban Review, 1*, 23–29.

Curcio, F., & Piserchia, E.A. (1978). Pantomimic representation in psychotic children. *Journal of Austism and Childhood Schizophrenia, 8*(2), 181–189.

Curry, N.E., & Arnaud, S.H. (1984). Play in developmental preschool settings. In T.D. Yawkey & A.D. Pellegrini (Eds.), *Child's play: Developmental and applied.* (pp. 273–290). Hillsdale, NJ: Lawrence Erlbaum Associates.

Dansky, J.L., & Silverman, I.W. (1975). Play: A general facilitator of associative fluency. *Developmental Psychology, 11*, 104.

Erickson, E. (1951). *Childhood and society.* New York: Norton.

Feitelson, D., & Ross, G.S. (1973). The neglected factor—play. *Human Development, 16*, 202–223.

Fewell, R.R. (1983). Working with sensorily impaired children. In S.G. Garwood (Ed.), *Educating young handicapped children* (2nd ed.) (pp. 235–280). Rockville, MD: Aspen Systems.

Fewell, R.R. (1984). Play assessment scale (4th ed.). Unpublished document. Seattle: University of Washington.

Fewell, R.R., & Kaminski, R. (1988). Play skills development and instruction for children with handicaps. In S.L. Odom & M.B. Karnes (Eds.), *Early intervention for infants and children with handicaps* (pp. 145–157). Baltimore: Paul H. Brookes Publishing Co.

Fraiberg, S., & Adelson, E. (1977). Self-representation in language and play. In S. Fraiberg (Ed.), *Insights from the blind: Comparative studies of blind and sighted infants* (pp. 248–270). New York: Basic Books.

Freud, A. (1970). The symptomatology of childhood. In R.S. Eissler, A. Freud, H. Hartmann, M. Kris, & S.L. Lustman (Eds.), *Psychoanalytic Study of the Child, 25.* New York: International Universities Press.

Fromberg, D.P. (1987). Play. In C. Seefeldt (Ed.), *The early childhood curriculum: A review of current research* (pp. 35–74). New York: Teachers College Press.

Garland, C.W., & Linder, T.W. (1988). Administrative challenges in early intervention. In J.B. Jordon, J.J. Gallagher, P.L. Hutinger, & M.B. Karnes (Eds.), *Early childhood special education: Birth to three.* Reston, VA: Council for Exceptional Children.

Garvey, C. (1977). *Play.* Cambridge, MA: Harvard University Press.

Gould, R. (1972). *Child studies through fantasy.* New York: Quadrangle Books.

Greenberg, R., & Field, T. (1982). Temperament ratings of handicapped infants during classroom, mother and teacher interactions. *Journal of Pediatric Psychology, 7,* 387–405.

Gregory, F. (1976). *The deaf child and his family.* London: Allen and Unwin.

Hammes, J., & Langdell, T. (1981). Precursors of symbolic formation and childhood autism. *Journal of Autism and Developmental Disorders, 11*(3), 331–346.

Harter, S. (1981). A model of intrinsic motivation in children: Individual differences and developmental change. In A. Collins (Ed.), *Minnesota Symposium on Child Psychology, 14.* Hillsdale, NJ: Lawrence Erlbaum Associates.

Hefferman, L., Black, F.W., & Poche, P. (1982). Temperamental patterns in young neurologically impaired children. *Journal of Pediatric Psychology. 7,* 415–423.

Herron, R.E., & Sutton-Smith, B. (1971). *Child's play.* New York: John Wiley & Sons.

Hill, P., & McCune-Nicholich, L. (1981). Pretend play and patterns of cognition in Down's syndrome children. *Child Development, 52,* 611–617.

Hohmann, M., Banet, B., & Weikart, D.P. (1979). *Young children in action.* Ypsilanti, MI: High Scope Educational Research Foundation.

Howard, A.C. (1986). Developmental play ages of physically abused and non-abused children. *The American Journal of Occupational Therapy, 40*(10), 691–695.

Hulme, I., & Lunzer, E. (1966). Play, language, and reasoning in subnormal children. *Journal of Child Psychology and Psychiatry, 7,* 107–123.

Isaacs, S. (1972). *Social development in young children.* New York: Schocken.

Jennings, K.D., Connors, R.E., Stegman, C.E., Sankaranarayan, P., & Medolsohn, S. (1985). Mastery motivation in young preschoolers. *Journal of the Division of Early Childhood, 9* (2), 162–169.

Krakow, J., & Kopp, C. (1983). The effect of developmental delay on sustained attention in young children. *Child Development, 54,* 1143–1155.

Li, A.K.F. (1981). Play and the mentally retarded. *Mental Retardation, 19,* 121–126.

Linder, T.W. (1983). *Early childhood special education: Program development and administration.* Baltimore: Paul H. Brookes Publishing Co.

Linder, T.W. (1999). *Read, Play, and Learn!: Storybook activities for young children. Teacher's guide.* Baltimore: Paul H. Brookes Publishing Co.

Lovell, K., Hoyle, H.W., & Siddall, M.C. (1968). A study of some aspects of the play and language of young children in delayed speech. *Journal of Child Psychology and Psychiatry, 9,* 41–50.

Mahoney, G., Glover, A., & Finger, I. (1981). Relationship between large and sensorimotor development of Down syndrome and nonretarded children. *American Journal of Mental Deficiency, 86*(1), 21–27.

McCune-Nicholich, L. (1980). *A manual for analyzing free play.* New Brunswick: Douglas College, Rutgers University.

McCune-Nicholich, L. (1981). Toward a symbolic functioning: Structure of early pretend games and potential parallels with language. *Child Development, 52,* 785–797.

McCune-Nicholich, L., & Fenson, L. (1984). Methodological issues in studying pretend play. In T.D. Yawkey & A.D. Pellegrini (Eds.), *Child's play: Developmental and applied* (pp. 81–104). Hillsdale, NJ: Lawrence Erlbaum Associates.

McKirdy, L.S. (1972). *Play and language in four- to-five-year-old deaf and hearing children.* New Brunswick: Rutgers University. (ERIC Document Reproduction Service No. EC 113 220)

Mead, M. (1975). *Growing up in New Guinea.* New York: William Morrow & Co.

Mogford, K. (1977). The play of handicapped children. In B. Tizard & D. Harvey (Eds.), *Biology of play.* Philadelphia: J.B. Lippincott.

Morgan, G.A., & Harmon, R.J. (1984). Developmental transformations in mastery motivation. In R.N. Emde & R.J. Harmon (Eds.), *Continuities and discontinuities in development.* New York: Plenum.

Motti, F., Cichetti, D., & Sroufe, L.A. (1983). From infant affect expression to symbolic play: The coherence of development in Down syndrome children. *Child Development, 54,* 1168–1175.

Musselwhite, C.R. (1986). *Adaptive play for special needs children.* San Diego, CA: College-Hill Press, Inc.

Neisworth, J.T., & Bagnato, S.J. (1988). Assessment in early childhood special education: A typology of independent measures. In S.L. Odom & M.B. Karnes (Eds.), *Early intervention for infants and children with handicaps: An empirical base* (pp. 23–49). Baltimore: Paul H. Brookes Publishing Co.

Newson, E., & Head, E. (1979). Play and play-things for handicapped children. In E. Newson & J. Newson (Eds.), *Toys and play things in development and remediation.* New York: Penguin Books.

Nicholich, L.M. (1977). Beyond sensorimotor intelligence: Assessment of symbolic maturity through analysis of pretend play. *Merrill-Palmer Quarterly, 23,* 89–99.

Parten, M. (1932). Social participation among preschool children. *Journal of Abnormal and Social Psychology, 27,* 243–269.

Pellegrini, A. (1980). The relationship between preschoolers' play and achievement in prereading, language, and writing. *Psychology in the Schools, 17,* 530–535.

Pellegrini, A., & Greene H. (1980). The use of a sequenced questioning paradigm to facilitate associative fluency in preschoolers. *Journal of Applied Development Psychology, 1,* 189–200.

Pellegrini, A. (1981). Speech play and language development in young children. *Journal of Research and Development in Education, 14,* 73–80.

Pellegrini, A.D. (1984). The effects of exploration and play on young children's associative fluency: A review and extension of training studies. In T.D. Yawkey & A.D. Pellegrini (Eds.), *Child's play: Developmental and applied* (pp. 237–255). Hillsdale, NJ: Lawrence Erlbaum Associates.

Pellegrini, A.D. (1987). *Applied child study: A developmental approach.* Hillsdale, NJ: Lawrence Erlbaum Associates.

Piaget, J. (1962). *Play, dreams, and imitations.* New York: Norton.

Quinn, J.M., & Rubin, K.H. (1984). The play of handicapped children. In T.D. Yawkey & A.D. Pellegrini (Eds.), *Child's play; Developmental and applied.* Hillsdale, NJ: Lawrence Erlbaum Associates.

Ricks, D., & Wing, L. (1975). Language, communication and the use of symbols in normal and autistic children. *Journal of Autism and Childhood Schizophrenia, 5(3),* 191–221.

Rogers, S. (1977). Characteristics of the cognitive development of profoundly retarded children. *Child Development, 48,* 837–843.

Rogers, S.J. (1982). Cognitive characteristics of handicapped children's play. In R. Pelz (Ed.), *Developmental and clinical aspects of young children's play.* Monmouth, OR: Westar Series Paper, No. 17.

Rogers, S.J., & Puchalski, C.B. (1984). Development of symbolic play in visually impaired infants. *Topics in Early Childhood Special Education, 3(4),* 57–64.

Rogers, S.J. (1986a). *Play observation scale.* Unpublished document. Denver, CO: University of Colorado Health Sciences Center.

Rogers, S.J. (1986b), Review of methods for assessing young children's play. *Journal of the Division for Early Childhood, 12* (3).

Rubin, K., & Maioni, T. (1975). Play preference and its relation to egocentrism, popularity, and classification skills in preschoolers. *Merrill-Palmer Quarterly, 21,* 171–179.

Saltz, E., & Johnson, J. (1974). Training for thematic-fantasy play in culturally disadvantaged preschoolers: Preliminary results. *Journal of Educational Psychology, 66,* 623–630.

Saltz, E., Dixon, D., & Johnson, J. (1977). Training disadvantaged preschoolers on various fantasy activities: Effects on cognitive functioning and impulse control. *Child Development, 48,* 367–379.

Sandler, A.M., & Wills, D.M. (1965). Preliminary notes on play in the blind child. *Journal of Child Psychology, 1,* 7–10.

Sharp, E. (1970). *Thinking is child's play.* New York: E.P. Dutton.

Sigman, M., & Ungerer, J. (1984). Cognitive and language skills in autistic, mentally retarded and normal children. *Developmental Psychology, 20*(2), 293–302.

Smilansky, S. (1968). *The effects of sociodramatic play on disadvantaged pre-school children.* New York: John Wiley & Sons.

Thompson, T., & Berkson, G. (1985). Stereotyped behavior of severely disabled children in classroom and free-play settings. *American Journal of Mental Deficiency, 89*(6), 580–586.

Tizard, B. (1977). Play: The child's way of learning. In B. Tizard & D. Harvey (Eds.), *The biology of play* (pp. 199–208). Philadelphia, PA: J.B. Lippincott.

United Cerebral Palsy National Collaborative Infant Project. (1976). *Staff development handbook: A resource for the transdisciplinary process.* New York: United Cerebral Palsy Association of America.

Vygotsky, L. (1967). Play and its role in the mental development of the child. *Soviet Psychology, 12*, 62–76.

Weiner, E.J., Ottinger, D.R., & Tilton, J.R. (1969). Comparisons of toy play behavior of autistic, retarded and normal children: A reanalysis. *Psychological Reports, 25*, 223–227.

Weiss, R. (1981). INREAL intervention for language handicapped and bilingual children. *Journal of the Division of Early Childhood, 4*, 40–51.

Westby, C.E. (1980). Assessment of cognitive and language abilities through play. *Language, Speech and Hearing Services in Schools, 11*, 154–168.

Williams, R. (1980, February). *Symbolic play in young language handicapped and normal speaking children.* Paper presented at the International Conference on Piaget and the helping professions, Los Angeles.

Woodruff, G., & McGonigel, M.J. (1988). Early intervention team approaches: The transdisciplinary model. In J.B. Jordan, J.J. Gallagher, P.L. Hutinger, & M.B. Karnes (Eds.), *Early childhood special education: Birth to three* (pp. 163–182). Reston, VA: Council for Exceptional Children.

Yawkey, T.D., Jones, K.C., & Hrncir, E.J. (1979). *The effects of imaginative play and sex differences on mathematics, playfulness, imaginativeness, creativity and reading capacity in five-year-old children.* Paper presented at annual meeting on the North Eastern Educational Research Association.

II

The TPBA Model

Transdisciplinary play-based assessment is conducted in an enticing play environment.

4

Conducting the Play Session

Transdisciplinary play-based assessment is designed to be modified to fit diverse state assessment requirements, variable staffing patterns, and the individual needs of children and families. This chapter addresses the fundamental aspects of conducting the TPBA play session. Team composition and roles are described. Facilities and materials that maximize the child's play interactions are suggested. A flexible structure for the TPBA is recommended, along with a description of methods for documenting behavioral observations during the play session. The transdisciplinary play-based assessment process is not a standardized approach, and thus may be altered to acquire the information required in the format that is most suited to the needs of the child, family, and team. The team, materials, and format advocated in this chapter offer a comprehensive view of the child. If a less inclusive picture of the child's development is needed, or if TPBA is implemented as a segment of total evaluation using other instruments, the session may be adapted.

GETTING READY FOR THE PLAY SESSION

A pre-assessment planning meeting is held prior to the play session. During this meeting, several aspects of the session are discussed: 1) activities and materials to be included in the play session, 2) the structure of the session, and 3) assignment of roles to team members. Before the evaluation, the parents are asked to complete a developmental inventory assessing their child's abilities at home. (See Chapter 11 for a discussion of parent involvement in the assessment process.) During the pre-assessment planning meeting, information from the parents' assessment is examined to obtain an idea of the child's developmental level and the parent's primary concerns and goals for the child. This information provides a basis for discussions with the parents during and after the play session, and also contributes to planning the structure of the session. (While watching the play session, the parent facilitator will refer to the parents' information provided during the planning session, confirming the parents' observations, identifying possible discrepancies, and referencing parental concerns.) The pre-assessment information can also be used for selecting the appropriate setting and materials for the play session. If, for example, the parents indicate that the child walks, climbs, plays with dolls, and stacks objects, the team can structure dramatic play, construction and manipulation, and motor activities that are appropriate for the child's level. By using parent observations to determine the child's approximate abilities, the team can plan whether to conduct the play session in the home or center, as well as the type of toys and activities that should be incorporated. For a child with severe motor impairments, for instance, the team will need to modify toys (switch-operated) and identify communication alternatives.

The structure of the play session is also discussed in the pre-assessment meeting. Based on the age of the child and the information derived from the parent assessment instrument, the team can structure the components of the TPBA play session (see Table 4.1). When observing a young infant, for example, the parents will need to be involved in the play throughout the session. When observing a child with severe impairments, the team may want the parent involved at the beginning to enable them to observe communication idio-syncracies and effective interaction styles, so that the play facilitator can model effective approaches. If parents have identified separation problems as an issue, the team may want to delay having the parents leave the room (for observation of separation reactions) until the end of the session.

In addition to planning the structure and activities of the session, the team will need to identify the facilitators, the videocamera operator, and any other resource team members whose presence is desired. (See the discussion below for more information about team members and their roles.) The parents may have indicated, for example, that the child ex-hibits behaviors that prohibit the family from participating in community activities. In this case, the team may want to ensure that a psychologist is present at the session. The pre-assessment planning meeting provides an opportunity to coordinate the efforts of team members to maximize observation during the play session.

THE TEAM

The transdisciplinary play-based assessment process adapts to the composition of any team. Team composition begins with the parent(s). In addition to the parents, a *minimum* team consists of three professionals[1]: a speech-language pathologist, occupational or physical therapist, and a teacher or psychologist. These particular disciplines are available in many programs, and their expertise relates directly to the Observation Guidelines. Other team members, such as a social worker, psychiatrist, or vision specialist, may be incorporated, depending on availability and on the needs of the child being assessed. Depending on the number of team members needed or desired, the following roles are assumed:

1. The play facilitator who interacts with the child being evaluated
2. The parent facilitator who interacts with the parent(s)
3. Observing team members
4. The videocamera operator who tapes the session

The teacher, frequently omitted from traditional assessment procedures, is often an important team member in the TPBA process. The well trained teacher is able to ascertain cognitive learning styles, interaction patterns, and functional skills that will be important in the classroom. The teacher also plays a role in defining specific recommendations for the child's future program.

Distinct team functions are assumed by the parent(s), the parent facilitator, the play facilitator, and the observing team members. The following section addresses each of these roles in greater depth.

---

[1]Obviously, parents can also be professionals. However, for the sake of clarity, parent team members are called *parents,* and those team members representing professional disciplines involved in the TPBA process are call *profes-sionals* throughout this book.

Table 4.1.   Sample format of a TPBA play session

Phase I	Unstructured facilitation	20–25 minutes
Phase II	Structured facilitation	10–15 minutes
Phase III	Child–child interaction	5–10 minutes
Phase IV	Parent–child interaction	
	A. Unstructured	5 minutes
	B. Separation	
	C. Structured	5 minutes
Phase V	Motor play	
	A. Unstructured	5–10 minutes
	B. Structured	5–10 minutes
Phase VI	Snack	5–10 minutes
	Total time	60–90 minutes

Parents

Parents are involved in the transdisciplinary play-based assessment process as both information providers and participants. The parents' role is important: to provide valuable developmental information and insight, and to enable the team to see how the child interacts and works with persons who are close to the child.

During the play session, the parents may be involved in one of several ways: 1) behind a one-way window (with actual participation in the play session when called for); 2) seated to the side within the playroom; or 3) accompanying the child if the age or behavior of the child necessitates the parents staying with the child. In the first two instances, the parent facilitator sits with the parents and involves them in the observation process. Of the three ways that parents can participate, the two that involve having the parent within the playroom are preferred. In this way, ongoing parent–child interaction and dependency can be monitored by observing the child's need to visually and/or physically "check in" with the parent. Flexibility is important, however. The method or combination of methods that is most effective should be used.

As previously mentioned, having parents complete an assessment inventory and developmental history before the TPBA is preferred. If an "intake" has not previously been completed, the play facilitator and parents can use the beginning of the session, while the child is playing, to exchange necessary information concerning the child's birth, medical and developmental history, and current educational or therapeutic status. The parents also are observers, discussing the play session and comparing the child's present activities with behaviors seen at home.

At some point in the session, the parents will be asked to leave the room for a few minutes; the team can then watch the child's reaction to separation from the parent. The parent is also asked to play with the child and to teach the child a task during the session. The child's response to the parent is observed and compared to interactions with the facilitator and a peer.

Parent Facilitator

The parent facilitator accompanies the parents and the child to the playroom, where the play facilitator and other team members await them. The parent facilitator may be the service coordinator, the social worker, or any member of the team with effective communica-

Several benefits are obtained by having the parent in the playroom with a parent facilitator: 1) the child is more comfortable; 2) the team can observe how often and in what ways the child needs to "check-in" with the parent; and 3) the parent and parent facilitator can compare the child's abilities at home with those being observed in the play session.

tion skills. The parent facilitator's role is to provide information to the parents about the process, to obtain knowledge about the child, and to involve the parents in the actual assessment. If there are questions after reviewing the parents' assessment data, the parent facilitator requests clarification. He or she also explains activities within the play session.

The parent facilitator informs the parents about their upcoming role in the assessment process, telling the parents that they will be asked to play with their child just like they do at home, using whatever activities are fun for both the child and the parents. (One or both parents may be involved in the play, as desired or needed.) The parent facilitator also determines when to ask the parents to leave the room for several minutes so that the child's reaction to separation may be observed. Later in the session, when the play facilitator indicates, the parent facilitator requests that one of the parents "teach" the child a task, such as how to put together a puzzle, so that the team can observe the child's learning style with the parent.

Play Facilitator

The role of the play facilitator, who will also be selected from the team, is to imitate the child's responses, model new behaviors, or, in some cases, "teach" the child a new skill. The play facilitator needs to be sensitive to the child, following his or her lead whenever possible. The intent of this interaction is to obtain a sample of behavior that is spontaneous, functional, and interactive. By following the child's lead, a quick rapport is more easily established, and the child is more likely to demonstrate his or her higher-level skills. Directives toward the child should be carefully interjected, and only when the play facilitator thinks the child will respond well. The facilitator structures the environment to encourage play, provides props, comments on the child's actions, and elaborates or extends the child's play. When appropriate, the facilitator clarifies actions or roles to help the child become more involved in dramatic scenarios.

The play facilitator also acts as the moderator of the different phases of the assessment process. He or she decides when enough time has been spent in a given phase, or when enough information has been obtained. Feedback from observing team members helps with the decision-making, and team members may request additional time or activities within any phase; the play facilitator can also request response or assistance from other team members as it is needed. As the team gains experience in conducting play-based assessments, they learn to incorporate the specific types of activities that individual team members find useful.

The person representing the discipline most closely associated with the primary reason for the child's referral is a logical choice. For example, for the child referred for motor problems, the occupational or physical therapist might be selected. In some cases, the team may also prefer to have the teacher or the psychologist be the play facilitator.

Other team members can enter the process, if necessary, but having the same play facilitator throughout the session is preferable. This allows maximum rapport to be established, and is less disrupting to the child. One of the problems with traditional assessment methods is that the child can become overwhelmed by being "passed" from one person to another. Having to interact with many different people, the child never has an opportunity to establish a relationship with any one. In the TPBA play session, other team members cue the play facilitator to attempt to elicit the desired behaviors, thus allowing the team members to gain information about the child without direct interaction with the child.

The play facilitator can also be the person with the most enticing manner with children. Selection of the parent facilitator can be done in a similar way, either by staff role or by selecting the person with the best parent communication skills. As teams become more experienced with the model, these roles tend to emerge and evolve.

Much of the success of the TPBA process rests upon two factors: 1) the sensitivity of the play facilitator in accurately reading the child's cues and being able to respond quickly and appropriately, and 2) the astuteness of the team in interpreting their observations of the child's behaviors. Videotaping the session is highly recommended, as it allows the team to reexamine important aspects of the assessment.

Observing Team Members

All team members are observers; however, those who are not directly interacting with the child and parents are responsible for documenting behavioral observations. Worksheets are provided for each developmental area. The worksheets are structured to allow team members to take notes relating to categories of the guidelines. The worksheets provide cues to remind observers of the content of the guidelines being used. Behavioral examples are noted on the worksheets to enable team members to document specific aspects of the child's performance. These notes will serve as a basis for team discussion and will be prioritized and summarized on the Summary Sheets. Team members are primarily responsible for observing "their" area of expertise, but all team members observe all developmental areas and contribute to cross-disciplinary discussion after the session.

Observing team members also act as consultants to the play facilitator, cuing him or her if specific activities are desired. At times, a team member may desire to interact directly with the child. The physical therapist, for instance, may want to "feel" the child's muscle tone. However, interjection by other team members should be minimized to maintain the continuity of the session.

Videocamera Operator   Most programs do not have the luxury of hiring a media specialist. For this reason, it is necessary for one of the team members to operate the videocamera. Operating these cameras takes some practice, as many home video aficionados have discovered. It is easy to end up with a final videotape that looks as if it were shot from a boat in the middle of a storm. To avoid this, the team may need some instruction from a media specialist. This may be done in an in-service training session. In some cases, the use of a tripod is helpful; however, if the child moves around very much, a tripod can be awkward.

The person filming the videotape has to understand what information is being sought from various activities. For example, certain activities lend themselves to fine motor observation. The videocamera operator may need to select the activities where a close-up of the hands is warranted, or the physical therapist on the team may want to see the child's full profile to look at posture. (During the pre-assessment planning meeting, team members can also discuss the activities and specific pictures they would like to see.)

Team members often wish they had been able to see other aspects not captured on the videotape. By discussing missing elements after each evaluation, team members will become more astute at videotaping when it is their turn to operate the camera.

FACILITY AND MATERIALS

Facility

TPBA play session is best conducted in a well-equipped, large room. A typical preschool classroom will work well. To facilitate the child's ability to make choices, the room should be arranged with distinct areas that are visible to the child. For example, a good arrangement might include a house area, a block area with trucks and buildings, an art area, a sand and/or water table area, a work table area with puzzles and manipulatives, and a gross motor area. A one-way window, if available, provides an unobtrusive way for many individuals to observe. If a one-way window is not available, observers can sit quietly to one side in the classroom. Once the child is engaged in the play experience, he or she is relatively oblivious to the observers. If this is not the case, the child's concern about, and interaction with, the observers may provide additional relevant information to be included in the assessment.

If a classroom facility is not available, the TPBA play session can be conducted in the parents' home or any room that can be set up with portable materials. The space should be large enough to arrange toys and materials in a way that encourages the child to choose from several activities.

Materials

The room (or rooms) used for the assessment process must contain a variety of colorful toys and equipment. The house area needs a variety of representational toys: table and chairs, sink, stove, refrigerator, doll bed, and other toys that promote the re-creation of familiar activities. Provision of real or toy household appliances, dishes, silverware, telephones, blankets, pillows, and so forth is important. Clothing such as hats, coats, shoes, dresses, capes, and gloves are excellent stimulators of dramatic play. Other settings, such as an area set up like a grocery store, may also be appropriate. Such settings and objects should be ones with which the child is very familiar. (Familiarity encourages the use of spontaneous behaviors that are part of the child's repertoire.) New or unusual situations and objects are also included to encourage the use of problem-solving behaviors.

Dramatic play in another form is fostered through the availability of miniature houses, garages, and farm sets that require the child to direct dolls through actions. Miniatures allow children who are older or functioning at higher levels to exhibit more complex representational skills. When incorporated into the block area, these toys can be combined with blocks, Legos, tinker toys, and other construction materials to make enclosures, bridges, or other props. The block area should also have cars, trucks, and toy hammers and saws, as well as other toys that encourage combinatorial and representational play.

The art area should contain various media for the child to demonstrate manipulative skill, representational understanding, and fantasy play. Pencils, crayons, paints, clay, paper, and scissors are the most common, but other media such as shaving cream, dough, or other materials may be appropriate. If the team wants to look at tactile responsiveness, unusual textures may be desired.

A sand-and-water table is also useful for facilitating play and looking at responses across developmental areas. The table can be filled with cause-and-effect toys such as funnels, water wheels, squeeze toys, or higher level representational toys for the child to build roads in the sand or take dolls on boat rides.

Another table, with manipulative toys, allows the team to observe specific skills not seen in the other areas. Puzzles, paper and crayons, peg boards, beads, cause-and-effect toys such as cash registers, and size and color sorters are brought out to assess different skills. This is the general area where team members can structure tasks they have not yet had the opportunity to see.

Gross motor equipment, such as steps, rocking boards, slides, balls, prone boards, barrels, balance beams, and tricycles, are also placed in an area. The equipment and materials needed for assessment of gross and fine motor development is further discussed in Chapter 9. The gross motor area is incorporated into a large preschool room or into a separate gross motor area. An outdoor play area is another option.

STRUCTURE OF THE TPBA PLAY SESSION

The TPBA model is meant to be flexible. Table 4.1 (see p. 43) provides an example of a workable format for the transdisciplinary play-based assessment for a preschool-age child. It may be modified, however, depending on the age and needs of individual children.

Phase I: Unstructured Facilitation

The first phase of the play session is the unstructured play phase. During this time, which lasts 20–25 minutes, the child takes the lead. The play facilitator follows the child, imitates the child's behavior or vocalizations, engages in conversation, and interacts with the toys in parallel, associative, or cooperative play (defined in Chapter 7), depending on which is appropriate to the child's level of development. By following the progression from parallel to associative and then cooperative play, the play facilitator ascertains the interaction level that is most comfortable to the child. Whenever possible, the play facilitator tries to "bump-up" the child's level by modeling a slightly higher level skill.

The child is free to move from area to area, depending on his or her interest and attention. During this time, the play facilitator pays close attention to the cues the child is giving through body language, interest, learning style, and patterns of interaction. The facilitator also notes which behaviors and skills the child spontaneously initiates and which behaviors the child performs only in imitation. In certain instances, the play facilitator can actually try to "teach" the child, using physical or verbal prompting and reinforcement for successful approximation. However, the use of teaching in this phase should be kept to a minimum. The directive approach tends to negatively influence the nature of the interaction with the child. Rapport builds easily when the facilitator is following the child's lead, and deteriorates rapidly when the interaction becomes more directive. A directive approach in this phase is acceptable if the child is highly motivated to do a task and is unable to do so, or if the child requests assistance.

Phase II: Structured Facilitation

The second phase of the session is more structured. During this phase, the child engages in cognitive and language activities that were not observed in the previous phase. The child is asked to perform spatial tasks such as puzzles or drawing, cause-and-effect tasks involving understanding how things work, higher-level problem-solving skills, and pre-academic and other developmentally appropriate skills. The facilitator is more directive in this phase, selecting tasks, requesting performance, and questioning. This phase, however, should retain as much of the child-initiated play quality as possible. Making the tasks into fun "games" is desired. The length of this phase will vary, depending on the age and attention of the child (5–10 minutes for very young or behaviorally difficult children or 10–15 for higher-functioning children). Although this seems like a short period of time for structured assessment, many other skills will be observed in the other, less structured, phases. For older children, the structured facilitation phase can take place at a small table or work area, but any area can be used.

Phase III: Child–Child Interaction

In the third phase, the child returns to the unstructured mode, this time with another child in the play environment. The presence of a familiar, slightly older child of the same sex who is nondisabled may result in the best interactions (Brooks-Gunn & Lewis, 1978; Doyle, Connolly, & Rivest, 1980; Guralnick & Groom, 1987). The developmental level of the two children should not be too disparate. The team will find it difficult to meet all of these criteria, and finding the perfect match is not critical. The primary purpose of this phase is to compare the child's interactions with another child.

The timing of the observation of child–child interaction will vary. If during the first phase, for example, the child is actively engaged in representational play, the new child can be introduced toward the end of the phase. Dramatic play encourages social interaction and verbal interchange; the block area is another area where associative or cooperative play takes place, particularly if trucks, dolls, and other representational toys are incorporated. The play facilitator will usually know when and where the peer can best be introduced after interacting with the child in Phase I.

The child–child phase allows observers to not only observe play interactions and social patterns, but also cognitive, language, and motor behaviors. Different responses may be seen with another child than those that occur with the adult facilitator. These differences are important to note.

The play facilitator still follows the lead of the child being assessed. However, if no interaction takes place between the two children, the play facilitator tries to initiate and reinforce interaction. The introduction of toys that encourage interaction is helpful. Telephones, balls, and cars, for example, promote interaction. The child–child phase lasts 5–10 minutes. The peer may be allowed to stay in the room and play after this phase if he or she is interested in another toy area, or if the two children are not interacting. If the other child interferes with facilitation of remaining segments of the TPBA, he or she should be removed from the room. The peer may return during the snack at the end of the session, so that further interactions can be observed.

Phase IV: Parent—Child Interaction

The fourth phase involves the parents. The parents are asked to engage in play with their child (individually if both are present). They are requested to repeat the types of play activities that they do at home. The parent is observed for about 5 minutes. During this time the child's interaction patterns with the parent are observed, as well as additional child skills and behaviors. Although this is a brief period, the child usually interacts with the parent in the same manner that he or she does at home. This may be confirmed by asking the parent if the child's behaviors and their interactions are typical of what they experience at home. Interaction patterns, language level with the parent, problem-solving style, and other developmental indicators may be different with the parent than with the facilitator. The child may, for example, be more verbally expressive with the parent, using more vocabulary and a higher level of syntax. The team may then use this opportunity to obtain a more representative language sample.

The purpose of the parent—child observation is primarily to gain more information about the child; however, the team may also observe indicators of difficulties within the parent—child interaction. This is useful information, but should not be used to form diagnostic conclusions. Further evaluation would be necessary before program recommendations could be made.

After the initial play time, the parent(s) are asked to leave the play room. The parent tells the child that he or she is leaving, but will return in a few minutes; the child's behavior during this separation is then observed. The child's emotional response to the absence of the parent(s) is noted, along with any other indicators of the child's emotional level of development. When the parent returns, the child's response is again noted, and the parent is then asked to perform a more structured task with the child. The task should be unfamiliar and slightly challenging to the child. Again, the child's response to the parent is observed, this time under a more stressful situation. The techniques used by the parent to "teach" or "help" the child are noted, along with the responsiveness of the child and other emotional, cognitive, language, and motor factors. Parent—child interaction patterns also become evident in this segment.

Phase V: Motor Play

Phase V involves a 10–20 minute session of motor play. The first part is unstructured, with the play facilitator following, encouraging and, when necessary, initiating motor play on various types of equipment. After several minutes of unstructured motor play, the facilitator directs the child through those activities that have not yet been observed. The motor therapist, if he or she is not the play facilitator, may want to join the child at this time in order to better observe the child's muscle tone, equilibrium, and so on. The decision to include the occupational or physical therapist will depend, in part, on the child and his or her response to new adults. The play facilitator's familiarity with assessing this area, as well as the therapist's observations and need to have "hands-on" contact with the child, are final factors. As previously noted, the therapist may also elect to see the child separately.

Phase VI: Snack

The final phase of the assessment is a snack. The child being assessed may be joined by the child brought in earlier. During snacktime, additional social interactions may be observed, along with self-help skills, adaptive behavior, and oral motor difficulties. Cursory guidelines for assessing oral motor skills are included as a screening in the communication and language guidelines (Chapter 8). A more in-depth process is not included, due to the intrusive nature of the oral motor examination. After observing the child eating a snack, how-ever, the speech-language and motor therapists can determine whether a further oral motor evaluation is necessary. The team may want to choose snacks that require the child to use different mouth and tongue movements.

RECORDING DEVELOPMENTAL OBSERVATIONS

During each of the phases discussed above, professional team members record the child's skills and behaviors. Observation Guidelines, developed for the TPBA model, assist team members in organizing these observations. Presented in outline formats, these guidelines provide a framework for detailed, qualitative observation of the child across the four key domains of cognitive, social-emotional, communication and language, and sensorimotor development.

Worksheets accompany each set of guidelines to direct team members in recording their observations. To avoid "yes" or "no" responses that would reduce the guidelines to simplistic checklists of behavior, the Observation Guidelines have been intentionally worded to encourage team members to think in qualitative terms. Instead of "acknowledges peer," for example, the social-emotional guidelines ask, "How does the child acknowledge the presence of a peer?" The effect is to make team members focus not only on *what* the child does but also *how* he or she does it. Sample worksheets, illustrated in the text, have been redesigned in more useful formats for this revised edition of *Transdisciplinary Play-Based Assessment* and are also available in packets of individual forms under the title *Transdisciplinary Play-Based Assessment and Intervention: Child and Program Summary Forms* (Linder, 1993a). These forms are completed during the TPBA while the child is being observed and after the TPBA when the videotape is being reviewed.

Before applying the guidelines to an actual play session, team members need to be knowledgeable about the guidelines in *all* domains, especially as they pertain to their partic-ular discipline. Reference to the guidelines during the play session will assist team members in analyzing the play and will ensure that activities that should be observed are not over-looked. Not every question listed in the guidelines, however, will need to be answered for every child. The team may wish to skip sections of the guidelines if observations were not possible, or if specific sections are not germane to the child assessed. The observation of child–peer interactions, for example, will be omitted if a peer was unavailable.

The TPBA approach also offers flexibility in other ways to individualize data collection. For example, guidelines for observation of social interactions in a group are offered in Chap-ter 7. If observation of the child in a group is necessary, this may be done within a classroom setting at a different time. When included, this observation will probably be done by one or two team members rather than the whole team.

The TPBA approach also allows for different styles of documenting observations. The revised Observation Worksheets are intended to make documenting behaviors easier. Each team member will need to experiment to find the approach that is the most efficient for him or her. Corresponding to the question format of the guidelines, the Observation Worksheets allow team members to record, under the appropriate category, specific behaviors they ob-serve while watching the play session. This step is particularly critical if the session cannot be videotaped. Organizing the data with the worksheets will facilitate report writing and documentation of conclusions, because the guidelines later serve as the outline for the final written report.

Because children do not perform behaviors in the order presented on the worksheet, however, some observers may find it more helpful to take straight raw data, writing down a continuous list of observed behaviors. The gathered observations can then be organized later into categories related to the guidelines. For sessions in which a videotape is used, team members may also take advantage of the opportunity to watch the play session again, either individually or as a team, to resolve any confusion or disagreement.

After the worksheets have been used to record the data, the Summary Sheet for each domain should be completed. These Summary Sheets, available in the TPBA/TPBI forms packets, allow team members to indicate relative strengths, or what the child is currently doing well, what the child is ready for, and areas that are in need of further evaluation. The Summary Sheets also enable team members to document their classification decisions. This step and other post-session steps in the TPBA process are discussed in the next chapter. Planning of intervention approaches and home- and center-based strategies beyond the development of service delivery plans and specific objectives are discussed in depth in *Transdisciplinary Play-Based Intervention* (Linder, 1993b).

REFERENCES

Brooks-Gunn, J., & Lewis, M. (1978). Early social knowledge: The development of knowledge about others. In H. McGurk (Ed.), *Issues in childhood social development* (pp. 79–106). London: Methuen & Co., Ltd.

Doyle, A., Connolly, J., & Rivest, L. (1980). The effect of playmate familiarity on the social interactions of young children. *Child Development, 51,* 217–223.

Guralnick, M.J., & Groom, J.M. (1987). Dyadic peer interactions of mildly delayed and nonhandicapped preschool children. *American Journal of Mental Deficiency, 92*(2), 178–193.

Linder, T.W. (1993a). *Transdisciplinary play-based assessment and intervention: Child and program summary forms.* Baltimore: Paul H. Brookes Publishing Co.

Linder, T.W. (1993b). *Transdisciplinary play-based intervention: Guidelines for developing a meaningful curriculum for young children.* Baltimore: Paul H. Brookes Publishing Co.

5

Interpreting the Observations and Planning for Intervention

As described previously, transdisciplinary play-based assessment serves multiple purposes within the total assessment process. TPBA contributes to understanding the extent to which a child demonstrates delays or deviations in development, assists in determining eligibility for services, provides direction for planning intervention goals and therapeutic or remedial strategies, relates child and family needs, and documents changes that occur as a result of intervention. This chapter describes how the developmental observations gathered from the TPBA guidelines can be used for assessment and to plan intervention programs for the child and family.

The team members' tasks are not complete after the play session. The crucial steps of interpretation and programming lie ahead. To successfully complete the TPBA process, team members are encouraged to proceed in the following order:

Step 1:   Schedule a post-session meeting
Step 2:   Analyze videotape (if available)
Step 3:   Correlate observations and guidelines
Step 4:   Complete Summary Sheets
Step 5:   Develop preliminary transdisciplinary recommendations
Step 6:   Convene program planning meeting
Step 7:   Write formal report

Each of these steps is described in detail below.

STEP 1:   SCHEDULE A POST-SESSION MEETING

After completing the TPBA play session with the child, the TPBA facilitators and observers should meet briefly to discuss initial impressions, raise questions, and share information. If possible, the post-session meeting should be held immediately after the play session to enable parents to participate. If this is not possible, scheduling of the post-session meeting should be arranged to encourage parent participation. The guidelines, as well as worksheets used during the play session, may be referred to at this time to stimulate cross-disciplinary discussion of the different domains. The participants will each generate different examples of behavior they observed in response to various categories on the TPBA guidelines, and additional notes may be added to the guideline worksheets.

As they exchange ideas, differences of opinion may arise. These exchanges foster cross-disciplinary understanding and promote accurate child and family assessment. For example, the speech-language therapist notes that during the play session the child's language utterances averaged 2–3 words. The psychologist interjects that the child's language seemed to be more mature when in interaction with the parent or a peer and speculates that the comfort with the parent and the interest in the peer is stimulating the child's higher-level language skills. The speech-language therapist relates that, yes, that could be a factor, but she wants to look at the tape and compare the language samples in various situations.

As team members share observations, hypotheses are formed concerning the factors influencing the child's development. Areas of concern as well as strengths emerge. These will later be recorded on the Summary Sheets. Allowing staff to hear what other team members have noted can help identify significant behaviors. Questions often arise for which no single team member has an answer. The ensuing discussion may lead to a plan for further evaluation of the area of concern. Team members leave the post-session meeting with new perspectives and, frequently, a desire to study the videotape in order to observe behaviors again.

STEP 2: ANALYZE VIDEOTAPE

In most cases, a videotape is available for team members to watch and analyze. Since children do not perform behaviors in guideline sequence, and because answering the questions on the guidelines while observing the session can be difficult, the videotape provides an excellent opportunity to note overlooked behaviors. Some team members like to watch the whole session again, taking comprehensive notes on critical aspects. Others like to reexamine only certain parts of the play session to answer certain questions or to take data on specific behaviors.

For example, the speech-language therapist may want to watch segments in order to acquire a more comprehensive language sample, the psychologist may want to watch a segment of the session in which the child verbalized strong emotional responses toward characters in the dramatic play; the teacher may want to look for conceptual abilities demonstrated throughout the tape; and the physical therapist may need to observe activities that show the child in different movement patterns. Qualitative aspects of behaviors also become more evident in a second viewing. Learning style, coping mechanisms, and interaction patterns may be more evident, as well.

The time-consuming nature of watching the entire play-based assessment again is not to be overlooked. Each team member needs to determine the aspects of the session he or she needs to examine in more detail, in order to streamline the process. But this step does allow observers to ensure that their Observation Worksheets have been fully completed (see Chapter 4). The guidelines are referred to after data have been organized by category, because the questions can then be answered with supportive documentation.

STEP 3: CORRELATE OBSERVATIONS AND GUIDELINES

Responses to questions in the guidelines fall into three categories: 1) *developmental level* of skills observed, 2) *professional judgment* concerning the quality of behaviors observed, and 3) *description* of specific aspects of behaviors or skills observed. This information will be used to determine the child's strengths and what he or she is ready for in relation to both skill levels and qualitative performance factors.

Following this step helps avoid the pitfalls encountered on criterion-referenced instruments or behavior checklists. Although a checklist may seem easier to use (as the observer merely places a + next to behaviors that the child is able to perform or a − next to behaviors that the child is unable to perform, and the latter become targets for intervention), this approach does not take into consideration other important variables. Quality of performance, for example, is difficult to note on a +/− checklist. The question format in the TPBA guidelines encourages team members to respond more fully to each area. A child, for example, may perform several skills at age level, but only in imitation of the facilitator. Therefore, generalization and spontaneous use of the skill become the qualitative objectives.

To assist team members in this documentation, age charts accompany each domain (see Chapters 6–9). These charts provide age ranges as a reference for skill acquisition. In the example above, the mean length of utterance for a 2-year-old may be obtained from the age charts. Similarly, descriptions and specific examples are needed to justify the conclusions reached about the child's abilities.

Professional knowledge and experiences with young children can provide a basis for clinical judgments regarding qualitative aspects of behaviors, but these judgments need to be documented through the use of behavioral examples. It is not sufficient to say that the language of a 2-year-old was qualitatively poor. The speech-language therapist might document that the child used age-appropriate sentence length (2–3 words for a 2-year-old), but the frequency of use was much less than expected (3 times in an hour).

Thus the raw data of observations are translated into qualitative statements about a child's strengths and needs. The worksheets and guidelines also encourage the team to develop objectives that are not directly derived from test items. With team input and careful analysis, descriptive examples and clinical judgments gathered at this step are then summarized, as discussed in the following step.

STEP 4: COMPLETE THE SUMMARY SHEETS

Summary Sheets that accompany the Observation Guidelines for each domain enable the observers to translate the data gathered on the worksheets into a more meaningful format (Figure 5.1). Each TPBA Summary Sheet has a column listing the major observation categories for that particular domain. Each observation categories column has several corresponding columns, including: a column to rate the child's performance, a column to justify or explain that rating, and columns to indicate the child's strengths and what he or she is ready for in that category.[1] (See Figure 5.2 for an outline of scoring criteria and procedures for using the Summary Sheets.)

In the ratings column, categories are marked with a [+] if the child exhibits skills that are within a standard range of development within that category, based on age charts (provided for each domain) or other references, the child demonstrates typical behavior patterns based on professional judgment and expertise, and the child shows good quality of performance based on professional judgment and expertise. A category in the ratings column is marked with a [−] if the child demonstrates any of the following: a delay in development (based on age charts or other references), a deviation from normal behavior patterns, or poor quality of performance. The [+] and [−] rating may resemble some checklist formats; however, unlike most checklists, a [−] in a Summary Sheet category does not automatically become an objective or goal for intervention. The [−] indicates a need to

---

[1]Summary Sheets have been revised to allow more space for writing observations and recommendations. Samples are included at the end of each Guidelines chapter, and Summary Sheets completed for Rachel M. are included in Chapter 11. A sample has been reproduced in Figure 5.1. The Summary Sheets included in this book are meant to be representative of what should be used in TPBA. The new forms are available in packets that include the TPBA worksheets and *Transdisciplinary Play-Based Intervention* (Linder, 1993b) planning forms (Linder, 1993a).

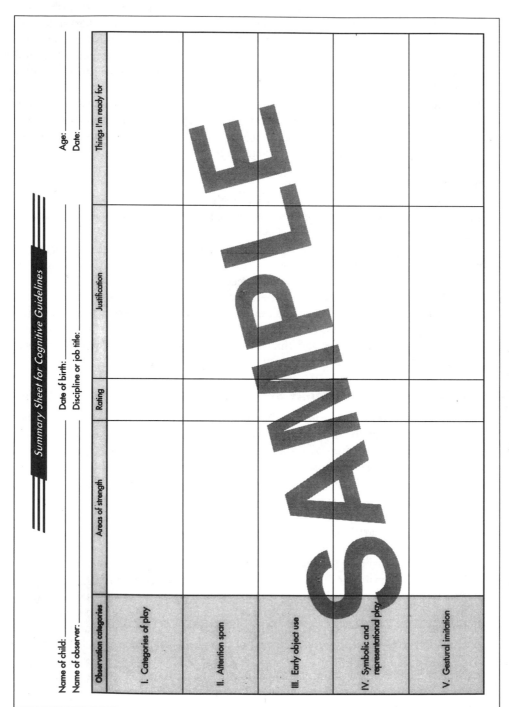

Figure 5.1. Sample portion of Summary Sheet (see Chapter 6 for a complete version).

56

SUMMARY SHEET INSTRUCTIONS

Definitions of scoring criteria:

+   Child demonstrates:
  1. skill within an appropriate range of development, based on age charts or other references; *and*
  2. typical behavior patterns, based on professional judgment and expertise; *and*
  3. good quality of performance, based on professional judgment and expertise.

−   Child demonstrates:
  1. delay in development based on age charts or other references; or
  2. deviation from normal behavior patterns; or
  3. poor quality of performance.

✓   Insufficient information was obtained. Further evaluation is required.

NA   Not applicable due to the age of the child, disability, or other factors.

NO   No opportunity to observe, but further evaluation is not recommended.

Procedures:

1. For each of the *Observation Categories* in the left column, indicate strengths the child exhibited within the area.
2. For each of the *Observation Categories* in the left column, indicate whether the child receives a rating of [+], [−], [√], [NA], or [NO].
3. Under the column heading *Justification,* write a brief explanation of why the child received the rating of [−] or [√]. Documentation of reason for [−] rating will assist in the identification of what the child is ready for. Documentation of reason for [√] rating may aid in selection of future assessment procedures.
4. Under the column heading *Things I'm ready for,* identify specific types of activities or developmental processes that the child is ready for in order to progress to higher-level skills.

Figure 5.2   Directions for using Summary Sheets.

examine the cause for concern and determine if intervention is needed, if support or recommendations to the family would be helpful, or if the area needs to be monitored in the future.

For example, if the child's representational play skills are delayed a [−] might indicate a need to facilitate the child's development in this area. But a [−] in the temperament area might indicate that the child's temperament characteristics are problematic or stressful to the family or team. In such a situation, intervention to change the child's temperament is not indicated, but suggestions for the family to help them cope with the child's style or to modify certain behaviors would be useful. Similarly, a child might demonstrate weak mastery motivation. The objective may not be to increase mastery motivation, but objectives to increase attention and problem-solving skills may result in improved mastery motivation.

It is important to rate each observation category listed on the Summary Sheet; however, not all categories can be rated with a [+] or [−], due to a lack of information. In some cases, this lack of information is related to a child's age, and further information may not be needed; however, in other cases further information will need to be obtained. In order to distinguish these different types of situations, three additional ratings have been designated.

If the category cannot be rated with a [+] or [−] because not enough information on that aspect of a child's behavior was obtained during the play session and further evaluation is required, a [√] is marked. The speech-language therapist, for instance, may want to evaluate receptive language in more depth. He or she would indicate the type of information that is desired in the things I'm ready for column.

If the category cannot be marked with a [+] or [−] because it is inappropriate for the age of the child, then it can be marked as not applicable [NA]. For example, the child under 3 years of age will not need to be observed in a group.

Finally, if there is no opportunity to observe an area, and further evaluation is not needed, [NO] may be indicated. If the child was not observed with a peer, for example, and the family indicates that social interactions with peers are a strength, [NO] could be marked in the category of peer interaction.

The three distinctions that are made between the [√], [NA], and [NO] ratings are particularly helpful for later stages of analysis and planning, and the ratings should be considered carefully. For example, if a child is referred for behavior problems with peers or if interactional difficulties are apparent in the play session, the peer interaction aspect of the evaluation is critical, and should be marked with a [√] rather than a [NO]. Observation of the child within a peer dyad and group should be included at some other date, and if it were rated with a [NO], this later evaluation would not be indicated.

The justification column is used to explain why a particular rating was given. This is especially important for a rating of [−] or [√]. A [−] given because of poor quality of performance or deviant behavior has implications for intervention. The justification is also important for the parents' understanding of the child's performance, because it clarifies that the [−] does not merely indicate that their child lacks this skill. The broader range of [−] justifications allows children to qualify for services for reasons other than just delayed skills. A [√] is justified by explaining what specific observations are lacking.

The strengths and things I'm ready for columns are also a very important part of the Summary Sheet, because they help to make it more than a checklist. Both columns should be completed for every category that has been rated with a [+] or [−].

The needs that are identified will provide the basis for determining service and intervention plans for the child and the family to enhance the development of the child. The statements that are written in the things I'm ready for column should reflect information gathered in the assessment process, rather than service needs. The physical therapist, for instance, might write that the child needs to increase stability, equilibrium responses, and weight shifting in order to build pre-walking skills, while the speech-language therapist may note that the child needs to increase spontaneous labeling of objects and to decrease imitative or echolalic speech. In addition, the teacher might indicate readiness for an increase in the length of scheme sequences, increase representational use of objects, and improve discrimination abilities.

The strengths column should *always* be completed in each observation category that has been marked with a [+] or [−]. The child will demonstrate a skill, style, approach, or attitude that can be identified as a strength. For example, the child's highest level of performance is a relative strength and can be listed as a beginning point. Parents should be informed that the [−] ratings are used to document the need for services and may point out areas for program planning, but they are not meant to mask the child's strengths.

Identification of strengths is as important as identification of activities and processes the child is ready for because both provide a better overall picture of the child, and also because the strengths column helps to balance the [−] ratings. The [−] rating assists the team in focusing on the concerns that surfaced in the assessment process. This rating also enables the team to identify the child whose skills may be at age level, but whose behavior patterns or qualitative aspects of performance dictate a need for intervention; these qualities may be overlooked in more tradition assessment approaches. The disadvantage of the way that the [−] ratings are determined is that the child may appear to have all [−] ratings; it is for this reason that the strengths column should always be completed.

Table 5.1 illustrates a process for determining strengths and things the child is ready for. A child may demonstrate a skill that is a relative strength and at the same time an area of concern. For instance, a child may be able to walk spontaneously, without modeling or physical assistance, but in a manner that is awkward and unstable. The team may recognize the skill as a relative strength, but still be able to identify the necessary underlying motor processes as an area of concern requiring further intervention.

When the team again meets with the parents, the information from the Summary Sheets, in combination with the results of the parents' assessment, will contribute to the formulation of the IEP or IFSP. For example, the parents may have selected several intervention priorities, including: 1) that the child learn to walk, 2) that the child be able to point to and name pictures in a book, and 3) that the child be able to play cooperatively with peers. The intervention team can then discuss how the observations and the indicated areas of readiness relate to the parents' goals, and, in fact, provide the basic foundations for building those skills. The transdisciplinary play-based intervention process (Linder, 1993b) begins at this point, as the intervention team and family plan how objectives will be incorporated into home activities, play interactions, and the school curriculum. The use of team planning sheets facilitates this process.

STEP 5: DEVELOP PRELIMINARY TRANSDISCIPLINARY RECOMMENDATIONS

After reviewing the observations and completing the Summary Sheets, those who participated in the post-session meeting should meet briefly to prepare for the full team program planning meeting. At this time, concerns that surfaced at that earlier meeting can be reviewed, intervention strategies can be offered, and areas of disagreement can be addressed. Disagreements and uncertainties are inevitable, given that team members come from disparate theoretical and experiential background, but the benefits of such interdisciplinary exchange strengthen the planning process. Exploring discrepancies at this point allows the team to debate contrasting views openly and identify the most salient aspects of each point of view. This exchange can then be summarized at the full team meeting, and parental feedback solicited.

In a post-analysis meeting after a transdisciplinary play-based assessment on a 3-year-old named Lisa, the team was unable to come to a consensus about her program needs. Lisa had two brothers, a 5-year-old who had been diagnosed as autistic, and a 3-month-old baby. Her language

Table 5.1. Framework for determining strengths and things the child is ready for

Observed skill	Interpretation
Spontaneously demonstrated	Relative strength
Demonstrated in imitation	Emerging skill; goal is to generalize and use spontaneously
Demonstrated with physical prompts or reinforcement	Potential target if skill is functionally important; goal is to elicit in imitation
Skill observed, but qualitatively immature	Area of readiness; goal to improve underlying processes
Age-appropriate skill not observed	Probably not yet ready for; need to build underlying processes

The team process is a vital aspect of the TPBA, and time must be scheduled for the team to plan, discuss, and develop functional recommendations that integrate all disciplines.

level was delayed 2 years, her cognitive skills as reflected in her play were delayed 1 year, and she displayed low affect, lack of initiation of interaction, and an inability to maintain interactions. Her motor skills were approximately age level, but the quality of her movements was poor. Lisa did exhibit a high level of mastery motivation on manipulative and cause-and-effect toys. In interaction with a peer, her vocalizations and positive affect increased. Her mother had reported that Lisa was not exposed to many toys at home, because her brother destroyed any toys available. Her mother also stated that the new baby and the brother with severe disabilities demanded almost all of her time. She felt exhausted and overwhelmed by the thought that Lisa might also have problems. Her husband, who worked two jobs, was not available as a support for her.

Lisa's teacher had indicated concern that Lisa was exhibiting characteristics similar to those of her brother, and should be placed in a behaviorally based program to systematically work on her skills. The psychologist felt that although some of those characteristics, such as poor interaction patterns, were present, Lisa demonstrated many strengths that led him to believe her potential was much greater. He felt that if she were placed in a regular preschool with peer language models, her language and interactions would improve greatly. The speech-language therapist felt that Lisa needed to be in a program with a strong language intervention component and individual speech therapy. The physical therapist felt that her motor needs could be addressed without individual therapy, but that placement in a regular preschool would not allow her to receive attention to her motor difficulties. After then presenting their ideas and discussing the interrelationship of language, cognitive, and social-emotional development for Lisa, the team outlined the advantages and disadvantages of the various options available. All team members agreed that Lisa's home environment was not enhancing her development and that some type of program would be beneficial. They also agreed that Lisa's mother needed support and assistance in dealing with an overwhelming situation, and discussed available options that could be presented to the parents. Due to the mother's self-expressed fragile emotional state and her fear of Lisa being diagnosed as having a disability, the team also discussed how the findings could be presented in a way that was sensitive to the needs of the family.

The important aspect of the above illustration is that the team identifies and discusses discrepancies in points of view, as well as the alternatives, based on those differences. Frequently, discussion will result in consensus. Alternatives are presented to the parents, as they are the ultimate decision-makers.

At this stage, goals or objectives for the child or family should *not* be written; however attendees may elect to consolidate suggestions in written form. When participants do not feel the need to write these suggestions, the Observation Worksheets and Summary Sheets are an adequate basis for the upcoming program planning meeting.

If the TPBA team has identified areas in need of further evaluation, then additional testing, observations, or interviews are scheduled and conducted prior to the program planning meeting.

STEP 6: CONVENE PROGRAM PLANNING MEETING

A full team meeting is next held to review assessment information, determine eligibility for services, and plan intervention goals for the child and family. Planning for TPBI can also begin at this meeting. At this stage, TPBA becomes part of the larger team assessment process (federally mandated) that examines the range of abilities and needs of the child as well as those of the family. TPBA can be used as the basis for developing individualized education programs (IEPs), required by IDEA (the Individuals with Disabilities Education Act) or individualized family service plans (IFSPs), mandated by PL 99-457 (Education of the Handicapped Act Amendments of 1986) and PL 102-119 (the Individuals with Disabilities Education Act Amendments of 1991). IFSPs are distinguished from IEPs in their provision of services to both children with disabilities and children at risk, 5 years of age and younger, and in their extension of services to the family. TPBA is valuable in meeting the family-focused mandates of PL 102-119, whose programmatic implications are dramatically affecting programs for infants, toddlers, and preschoolers. The elements of the IFSP can be drawn from the information obtained from TPBA and other formal and informal assessments of the child and family. Later in this chapter, specific examples of this correlation are provided.

Consistent with the philosophy of the IFSP, parents assume a preeminent role; their importance on the team cannot be overstated (Brinkerhoff & Vincent, 1986). The family will determine which needs they want to address and identify the priorities in relation to their child's progress. Families should also be allowed to determine the degree of intervention in their lives.

The TPBA team that conducted Lisa's assessment suggested that Lisa's mother might benefit from having some time to spend with the new baby and that Lisa would profit by spending time with other children who could talk and play with her. The change in Lisa's vocalizations in the play session with the peer was cited as an example. The team suggested enrolling Lisa in a regular preschool for half days to allow her increased play and interaction opportunities. Concerns about Lisa's development were addressed, and Lisa's mother concurred that she was concerned about Lisa's language, but stated that she didn't feel she needed to be in a program "like her brother's." She felt that individual speech-language therapy twice a week would be sufficient. Plans were made for the speech-language therapist to see Lisa after preschool 2 days a week. Alternative supports for the mother were also discussed at this time, and plans for a review in 3 months were made.

Each professional who is on the team has been selected because of his or her area of expertise; however, it is important that the professionals discuss their data in a general manner, so that other professionals, and especially the parents, will not be excluded from the discussion. Showing respect for all areas of expertise, including the parents', will make the meeting less stressful and more meaningful. Conducting the meeting in this manner enables the parents to participate more actively. Indeed, Brinkerhoff and Vincent (1986) found that parents became more involved in the decision-making process when they were given a significant role and prepared in advance for the meeting. Conducting the meeting in a comfortable setting at a time that is convenient for parents is also important. Other ways to improve the process include reducing the number of professionals at the meeting, keeping procedures on an informal basis, eliminating jargon, and relating information to the daily life of the child and family.

At the end of the program planning meeting, a Cumulative Summary Sheet is completed. This form (Figure 5.3) summarizes the areas of strength and readiness as well as identifying the team who will work with the child and family. This form is a brief, jargon-free summary that the parents can take home with them. A more comprehensive final report is written after the meeting. In addition, the family may develop with the team, either at the staffing or at a subsequent meeting, a transdisciplinary play-based intervention plan (Linder, 1993b).

STEP 7: WRITE FORMAL REPORT

The TPBA process ends with a formal written report. The quantitative and qualitative description of the child's performance that has emerged in the previous seven steps enables the team to write a comprehensive, functional report that serves as the basis for program planning and intervention. This report can follow the outline provided below and should include the information generated for the IFSP or IEP. The information in the report also forms the basis for the transdisciplinary play-based intervention plan (Linder,1993b) as recommendations will be interpreted into home and school activities.

While the format of the report is similar to that of standard assessment reports (Linder, 1983), the content and style are distinct. The TPBA report provides comprehensive, detailed information on the child's abilities, concerns or areas of readiness, instructional targets, learning style, environmental demands, and recommended approaches to intervention. In contrast, many other professional reports are limited to descriptions of items the child passed or failed on various tests, documentation of various test scores, and age levels. This information is useful for determining eligibility for programs, but does not provide sufficient direction to parents or staff who will provide intervention to the child and family. The following outline provides a sample structure for a TPBA report:

I.   Identifying information
   A.   Name
   B.   Date of birth
   C.   Age
   D.   Sex
   E.   Parent name(s)
   F.   Address
   G.   Names of assessment team members
   H.   Dates of assessment
II.   Reason for referral and person initiating referral
III.   History
   A.   Birth weight and duration of gestation
   B.   Pregnancy, labor and delivery, and neonatal period
   C.   Significant illnesses
   D.   Convulsions: Include type of episodes, age of onset, frequency, duration, association with fever, and treatment
   E.   Developmental history: Indicate areas in which progress was noted
   F.   Educational experiences

Cumulative Summary Sheet

Name:_____ Date:_____

Address:_____

_____

_____

Areas of strength

Cognitive:

Social-emotional:

Communication and language:

Sensorimotor:

Primary things I'm ready for:

Secondary things I'm ready for:

Identified intervention team members:

Signatures of persons present at the meeting:

Name	Title	Agency

Persons not in attendance to whom a report will be sent:

_____ _____ _____

_____ _____ _____

_____ _____ _____

Parental consent:

I have been informed of my rights, and I am in agreement with the assessment findings and the program plan for my child and my family.

Signature: _____ Date:_____

Signature: _____ Date:_____

Figure 5.3. Cumulative Summary Sheet.

IV. Method of assessment
    A. Description of transdisciplinary play-based assessment process, including the setting in which observations were made, persons present, format of the observations, and description of the context of the assessment

  B. Normative tests and scales administered and reference citations
  C. Informal or criterion-referenced tests administered
  D. Formal and informal interviews conducted, including who was interviewed, by whom, and for what purpose
  E. Environmental assessments conducted, including measures used, dates of assessment, purpose of assessment, and person conducting assessment
 V. Interpretation of assessment results
  A. Developmental skills, patterns, and qualitative aspects of behavior observed in each developmental area—cognitive, social-emotional, communication and language, sensorimotor, and adaptation
  B. Summary of major areas of need
 VI. Recommendation
  A. Need for additional assessment
  B. Recommended services
  C. Long-term objectives
  D. Transdisciplinary play-based intervention strategies or other specific intervention strategies
  E. Family support and home intervention

(Adapted from Linder, 1983, pp. 112–113.)

The final report must be a transdisciplinary effort. Each professional participating on the team will contribute to the report in areas pertaining to his or her discipline. Typically, basic disciplines such as teaching, speech-language pathology, occupational therapy, physical therapy, psychology, and nursing may be represented, although staffing limitations in rural or small programs may result in participants assuming responsibility for more than one area.

The report should be readable and useful to parents and members of various disciplines. Professional jargon should be eliminated, or, if essential, defined. Team members can assist each other in clarifying confusing sections of the report, relating findings from one developmental area to another, and developing interrelated functional intervention approaches. This collaborative exchange is valuable, not only because it results in a transdisciplinary assessment document, but also because it initiates an ongoing transdisciplinary planning dialogue. Transdisciplinary play-based intervention (Linder, 1993b) integrates prioritized assessment information into home and school intervention plans and also incorporates a process for periodic play observation updates and consequent program modification.

When the report is completed, the parents must have an opportunity to examine it. One of the professional team members can meet with the parents to review the document, and relate it to the information that was generated at the earlier full team meeting (discussed in Step 6). If the parents have additional information or desire modifications, the report should be changed.

TPBA AND THE IFSP

As the preceding seven steps have shown, transdisciplinary play-based assessment can be an integral part of developing an IEP or IFSP. Although the very nature of an IFSP calls for individuality in format, eight basic content areas are mandated by Part H of IDEA:

1. A statement of the child's present levels of performance in cognitive, speech-language, psychosocial, motor, and adaptive (self-help) skills
2. A statement of the family's resources, priorities, and concerns related to enhancing the child's development

3. A statement of major outcomes to be achieved for the child and family, and the criteria, procedures, and timelines for determining progress toward the stated goals
4. The specific early intervention services necessary to meet the unique needs of the child and family, including the method, frequency, and intensity of service
5. A statement of the natural environments in which early intervention services will be provided
6. The projected dates for the initiation of services and the expected duration
7. Identification of the service coorindator
8. Procedures for transition from the infant intervention program into the next program

The above content areas, in relation to how they can be completed using TPBA, are discussed below. Throughout the discussion, the TPBA process used for Jenny L., a 3-year-old with quadriplegia, is described in examples.

Present Levels of Development

One of the early sections of the IFSP should be a review of the child's present level of performance in all domains. Part H of IDEA requires a statement of the infant's or toddler's present levels of physical development, cognitive development, language and speech development, psychosocial development, and adaptive skills. Applicable here will be all the information gathered from the TPBA about the child's strengths and areas of readiness.

When writing the IFSP, parents and professionals can look back on specific parts of the TPBA process to extract observations about the child's present performance level. The developmental inventory (completed by the parents prior to the play session), observations from the TPBA worksheets, and information from the program planning meeting can all be used. If necessary or as appropriate, the information on skills, processes, and patterns observed in TPBA can be supplemented with other instruments.

In Jenny's play session, her cognitive abilities were assessed as slightly delayed, as demonstrated by her ability to use eye-pointing to direct the facilitator through a sequence of dramatic play behaviors, her laughter at incongruous actions in dramatic play, and her ability to classify objects by matching them with eye-pointing. Her interaction skills were limited, due to verbal and motor limitations, but she was able to initiate interactions through vocalization and eye-pointing, and to maintain an interaction if the person engaging her was responsive to her need for wait time, soft affect, and measured responses. Her receptive language also appeared to be only slightly delayed, as she was able to identify concepts through eye-pointing, and she understood the facilitator's directions to "use your eyes to tell me what to do with the baby now." Jenny was limited in the sensorimotor domain. She had poor head and trunk control, minimal use of her hands and arms, was unable to support weight on her arms or legs, and was dominated by primitive reflexes.

*During the program planning meeting, Jenny's parents and the other members of the team identified many of her **strengths**, such as: 1) her pleasant temperament; 2) her mastery motivation; 3) her ability to communicate with gaze, vocalization, and gross gestures; and 4) her cognitive understanding. Jenny's parents confirmed that Jenny understood "everything." They were surprised to see her ability to direct the play sequence with her eyes, and said that they had tried the same play successfully at home several times since the play session had taken place.*

Mr. and Mrs. L. indicated that their priorities for Jenny were to increase her independence in play and adaptive skills, particularly in feeding. They also wanted her to learn to communicate more effectively and to learn how to operate an electric wheelchair. The other team members concurred, and suggested incorporating technology into her intervention program so that she could begin to use switch-operated toys, computers, and other mechanical devices for self-initiated play, communication, self-feeding, and mobility.

As the preceding example underscores, equal specification of strengths and identification of what the child is ready for is important.

Family's Strengths and Resources, Priorities, and Concerns

The IFSP calls for assessment of the family's strengths and resources, priorities, and concerns. Comprehensive approaches to family assessment have been developed that include assessment of overall family needs, family stress, critical life events, family roles and supports, family environments, family functioning style, and family–child interactions (Bailey & Simeonsson, 1988; Dunst, Trivette, & Deal, 1988). These resources, priorities, and concerns are to be viewed in relation to enhancing the development of the child. If an IFSP is being developed, prior to the TPBA program planning meeting the professional members on the team will have completed an assessment of family resources, priorities, and concerns to complement the information gained through TPBA.

TPBA data relevant for family assessment, for example, can come from observations of parent–child interaction during the play session. Then, in the program planning meeting, these characteristics can be discussed, and parents and professionals can jointly determine if interaction skills are an area to be addressed within the IFSP goals and objectives for the child and family. In addition, if an instrument such as the Daily Routine Form (discussed later in Chapter 11) has been completed, the team can incorporate information about the family's typical day to identify stressful or pleasurable interaction times. This will facilitate planning appropriate intervention times for the child and family. In the transdisciplinary play-based intervention process, the family will identify times during which they naturally interact with their child. These times will then be integrated into the planning of play and pleasurable activities that will incorporate the child's objectives. Specific considerations with regard to preparations, cues and prompts, positioning, and so forth are also relevant to implementation of a plan.

Jenny's family had many strengths. They had adjusted to Jenny's style of interaction, and were able to read Jenny's cues and respond appropriately. They gave Jenny much affection and attention. Analysis of their daily routine revealed that at least one member of the family was with Jenny almost every minute of the day. The family, including Jenny's mother, father, and two older brothers, had distributed roles and responsibilities for Jenny so that everyone assisted, but Jenny's mother had primary caregiving responsibilities during the day.

The strengths of the family were identified as: a strong commitment to Jenny and to each other, sensitivity to Jenny's cues, and responsiveness to her style of interaction and learning. In addition, family members expressed willingness to take extra time to interact with Jenny.

Although these parent–child interaction patterns were recognized as strengths, Mr. and Mrs. L. indicated a desire to further learn how to interact with Jenny by using alternative forms of communication, and increasing their knowledge of technological applications.

Other priorities identified included increasing Jenny's independence in feeding and facilitating her brother's ability to play with her. The team also questioned Mrs. L. about whether she wanted more time to herself to pursue her own endeavors. Mrs. L. responded that she had not been involved in any outside activities since Jenny was born. She stated that now that Jenny was going to be in preschool for several hours a day, perhaps it was time for her to identify some personal interests and think about new activities for herself.

Identification of the strengths, resources, priorities, and concerns of the family in relation to the child should be, in the assessment and planning phases, a family-directed, nonintrusive process. If team members identify areas of strength or priorities that are not considered so by the family, these may be presented in the planning meeting but judged by the parents to be unimportant or irrelevant to the child's program. This is their prerogative.

Major Outcomes

The outcomes that are expected to be achieved from intervention for the child and the family need to be expressed in specific goals and objectives on an IEP or IFSP. Major outcomes, or long-term goals, derive directly from the identified priorities and are to be reviewed on a regular basis. In order to mark progress toward these goals, short-term objectives should be stated as specifically as possible, because they provide direction to the team and family for intervention. Worthwhile objectives must be functional, socially valid, realistic, achievable, and address all phases of learning (Wolery, 1989).

A skill is *functional*, according to Wolery, if it is immediately useful and: 1) results in increased independence for the child (e.g., ability to dress self); 2) allows the child to learn other more complex skills (e.g., ability to imitate); 3) allows the child to be placed in a less restrictive environment (e.g., ability to attend to a task for 5 minutes; or 4) results in the child being more easily assisted or encouraged by the family and others.

Socially valid objectives are those that are relevant to the child and family. The IFSP process should ensure that socially valid objectives are included in the child's program plan. The TPBI process ensures that socially valid, pleasurable activities become part of the child's day. Suggestions for interaction with family members are reflected on the Team Ideas for Play (TIP) Sheets (see Linder, 1993b) generated by the intervention team, which includes family members.

Realistic and *achievable* objectives are more likely to be developed if "the assessment activities take place in natural situations, occur over time, and involve familiar adults when testing is used and when assessment results are validated" (Wolery, 1989, p. 489). Since the TPBA process is conducted in the home or classroom, involves the parents, and may involve observations in the child's classroom as well, it will result in more realistic objectives. Objectives need to be challenging, but not so long-term that parents will become discouraged at the child's lack of progress. It is better to set short-term objectives and update them frequently.

Haring, White, and Liberty (1980) organize *learning* into five phases: acquisition, fluency, maintenance, generalization, and adaptation. Wolery recommends that, when appropriate, goals and objectives be written to address these phases of skill acquisition, to ensure that the child uses the skill optimally.

After Jenny's strengths and needs were identified, six objectives were outlined:

1. *Jenny will be able to operate three developmentally appropriate switch-activated toys independently for 5 minutes on 3 consecutive days.*
2. *Jenny will be able to sequence four dramatic play events with her older brother, using eye-pointing and vocalizations in three different scenarios involving a baby doll.*
3. *Given proper positioning and adaptive equipment, Jenny will be able to drink from a cup with a straw by herself.*
4. *Jenny will be able to start and stop an electric wheelchair on command, using an adapted hand switch on consecutive trials over 5 days.*
5. *Jenny will be able to play one computer game, requiring her to push one adapted button, with any member of her family.*
6. *Given a communication board with pictures of familiar people, objects, and activities in her environment, Jenny will be able to eye-point to symbols for "I want" and "where is" in combination with three referents, and be able to request people, objects, or activities.*

The objectives were than transferred to a TIP Sheet and ideas for incorporating interactions into Jenny's day were brainstormed and also written on the TIP Sheet.

Several family goals were developed from Mr. and Mrs. L.'s suggestions, which evolved from their involvement in the play-based assessment. Three of these included:

1. *Jenny's brothers, Brad and Mark, will be able to use turn-taking in dramatic play, with Jenny directing the actions through vocalizations and eye-pointing.*
2. *Mr. and Mrs. L., Brad, and Mark will take a course for parents of children with disabilities at the Computer Access Center at Children's Hospital, in order to learn how to use computers.*
3. *All members of the family will be able to interact with Jenny on one computer game.*

The objectives that were delineated as part of the IFSP process were derived through a problem-solving process that involved the parents' discussion of their concerns and desires for Jenny, their available family resources, and their own priorities and interests. They were then greatly invested in the implementation of the program plan. The information gained from the TPBA and incorporated into the TPBI gave them a foundation for viewing Jenny and a framework for interacting with her in natural ways in typical environments.

The statement of major outcomes must also include criteria, procedures, and timelines for determining progress toward those stated goals. Criteria for accomplishing the outcomes or goals are stated within the written objectives or identified separately. Procedures may include informal observation, formal testing, parent report, and others; a partial or complete transdisciplinary play-based assessment could be included in these procedures. The Team Assessment of Play (TAP) Sheets (Linder, 1993b) used in the TPBI process allow both interventionists and family members to conduct ongoing naturalistic observations of the child and make appropriate modifications of objectives and strategies. The family, within the constraints of legal mandates, may determine how frequently these updates are desired. In addition, timelines for assessing progress toward goals and objectives must be established. In this regard, communication with families needs to be continuous, and objectives need to be modified as each is attained. Indeed, Part H of IDEA requires that program plans be reviewed with parents every 6 months, and that a complete IFSP evaluation be conducted annually. (Annual re-evaluation is also called for by IDEA.)

Early Intervention Services Needed

For any one family, there are specific early intervention services and agencies that will be necessary to meet their needs. According to Part H, the services and agencies that are appropriate for the family should be clearly stated in the IFSP. Using a problem-solving approach, the parents and professionals on the team can together determine the service delivery approach that best meets the child's and family's needs.

The method, frequency, and intensity of service delivery need to be individualized. Indeed, each family is unique, and their needs for and responses to service delivery represent a continuum (Hutinger, 1988), from maximal involvement to minimal interest. Parents and professionals choose as a team from basic service options, including home-based, center-based, integrated, part-time, or full-time programs. In order to arrive at the options that are most appropriate for the child and family, many factors should be examined. The family's schedule, interests, emotional availability, and other concerns are important considerations.

Jenny's family chose to enroll her in a half-day integrated preschool, with support from consulting specialists. Jenny would also receive individual speech-language, occupational, and physical therapy twice a week. Mr. and Mrs. L. requested that home visits be made once a month to monitor Jenny's progress at home. The team and Mrs. L. decided that Mrs. L. would accompany Jenny to school for the first week, to help the teacher learn Jenny's cues and interaction style. A "back-and-forth" notebook would then be kept, so that the parents and intervention team would be able to coordinate home and school programs. A conference was planned for the end of the first month, to evaluate Jenny's transition into preschool.

Natural Environments

Current legislation, specifically PL 102-119, requires "a statement of the natural environments in which early intervention will be provided." This requirement reflects the growing awareness of the importance of generalization of skills and abilities across all of the environments of the child's life. Intervention cannot take place in isolated settings, with only specialized professionals and therapeutic equipment. In order to be maximally effective, intervention must be conducted in the environments in which children need to *use* their abilities—in other words, in the home, school, child care center, and other community settings that require the child to use skills functionally. The TPBA process identifies functional skills and processes that are needed by the child across numerous environments. Rather than pinpointing isolated skills, the processes and abilities targeted for intervention are those that serve as a foundation for many skills across many environments. Planning for transdisciplinary play-based intervention (Linder, 1993b) involves integrating objectives into the child's natural environments. *For example, Jenny's natural environments included home, school, and community settings such as the grocery store. Identification of these settings in the IFSP assisted the intervention team and family to focus on strategies for functionally using the skills identified in her objectives within these environments. When the team members developed Jenny's Team Ideas for Play (TIP) Sheet during transdisciplinary play-based intervention, they paid particular attention to generating ideas for home, school, and community. Jenny's sixth objective read, "Given a communication board with pictures of familiar people, objects, and activities in her environment, Jenny will be able to eye-point to symbols for 'I want' and 'Where is' in combination with three referents and be able to request people, objects, and activities." On her TIP Sheet, the family identified Jenny's favorite objects and toys at home, foods at the grocery store, people in the neighborhood, and so forth. They found pictures for her communication board and then integrated opportunities for Jenny to request these special people, objects, and activities into her day. The encouragement of the application of her skills across daily environments thus accelerated the acquisition of communication skills.*

Dates for Service Initiation and Duration

For each identified service, the team and family need to determine when services will begin and the projected length of time that services will be needed.

Jenny was evaluated in September and her program plan was designed to begin as soon as she could be enrolled in the integrated preschool. Consultative services with the family and preschool staff were also designated to begin immediately. The team projected that Jenny would be enrolled in the preschool throughout the academic year. The services to the family were projected to be more short term. Weekly consultation with the family was planned, with the speech-language, occupational, and physical therapists monitoring progress on language, positioning and self-feeding objectives. It was anticipated that teaching Jenny's brothers how to follow Jenny's lead in play would take one month, based on meeting weekly. The classes at the Computer Access Center were to continue as long as the family felt them to be beneficial. Progress would be monitored monthly. The team and Mrs. L. agreed to re-evaluate how Mrs. L. was feeling about her own activities by the end of November.

Identification of Service Coordinator

Prior to Part H, parents' choices with regard to services were limited to what was offered at the planning meeting, which was usually only the services provided by the agency conducting it. The Part H legislation recognizes that families of young children with disabilities have many priorities and concerns requiring the coordination of numerous diverse services, many of which may be in other agencies. A service coordinator (formerly known as a case manager) is to be assigned to assist families in acquiring access to services.

Families who have just learned that their child has special needs are often overwhelmed by the implications. They do not have the energy or the psychological resources to be able to tackle the intricate network of service providers. At this point, a service coordinator is a welcome support. As families become more familiar with services and more knowledgeable about their child's needs, they become stronger advocates, and many begin to assume the role of service coordinator for their child. In reality, parents are always the child's service coordinator, because they make the ultimate decisions concerning the child and family needs. At various times, however, when transitions between services are made, when new services are required, or when stresses are great, the family may desire assistance in coordinating programs for their child and family. At these times, the service coordinator can assume greater responsibility to expedite service delivery, support the family, and act as an advocate on the child's behalf.

Although Part H states that the service coordinator should be from the profession most immediately relevant to the infant's or toddler's and family's needs, many different approaches to service coordination will undoubtedly be taken. The family should decide who they would like as a service coordinator, since this person will be responsible for ensuring the implementation of the IFSP, and for coordinating the services required. In all cases, the parents can be listed as co–service coordinators. The responsibilities of the professional service coordinator should be clarified, because the responsibilities will vary depending on the wishes of the family (Bailey & Simeonsson, 1988).

Jenny's parents were vocal and quite capable of advocating on her behalf. They felt that professional assistance would be necessary only when they needed information or they ran into problems acquiring the services that the team had identified within the community. They requested that the physical therapist be named as the co–service coordinator, because most of the specialized services that Jenny and the family would need related to her physical disability. They also felt that they would be consulting with the physical therapist on a regular basis, and having her assist with service coordination would reduce the number of professionals with whom they had to interact.

Procedures for Transition

Parents identify the times when their child is making a transition into a new program as particularly stressful (Barber, Turnbull, Behr, & Kerns, 1988). Changes are difficult for the child and family. Schedules vary, staff are different, services are revised, expectations for child and family are altered, and support systems are modified; the requirement to address procedures for transition in the IFSP is included for this reason. The team and family should determine what will be done to ease transition, and who will assume various responsibilities.

Jenny's mother decided to personally assist Jenny with the transition into preschool. The plan for Jenny's mother to communicate frequently with the teacher and therapy team was also intended to facilitate transition. Mr. and Mrs. L. felt that their support system would increase in the new program and that no additional supports would be necessary. Mrs. L. said that she would like to become involved in school activities with other parents as a means of becoming part of the new school. This was noted in the program plan, with the name of the person to contact in the parent–teacher organization. The suggestion was made that TIP Sheets with intervention ideas for Jenny could be shared with the preschool teacher. This would give the teacher an idea of what was being done at home that could be enhanced in school.

Once completed, the IFSP becomes the working document to guide intervention and the evaluation of the effectiveness of the program for the child and family. Transdisciplinary play-based assessment can be a significant component in the assessment planning process. TPBA/TPBI sets an informal tone, establishes the partnership with the parents, and provides worthwhile information about child and family needs.

REFERENCES

Bailey, D.B., Jr., & Simeonsson, R.J. (1988). *Family assessment in early intervention.* Columbus, OH: Charles E. Merrill.

Bailey, D.B., & Wolery, M. (1989). *Assessing infants and preschoolers with handicaps.* Columbus, OH: Charles E. Merrill.

Barber, P.A., Turnbull, A.P., Behr, S.K., & Kerns, G.M. (1988). A family systems perspective on early childhood special education. In S.L. Odom & M.B. Karnes (Eds.), *Early intervention for infants and children with handicaps: An empirical base* (179–198). Baltimore: Paul H. Brookes Publishing Co.

Brinkerhoff, J.L., & Vincent, L.J. (1986). Increasing parental decision-making at the individualized educational program meeting. *Journal of the Division of Early Childhood, 11*(1), 46–58.

Dunst, C., Trivette, C., & Deal, A. (1988). *Enabling and empowering families: Principles and guidelines for practice.* Cambridge, MA: Brookline Books, Inc.

Haring, N.G., White, O.R., & Liberty, K.A. (1980). *An investigation of phases of learning and facilitating instructional events for the severely handicapped.* Bureau of Education for the Handicapped, Project No. 443CH70564. Seattle, WA: University of Washington, College of Education.

Hutinger, P.L. (1988). Linking screening, identification, and assessment with curriculum. In J.B. Jordan, J.J. Gallagher, P.L. Hutinger, & M.B. Karnes (Eds.), *Early childhood special education: Birth to three.* Reston, VA: Council for Exceptional Children.

Linder, T.W. (1983). *Early childhood special education: Program development and administration.* Baltimore: Paul H. Brookes Publishing Co.

Linder, T.W. (1993a). *Transdisciplinary play-based assessment and intervention: Child and program summary forms.* Baltimore: Paul H. Brookes Publishing Co.

Linder, T.W. (1993b). *Transdisciplinary play-based intervention: Guidelines for developing a meaningful curriculum for young children.* Baltimore: Paul H. Brookes Publishing Co.

Wolery, M. (1989). Using assessment information to plan instructional programs. In D.B. Bailey & M. Wolery (Eds.), *Assessing infants and preschoolers with handicaps.* Columbus, OH: Charles E. Merrill.

III

The TPBA Guidelines

Part III provides the team with the working mechanisms of the transdisciplinary play-based assessment process. Included are guidelines for observing cognitive, social-emotional, communication and language, and sensorimotor development. These are the core of the TPBA process. The guidelines can be used with children from infancy to 6 years of age. Older children who are functioning within that range can also be assessed using the guidelines.

The TPBA process differs from other play scales in two major ways. First, earlier scales have primarily focused on cognitive development, with a few tools addressing language and social interaction in a cursory fashion. TPBA encompasses four domains, with each set of guidelines affording a comprehensive examination of critical aspects of that developmental domain. TPBA is one of the few assessment measures available that assesses motor development within the context of play.

Second, many play observation scales were designed to be used in research studies. The TPBA Observation Guidelines were specifically developed to provide direction to developmental specialists, teachers, therapists, and families with respect to the content and process of intervention. In addition, the TPBA Observation Guidelines yield developmental information pertaining to the child's present level of performance in all areas.

Although these guidelines are designed to be implemented by specialists in the respective developmental domains, it is recognized that all professional disciplines may not be available in every program. For this reason, the chapters and guidelines are written so that they could be used and understood by any discipline. Toward this end, an attempt has been made to eliminate all unnecessary professional jargon. Whenever specific professional terms are needed, they are defined for the reader. In this way, the instrument can be used in a transdisciplinary method, making observation and discussion across domains possible. Professional expertise is preferred, however, and results in increased clinical accuracy.

All of the chapters in Part III employ the same format. A discussion of the content of the guidelines is followed by the guidelines for observation of the domain, age charts, Observation Worksheets, and domain Summary Sheets. The guidelines are divided into major sections for every domain. Within the chapters, each section of the guidelines is discussed by briefly reviewing the literature related to that section, addressing the observation questions, providing examples to illustrate the observations, and commenting on implications for intervention. This format is used to make it easier for the reader to understand the rationale for inclusion of the section, how to observe specific behaviors, and important qualitative aspects of each section of the guidelines. The implications for intervention (indicated by a ☞) assist the reader in linking findings from the TPBA to intervention strategies. The examples used in the observation sections are used again to demonstrate the implication for intervention for these specific children.

The *Observation Guidelines* included with each chapter are based on numerous developmental theories and research in child development. Targets for observation were derived from existing instruments, from the literature, and from experience with children with special needs. The guidelines are meant to help team members identify the child's present level of functioning, as required in Part H, and to provide specific recommendations for developing functional intervention strategies.

Age ranges are provided when applicable to provide approximate age expectations, based on the literature currently available, for various skills discussed in the guidelines. The ranges may be used as a reference for determining the child's estimated developmental levels across different skills.

Observation Worksheets are also provided in each chapter of Part III. These worksheets are intended to be used by observers during the play session and after the session, when reviewing the videotape. They include the major categories addressed on the guidelines. Observers note specific behaviors observed under each category on the worksheet. These behaviors can then be cited in answering the questions on the guidelines.

Summary Sheets for each domain are also included in each chapter. These forms address major sections of the domain. (A thorough discussion of how to complete the Summary Sheets appears in Chapter 5.) The responses to the questions on the guidelines assist professionals in being able to complete the Summary Sheets that outline strengths, areas of and reasons for concern, and things the child is ready for. The information from worksheets, when related to the guidelines and summarized on the domain summary forms provides the basis for program planning and development of strategies for intervention. Each chapter is independent, but interrelated with the other domains; therefore, transdisciplinary discussion is important throughout the process.

A separate pad of child and program forms is available to assist the professional in integrating assessment information into specific plans for home, school, and community. Each pad contains the Observation Worksheets and Summary Sheets needed to assess one child in each area of TPBA, as well as TIP/TAP Sheets and program planning sheets for curriculum development (Linder, 1993; sold five pads per package—see p. *ii* for ordering information). After completion of the TPBA, the team can use the information on the TPBA Observation Worksheets and Summary Sheets to derive a functional set of objectives and intervention suggestions that are then written on the home and school TIP Sheets. Planning for a group of children in a classroom setting is the next step and can be structured through team planning on the program planning sheets.

REFERENCE

Linder, T.W. (1993). *Transdisciplinary play-based assessment and intervention: Child and program summary forms.* Baltimore: Paul H. Brookes Publishing Co.

6

Observation of Cognitive Development

This chapter provides a framework for observing cognitive development during the TPBA play session. Complete guidelines are provided in question format at the end of the chapter, as is done for the other domains. Included in the cognitive domain are categories of play, attention span, early object use, symbolic and representational play, gestural imitation, problem-solving approaches, discrimination/classification, one-to-one correspondence, sequencing ability, and drawing ability. The nondirective nature of the assessment process precludes evaluation of cognitive aspects such as memory or computation skills; further evaluation may be required if information on these cognitive skills is desired.

The cognitive chapter and accompanying guidelines are meant to be used in conjunction with the other chapters and Observation Guidelines in Part III. All areas are interrelated, and no one area can stand alone.

CATEGORIES OF PLAY

Various researchers have categorized a child's play and non-play behaviors. Weisler and McCall (1976) differentiate exploration from play, explaining that exploration is a more stereotypical examination of objects or situations for the purpose of acquiring information. Play is seen by these researchers as occurring after the child has enough information about an object or a situation to decide how the object can be used or the situation can be modified (Hutt, 1979; Rubin, Fein, & Vandenberg, 1983). Other researchers see exploration as a type of play (Garvey, 1977; Musselwhite, 1986; Wehman, 1979).

Range of Categories

Within TPBA, and also cited elsewhere, play is differentiated as being: 1) exploratory (or sensorimotor), 2) relational, 3) constructive, 4) dramatic, 5) games-with-rules, or 6) rough-and-tumble (Piaget, 1962; Rubin, 1984; Rubin et al., 1983; Smilansky, 1968). Children may primarily engage in one type of play or they may exhibit various types of play, depending on their developmental level and their interests.

Exploratory or Sensorimotor Play
Called *functional play* by Rubin (1984), exploratory play is defined as "an activity which is done simply for the enjoyment of the physical sensation it creates" (p. 3). However, in order to differentiate this play from relational (sometimes called *functional*) play in this discussion, the term exploratory play is used rather than functional play. Examples include repetitive motor movements, such as pouring water in and

out of containers, making noises with the mouth or objects, and repeatedly climbing up and down steps.

Relational Play   Relational play denotes the child's ability to use objects in play for the purposes for which they were intended (Fenson, Kagan, Kearsley, & Zelazo, 1976). This includes using simple objects correctly, such as a brush for the hair; combining related objects, such as a truck and driver; and making objects do what they are made to do, such as pumping the handle on a top.

Constructive Play   "Manipulation of objects for the purpose of constructing or creating something" is how Rubin (1984, p. 4) defines constructive play (Smilansky, 1968). The difference between exploratory, relational, and constructive play is that in constructive play the child has an end goal in mind that requires the transformation of objects into a new configuration. Examples include building a fence with blocks or making a face from clay.

Dramatic Play   Also called *symbolic play* (Chance, 1979; Piaget, 1962), dramatic play (Rubin, 1984; Smilansky, 1968) involves the child pretending to do something or be someone. The child pretends with objects (drinks from a cup), pretends without objects (brushes his or her teeth with a finger), or pretends through other inanimate objects (has dolls pretend to feed the animals).

Games-with-Rules Play   Games with rules (Rubin, 1984, Smilansky, 1968) involve the child in an activity with accepted rules or limits. The game implies shared expectations and a willingness to conform to agreed-upon procedures (Garvey, 1977). An element of competition may also be suggested, either with another child or with him- or herself (Rubin, 1984). The game can be a preset standard game, such as the card game "Go Fish," or it can be a game with rules that the child makes up.

Rough-and-Tumble Play   Boisterous and physical are two ways to describe rough-and-tumble play. Garvey (1977) defines rough-and-tumble play as "action patterns that are performed at a high pitch of activity, usually by a group" (p. 35), although two people can also engage in rough-and-tumble play. It can include such things as running, hopping, tickling, playful "punching," or rolling around on the floor. Aggressive behavior, in contrast to rough-and-tumble, is *not* done in a playful manner.

These six categories of play must be considered by the TPBA team. The child being assessed may engage in primarily exploratory or sensorimotor behaviors, examining objects and determining their characteristics. Such behaviors include mouthing, looking, touching, or repeating an activity in a repetitive fashion. Young infants of 6–9 months may explore a toy by looking at it, touching it, or mouthing it—all sensory exploration. An older child with disabilities may engage in similar behavior with a toy or may repeat an action, such as throwing blocks, just because he or she likes the sensations received from this action.

The child from 9 months on may be seen playing with toys in functional or relational ways, using them as they were intended, seeing relations and combining toys that are functionally related (Fenson et al., 1976). For example, the child may relate common objects such as a bowl and a spoon, items that are functionally encountered every day. This ability to relate objects increases and is predominant from the first to the second year of life (Fein & Apfel, 1979; Fenson et al., 1976; Rosenblatt, 1977; Zelazo & Kearsley, 1980). A child with disabilities may show prolonged relational play.

Susan, age 4, was observed putting several related objects together during the TPBA play session. She put a glass in a cup, a hat on a doll, a shoe on her foot, and a cloth to her face; however, she had not yet acquired the ability to combine functions or use this relational knowledge in more complex play sequences.

The team should observe whether the child can use his or her relational knowledge to construct or create a new configuration. Although the child of 1 year can combine two blocks, true construction is not seen until the child creates a structure with the blocks. The 2-year-old may be seen stacking blocks and knocking them down, but constructive play is not predominant until the third year. The 3- to 3½-year-old will build enclosures. From 3½ years on, the child will build three-dimensional structures that represent buildings (Westby, 1980). It is important here to differentiate between simple relational play and constructive play. Stringing beads or combining pop beads may be seen as relational play, because the child is relating like objects in a meaningful way; however, combining beads to make a necklace can be seen as constructive play. The latter is a higher-level ability, requiring the child to combine objects into a new representation.

Some children prefer dramatic or symbolic play. Relational play leads the child into exploration of interrelationships among objects and events. From this exploration evolves an understanding of spatial relations, causal relations, and categorical relations, all elements observed in dramatic play. Early representational play, such as pretending to drink from a cup, can be seen around 1 year of age, but dramatic play with sequences of pretend acts does not predominate until after 2 years of age (Belsky & Most, 1981; Fenson & Ramsay, 1981; McCune-Nicholich, 1981). From 2 years to 6 years of age, dramatic play becomes more elaborate, combining materials and events in increasingly more complex ways. The child becomes less controlled by the objects and materials at hand and better able to plan events and roles within dramatic play (Garvey, 1977). Most preschool-age children find dramatic play a satisfying means by which to act on their knowledge of the world.

Sally, age 5, was observed in a play session pretending to put gas in the car, driving to the grocery store, getting groceries, and coming back to prepare dinner for her "guests." She used real, substitute, and pretend objects in her scenarios. When the facilitator introduced Sally to the block and manipulative areas, Sally proceeded to pick up "cakes" (blocks) for her party and "drive" back to the house area. Sally clearly preferred dramatic play to other types of play.

Play involving games with rules may be harder to observe in the TPBA play setting. The parent may be asked if the child initiates or likes to participate in games with rules, such as "Duck-Duck-Goose." The child does not seek out games with rules until the child has a social understanding of roles in games, a concept of competition, or winning and losing, and a grasp of the idea of rules or guidelines that remain the same from situation to situation (Piaget, 1962). Games with rules become important to the child over 5 years of age. Younger children may like to play games with rules, but they change the rules to meet their own needs. When observing the older child in the TPBA play session, it may be possible to entice the child into a favorite card game or competitive ball game with rules that the child creates alone or with the facilitator. Observers can then note how well the child understands and maintains the rules, how important winning is to the child, and how persistent the child is in this type of play.

Spontaneous rough-and-tumble play can be observed in younger children, around age 3, but is most predominant in children from 4 through 5 years of age (Garvey, 1977). Rough-and-tumble play is most easily observed in a group or classroom situation, where children are familiar with each other. If the observers have an opportunity to watch the child's class or talk to the child's classroom teacher, involvement in rough-and-tumble play can be investigated. During the actual play session, the facilitator may try to engage the child in rough-and-tumble activities. Many children thoroughly enjoy this activity, but others are not at all interested, and, in fact, may find even playful physical interaction to be unpleasant. For still other children, this type of play may provide a route to interaction not available in other forms of play.

Robert, a nonverbal, noninteractive 5-year-old, did not engage with the facilitator in rela-

tional, dramatic, or constructive play. When movement became the basis of the interaction, how-ever, Robert became interested in the facilitator. They ran, jumped, and chased each other. The facilitator tickled and rocked Robert, and he responded by seeking more of the same type of inter-action. After these interactions, Robert was also able to focus on the facilitator and imitate other behaviors.

☞   Knowing the child's primary mode of play is important to those who will work with the child. First, they will understand something about the child's developmental level in play. Second, they will be able to incorporate the child's preferences into intervention activities. Third, the staff will be better able to make recommendations to the parents about play activities at home. During the TPBA play session, the team has an opportunity to observe the child in various types of play activities, and patterns and preferences become apparent very quickly.

In Robert's school program, the day was structured into activities that the teacher directed. Robert was reinforced with yogurt-covered raisins for correct responses. Robert did not interact with teachers, therapists, or peers. He performed, when he chose to perform, with robot-like re-sponses and little positive affect.

After the play session, recommendations were made to the intervention team to increase sensorimotor activities and rough-and-tumble play at the beginning of Robert's day. A particular team member was selected to relate to Robert in order to develop ongoing playful interactions that Robert could anticipate. Sensorimotor activities were incorporated throughout the day, as Robert had shown a preference for these in the play session.

After only a few weeks, Robert sought interactions more frequently with the team member with whom he played, his vocalizations increased, and he said "more" during the rough-and-tumble times. Robert's attention span immediately following sensorimotor and rough-and-tumble activities also increased. Therefore, this information about Robert's primary play modalities changed the content, process, and schedule of his day. In addition, Robert's parents spent more time with him in similar type of activities at home, and thus were able to improve their interactions with him.

ATTENTION SPAN

A child's ~~ability to focus attention on a given activity~~ is viewed by many teachers as an important cognitive ability. Children who cannot attend well are frequently seen as "hyper-active," "easily distracted," or "immature," and are consequently referred for further evalua-tion. What is often overlooked, however, is that a child may attend differentially to various activities, or attend better at various times of the day and with different people. Although there are no norms regarding the appropriate length of attention span for any given age level, the qualitative aspects of attention are worthy of observation and documentation.

Attention Preferences

Observing the child for an hour to an hour and a half gives team members an opportunity to watch for fluctuations in attention span across stimuli, in different types of play, or during different parts of the session. As mentioned in the previous section, the team should attend to the categories of play activities that captivate the child for the longest periods of time.

While observing the play session and viewing the videotape after the session, team members need to note the amount of time the child spends engaged in the various catego-

---

☞ indicates discussion of implications for intervention. Readers will see this symbol throughout each of the guidelines chapters.

ries of play. Does the child spend more time in simple exploration, or in one of the other categories of play? In the same way, it should be noted which types of activities engage the child for the least amount of time. Also of importance is the sequence of the child's attention. What the child chooses to do first or second and at various times during the session (beginning, middle, end) may reveal interests that affect attention. The team also has an opportunity to observe the child interacting with the facilitator, the parent(s), and a peer; the child's attention span may vary with different people.

Also of importance is whether the child is particularly attracted by certain characteristics of play objects or situations. Some children select objects that have strong visual features, such as bright colors, tiny pieces, or similar parts (e.g., wheels). Others attend for longer periods of time to objects that make noise or objects that have distinct tactile characteristics.

☞ All of this information may provide clues about the child's interests, strengths, and weaknesses.

Three-year-old Tina's attention was particularly focused when tactile materials were involved. She rubbed the facilitator's socks, explored the texture of the sand in the sand table without playing with objects on the table, and sat in and manipulated packing "peanuts." All of these are activities, demonstrating lower-level play skills. However, she was also observed to engage in simple dramatic play for a long period of time, demonstrating a capacity for higher-level cognitive thinking.

After observing the patterns of Tina's interactions with people and objects, it became clear that this child's need for tactile input was negatively affecting her ability to focus on and use objects in more functional ways. Recommendations were made for further sensory evaluation. In addition, recommendations were made to the intervention team regarding how to facilitate the child's involvement in higher-level cognitive play by incorporating her interests and strengths. For instance, by using materials with strong tactile input in the dollhouse, such as furry doll blankets, Bristle blocks for "food," silky material for a table cloth, or rough towels to dry the baby, Tina's attention was captured. The staff was then able to engage her in representational play with those materials.

Information on the child's attention preferences may also enable the team to arrange the child's schedule and activities to optimize the child's focus of attention, and thus encourage his or her learning.

Maggie's attention span was longer at the beginning of the session than at the end, and dramatic play held her attention for longer periods of time than did constructive play. This information allowed Maggie's teacher to arrange the schedule for her so that constructive type play came early in the day and dramatic play came later. This helped to maximize Maggie's attention throughout the day.

Locus of Control

Another aspect of attention is how much external reinforcement is needed to maintain the child's focus of attention. Some children will control the flow of the entire play session, selecting, attending to, and changing activities without the need for adult direction or reinforcement. Other children will need various degrees of direction, support, and reinforcement to maintain active involvement in the session. The team needs to evaluate the type of reinforcement to which the child responds most positively. For some children, verbal encouragement will be enough, while for others physical support or prompting will be needed.

During the TPBA play session, Shawna (3 ½ years old) flitted from activity to activity with little internal motivation to stay with an endeavor. When the facilitator showed excitement over

Shawna's ability to stack up a tower of blocks, Shawna looked at her, then proceeded to stack the blocks again. The facilitator used verbal reinforcement and also physically hugged Shawna when she accomplished a challenging task; Shawna consistently responded by smiling and repeating whatever had earned her praise.

Luther, a 5-year-old referred by his teacher due to complaints of a short attention span, was observed in the play session to have an adequate attention span. He needed the facilitator, however, to imitate his play, model for him, and comment on his actions. When left alone, his attention shifted rapidly from activity to activity. As he was frequently not in a one-to-one situation with his teacher, the difference in his behavior was evident.

☞   The type and amount of external reinforcement that is needed to assist the child in maintaining active involvement is relevant to all staff who will be working with the child, as well as to the parents.

In Shawna's case, one-to-one attention and verbal praise were highly effective in improving her attention to activities. In the mainstreamed preschool setting, her teacher was encouraged to not only use verbal praise, but also to teach the other children in the class to praise Shawna's positive performance as well. In this way, Shawna would receive one-to-one attention when the teacher was unavailable.

For Luther, recommendations concerning how to use imitation and modeling in facilitating play, how to pair him with a higher-level peer, and how to select optimal interest play activities were made.

Distractibility   A final concern in the area of attention span is how easily the child is distracted. Sudden shifts in the child's attention should be noted, along with whether these occur due to a change in interest, or whether visual or auditory stimuli draw the child away from play. If other activities are taking place near the child, they may or may not be distracting to the child. Again, this may be useful information for interventionists, and environmental modifications can be made to reduce distractions.

As stated previously, the area of attention span is one that has little normative data on which to base judgments of age appropriateness. Professional judgment will need to be made concerning how problematic attention deficits may be. The important element here is not diagnosing a disorder, but rather, documenting the aspects of play, the sequence of play, and the facilitation methods that most *enhance* the child's attention.

EARLY OBJECT USE

Schemes are a Piagetian concept defined as a basic unit of knowledge, a mental structure that represents both the internal and external aspects of the child's world (Ginsberg & Opper, 1988). Schemes may relate to physical behaviors, mental images, or complex belief systems (Piaget, 1962). The child's first schemes are sensory in nature; looking, tasting, touching, smelling, hearing, and moving all provide input to the brain. The messages left in the brain as a result of sensory and motor input gradually become integrated and coordinated, resulting in the child's ability to use more complex schemes, sequences of schemes, and increasingly more abstract schemes. This developmental process results in the child's ability to engage in the more sophisticated categories of play.

Objects are not important to the infant in the first 2 or 3 months of life. The infant gets enjoyment out of repeating actions for their own sake; Piaget calls these repetitive actions *primary circular reactions*. Even after the child has acquired an interest in manipulating objects, play is focused on the action that can be performed with the object (mouthing, banging, shaking), rather than the object itself (Lamb & Campos, 1982). Actions on objects in this stage relate to the sensorimotor play discussed earlier.

Between 6 and 9 months of age, the child begins to pay attention to the characteristics of objects, and his or her play becomes more exploratory. The child is still tuned in to perceptual attributes, such as color, size, and shape, but is increasingly aware of characteristics of objects such as texture and weight (Fewell & Kaminski, 1988). His or her range of schemes is increasing to include pushing, pulling, waving, turning objects over, poking, and tearing.

By 8–9 months of age, an important change occurs in the child's play. He or she begins to be able to combine schemes into "relational play" (Fenson et al., 1976). The child may now put objects into a container or stir with a spoon in a bowl. This play is important in several ways. First, it denotes the child's ability to see the relationship between the "meaning" of two objects and demonstrates cause-and-effect understanding; second, it demonstrates the child's ability to sequence two schemes (e.g., grasping and stirring); and third, it shows the child's developing understanding of spatial relations. The simple combining of objects, such as stirring with a spoon, may also denote the first rudimentary attempts at representing what is known about the world.

By 12 months of age, a child's understanding of the relation between actions and resulting consequences is reflected in the play in which the child engages, acting on objects with a great variety of schemes in order to discover the characteristics of those objects and to see the effects of his or her actions. Pushing buttons, turning handles, and opening and shutting lids and doors are just part of the child's growing repertoire.

In addition, the child's play shifts from simple exploration of objects and application of the same schemes to all objects, to play, which demonstrates an understanding of the functions of objects (Belsky & Most, 1981; Fenson et al., 1976; Zelazo & Kearsley, 1980). The child will push cars, put a comb to his or her hair, put a spoon to his or her mouth, and differentiate schemes according to the type of toy with which he or she is playing, such as blowing in a noise maker instead of banging it. These developing abilities—to see the relationships between objects, to apply discrete schemes to different objects, and to use objects according to their appropriate functions—are first steps in the development of a conceptual system that will help the child make sense of the world.

Observation of people has brought the child to the point where he or she can now imitate actions with objects. Imitation of adults' actions takes on increasingly greater significance, and will lead the child into constructive and symbolic play. Rudimentary constructive play begins soon after the child has begun relational play; the child will stack two blocks shortly after the first year (Bayley, 1969). But true constructive play requires the ability to conceptualize what one is trying to construct, and is thus closely related to the development of representational skills.

Type and Range of Schemes

The previously discussed literature serves as background for the section of the guidelines relating to the child's play schemes. It is important to observe the child's play throughout the session, since the developmental level that the child exhibits may vary from activity to activity. Although all of the schemes and object play just described should be exhibited by around 12 months of age, they are included here as an important aspect of play observation because many children with disabilities reveal deficits in these early behaviors.

The type of schemes that were observed during the play session should be noted. In addition, the percentage of schemes that were developmentally immature (e.g., mouthing, banging, shaking) versus the percentage that were complex, more adaptive schemes (e.g., pushing, poking, pulling, turning) provide important insights about the child. The child may use a great variety of schemes, or may be limited to repetition of the same actions over and over. Therefore, the frequency of use of various schemes is also important.

Scheme Use and Generalization

The child's ability to generalize schemes appropriately across multiple objects (e.g., stirs in cup, stirs in pot, stirs on plate) and to adapt schemes to new objects (e.g., turns key in lock, turns handle of a door, turns cap on bottle) is also important. For example, a child may demonstrate a variety of schemes within the session, but his or her pattern of object use might be predominantly one of mouthing and throwing. In other words, this child may have the ability to use objects more appropriately, but qualitatively his or her actions on objects are limited.

Linking of Schemes

In addition to the variety and generalization of schemes, the team should watch the child's ability to link schemes into meaningful sequences. For example, shortly after 12 months of age, a child might grasp a block and place it on the table, then grasp another block and place it on top of the first. An example of a higher-level scheme sequence would be evident in the child who pretends to get the food from the refrigerator, puts it on the table, and feeds the baby. This type of sequence might be seen around 2 years of age (Fewell, 1983). In dramatic play, the highest form of sequencing would be exhibited in script play, where the child is able to act out a long string of related scheme sequences into a story. The child might fix dinner, serve it, wash the dishes, and go to bed. This shows an ability not only to link schemes, but also relate each sequence into an integrated whole with a beginning, a middle, and an end (Curry & Arnaud, 1984; Westby, 1980). Script play develops around 3 years of age (Westby, 1980). The ability to plan and conceptualize time, action sequences, and role behaviors in this play can be seen as precursors to academic listening, storytelling, and reading skills.

For all of the previously mentioned areas of scheme use, observations are made about whether the child: 1) spontaneously uses the schemes, 2) will imitate schemes after modeling, or 3) needs physical or verbal prompting to engage in play. Again, the child's behavior will vary depending on the type of play, the familiarity of the toy, the familiarity of the person interacting with the child, and the child's motivation level.

☞   Both type and quality of schemes used by the child are certainly relevant to the intervention team. By examining the observation data, the team can determine which schemes the child is ready to add to his or her repertoire, as well as which ones are present but not being generalized or adequately incorporated into functional skills.

Looking at the number of schemes or behaviors in a sequence that a child is able to combine is also relevant to intervention. If the child has been observed to primarily combine two or three schemes in a sequence, the team can work on "bumping up" the child's sequence to three or four steps.

In dramatic play, Justin was able to act out pulling his revolver and shooting the facilitator several times (a favorite game with his mother and father). This two-step sequence was typical of Justin's play. Recommendations were made to expand Justin's sequences. In the above scenario, a step was added to put a bandage on the wounded person—an expansion that was easily adopted by Justin, as were other expansions of his sequences. He merely needed a model for the next step in a sequence and several practice times. Using themes and toys that were motivating to Justin was also important.

SYMBOLIC AND REPRESENTATIONAL PLAY

Symbolic Object Use

The development of symbolic use of objects follows the child's ability to use a wide range of schemes, and to use them functionally with objects. At the same time, the child's memory of events is increasing, and he or she is beginning to associate specific labels (another form of symbol) with objects, people, and events. The emergence of symbolic play, which also denotes the development of representational thought, begins between 12 and 15 months of age, with the child pretending to engage in real life activities, such as eating or sleeping (Fein & Apfel, 1979; Fenson et al., 1976). The pretend activities center on the child's own body and actions (Nicholich, 1977; Watson & Fischer, 1977; Westby, 1980). Not until after 16 months of age is the child able to focus the pretend play on other people and objects (Fewell, 1983; Westby, 1980). The child will first direct actions toward persons (e.g., feeding mother) and then will direct actions toward inanimate others (e.g., feeding the stuffed dog) (Fein & Apfel, 1979). Around 2 years of age, the child is capable of having the inanimate object perform actions (e.g., having the doll wash itself) (Watson & Fischer, 1977).

As the child becomes capable of *decentering* (Piaget, 1962), he or she can focus attention on other persons. Play also becomes more *decontextualized* (Werner & Kaplan, 1963), a term that refers to the child's ability to use something other than the actual object, or to use an object away from its normal context. Between 18 and 24 months of age, the child gradually increases the ability to use nonrealistic objects in pretend play (Elder & Pederson, 1978; Watson & Fischer, 1977). Initially, the substitute objects must appear similar to the actual object (Ungerer, Zelazo, Kearsley, & O'Leary, 1981). After 2 years of age, the child becomes increasingly capable of using more abstract representations of the actual object, until around 3 years of age, when the child begins to use imaginary objects. During the ages of 4 and 5 years, the child is capable of creating imaginary characters within play (Garvey, 1977).

Symbolic Play Roles

Watson (1981) has also explored the sequence by which children acquire an understanding of various roles within their play. His study showed that most 3 ½-year-old children could make a doll carry out several activities, which indicated that they understood the social roles of a character (e.g., doctor). Most 4-year-old children could act out a doctor-and-patient interaction with dolls, indicating that they understood the relationship between the two. Most 5-year-olds were able to increase their role understanding to three interacting dolls, with themselves directing the interaction. Six-year-old children demonstrated an understanding of how a character can assume more than one role at a time (doctor and father), which they related to another character who had more than one role (patient and daughter). Watson termed this *role intersection*. The child's play thus demonstrates a growing understanding of categories of behavior and differentiation of those categories into various roles. By observing the child's play, the level of role understanding can be ascertained.

During the observation of dramatic play, the team observes the child's ability to use objects symbolically. In other words, the team examines the degree to which the child is capable of using one object to represent another (abstraction). As previously discussed, the child will first need the real object for an activity. He or she may then substitute a realistic object for the real object (e.g., a stick for a toothbrush), and then an unrealistic object (e.g., a banana for a telephone). Finally, the child will be able to pretend an object exists without any prop.

Examination of the roles the child is capable of assuming is another crucial element of symbolic play (Arnaud & Curry, 1973). As noted by Watson (1981) and Watson and Fischer (1977), the sequence can be observed by attending to whom or what the child's actions are directed—self, object or toy, or another person. The actions that the child portrays demonstrate that he or she understands behaviors that are important to specific roles he or she assumes. For example, the child who is playing "gas station" may show an understanding of the role of a gas station attendant by filling the gas tank, putting in oil, and fixing a flat tire.

Another element of role understanding is seen in observation of the child's play with dolls and props (e.g., soldiers and tanks, or hospital, doctors, nurses, patients). If appropriate to the child's level of functioning, the team should provide the child with the opportunity to play with miniature dolls in a scene such as a house, hospital, farm, or gas station; the team can then ascertain the child's level of role comprehension. Observers should document the actions and words of the child that denote comprehension of roles and responsibilities.

For example, in the hospital scene the child might have the patient doll say, "I don't feel good," to which the nurse doll replies, "I'll take your temperature and give you some medicine." The doctor doll then enters and says, "You're going to need an operation." By observing how the child directs the scene, it is possible to see that the child is capable of understanding and directing three characters. The characters all relate to the patient, however, and not to each other in this example.

Representational play also gives the facilitator a chance to explore the child's expression of emotions related to themes of concern to the child. Evaluation of this aspect of emotional development will be discussed in more detail in Chapter 7.

☞   Symbolic and representational play skills have implications for both the cognitive and emotional areas of intervention. Dramatic play can provide an arena for the expression and facilitation of almost every type of cognitive skill, and should therefore hold a fundamental role in the total intervention program. Through modeling, expanding, questioning, and problem-solving, the team can move the child to the next level of symbolic object use, role understanding, and scenario development.

During the play session, 4-year-old Betsy was observed playing with the toy bus. She was able to put the toy people in the bus, drive them to the house, and take them out. Then she would repeat the sequence again and again. Because Betsy seemed intrigued by buses (she took one to school every day), the team decided to use the theme of the bus for dramatic play in Betsy's intervention program.

The teacher set up chairs to form a "bus," and everyone had dress-up coats, hats, and purses. The occupational therapist made suggestions for positioning several children, and the speech-language therapist incorporated suggestions for language skill development that fit with the scenario. The teacher and therapists modeled the various roles of bus driver, rider, and new passengers getting on the bus.

Betsy was teamed with the teacher as the bus driver. She imitated putting the keys in the ignition, turning on the bus, and driving. After several successful "trips," the teacher hid the real keys and substituted a ring of plastic toy "fish," which looked similar to the real keys. Betsy had no problem understanding this substitution in the now familiar role-play. The team then expanded the role-play to picking up passengers, waving to people on the street, getting gas, and, finally, having a flat tire. Betsy also, at times, acted as the passenger and the gas station attendant.

The scenarios were acted out over several weeks with team facilitation. The team then withdrew from the role-plays and watched as the children created their own modifications. Betsy was now able to switch roles on her own and use various types of real and substitute props. When observed with a toy bus and miniature people, Betsy's play now reflected the ideas that she had acted out in scenarios with the class. The team used the same approach with many diverse themes throughout the year.

IMITATION

Imitation is one of the primary means by which children learn. The development of symbolic thought and dramatic play derive from "internal imitation" (Ginsberg & Opper, 1988). Early imitation behaviors are both physical and vocal, as the child begins to represent things by recreating actions. By age 4–8 months, the infant will imitate the actions of others if those actions are already part of his or her repertoire. Imitation of sounds and gestures that are not in the child's repertoire follow from ages 8–12 months, although reproductions are frequently not accurate. By 12–18 months of age, the child's imitative abilities are more systematic, and the child is more adept at immediate imitation of a model. The older child is able to perform these acts mentally; from 18 months to 2 years of age, the child develops the capacity to mentally represent an act that is not perceptually present (Dunst, 1980; Ginsberg & Opper, 1988). This mental representation allows the child to perform deferred imitation, or imitation of actions seen at a previous time.

The relationship to dramatic play therefore becomes clear. In dramatic play, the child is able to act out scenes and sequences that he or she has previously seen in the environment. As previously noted, at first the imitated scheme sequences are short, increasing in length as the child's representational abilities increase. The child of 4 and 5 years of age can also create new sequences and scripts made up of "pieces" of actions that were seen in different times and different places. Such a child now has a storehouse of memories of actions, roles, scenarios, and relationships from which to draw (Garvey, 1977). Cognitively, the child's imitative abilities are now limited only by his or her previous experiential base and capacity to draw on those experiences to formulate new ideas for play.

Level of Imitation

Observations of the child's imitative abilities include looking at the developmental level of the child's skills. Can the child imitate simple visible gestures (gestures that he or she can see self perform, such as clapping), invisible gestures (those that he or she cannot see, such as pursing lips), and familiar or unfamiliar sounds or words? Younger children can only imitate sounds that are in their repertoire, whereas older children can imitate sounds that are new to them (e.g., making a "whooshing" noise with a toy car). When observing sound imitation, it is important to look at the child's overall imitative abilities, because an inability to imitate some sounds may indicate an oral motor or articulation problem rather than delayed imitative abilities. Children may also demonstrate different levels of skill in gestural and vocal imitation (Dunst, 1980; Uzgiris & Hunt, 1975).

In toy play, the team should note whether the child can imitate single schemes or more complex scheme sequences. For example, if the child can imitate putting a block in a can, he or she may also be able to imitate putting a block in the can and then shaking the can. Whether the child is capable of imitating sequences of representational play, such as washing the doll, wrapping it in a towel, and putting it to bed, should also be noted. In addition, the team needs to observe whether the child can imitate problem-solving approaches, including tool usage, such as imitating the facilitator using a stick to get the latch open on a water wheel.

The level of drawing that the child can imitate, from simple marks and strokes to more complex spatial configurations, such as circles, squares or triangles is also important. Is the child able to imitate representations of people, houses, flowers, or other likenesses that are known to him or her? And, finally, can he or she imitate unfamiliar, complex figures and/or representations?

Timing of Imitation

The timing of the child's imitations is also important to note. Some children may demonstrate a delayed response, but they are still be able to replicate the facilitator's actions. Several seconds, or even minutes, after the facilitator has demonstrated an action, the child may repeat the behavior. This delayed response may indicate that the child has difficulty processing the information. The team should note whether the stimuli presented were auditory, visual, kinesthetic, or a combination of these, in order to better understand the type of processing problem the child is experiencing.

Another type of delayed imitation, *deferred imitation*, is not problematic. Deferred imitation, or the ability to imitate behaviors and roles previously seen, is an important skill for the toddler and preschooler. Observation of deferred imitation will give the team insight into the experiential background of the child. One abused child, who had previously been hospitalized for inflicted wounds, chose to act out hospital scenes where she alternately played the roles of doctor and patient. In deferred imitation, the child can reproduce experiences from memory at will. When a delay in imitation is due to slowness of processing, the child cannot imitate immediately.

Team members also observe the context in which the child's imitations take place. Many children with disabilities will imitate gestures, vocalizations, or sounds, but not in the contexts for which they were intended. For example, the child may repeat words or phrases previously heard, but the context in which he or she uses them is inappropriate.

At the beginning of his play session, Freddie entered the play room and said to the facilitator, "Bye, nice to see you again." He wasn't leaving and he had never met the facilitator before. Throughout the session, Freddie interjected words and phrases that he had heard previously or that the facilitator had just said.

In some cases, this type of behavior reflects echolalic speech, but in others, it may indicate processing difficulties or emotional disturbances. Only the *overall pattern* of behavior can help to differentiate the underlying problem.

Turn-Taking

Turn-taking is frequently an imitative behavior; the team should observe turn-taking in each area of development, including the physical movements or sensorimotor acts that the child imitates and seeks to continue through several turns. Chasing, tickling, and jumping are examples of physical turn-taking, in which the child may imitate the facilitator in back-and-forth play. Vocal imitative play may also be initiated by the child with the intent of continuing the game. Rhyming words is an example. (Conversation is also turn-taking, but usually without imitation.) Turn-taking behavior may take place with objects, such as a ball in representational play, such as taking turns talking on the phone, or in structured games, such as cards; it is important to note during which situations it takes place.

If the child does engage in turn-taking within activities, he or she may imitate the facilitator's turn or modify it and add variations on the theme. For example, in taking turns throwing the ball back and forth, the child may change the turn by bouncing or kicking the ball to the facilitator. These qualitative aspects of imitation are not only important to cognitive development, but to social development as well. Turn-taking is critical to communication and social interaction. The ability to modify a turn is necessary to keep a partner interested, and therefore helps to maintain an interaction.

Observers need to assess how much of the child's play is spontaneous and how much of it is exhibited in imitation. Children with disabilities may exhibit many skills in imitation that are seen less frequently through spontaneous initiation. This has important implications for intervention, because behaviors that can be imitated are obviously within a child's capability, and may be viewed as emerging skills. Imitated skills may become targets for intervention, so that these behaviors can become spontaneous.

Betsy was able to perform many more steps in her "bus" role-play after she had imitated her intervention team on numerous occasions. By making the experiences highly motivating and repeating the variations until they were incorporated into Betsy's understanding, the team was able to move Betsy from imitation to spontaneous use of these skills.

Children who do not consistently imitate adults or peers, or who imitate only certain categories of play, can be assisted in several ways. When imitation skills are minimal, the team will need to begin with low-level schemes that are within the child's spontaneous repertoire, and prompt and reinforce the imitation of those behaviors. Increasing attention, by using highly motivated stimuli and exaggerated movements and affect, may improve the potential for imitation. The actions the child does imitate may be generalized to new toys and expanded by slight modification.

PROBLEM-SOLVING APPROACHES

From a Piagetian framework, problem-solving is one section of the sensorimotor stage. Many instruments designed to assess infants incorporate a detailed assessment of the child's problem-solving skills (Dunst, 1980; Uzgiris & Hunt, 1975). Object permanence, means–ends behavior, and spatial understanding are viewed as separate areas for assessment on these ordinal scales. As the child gets older, however, the ability to solve more complex problems depends on the integration of these skills. For this reason, problem-solving in the play-based assessment has integrated key developmental skills from each of these areas.

The young infant is learning to relate information from his or her sensory systems, including vestibular input, proprioception, vision, hearing, touch, taste, and smell. The child is organizing this information along with a growing understanding of objects and people, a foundation that gives the child a better means to get needs met and accomplish goals. Needs and goals are also changing as the child matures; therefore, the problems he or she needs to solve are different at various developmental levels. The following, based on the work of Piaget (1962) and Uzgiris and Hunt (1975) summarizes how problem-solving evolves as the child develops:

From ages 6 to 9 months, the child's basic problem is how to acquire the objects he or she wants, and how to make an interesting event recur with body movement.

From ages 9 to 12 months, the child is learning how to perform actions and how to use adults to achieve desired results.

From ages 12 to 18 months, the child is learning more about what makes things work. He or she knows objects, their parts, their mechanisms, their relationships to other objects, and how people can have an affect on objects.

From ages 18 to 24 months, the child is learning to think about his or her actions. Combined with increasing fine motor skills and emerging language skills, the child can explore with more precision and take instruction from adults.

From ages 2 to 4 years, the child's problem-solving involves taking acquired knowledge and applying it to new situations. Problem-solving involves reasoning from situation to situation.

From age 5 on, the child's problem-solving relies less on perceptual problem-solving and more on building an integrated understanding of the rules governing how things work.

Means—End and Cause-and-Effect

During the play session, team members need to observe the means the child uses to accomplish goals, and how the child who is challenged by an activity, situation, or event attempts to attain the desired end. The team may observe problem-solving skills by arranging the environment so that the child encounters new toys and materials that are highly motivating yet challenging. Toys such as cash registers, key and lock boxes, and pop-up toys with different types of door-opening devices can be incorporated into the play time. Naturalistic observation of problem-solving during role-play or building with blocks is just as relevant, however, because it demonstrates how well the child has generalized skills to new situations. For example, how the child figures out how to open the oven door in the dollhouse, or what the child does when the pan won't fit in the refrigerator will provide information about skill generalization and problem-solving.

Problem-solving within motor activities is also important. As the child encounters unfamiliar gross motor toys or maneuvers through an obstacle course, his or her gross motor problem-solving (or motor planning) can be seen. Observation of fine motor manipulation of toys that require movement of small pieces to activate is also helpful.

The team can also observe problem-solving that occurs within social situations. Social problem-solving is addressed in Chapter 7.

The team should be able to ascertain how much the child is able to solve problems alone and how much the child relies on adults or peers to solve problems. The child may be able to use tools to accomplish the goal, such as getting a chair to reach a toy that is too high. The older child may employ more complex types of tool use, such as figuring out how to use a lever or pliers to open something.

Trial-and-Error

The facilitator can set up situations that will require problem-solving by having toys that do not work quite right or by creating a problem situation. The facilitator, while building with the child in the block area, might ask, "What can we use for a roof for our house?" and then, "I wonder what we can do to get the roof to stay on." The facilitator should give the child enough time to allow for trial-and-error approaches. Some children may try the same tactic repeatedly, while others will alter strategies when they are ineffective. If the child is unable to attempt any solution, the facilitator can model for the child and see if the child can expand on the idea.

Advance Planning   Another aspect of problem-solving is whether or not the child shows evidence of thinking ahead or reflecting about the problem at hand. The child may use visual scanning to search for a solution, physically try all alternatives, or use verbal mediation to think through the problem. For example, many children will verbalize their problem-solving: "I don't think it fits here. Does it go this way? No. Does it go that way? I think I'll put it here." Observing these qualitative aspects of problem-solving yields valuable information for the intervention team.

☞   Many children with disabilities have limited problem-solving abilities. Knowing the problem-solving approaches that the child typically employs gives the intervention team an opportunity to alter the environment and facilitation methods in order to challenge the child without frustrating him or her.

When Marybeth was observed in the play session, she seldom attempted to activate a toy or obtain items she wanted. She primarily gestured for items or handed toys to an adult to activate. When a toy did not do what she wanted it to do, Marybeth would throw the toy and cry. Clearly her problem-solving skills were limited.

The assessment team recommended providing Marybeth with very simple, easily activated toys so that she could achieve success quickly and consistently before being offered more challenging toys. They also recommended that the team model ways of accomplishing her goals using verbalization and physical movement. The area in which Marybeth was playing was arranged so that very little movement was necessary initially. Required movement was gradually increased as the occupational therapist worked on her movement patterns. In addition, the speech-language therapist worked with the teacher on interpreting Marybeth's gestures and giving her desires appropriate verbalizations.

Mark is an example of an older child who was able to analyze a situation, but showed limited response options. He would try the same solution again and again, unsuccessfully. The team encouraged Mark to verbalize what he was doing, in order to monitor his thinking. They also encouraged Mark to "think of another way," and praised him for each new attempt he made. In addition, the teacher modeled for Mark by talking about the pieces and what was working and not working for him as he tried to solve the problem himself. This approach was employed in the classroom for all of the activities that required Mark to analyze a situation and determine a solution.

Knowledge gained in the TPBA about which strategies are effective in helping a child move to higher or qualitatively stronger performance levels is directly transferable to TPBI. Discussion of what "worked within the TPBA is as important as determination of the child's skills and abilities.

DISCRIMINATION/CLASSIFICATION

Concept development results from a differential awareness of relations among people and objects. As this differential understanding develops, higher-level classification systems evolve. Discrimination, or the ability to distinguish between sensations, can be seen very early. As early as 3 days of age, the young infant who is being breastfed can discriminate the smell of his or her mother's breast pads from others, as well as her voice and face (Stern, 1985). This sensory discrimination becomes more finely tuned as the child matures. From the ages of 2 to 6 months, the infant has a growing sense that he or she and mother are quite separate, physically and emotionally, and that mother is different from other humans (Stern, 1985). Differential awareness of self and others is a critical link between cognitive and social development (Fewell & Vadasy, 1983). Social discrimination, or awareness of differences among people, allows the child to respond and interact uniquely to each individual. This social awareness parallels the infant's developing awareness of *object use and function*, finding out how various objects respond to the same and dissimilar movements. By 9 months of age, the infant's ability to respond differently to unique objects increases. From 9 to 12 months of age, the child begins to see relationships between objects and to combine related objects, such as a shovel and a pail (Fenson et al., 1976). Increased fine motor abilities, combined with greater understanding of parts of objects, also allows the child to experiment with putting things together (a top on a box) through nonsystematic trial and error (Belsky & Most, 1981). Improved problem-solving abilities enable the child to further refine classification skills as he or she learns what fits together, goes in, turns, pulls, goes on top of, and so on. The child is beginning to perform functional classifications as he or she discovers which things roll, which make noises, which bounce—in other words, which things are used for the same purpose (Morgan & Watson, 1989). He or she also begins to match objects with related parts, such as a lid on a tea pot. Continual experimentation and comparison of objects leads to the ability to match by color, shape, and size. By 2 years of age, the child can place a circle or square into a puzzle, and by 3 years of age the child can discriminate a triangle (Kusmierek, Cunningham, Fox-Gleason, Hanson, & Lorenzini, 1986). Also by 3 years of age, he or she has learned to discriminate size and is able to build three-dimensional block constructions (Cohen & Gross, 1979). Combining his or her increasing representational skills, spatial understanding, and problem-solving skills, the 4- to 5-year-old can put together complex puzzles and build elaborate symmetrical or asymmetrical block structures (Morgan & Watson, 1989).

The previously described skills, which allow the child to engage in a rich repertoire of manipulative, constructive, and imaginative play, also set the foundation for the development of preacademic skills. *Preacademic skills*, as defined by Wolery and Brookfield-Norman (1988), are "cognitive abilities that are necessary for later school learning" (p. 109). Reading, writing, and math abilities, considered fundamental to school success, are built on the development of discrimination skills, classification skills, sequencing abilities, one-to-one correspondence, and drawing skills. Each of these areas is considered in the TPBA process as a separate category. However, the *integration* of these abilities is what contributes to the development of strong academic skills (Furth, 1975). Because TPBA looks at the child's development from infancy to 6 years of age, a preacademic category is not consistent with that age span, and separate categories have therefore been maintained.

Preacademic skills, such as differentiation of sounds and phonemes, letters and words, and sound/letter associations, have not been included in the play-based assessment. These skills are difficult to elicit in a play context, unless the facilitator is "playing school." These skills develop in the preschool-age child, however, and a child who is interested in looking at books can be evaluated on several preacademic tasks.

During the play session, the team will have many opportunities to observe how the child combines objects, matches objects, combines pieces into a whole, sorts, and nonverbally classifies objects. The verbal child is usually talking while playing, allowing the team to ascertain the labels, descriptions, and classifications that the child assigns to objects, ac-

Preacademic skills are built on the development of discrimination and classification skills, sequencing abilities, and one-to-one correspondence. In the TPBA play session, these fundamental cognitive abilities are observed in child-selected activities.

tions, and events. The facilitator may elicit concepts and classification knowledge while playing with the child. For example, the facilitator might dump out a pile of varicolored beads of different sizes to make a necklace for the doll or the child. The child may automatically classify by color or size. If not, the facilitator might suggest, "Let's make one out of all the big beads," or at a higher level, "Let's make one out of small yellow beads." In the house area, the facilitator may inspire relational thinking by identifying a piece or part of a toy, and then requesting the child's help in finding the parts that go with it. Sorting can be encouraged by putting out a basket of plastic food and containers and suggesting that "we put away the groceries." The child should select a classification method to solve the problem.

The team notes behaviors that demonstrate the child's ability to combine related objects, to combine objects in sets, to discriminate objects by color, shape, or size, and to classify by category, function, or association. More complex classification or matching may be observed in solving puzzles or creating block constructions as well.

Many curricula approach discrimination and classification skills as table-top activities, requiring picture cards, puzzles, or packaged materials. Cards that ask a child to find the home that matches the animal or the nail that matches the hammer are common curricular materials for developing classification skills. These materials are probably best used as an ongoing evaluation measure rather than a teaching tool. Most of the classification skills at the preschool level are taught in a more meaningful way, using real or simulated materials in dramatic play situations. The child can therefore integrate associations, relationships, and new concepts at a concrete level. Teaching "animal homes," for example, can be done through visits to and/or re-creations of a farm, a zoo, or a camping trip in the woods.

Ellen, a 4-year-old from the inner city, showed delayed concepts and classification skills in the play-based assessment. Recommendations included providing Ellen with experiences to enrich her concept base, and helping her to draw conclusions about similarities and differences. The team organized a unit on camping that included a field trip with a hike in the woods and a visit to a camping store. The class set up a "camp" that they planned and created in the classroom, based on their experiences, observations, and problem-solving with the team. The camp included trees, a river, and animals. They set up a tent and sleeping bags, brought in wood for a fake fire, dishes, and other camping essentials. Each day, the team presented scenarios related to camping— fishing, hiking, cooking, washing, playing cards, and so on. They helped the children compare experiences in the woods to experiences at home. They classified foods, animals, shelters, and tools. Ellen loved this unit, and became a leader in organizing activities. She grasped new concepts easily and, with assistance, was able to draw relationships between ideas. In this example, TPBI was planned to incorporate the cognitive processes that the TPBA determined Ellen was ready for.

ONE-TO-ONE CORRESPONDENCE

Understanding of number concepts does not occur until the child is 4 or 5 years of age, but the precursors to number knowledge develop throughout infancy. As the child learns to label and classify objects, he or she is laying the foundation for the development of one-to-one correspondence. Bailey and Wolery (1984) identify comparing, labeling, measuring, and using symbols related to quantity as premath skills. Comparing quantity involves knowledge of one-to-one correspondence, ability to sequence, and ability to make basic concept judgments, such as one/many, more/less (Cohen & Gross, 1979; Williams et al., 1978). Labeling quantity includes counting by rote and rational counting, while measuring quantity includes understanding quantification concepts such as weight, length, time, and money. The child also learns to identify written numerals with the correct verbal label

(Bailey & Wolery, 1984). At the same time, the child learns that an object can be called more than one thing (a boat and a ship), that it can have abstract characteristics such as color (the red boat), and that if there is more than one the word becomes plural (boats) and is labeled with a number (2 boats). Gelman and Galliste (1978) found that children of 2–3 years of age understand the underlying principles of counting. Two-year-olds were able to correctly use one-to-one correspondence to count 2 or 3 items. Three-year-olds were able to count 3–5 items correctly. During the fourth year, the child counts up to 20 objects in a fixed order (Cohen & Gross, 1979). Ordering the measuring concepts are also acquired during the preschool years.

According to Piaget, the ability to represent the world in more abstract concepts is linked with concrete objects and events. Flavell (1977) explains several reasons for this connection. First, the child depends on what he or she sees to make judgments, and is therefore perception-bound. Second, attention focuses on a specific attribute rather than many. Third, the child attends to the final state of an action, rather than the transformational process. And, finally, he or she is unable to reverse thinking processes to re-create an action. TPBA, done with concrete objects and events, is consequently a natural means for assessing the preschool-age child's cognitive skills. The facilitator needs to have in mind the type of skills to elicit and creative ways of stimulating the child's discussion of such concepts.

The facilitator can arrange many opportunities for the child to count, to compare quantities, and to measure. In the block area of the playroom, cars, people, and blocks can be counted, and comparisons of sizes and number, measurements of light and heavy, and distinctions between short and long can be made. In the house area of the playroom, similar comparisons are possible. One-to-one correspondence with pictures and words on containers or in books can be incorporated as well.

When 4 ½-year-old Becka was playing in the house area, she poured water into glasses for herself and the facilitator. The facilitator asked her, "Which one of us has more juice?" Becka said that she had more because hers was taller. She understood the concepts of more and taller. When they made "cookies" out of clay, Becka said she was going to make a few more. She then counted the cookies in a row, pointing to each one separately, correctly up to 14. After counting to 14, she skipped several numbers and ended up with a total of 20 (there were actually 17). The facilitator then moved the cookies out of the row into a random arrangement and said, "I wonder how many cookies there are now?" Becka counted several cookies more than once, missed others, and ended up with 19. Her number skills and concepts were also observed in the block area, when she built a structure and talked about the size of blocks she needed, how tall her structure was, and the length of the road she needed to build.

When assessing the preschool-age child, the facilitator needs to creatively incorporate situations and materials that will allow the child to demonstrate one-to-one correspondence and other preacademic skills. Comments and subtle questions that do not seem like interrogations can extract the child's conceptual level of understanding.

Determining the child's level of understanding of one-to-one correspondence has direct implications for the intervention program. Based on the child's understanding, activities and situations can be designed to meet the child's developmental level.

Becka's teacher was able to plan activities that enabled Becka to work on number concepts above 14. She also worked on Becka's ability to estimate the number of objects in a group. Knowing Becka's concepts allowed the teacher to individualize activities. When lower-level children were working on other concepts, the teacher was able to modify the activity so that Becka experimented with size and measurement concepts at her own level.

One-to-one correspondence is best taught using concrete materials in situations that require the child to match objects to other objects. Whether setting the table for a snack, finding the right number of chairs for the children in a group, or putting hats on all the dolls, the child is acquiring one-to-one correspondence skills. The adult may assist the child in labeling the objects with the appropriate number. Counting by rote, without actual objects to associate with the number, does not promote one-to-one correspondence.

SEQUENCING ABILITY

Sequencing, or the ordering of objects or concepts, is related to the previous areas of classi-fication and one-to-one correspondence. The child's early sequencing abilities are related to the linking of schemes (see p. 82) and differentiating sensory input. The child develops an ability to sequence events in the environment, beginning with schemes and moving to sequences of ideas in conversation, stories, and dramatic play (Curry & Arnaud, 1984; Fenson et al., 1976; Westby, 1980). At the same time, the child detects differences between sounds, textures, tastes, degrees of light (Cohen & Gross, 1979; Fewell & Vadasy, 1983), sizes, and color. Eventually, the child is able to compare a series of elements and place them in order from one end of a continuum to another, beginning with two elements and increas-ing to a large number of comparisons in adulthood. It is this ability to compare and order units that enables the child to develop true number concepts (Achenbach & Weisz, 1975; Ginsburg & Opper, 1988; Piaget & Inhelder, 1964). The child must be able to see the rela-tionship between the element that precedes and the element that follows any one element in the series, and understand the equivalence of units. During the preschool years, the child is developing more sophisticated reasoning abilities and moving from perceptual problem-solving to logical problem-solving.

Observation of sequencing and seriation abilities (e.g., skill in placing the elements in a series in order) can be seen in the child's play with objects and in representational play. Observation of the linking of schemes, discussed earlier, leads to the more advanced skills of story building recognized in the child's dramatic play. In this observation, the team can distinguish whether the child's play demonstrates a logical sequence, a comprehension of beginning, middle, and end, and an awareness of time progression. This will be reflected in the child's actions and conversation.

Five-year-old Mindy's dramatization depicted planning dinner, going to the store for groc-eries, putting the groceries away, eating dinner, cleaning up, and going to the movies. Her story was logically organized and revealed an understanding of the passage of time and daily activities. Each step of the chain of events was punctuated with shorter sequences illustrating other relational concepts. She sorted her groceries and placed them on the shelves in order of size (at the suggestion of the facilitator), counted place settings for dinner, set equal amounts of food on each plate, and stacked the dishes by size. Mindy chatted with the facilitator, describing each of her actions. She was also able to "read" to her doll when she put it to bed, telling the story in detail from the pictures in the book. Mindy demonstrated age-appropriate sequencing abilities.

As with the other areas previously discussed, observations of sequencing abilities translates directly into intervention strategies. The team can determine the average number of events in a story sequence in the child's dramatic play and recommend the level of expan-sion appropriate for the child. Sequence concepts such as number, time, and size can also be incorporated into daily activities, if the play-based assessment detects deficiencies in these areas.

Mindy showed no deficiencies in her sequencing abilities, so the team could plan to expand and enrich her existing abilities. Mindy easily planned and organized activities with which she was familiar, so the intervention team decided to develop play scenarios that were less practiced. In this way, her imagination could be challenged and she could act as the leader, modeling for others in the group.

Using a storybook curriculum, the team decided to set up a center with the theme of "Goldilocks and the Three Bears." After reading the story to the group, the children planned what would be needed for each stage of the story. Mindy, as expected, had many ideas and was able to plan what was needed for Goldilocks to head into the woods and what would happen when she met the bears. They planned another center for the bears' house. With assistance from the team on the first performance of the story, Mindy was then able to remember and develop the story on her own. She became the "star" of the play as Goldilocks, and the "director" of the scenes involving the three bears. During unstructured play activities, Mindy frequently organized a group to repeat the story again.

DRAWING ABILITY

Drawing ability has long been considered an avenue to interpreting the maturing mind of the child (Luquet, 1913), and is included in many tests of intelligence and cognitive development. The child's first marks on paper are experimental and sensory. As the child gains more fine motor control and greater understanding of cause and effect, he or she begins to gain control over the random scribbling. Between 15 months and 3 years of age, lines and arcs are made, with the circle emerging around 3 years of age (DiLeo, 1977). Shortly after learning to draw a circle, this child realizes that the circle can be made to represent something in reality, the face. The child now enters the world of representation through drawing. As the child's dramatic play reflects his or her representation of the world, so, too, does the child's drawing. Between the ages of 3 and 4 years, the child makes crude attempts to represent people and objects. By 4, he or she can draw a recognizable person, although the legs may originate from the head. Between ages 4 and 5, the child adds a trunk and arms to the person, as well details such as hair or fingers. The person is always drawn in what Luquet (1913) termed *intellectual realism*; the child draws what he knows rather than what he sees. The person is always drawn from the front view, never in profile. The child also draws other identifiable objects, such as a house, tree, or car, always from the most recognizable angle. From age 5 on, the child's drawing abilities become more refined. Bodies become better proportioned, and legs are no longer seen through pants and skirts. Pictures begin to tell a story and reflect the emotions of the child.

The child's ability to manipulate a pencil also results in the acquisition of prewriting skills. Between the ages of 2 and 3, the child is able to copy circles, vertical lines, horizontal lines, and a cross. By age 5, the child can copy squares, triangles, diamonds, and most letters and numbers, although these attempts may be large and irregular (Cohen & Gross, 1979). From 5 years on, letters and numbers become more even, and the child can write his or her name and copy simple words (Cohen & Gross, 1979). The development of drawing and writing abilities is obviously related to fine motor proficiency and cognitive competence in classification, sequencing, and one-to-one correspondence, and deficiencies in these areas will be reflected in the child's drawing. Social-emotional development is also reflected in the older child's drawing, but this analysis is beyond the scope of the play-based assessment. However, psychologists may wish to incorporate analysis of the child's drawing into their evaluation.

TPBA is intended to be child-directed. As such, the child may not choose to use paper and pencil. The environment needs to entice the child to draw. Most children will take advantage of an easel and paint or crayons and paper; however, the facilitator is not limited to these media. Shaving cream on a mirror, finger paints, clay, and other options are appealing to many children. If the child does not spontaneously initiate drawing, the facilitator may model a fun activity. Most preschool children love to paint on an easel, and can be inspired to create a picture and label it with their name. The facilitator can then model painting different shapes and letters. Observations are made of the child's level of representational skills in drawing people, and his or her level of prewriting skills or drawing of lines, shapes, and letters.

Brendon, a 5-year-old, nonverbal child with autism, was encouraged to demonstrate his skills using shaving cream on a mirror. He wrote his name, then drew a cross, a circle, and a square, but was not interested in drawing a person. His drawing skills reflected much higher cognitive capability than was seen in other areas of his play.

☞   The area of drawing cannot be examined in isolation. In combination with recommendations from fine motor and other cognitive areas, the team can suggest an appropriate level of activities to encourage the child's drawing mastery.

In Brendon's case, drawing lines, shapes, and letters was a strength. Representational skills, as reflected in play and drawing of people, were weak. This was consistent with his lack of knowledge of self and others, and his ineffectual interpersonal skills. Brendon had developed "splinter" skills in writing as a result of his preschool program. Recommendations for Brendon took into account his varying levels of development. He needed to work on beginning representational skills and self-identity through tactile and interactional methods. He could also continue to enjoy copying and drawing symbols, which required mechanical fine motor proficiency that was within his ability level. His comprehension of these symbols, however, was limited. His parents believed that he was beginning to learn to read because he was able to copy letters. Consultation with the parents was required to describe Brendon's different levels of comprehension and the skills that he still needed before he would be able to read.

SUMMARY

Cognitive development covers a broad range of skills, not all of which are incorporated into the cognitive guidelines of the transdisciplinary play-based assessment. However, the areas addressed are observable in play and translate directly into infant, toddler, or preschool curricula. All areas complement and must be used in tandem with the social-emotional, communication and language, and sensorimotor domains.

REFERENCES

Achenbach, T.M., & Weisz, J.R. (1975). A longitudinal study of developmental synchrony between conceptual identity, seriation, and transitivity of color, number, length. *Child Development, 46,* 840–848.

Arnoud, S.H., & Curry, N.E. (1973). *Role enactment in children's play: A developmental overview* (Film). Valhalla, NY: Campus Film Distributors.

Bailey, D.B., & Wolery, M. (1984). *Teaching infants and preschoolers with handicaps.* Columbus, OH: Charles E. Merrill.

Bayley, N. (1969). *Bayley scales of infant development.* New York: The Psychological Corporation.

Belsky, J., & Most, R.K. (1981). From exploration to play: A cross-sectional study of infant free play behavior. *Developmental Psychology, 17*(5), 630–639.

Chance, P. (1979). *Learning through play*. New York: Gardner Press.

Clark, T.C., Morgan, E.C., & Wilson-Vlotman, A.L. (1984). *The SKI * HI curriculum: Early home programming for hearing impaired children*. Logan, UT: The SKI * HI Institute.

Cohen, M.A., & Gross, P.J. (1979). *The developmental resource: Behavioral sequences for assessment and program planning*. New York: Basic Books.

Curry, N.E., & Arnaud, S.H. (1984). Play in developmental preschool settings. In T.D. Yawkey & A.D. Pellegrini (Eds.), *Child's play: Developmental and applied*. (pp. 273–290). Hillsdale, NJ: Lawrence Erlbaum Associates.

DiLeo, J.H. (1977). *Child development: Analysis and synthesis*. New York: Brunner/Mazel.

Dunst, C.J. (1980). *A clinical and educational manual for use with the Uzgiris and Hunt Scales of Infant Psychological Development*. Baltimore: University Park Press.

Elder, J.L., & Pederson, D.R. (1978). Preschool children's use of objects in symbolic play. *Child Development, 49*, 500–504.

Fein, G.G., & Apfel, N. (1979). Some preliminary observations on knowing and pretending. In N. Smith & M. Franklin (Eds.), *Symbolic functioning in childhood* (pp. 87–100). Hillsdale, NJ: Lawrence Erlbaum Associates.

Fenson, L., Kagan, J., Kearsley, R., & Zelazo, P. (1976). The developmental progression of manipulative play in the first two years. *Child Development, 47*, 232–236.

Fenson, L., & Ramsay, D. (1981). Effects of modeling action sequences on the play of twelve-, fifteen-, and nineteen-month-old children. *Child Development, 52*(3), 1028–1036.

Fewell, R.R. (1983). New directions in the assessment of young handicapped children. In C.R. Reynolds & J.H. Clark (Eds.), *Assessment and programming for young children with low incidence handicaps* (pp. 1–41). New York: Plenum.

Fewell, R.R., & Kaminski, R. (1988). Play skills development and instruction for young children with handicaps. In S.L. Odom & M.B. Karnes (Eds.), *Early intervention for infants and children with handicaps: An empirical base* (pp. 145–158). Baltimore: Paul H. Brookes Publishing Co.

Fewell, R.R., & Vadasy, P.F. (1983). *Learning through play*. Allen, TX: Developmental Learning Materials.

Flavell, J.H. (1977). *Cognitive development*. Englewood Cliffs, NJ: Prentice-Hall.

Furth, H. (1975). *Thinking goes to school: Piaget's theory in practice*. Oxford University Press.

Garvey, C. (1977). *Play*. Cambridge, MA: Harvard University Press.

Gelman, R., & Gallistel, C.R. (1978). *The child's understanding of number*. Cambridge, MA: Harvard University Press.

Ginsberg, H.P., & Opper, S. (1988). *Piaget's theory of intellectual development*. Englewood Cliffs, NJ: Prentice-Hall.

Hedrick, D.L., Prather, E.M., & Tobin, A.R. (1984). *Sequenced inventory of communication development—Revised*. Seattle: University of Washington Press.

Hutt, C. (1979). Exploration and play. In B. Sutton-Smith (Ed.), *Play and learning* (pp. 175–194). New York: Gardner Press.

Kusmierek, A., Cunningham, K., Fox-Gleason, S., Hanson, M., & Lorenzini, D. (1986). *South metropolitan association birth to three transdisciplinary assessment guide*. Flossmoore, IL: South Metropolitan Association for Low-Incidence Handicapped.

Lamb, M.E., & Campos, J.J. (1982). *Development in infancy*. New York: Random House.

Luquet, G.H. (1913). *Les dessins d'un enfant: Etude psychologique* (Child drawings: A psychological study). Paris: Libraire Felix Alcan.

McCune-Nicholich, L. (1981). Toward symbolic functioning: Structure of early pretend games and potential parallels with language. *Child Development, 52*, 785–797.

Morgan, E., & Watson, S. (1989). *Insight developmental checklist* (2nd ed.). Logan, UT: HOPE, Inc.

Musselwhite, C.R. (1986). *Adaptive play for special needs children*. San Diego, CA: College Hill Press.

Nicholich, L. (1977). Beyond sensorimotor intelligence: Assessment of symbolic maturity through analysis of pretend play. *Merrill-Palmer Quarterly, 16*, 136–141.

Piaget, J. (1962). *Play, dreams, and imitation in childhood*. New York: Norton.

Piaget, J., & Inhelder, B. (1964). *The early growth of logic in the child*. New York: Norton.

Rosenblatt, D. (1977). Developmental trends in infant play. In B. Tizard & D. Garvey (Eds.), *Biology of play* (pp. 33–44). London: WM. Heineman Medical Books Ltd.

Rubin, K.H. (1984). *The play observation scale.* Unpublished manuscript. University of Waterloo, Ontario, Canada.

Rubin, K.H., Fein, G.G., & Vandenberg, B. (1983). Play. In E.M. Hetherington (Ed.), *Handbook of child psychology: Socialization, personality, and social development* (pp. 693–774). New York: John Wiley & Sons.

Smilansky, S. (1968). *The effects of sociodramatic play on disadvantaged preschool children.* New York: John Wiley & Sons.

Stern, D. (1985). *The interpersonal world of the infant: A view from psychoanalysis and developmental psychology.* New York: Basic Books.

Ungerer, J.A., Zelazo, P.R., Kearsley, R.B., & O'Leary, K. (1981). Developmental changes in the representation of objects in symbolic play from eighteen to thirty-four months of age. *Child Development, 52,* 186–195.

Uzgiris, I.C., & Hunt, J.M. (1975). *Assessment in infancy: Ordinal scales of psychological development.* Urbana: University of Illinois Press.

Watson, M.W. (1981). The development of social roles: A sequence of social-cognitive development. In K. Fischer (Ed.), *Cognitive development: New directions for child development* (Vol. 12) (pp. 33–42). San Francisco: Jossey-Bass, Inc.

Watson, M.W., & Fischer, K.W. (1977). A developmental sequence of agent use in late infancy. *Child Development, 48,* 828–836.

Wehman, P. (1979). Instructional strategies for improving toy play skills of severely handicapped children. *AAESPH Review, 4*(2), 125–135.

Weisler, A., & McCall, R.B. (1976). Exploration play: Resume and redirection. *American Psychologist, 31,* 492–508.

Werner, H., & Kaplan, B. (1963). *Symbolic formation: An organismic development approach to language and the expression of thought.* New York: John Wiley & Sons.

Westby, C.E. (1980). Assessment of cognitive and language abilities through play. *Language, Speech and Hearing Services in Schools, 11,* 154–168.

Williams, W., Coyne, P., Despain, C.J., Johnson, F., Scheuerman, N., Stengert, J., Swetlik, B., & York, R. (1978). Teaching math skills using longitudinal sequences. In M.E. Snell (Ed.), *Systematic instruction of the moderately and severely handicapped.* Columbus, OH: Charles E. Merrill.

Wolery, M., & Brookfield-Norman, J. (1988). (Pre)Academic instruction for handicapped preschool children. In S.L. Odom & M.B. Karnes (Eds.), *Early intervention for infants and children with handicaps: An empirical base* (pp. 109–128). Baltimore: Paul H. Brookes Publishing Co.

Zelazo, P., & Kearsley, R. (1980). The emergence of functional play in infants: Evidence for a major cognitive transition. *Journal of Applied Developmental Psychology, 1*(2), 95–117.

6

Observation Guidelines for Cognitive Development

I. Categories of Play
    A. What range of categories are observed in the child's play?
        1. Exploratory or sensorimotor play
        2. Relational or functional play
        3. Constructive play
        4. Dramatic or symbolic play
        5. Games-with-rules play
        6. Rough-and-tumble play
    B. Primary category in which the child engages
II. Attention Span
    A. Attention preferences
        1. What is the average length of time the child spends per activity?
        2. What activities engage the child for the longest time?
            a. Observation
            b. One of the categories listed in I., A.
        3. What activities engage the child for the shortest time?
        4. Does the child demonstrate a sensory preference?
            a. Visual preference—the child attends longer to the visual features of objects or to objects that have strong visual features
            b. Auditory preference—the child attends longer to toys with auditory features
            c. Tactile preference—the child attends longer to toys that provide strong tactile input
            d. Vestibular preference—the child attends longer in activities that provide movement or vestibular input
    B. Locus of control
        1. Does the child select activities and stay with them without external prompting or reinforcement?
        2. What type of external support, direction, or reinforcement is needed in order for the child to maintain attention in an activity?
            a. Verbal
            b. Physical
            c. Other
        3. Distractibility—Do external stimuli interfere with an activity?
            a. Do visual stimuli (materials, toys, etc.) distract the child?
            b. Do auditory stimuli (bells, voices) distract the child?

        c.   Do nearby activities distract the child?

        d.   Do people in the room distract the child?

III.   Early Object Use

    A.   Type and range of schemes

       1.   What type and number of low-level schemes were observed (mouthing, banging, shaking, etc.)?

       2.   What type and number of more complex adaptive schemes were observed (pushing, poking, pulling, throwing)?

       3.   Does the child use a large variety of schemes?

       4.   How frequently does the child use various schemes?

    B.   Scheme use and generalization

       1.   Which schemes does the child use spontaneously?

         a.   Indiscriminate use of scheme with all objects (i.e., mouths all objects)

         b.   Selective appropriate use of schemes (i.e., stirs with spoon)

         c.   Generalization of schemes to similar objects (i.e., opens all things with doors, lids)

       2.   Scheme use after modeling by facilitator

         a.   What higher level schemes can be instigated through modeling?

         b.   What prompting is necessary (vocal, gestural)?

    C.   Linking of schemes

       1.   What behaviors demonstrate linking of schemes in a related sequence (filling a pitcher, pouring into a cup, then pretending to drink)?

       2.   What events demonstrate linking of schemes in representational "script" play (child fixes dinner, serves it, washes dishes, and goes to bed)?

IV.   Symbolic and Representational Play

    A.   Symbolic object use

       1.   To what degree is the child capable of abstracting a concept—or using one object to represent another?

         a.   Real objects needed for activity

         b.   Realistic object may substitute for real object

         c.   Unrealistic item may be substituted for real object

         d.   Can pretend an object exists without a prop

    B.   Symbolic play roles

       1.   What roles is the child capable of assuming in representational play?

       2.   Toward whom or what are the child's pretend actions directed?

         a.   Self

         b.   Object or toy (baby doll)

         c.   Another adult

       3.   How does the child demonstrate understanding behaviors important to specific roles that he or she assumes (gas station attendant pumping gas with hose)?

       4.   To what degree can the child direct the play scenario without being a player or role taker (has soldiers fighting, etc.)?

       5.   When the child is directing actors (person, doll, puppet, or symbolic substitute for actor) in scenarios, how does he or she indicate understanding of the behaviors of the actors (has store clerk doll act out stocking the shelves, checking out groceries)?

       6.   What level of role interaction is demonstrated in the child's play (having doll assume more than one role at a time, such as mother and wife)?

V.   Imitation

    A.   Level of imitation

        1.   Simple visible gestures (child can observe his or her imitative actions, such as clapping hands)

        2.   Simple invisible gestures (child cannot observe his or her imitative actions, such as patting top of head)

        3.   Single scheme imitations using objects

        4.   Complex imitations—sequence of schemes using gestures or objects (see also symbolic play)

        5.   Imitation of problem-solving approaches

        6.   Imitation of dramatic play sequences

           a.   Familiar

           b.   Unfamiliar

        7.   Imitation of drawing

           a.   Within child's repertoire

           b.   Novel

B.   Timing of imitation

        1.   Are the majority of imitations immediate (right after model)?

        2.   Are the majority of imitations delayed (after several elapsed seconds)?

        3.   What examples of deferred imitation are seen (imitation after a period of elapsed time, such as Mom washing dishes)?

           a.   Are deferred imitations replicated within the appropriate context?

           b.   What behaviors denote deferred imitation in inappropriate or non-meaningful contexts?

C.   Turn-taking

        1.   What type of imitative sequences or turn-taking play takes place?

           a.   Physical movement or tactile play (bouncing, tickling)

           b.   Vocal imitative play (vocalizations, words, rhymes)

           c.   Imitative turn-taking with objects

           d.   Imitative turn-taking in representational play

           e.   Imitative turn-taking in structured games

        2.   Does the child modify the turn-taking game by changing some aspect of the behavior?

        3.   Does the child repeat a modification made by another person in the turn-taking?

VI.   Problem-Solving Approaches

A.   What interest does the child show in cause-and-effect objects and events?

        1.   Does the child use physical "procedures" or bodily movement to make events recur?

        2.   What behaviors were observed where the child uses the adult as an agent to make something recur?

        3.   What behaviors were observed where the child acted as the agent to make something recur?

        4.   What behaviors were observed where the child used an object as a tool to solve a problem?

B.   What means does the child use to accomplish goals? How does he or she figure out challenging tasks?

        1.   Does the child use a repetitive approach, doing the same act over and over to cause something to happen (continually bangs box to get it open)?

        2.   What evidence was observed of trial-and-error problem-solving using alternative approaches to achieve a goal?

        3.   What evidence is observed of advance planning in problem-solving?

           a.   The child uses physical searching behaviors in selecting an approach

       b.   The child uses visual scanning to select an approach

       c.   The child uses verbal mediation (talking to self) or questioning of another to select a problem-solving approach

VII.   Discrimination/Classification

    A.   How does the child show knowledge of classification of concepts?

       1.   What behaviors demonstrate combining related objects (spoon and plate)?

       2.   What behaviors demonstrate combining like objects in sets (trucks all together)?

       3.   What behaviors demonstrate spatial matching (stacking same size blocks or lining up like objects)?

       4.   What behaviors demonstrate sorting or matching objects by color?

       5.   What behaviors demonstrate sorting or matching objects by shape?

       6.   What behaviors demonstrate sorting or matching objects by size (big, little)?

       7.   What behaviors demonstrate that the child can sequence objects by size (nesting or stacking in order)?

       8.   What behaviors demonstrate that the child can sort or match objects by functions (things that roll)?

       9.   What behaviors demonstrate sorting or matching by a more complex functional relationship (stop signs on road in block area)

      10.   What behaviors demonstrate that the child can identify objects by attributes?

         a.   Single attributes

         b.   Multiple attributes (big, blue square)

      11.   What behaviors demonstrate that the child can match simple patterns or designs (puzzles, Lotto)?

      12.   What behaviors demonstrate that the child can match more complex patterns or designs (parquetry blocks)?

      13.   What behaviors demonstrate the child's ability to group or label objects within a classification or categorical system (e.g., an apple is a fruit, a poodle is a dog, a dog is an animal)?

VIII. One-to-One Correspondence

    A.   How does the child demonstrate understanding of number concepts?

       1.   How does the child demonstrate ability to count discrete objects using the correct number (can use corresponding number for separate objects, rational counting)?

       2.   How high can the child count by rote?

    B.   What concepts demonstrate the child's ability to compare quantities (big/little, one/many, more/less, equal/not equal)?

    C.   What evidence is shown of understanding measurement concepts (heavy/light, full/empty, short/long, before/after, hot/cold)?

    D.   Does the child demonstrate any understanding of conservation of number (changing the configuration doesn't change the number of items)?

    E.   Does the child demonstrate one-to-one correspondence with words and pictures?

       1.   Identifies pictures in books with the correct word or action

       2.   Identifies words in print that correspond to pictures or common objects (labels on food cartons)

IX.   Sequencing Ability

    A.   What behaviors demonstrate sequencing ability?

       1.   Sequencing of schemes (See Linking of Schemes, III., C.)

       2.   Sequencing (seriation) of concepts

         a.   Number

         b.   Size

c. Sensory input (textures, smells, sounds)
3. Sequencing of stories
   a. In dramatic play
   b. Through pictures in a book
4. Sequencing of time
   a. In dramatic play
   b. In conversation

X. Drawing Ability
   A. What developmental level is represented in the child's drawing of lines and shapes?
   B. What developmental level is represented in the child's drawing of people or objects?

6

Age Ranges

Categories of Play

0–24 mo.	Exploratory or sensorimotor play
9–24 mo.	Relational or functional play (predominates from 15–21 mo.)
24 mo. +	Constructive play (predominates from 36 mo. on)
21–72 mo.	Representational/symbolic play
36 mo. +	Rough-and-tumble play (predominates 4–5 yr.)
60 mo. +	Games-with-rules play

Early Object Use

3– 6 mo.	Focus on action performed by objects (banging, shaking)
6– 9 mo.	Begins to explore characteristics of objects Range of schemes expands (e.g., pulling, turning, poking, tearing)
8– 9 mo.	Begins to combine objects in relational play (e.g., objects in a container)
9–12 mo.	Begins to see the relation between complex actions and consequences (opening doors, putting on lids) Differential use of schemes according to the toy played with, functional use of toys (e.g., pushes cars, throws ball)
12 mo. +	Acts on objects with a variety of schemes
12–15 mo.	Links schemes in simple combinations (puts person in car and pushes car)
24–36 mo.	Links multischeme combinations into a meaningful sequence (puts paste on toothbrush, puts cap on tube, brushes baby's teeth)
36–42 mo.	Links schemes into complex script

Adapted from Clark, Morgan, & Wilson-Vlotman, 1984; Kusmierek et al., 1986.

Symbolic and Representational Skills

12–16 mo.	Simple pretend play directed toward self (eating, sleeping)
12–18 mo.	Can focus pretend play on animate and inanimate objects and others Combines simple schemes in acting out familiar activity
18–24 mo.	Increased use of nonrealistic objects in pretending (similar to real) Can have inanimate objects perform actions (doll washes self)

(continued)

Symbolic and Representational Skills   *(continued)*

24–36 mo.	Can use more abstract representation of object in play Uses multischeme combinations (feed doll with bottle, pat it on the back, put it to bed)
36–48 mo.	Plans out pretend situations in advance, organizing who and what are needed for role-play Events in play are sequenced into scenario that tells a story
36–42 mo.	Can use imaginary objects in play Acts out sequences with miniature dolls (in house, garage, airport, etc.)
42 mo. +	Can make dolls carry out several activities or roles Creates imaginary characters Can direct actions of two dolls, making them interact within two roles
60 mo. +	Organizes other children and props for role-play Can direct actions of three dolls, making them interact
72 mo. +	Can direct dolls, where each doll plays more than one role (father and doctor, daughter and patient)

Adapted from Fewell, 1983; Nicholich, 1977; Watson, 1981; Watson & Fischer, 1977; Westby, 1980.

Imitation Skills

4– 8 mo.	Imitates vocalizations and actions that are part of his or her repertoire
6– 9 mo.	Imitates actions he or she can see performed that are in his or her repertoire
8–12 mo.	Imitates sounds and gestures not part of his or her repertoire
9–12 mo.	Imitates unseen patterns composed of familiar actions
12–15 mo.	Imitates novel movements
12–18 mo.	Immediate imitation of a model
15–18 mo.	Imitates drawing of a stroke
18–24 mo.	Recognizes ways to activate toys in imitation of adult Deferred imitation
21–24 mo.	Varies own imitation creatively from that of model
27–30 mo.	Imitates drawing of a face
36–60 mo.	Demonstrates increasingly complex role imitation (See Symbolic and Representational Play)
48–60 mo.	Imitates scenes from different aspects of life; pieces together into new script

Adapted from Clark, Morgan, & Wilson-Vlotman, 1984; Cohen & Gross, 1979; Kusmierek et al., 1986.

Problem-Solving Skills

6– 9 mo.	Finds object after watching it disappear Uses movement as a means to attain an end Anticipates movement of objects in space Attends to environmental consequences of actions Repeats actions in order to repeat consequences
9–12 mo.	Demonstrates tool use after demonstration Uses goal-directed behavior Performs an action in order to produce a result
12–15 mo.	Uses an adult to achieve a goal Attempts to activate simple mechanisms Rotates and examines three-dimensional aspects of an object Uses nonsystematic trial-and-error problem-solving
18–21 mo.	Attends to shapes of things and uses appropriately Uses some foresight before acting

(continued)

Problem-Solving Skills   *(continued)*

	Uses a tool to obtain a desired object
	Invents means to attain a goal through thought processes rather than just trial-and-error
	Operates a mechanical toy
	Can foresee effects or infer causes
21–24 mo.	Recognizes operations of many mechanisms
	Matches configurations, such as circle, square, triangle
	Manipulates objects into small openings
24–27 mo.	Discriminates sizes
24–30 mo.	Can build with blocks horizontally and vertically
27–30 mo.	Relates one experience to another, using logic and knowledge of previous experiences
	Can plan actions in his or her mind without acting them out
	Can relate one experience to another using "if . . . then" logic
36–48 mo.	Can build vertical block structure requiring balance and coordination (nine cubes)
	Can put graduated sizes in order
	Uses representational thinking in constructions
48–60 mo.	Can construct complex structures with vertical, horizontal, and symmetrical aspects
	Can integrate spatial, cause-and-effect, and representational thinking into problem-solving

Adapted from Clark et al., 1984; Cohen & Gross, 1979; Kusmierek et al., 1986.

Discrimination/Classification Skills

2– 6 mo.	Growing sense of difference between self and mother and mothers and others
6– 9 mo.	Differentiates primary caregiver from others
9–12 mo.	Combines related objects
15–18 mo.	Begins to spontaneously cluster objects that share physical or functional similarities
	Matches objects with relational parts (round lid on tea pot)
16–19 mo.	Discriminates circle and square on form board
24–27 mo.	Matches objects by color, shape, and size
	Recognizes part/whole relationships (can identify parts and the objects with which they go)
	Discriminates size (can nest four boxes)
24–36 mo.	Discriminates circle, square, and triangle
	Matches object to picture of the object
	Matches picture of object to another picture of the object
30–33 mo.	Matches objects that have the same function (comb and brush)
36–48 mo.	Can sort by one criterion (shape or color) without getting confused
48–60 mo.	Can sort objects by size (large, medium, small)
	Can sort a group of objects in several different ways
	Can classify objects into categories (toys, food, animals)
	Matches or identifies basic symbols
	Identifies different coins
	Identifies left and right
	Can put together complex puzzle
	Can build elaborate symmetrical or asymmetrical block structures
60–72 mo.	Can identify objects that do not belong in a group
	Can identify abstract characteristics (living, as opposed to nonliving)
	Matches letters
	Discriminates and names letters

Adapted from Clark et al., 1984; Cohen & Gross, 1979; Kusmierek et al., 1986.

One-to-One Correspondence

24–36 mo.   Can count by rote to five
             Understands concept of one
             Can count two to three objects
36–48 mo.   Can count up to five objects
48–60 mo.   Can count up to ten objects
             Understands "more," "less," "same"
             Can count objects, enumerating each object once
             Identifies and names numbers
             Can match the number of items in a set to the correct number
             Understands concept of zero

Adapted from Cohen & Gross, 1979.

Sequencing Abilities (see *Early Object Use* for early sequencing abilities)

36–42 mo.   Understands big, little
36–48 mo.   Understands questions about what is going to happen next
36–52 mo.   Understands tall, short
42–52 mo.   Understands tallest, largest, shortest, smallest
48–60 mo.   Counts objects in sequence with one-to-one correspondence
             Can put three pictures in a sequence to tell a story
             Knows sequence of reading book, from left to right and top to bottom
             Knows first, middle, and last
60–72 mo.   Can place objects in order from shortest to tallest, and smallest to largest
             Identifies first, last, middle
             Combines letters into words

Adapted from Clark et al., 1984; Cohen & Gross, 1979; Kusmierek et al., 1986.

Drawing Skills

12–24 mo.   Imitates scribbling
24–30 mo.   Imitates vertical stroke, horizontal lines, circular strokes
30–36 mo.   Imitates cross
             Draws lines, strokes, and arcs spontaneously
             Makes first spontaneous unrecognizable forms
36–48 mo.   Draws circle
             Draws face of a person
48–60 mo.   Draws stick figure
             Copies square, triangle, diamond
             Copies diagonal and V strokes
             Adds trunk and arms to person
             Draws identifiable objects without model
             Copies own name in large, irregular letters
             Copies numbers unevenly
60–72 mo.   Copies rectangle
             Copies letters and numbers with more accuracy, but still has many errors

Adapted from Clark et al., 1984; Cohen & Gross, 1977; Kusmierek et al., 1986.

Cognitive Observation Worksheet

Name of child: _____ Date of birth: _____ Age: _____

Name of observer: _____ Discipline or job title: _____ Date of assessment: _____

On the following pages, note specific behaviors that document the child's abilities in the cognitive categories. Qualitative comments should also be made. The format provided here follows that of the Observation Guidelines for Cognitive Development in **Transdisciplinary Play-Based Assessment.** *It may be helpful to refer to the guidelines while completing this form.*

I. Categories of Play

A. Range of categories

   1. Exploratory or sensorimotor:

   2. Relational or functional:

   3. Constructive:

   4. Dramatic or symbolic:

   5. Games with rules:

   6. Rough and tumble:

B. Primary play category:

II. Attention Span

A. Preferences

   1. Time per activity:

   2. Longest engaging activities:

   3. Shortest engaging activity *(circle one):*

     a. Visual   c. Tactile

     b. Auditory   d. Vestibular

(continued)

B. Locus of control
    1. Prompting or reinforcement:

    2. Type of reinforcement *(circle those that apply)*:
        a. Verbal   b. Physical   c. Other:
    3. Distractibility *(circle those that apply)*:
        a. Visual stimuli   c. Nearby activities
        b. Auditory stimuli   d. People

III. Early Object Use

A. Type and range of schemes
    1. Low-level schemes:

    2. More complex adaptive schemes:

    3. Variety of schemes:

    4. Frequency of various schemes:

B. Scheme use and generalization
    1. Schemes used spontaneously *(circle those that apply)*:
        a. Indiscriminate use with all objects
        b. Selective appropriate use
        c. Generalization to similar objects
    2. Scheme use after modeling
        a. Higher-level schemes:

        b. Necessary prompting:

C. Linking of schemes
    1. Behaviors in a related sequence:

    2. Events in representational "script" play:

(continued)

Cognitive Observation Worksheet

Name of child: _____ Date of birth: _____ Age: _____

Name of observer: _____ Discipline or job title: _____ Date of assessment: _____

IV. Symbolic and Representational Play

A. Symbolic object use

1. Abstracting a concept *(circle one)*:

   a. Necessary real objects   c. Substituted unrealistic objects

   b. Substituted realistic objects   d. Pretend objects, no props

B. Symbolic play roles

1. Roles assumed in representational play:

2. Direction of pretend actions *(circle those that apply)*:

   a. Self   b. Object or toy   c. Adult

3. Demonstration of behaviors with roles:

4. Ability to direct play with action figures:

5. Understanding of behaviors of characters when directing play:

6. Level of role interaction:

V. Imitation

A. Level of imitation

1. Simple visible gestures:

2. Simple invisible gestures:

3. Single-scheme imitations using objects:

4. Complex imitations:

5. Imitation of problem-solving approaches:

6. Imitation of dramatic play sequences *(circle those that apply)*:

   a. Familiar   b. Unfamiliar

7. Imitation of drawing *(circle those that apply)*:

   a. Within child's repertoire   b. Novel

(continued)

B. Timing of imitation
   1. Majority immediate? *(yes or no)*
   2. Majority delayed? *(yes or no)*
   3. Examples of deferred imitation *(circle those that apply)*:
      a. Within appropriate context   b. Within inappropriate or nonmeaningful contexts

C. Turn-taking
   1. Type of imitative sequences or turn-taking play *(circle those that apply)*:
      a. Physical movement or tactile play
      b. Vocal imitative play
      c. Imitative turn-taking with objects
      d. Imitative turn-taking in representational play
      e. Imitative turn-taking in structured games
      Examples:

   2. Modification of turn-taking game? *(yes or no)*
   3. Repeat modifications by others? *(yes or no)*

VI. Problem-Solving Approaches

A. Interest in cause-and-effect objects and events
   1. Physical "procedures" or bodily movement for recurrence? *(yes or no)*
   2. Behaviors with adult as agent:

   3. Behaviors with child as agent:

   4. Use of object to solve problem:

B. Goals accomplished? *(yes or no)*   Figures out challenging tasks? *(yes or no)*
   Examples:

   1. Repetitive approach? *(yes or no)*
   2. Alternative approaches? *(yes or no)*
   3. Evidence of advance planning *(circle those that apply)*:
      a. Physical searching   b. Visual scanning   c. Verbal mediation

VII. Discrimination/Classification

A. Knowledge of classification of concepts
   1. Combining related objects:

(continued)

Name of child: _____ Date of birth: _____ Age: _____

Name of observer: _____ Discipline or job title: _____ Date of assessment: _____

2. Combining like objects:

3. Spatial matching:

4. Sorting or matching by color:

5. Sorting or matching by shape:

6. Sorting or matching by size:

7. Sequencing by size:

8. Sorting or matching by function:

9. Sorting or matching by complex functional relationship:

10. Identifying objects by attribute
    a. Single attribute:

    b. Multiple attributes:

11. Matching simple patterns or designs:

12. Matching more complex patterns or designs:

13. Grouping or labeling within systems:

(continued)

VIII. One-to-One Correspondence

    A. Understanding of number concepts

        1. Counting of discrete objects with correct number? *(yes or no)*

        2. Counting by rote? *(yes or no)*

    B. Comparing quantities:

    C. Understanding of measurement quantities:

    D. Understanding of conservation of number:

    E. One-to-one correspondence with words and pictures

        1. Pictures in books:

        2. Words with common objects:

IX. Sequencing Ability

    A. Demonstration of sequencing ability:

        1. Schemes:

        2. Concepts:

            a. Number:

            b. Size:

            c. Sensory input:

        3. Stories:

            a. In dramatic play:

            b. Through pictures in books:

(continued)

Cognitive Observation Worksheet

Name of child: _____ Date of birth: _____ Age: _____

Name of observer: _____ Discipline or job title: _____ Date of assessment: _____

4. Time:

    a. In dramatic play:

    b. In conversation:

X. Drawing Ability

    A. Developmental level in lines and shapes:

    B. Developmental level in people or objects:

Additional Comments

Summary Sheet for Cognitive Guidelines

Name of child: _____   Age: _____

Name of observer: _____   Date of birth: _____

Discipline or job title: _____   Date: _____

Observation categories	Areas of strength	Rating	Justification	Things I'm ready for
I. Categories of play				
II. Attention span				
III. Early object use				
IV. Symbolic and representational play				
V. Gestural imitation				

(continued)

Summary Sheet for Cognitive Guidelines

Name of child: _____   Age: _____

Name of observer: _____   Date of birth: _____   Discipline or job title: _____   Date: _____

Observation categories	Areas of strength	Rating	Justification	Things I'm ready for
VI. Problem-solving approaches				
VII. Discrimination/ classification				
VIII. One-to-one correspondence				
IX. Sequencing ability				
X. Drawing ability				

SAMPLE

7

Observation of Social-Emotional Development

Examination of the social-emotional development of the child is a vital aspect of the play-based assessment procedure. With the exception of children referred for specific emotional problems, traditional evaluation procedures give minimal attention to the social-emotional domain. Assessments of abilities in cognitive, communication and language, and sensorimotor areas indicate *what* the child can do, but these instruments do not indicate *how* the child has acquired these proficiencies or how he or she *uses* them in interaction with others. This chapter provides Observation Guidelines for determining the developmental level of the child's social skills as well as the qualitative aspects of the child's social-emotional development. Areas addressed include: 1) temperament; 2) mastery motivation; 3) social relations with the facilitator, with the parent(s), and with peers; 4) emotional characteristics of play; and 5) awareness of social conventions.

The Observation Guidelines for social-emotional development are not a comprehensive evaluation of the social-emotional area and, as such, are insufficient for a diagnostic evaluation of emotional disturbance. They will, however, enable observers to identify problem behaviors and patterns of interaction that may negatively affect the child's development. In the case of a child who appears to have severe emotional problems, further evaluation will be recommended. A more in-depth evaluation could take into account the parent–child interaction, family dynamics and other ecological factors, and the child's fantasy world, anxieties, and defense mechanisms. The transdisciplinary play-based assessment can provide initial information regarding some of these areas, but additional evaluation of specific concerns may be necessary.

TEMPERAMENT

Temperament, defined here as the behavioral style of the child, is an important attribute in the child's social interactions. Individual differences in temperament may influence the child's social and cognitive performance in school (Keogh, 1986; Pullis & Cadwell, 1985). Temperament characteristics are observed throughout the TPBA play session. No age ranges for temperament are provided in the chapter, since temperament characteristics do not appear to be age-related. The team records descriptive information about the child's behavioral style, and professional judgment is used in identifying areas of temperament that may be of concern. Specific areas of temperament may provide valuable data that can be useful in planning intervention.

The area of temperament was first addressed as part of the nature-versus-nurture controversy, when researchers were trying to determine what aspects of personality (if any) were genetically, as opposed to environmentally, determined. The work of Thomas, Chess, Birch, Herzig, and Korn (1963) and Thomas, Chess, and Birch (1968) is seminal in this effort. They identified nine areas of temperament, including: 1) activity level, 2) approach/withdrawal, 3) distractibility, 4) intensity of response, 5) persistence, 6) quality of mood, 7) rhythmicity, and 8) threshold of response. These dimensions were assessed through scales that parents and teachers completed. Through their studies, Thomas et al. (1963, 1968) identified three different constellations of temperament traits that seemed to fit most of their subjects: the "easy" child, the "difficult child," and the "slow-to-warm-up" child.

Thomas and his colleagues followed their subjects for over 20 years. Results revealed that, although many aspects of temperament were modified over time, other aspects were relatively stable. More important, they discovered that the "goodness of fit" or match between the child's temperament and the demands of his or her environment was critical to the child's successful adaptation (Thomas & Chess, 1977). Barbara Keogh, in her work with children with disabilities discovered a similar relationship between a teacher and a child's temperament (1982a, 1982b, 1986). Clearly, there are aspects of temperament that are relevant to the child's behavior and social interactions with others.

Other researchers have investigated different approaches to temperament. Buss and Plomin (1975) identified four broad dimensions of temperament: emotionality, activity, sociability, and impulsiveness. Rothbart and Derryberry (1981) have studied the child's somatic activity, emotional activity, and self-regulation. Pullis and Cadwell (1985) found that the nine categories previously mentioned by Thomas and Chess (1977) can be grouped into three higher-order temperament factors: task orientation, adaptability, and reactivity. Inhibition and lack of inhibition have been identified as factors predicting social characteristics (Kagan, 1988). Still other aspects, such as the parent's personality, are summarized by Goldsmith and Campos (1982).

Three temperament factors were selected for transdisciplinary play-based assessment: activity level, adaptability, and reactivity. These were chosen for ease of observation and relevance to intervention. The previously mentioned facets have also been incorporated, either within these three categories or within other areas of TPBA observations.

Temperament observations can be interpreted only after sufficient observation time. Discussion with the parent regarding each factor may also be helpful in order to ascertain typical patterns of behavior. Temperament is frequently assessed through a parent-administered scale in which the parent is asked to rate the child's temperament on different dimensions (Carey & McDevitt, 1978; Keogh, Pullis, & Cadwell, 1980; Persson-Blennow & McNeil, 1979). For purposes of TPBA, the parent facilitator may want to ask the parent about each area, giving specific examples of how each might be exhibited in the child's daily life, to assist the parents in fully answering.

Activity Level

Activity level relates to the child's general arousal as expressed via the motoric system (Goldsmith & Campos, 1982). Is the child moving constantly from one toy or area to the next? Some children may demonstrate a lack of sustained attention to a toy or activity, and may "flit" from toy to toy. Activity level may also be observed during the child's engagement with a particular toy. The child may sit at a table playing with an object, but constantly "fidget," moving his or her legs, arms, or fingers, or standing up and down. At the other extreme is the child who rarely moves around. This child stays in one area and is content to move slowly through activities. He or she may appear lethargic, and may not move from area to area without encouragement. Activity level varies along a continuum. Observers are concerned about identifying any extreme behaviors that may negatively affect the child's performance and social interactions.

Variation of activity level within the observation time period is also important. Is the child very active at the beginning or end of the session? Does the activity level fluctuate, for example, when stressful or challenging situations are presented? Some children may only exhibit excessive motor activity on gross motor toys, such as spin boxes, swings, and slides. The variation in activity level may be an important indicator of the child's interest and motivation, or in the case of the child whose activity level decreases at the end of the session, may merely indicate fatigue. If the facilitator senses that variations are related to interests, activities can be modified (e.g., removing the child from the motor area for a while and returning later) to see whether the behavior changes.

Activity level should not be confused with attention span. A child may be very active and still have a good attention span, or be very inactive and have a poor attention span. A very high level of motor activity, however, may negatively affect attention span. See Chapter 6, Observation of Cognitive Development, for additional discussion of attention span.

☞ Having an awareness that a child has a particularly high or low activity level can assist the teacher in program planning.

Jason was observed in the play assessment to have a low activity level. Suggestions were made to help increase his active involvement. The occupational therapist recommended adding tactile and motor-alerting components to each activity to assist in increasing Jason's sensory awareness. The speech-language therapist recommended using variations in inflection and a high level of personal animation in order to increase motor responsiveness.

For the child with a high activity level, techniques that have a calming effect (e.g., using low lights, speaking slowly, or using deep pressure in touching the child) would be appropriate. If the teacher is cognizant of the child's activity level, activities can be modified to maximize the child's involvement.

Adaptability

The category of adaptability refers to the child's response and adaptation to new stimuli. How does the child initially respond to unfamiliar people, objects, or situations? For many children, the playroom may be an unfamiliar setting. Questions regarding how the child reacts upon entering the room, and whether he or she appears anxious, cautious, eager, or ready for this new experience, may be examined. Perhaps the child is cautious at first, but quickly settles and appears comfortable. The team can observe how quickly the child relates to the unfamiliar adults in the room, and whether he or she approaches the toys in the room, or avoids the unfamiliar adults. The child's selection of toys is also relevant. Does he or she seek out familiar or unfamiliar toys? (The parent facilitator will need to check with the parent to ascertain what is familiar and what is unfamiliar.) The behavior that the child exhibits while moving from toy to toy and from area to area should be noted.

The manner in which the child indicates his or her interest or withdrawal is also suggestive. Interest may be evident if the child smiles, touches, verbalizes, or seeks proximity to people or objects. The child who is inhibited may move away from people or objects, resist eye contact, protest or cry, or seek proximity to more secure people (e.g., parent) or objects (e.g., known toys or transition objects that they have brought along).

☞ indicates discussion of implications for intervention. Readers will see this symbol throughout each of the guidelines chapters.

Adaptability also refers to how the child adjusts after being introduced to new people, situations, or objects. Observations about the length of time it takes for the child to feel comfortable, and the mechanisms that the child uses to make the adjustment will provide information about adaptability. One child will hang back at first, then gradually move into or toward the new situation, person, or object. Another may vocalize to assure him- or herself: "That looks like a fun slide." Another child may use a parent as a base of security—entering an activity with the parent, but remaining after the parent has withdrawn. Yet another may need continuing verbal assurances and reinforcement from the parent or other adults. A few may not adapt at all, but will continue to avoid the new or unusual.

Briana was slow to adapt to new people and situations in the TPBA play session. She needed to sit with her mother while playing. The facilitator gradually introduced herself into the play until Briana was comfortable. Once she adapted, Briana was able to enjoy her interactions with the facilitator. Briana also had difficulty transitioning to a new play area; she started to cry unless the play facilitator selected a favorite toy and took it with her to the new area. Once involved in playing in the new environment, she was again content.

Information on adaptability can help staff determine when and how to introduce new people, situations, and objects to the child, so as to minimize negative responses.

The team was able to make recommendations regarding Briana's adaptability. They suggested that educational staff give Briana plenty of advance warning concerning changes that were about to occur, and that they provide her with information about unfamiliar people and situations. Transition objects and activities were recommended to help her feel more secure about the introduction of new activities or situations. In addition, they suggested that Briana needed to be given time to adjust to new people and situations. Her initial response was to withdraw, but sensitive handling allowed her to adjust and become comfortable with altered situations.

Anna, a 4-year-old, seemed shy and withdrawn. She would sit passively when toys were presented. The observers noted that when the facilitator played with the toy and showed her enjoyment, Anna slowly joined her in parallel play. She needed time and modeling to feel secure in exploration. The team recommended that wait-time and modeling be incorporated into Anna's program.

Pushing a child too fast or too hard may cause further resistance or withdrawal. Respecting the child's "warm-up" time may ease the tension between staff and the child, and may result in more programmatic gains for the child.

Reactivity

Reactivity refers to the amount of stimulation needed in order to evoke a discernible response from the child, and the intensity of the child's response to the stimulation. Some children need intense stimuli to evoke a response, while others need very little. The category of stimuli that are presented may also affect the need for greater intensity of stimulation. Children with sensory deficits, for example, may need a greater level of input into their weaker visual, auditory, or tactile modalities. Children may also respond differently to stimulation that is either object- or social-oriented. For example, a child with autism may respond positively to interaction with objects, but may respond negatively (or not at all) to social interaction.

By observing the *types* and *amounts* of input the child seeks, as well as the level of input needed to maintain pleasurable interaction, the observers on the TPBA team may identify deficit areas and gain valuable information to facilitate intervention. Team members should, therefore, observe the type and amount of stimulation needed to initiate and maintain a response. For example, the speech-language therapist can observe the type and amount of auditory input needed, the level of verbalization, the degree of intonation, and the volume required to elicit and maintain responses. Smiling, vocalization, or action are indicators of a positive response. Observers should also note the level of input that causes the child to "shut down" or turn away. Looking away, crying, and cessation of verbalization or action may be cues to a negative response to input. The physical or occupational therapist, educator, and psychologist are particularly interested in the optimal level and amount of stimulation for the child.

In addition to how much stimulation is needed to elicit a response, the *intensity* of the child's reaction is informative. The level of affect and energy should be noted when the child engages in play with objects or people in varied situations. Many children with severe disabilities may enjoy a playful experience, such as a pop-up toy, but their reaction may be a grimace or a jerky body movement. The degree to which the child indicates pleasure, displeasure, anxiety, frustration, or other emotions is important, including how intense the reactions are and the mode in which they are exhibited.

An abused child, Anna, demonstrated little response to the stuffed animals in the house area, but became quite animated and angry with the dolls, spanking them, scolding them, and putting them to bed "without nothing to eat." The facilitator allowed the child to develop related themes in her play. Anna showed average or even low-level intensity of reaction to most toys in the play session, but her intensity of response increased in relation to the emotionally charged areas of her life.

A child's intensity of reaction to people varies, too. *Anna was comfortable with a female facilitator, but showed withdrawal and anxiety with a male facilitator. This finding was potentially related to the identity of her abuser.* Although observations such as this one are not easily interpreted, it is still important to note any discrepancies in intensity of response to various situations, people, and toys, since the results of further investigation may have programmatic implications.

Intensity of reaction may also be noted with regard to frustration tolerance. How intensely does the child react to failure? He or she may demonstrate a range from little change in affect to severe tantrums. Circumstances that provoke variation in intensity of response during TPBA play session are noteworthy. Patterns of response may then be investigated.

☞ Teachers, therapists, and parents must frequently provide high levels of input to children with disabilities in order to obtain positive responses. Unfortunately, the "window" of response is often small, resulting in an overestimate of the child's tolerance; for example, the brief positive response to stimulation suddenly shifts to a cry of protest when stimulation is too long or too intense (Field, 1983). Observations of thresholds of responsiveness can help to gauge the level and amount of input that children need and can tolerate. Keeping a child's input at a pleasurable level will result in more effective intervention.

Carl, a child with autism, responded minimally to low intensity auditory or visual input, but laughed and engaged in turn-taking when a tickling game started. This behavior continued with high intensity for several minutes, and was then followed with a quiet turn-taking and imitation game of drinking water and making faces. This was the most positive interaction observed during the assessment period. The information gained from this allowed staff to recommend a program for Carl that called for intense interactive motor and sensory input prior to activities that required attention and imitation.

The team who will be working with the child should find it useful to know which activities elicit a strong positive or negative response from the child.

For Anna, the child who had been abused, the teacher and psychologist recommended working with her to express her fears and anxieties. They also modeled caring and nurturing behavior to Anna and the dolls. One of the goals for Anna was to develop alternative ways for her to express her feelings and emotions. Another long-term goal was for Anna to be able to develop safe, secure relationships with adults of both sexes.

MASTERY MOTIVATION

Assessment of the child's abilities in various areas indicates what the child can do but not *how the child is learning* (Brockman, Morgan, & Harmon, 1988). The development of individualized intervention programs demands a more specific process assessment. The examination of mastery motivation provides insight into the developmental domains upon which the child is focusing energy. The degree of persistence, approach to problem-solving, and effectiveness of efforts in each developmental area can be determined. Scarr (1981) and Yarrow, Klein, Lomanaco, and Morgan (1975) maintain that mastery motivation may be as predictive of later success as standardized tests, and may be *more* predictive. Mastery motivation is inextricably intertwined with cognitive development. A reciprocal relationship, therefore, appears to exist between persistence and competence (Yarrow, Morgan, Jennings, Harmon, & Gaiter, 1982).

The cognitive areas of attention span, object use, symbolic play, and problem-solving in TPBA overlap with mastery motivation. Mastery motivation is included as a separate area in social-emotional development because it influences the development of skills in all areas.

Research in mastery motivation stems largely from the work of White (1959), who developed a theory of *effectance motivation* identifying the child's innate motivation to master and control the environment. His theory is consistent with the prominent theories of Piaget (1936) and Hunt (1965), who espoused the child's active role in his or her own learning. Interest in mastery motivation has grown, resulting in studies examining: 1) the assessment of mastery motivation (Emde, Gaensbauer, & Harmon, 1981; Gaensbauer & Harmon, 1981; Morgan, Harmon, Pipp, & Jennings, 1983), 2) the development of mastery motivation in children who have disabilities and those who do not (Brockman et al., 1982; Harter, 1977, 1978, 1981), 3) the developmental changes in mastery motivation (Harmon, Morgan, & Glicken, 1984; Morgan & Harmon, 1984), and 4) the relationship of cognition to mastery motivation (Gaiter, Morgan, Jennings, Harmon, & Yarrow, 1982; Jennings, Harmon, Morgan, Gaiter, & Yarrow, 1979). As reflected in the age ranges included at the end of the chapter, these studies have shown that mastery motivation is demonstrated in distinct ways at different ages. Jennings et al. (1979) found that "infants' motivation to affect and explore their environment leads them to explore and play with objects about them. This motivation results in increasingly competent interactions with the environment" (p. 386). Children who showed greater ability to sustain focused attention during free play completed more tasks successfully and persisted longer on problem-solving tasks. The infant's quality of exploration, or cognitive maturity, was more important than the amount of exploration. In particular, ability to produce effects with toys was related to mastery motivation.

Morgan and Harmon (1984) reviewed the literature related to characteristics of mastery motivation at different ages. They note that at 9 months of age there is a shift from more general exploration to task-directed behavior. The child repeats successful cause-and-effect, combinatorial, or means–ends tasks. By 15 months of age, the child persistently works at multipart tasks, such as puzzles and formboards, or means–ends tasks, such as lock boards or cash registers. As the child reaches the preschool years, the child with high levels of mastery motivation prefers challenging tasks to easy tasks. By 4 years of age, the child self-initiates mastery activities and organizes problem-solving without asking for assistance.

During the play session, it is important to have age-appropriate toys that can provide a moderate challenge to the child. Toys that allow the child to produce an auditory or visual effect using buttons, levers, or dials are needed. For older children, combinatorial toys such as pegboards, formboards, and shape sorters are suitable for eliciting mastery motivation. Barriers can also be erected that require the child to circumvent an obstacle to attain a goal. Tasks for preschool-age children may be observed in the same areas, but using higher-level, more complex toys or activities. Building a complex block structure with angular blocks or completing a challenging puzzle may interest the child. The TPBA process of following the child's lead also offers the team an opportunity to observe the level of challenge involved in activities selected by the child. The facilitator may also allow the child to choose from toys (particularly relevant for children 3½ years of age and older) posing varying degrees of difficulty.

Team observations will include determining how the child responds to challenging objects or situations. The child may respond by examining, exploring, or using the object appropriately. The child may also exhibit persistent task-directed behaviors in certain types of activities. How often the child repeats successfully completed, challenging activities and the level of task that the child selects are also observations that can be made by the team. In addition, the team can determine the amount of assistance the child requests in completing tasks, and the degree to which the child prefers to figure out problems without adult assistance.

Sandy, a 2½-year-old child with a visual impairment, was observed during play session. His behavior was characterized by brief encounters with toys, in which he would bang or shake them. He tactually explored objects, but did not attempt to use the objects functionally. His cause-and-effect abilities were limited; he smiled at toys that produced sound effects, but did not attempt to generate the same result again. His persistence level was low on tasks in all developmental domains, but was highest in motor activities. When bounced on the facilitator's knee, tickled, or moved rhythmically in time to music, Sandy would smile and move his body to get the facilitator to repeat the action. Overall, Sandy's behavior was characterized by simple, unsustained exploration.

☞   Mastery motivation is encouraged in an environment that allows the child freedom to initiate and follow through on activities. Having toys and materials available that are developmentally challenging is vital to the TPBA process. Minimizing the use of external reinforcement is also important. Many children with disabilities "perform" to please the adults rather than to derive pleasure from the activity. Eventually, the child can lose intrinsic motivation and will strive to master a task only when they are reinforced (Brockman et al., 1988). For this reason, teams need to be cognizant of the amount of reinforcement they are giving the child. Many children with disabilities are clearly not strongly motivated internally, and need support and encouragement to increase initiations, explorations, and problem-solving. Reinforcement should be withdrawn as the child self-initiates mastery.

For Sandy, recommendations were made to use toys with maximal result for minimal input. A top that spun, made music, and lit up when a simple button was touched was one of the toys adapted for Sandy. A voice-activated, bright musical mobile was placed in his crib. His team and parents simplified and incrementally increased the complexity of all activities presented to Sandy. Their goal was to increase his motivation to affect his environment.

SOCIAL INTERACTIONS WITH THE PARENT

TPBA measures social functioning through observations of the child with parent(s), facilitator, a peer, and in a group. As discussed in Chapter 4, the parent is asked to interact with the child in a nonstructured play situation and in a more structured teaching task. The child's relationship to the parent is also observed when the parent is not directly interacting with the child, but is in the room watching the play session. The infant or young child should begin the session and remain with the parent as long as is necessary to ensure the child's optimal performance.

The importance of parent–child interaction to the child's development and the effect of a disability on interaction patterns is discussed in Chapter 11; the reader is referred to that chapter for additional information.

Rheingold (1966) proposed four principles on which infants' social behaviors are based: 1) the infant's responsiveness to social stimuli, 2) the infant's initiation of social contact, 3) the infant's modification of adult behavior, and 4) the adult's modification of infant behavior. These early social exchanges may be the foundation for the development of later cognitive abilities (Ramey, Farran, & Campbell, 1979), language development (Bruner, 1977), and social skills (Tronick & Gianino, 1986). Parent and child are equal contributors to interactions; therefore, either party may lack appropriate behaviors or possess unusual response patterns (Comfort, 1988; Goldberg, 1977).

Early literature on parent–child interaction emphasized the parent role in the dyad. Bell's (1968) review, however, highlighted the significant contribution that the infant makes in interactions. This is no less true with infants and young children who have disabilities. Looking at child characteristics and the impact that they have on parents and others provides insight into intervention approaches that will improve transactional patterns and social skills (Affleck, McGrade, McQueeney, & Allen, 1982).

Parents' feelings of competence during interactions with their child depend on the child's readability, predictability, and responsiveness (Goldberg, 1977), all of which may be problematic in the child with a disability. As Walker (1982) has mentioned, the social interactions of the young child with disabilities are frequently quite different than those of the child who does not have disabilities:

1. The amount of social interaction is reduced, as interactions with adults are mainly of a caregiving or teaching nature.
2. There is little spontaneous or child-initiated social contact.
3. The interactions that do occur are not of a truly socially interactive nature.
4. The children do not seem to be aware of the reciprocal nature of communication.
5. Interactions with caregivers may display one-sided activity or extremes of activity and inactivity. (Adapted from Walker, 1982, p. 218)

The level of affect displayed by the child is important, since a child who is smiling and laughing or obviously enjoying an activity is more pleasurable to engage. High-risk children or children with disabilities may show less affect for many reasons. A higher threshold of responsivity may make the child difficult to captivate (Field, 1983), low muscle tone may contribute to less facial animation (Emde, Katz, & Thorpe, 1978), and an inability to understand and interpret adult cues may reduce the child's ability to read the parent's affect (Brazelton, Tronick, Adamson, Als, & Wise, 1975).

Activity between the partners is another important aspect of social interaction. Walker (1982) noted in her research that infants who were deaf-blind were inactive a much greater percentage of the time than typical babies. Other investigators have also found that the overall activity level of children with disabilities is lower than that of peers without disabilities (Hanzlik & Stevenson, 1986).

Researchers also consistently find that children at high-risk and those who have disabilities initiate interactions with their parents less frequently than children who are not at-risk or do not have disabilities (Cunningham, Reuler, Blackwell, & Deck, 1981; Field, 1979, 1983; Hanson, 1984; Jones, 1978; Wedell-Monig & Lumley, 1980). Such children are placed in the role of responders rather than active transacters within their environments. Changing initiation patterns, therefore, becomes a crucial area for intervention.

The Child's Interaction with the Parent

Within the play-based assessment guidelines, the team observes the extent to which the child's interactions with his or her parents display the characteristics discussed above. Identification of problems can lead to recommendations that will strengthen social interactions with parents and others. Social interactions are one channel through which the child acquires communication skills and learns about the world. Given that the parents are the primary caregivers, controlling the child's environment and providing opportunities for interaction, observation of the child in interaction with his or her parent(s) becomes a critical area for assessment.

During the play session, the team should observe the child's affect during interactions with the parent. Observations regarding whether the child appears to enjoy the activities and the ways and the frequency of the child's indication of pleasure need to be made. Smiling or laughter, physical body movement, or intense attention are indications of pleasure that should be noted, although they are not the only indications that a child may make.

When her mother presented a doll to Jenny, a 3-year-old with quadriplegia, she showed pleasure by grimacing, increasing her tone, and making "jerky" movements with her arms—all behaviors that could be interpreted as a negative *response. Her mother was familiar with her cues, however, and correctly interpreted her behaviors as excitement.*

A child's differential response to various types of stimulation is also important. Is there increased positive response to vocal, tactile, or kinesthetic input?

Jenny responded positively to her mother's soft voice. She showed mixed pleasure and anxiety when moved. Slow movement appeared to be pleasurable, and quick movement seemed to produce anxiety.

Response to the parent's affect can be meaningful. If the parent shows happiness, excitement, frustration, anger, or sadness, does the child indicate that he or she is interpreting and reacting to these emotions?

Jenny watched her mother's face for reactions. When her mother showed excitement in response to her activity, Jenny opened her mouth and emitted a groan that sounded like a laugh. Clearly, she recognized her mother's affect.

Along with reading the parent's cues, the team may observe cues the child is sending to the parent, not only of pleasure and displeasure, but of comfort, anxiety, and needs. The very young child or the child with severe disabilities gives primarily gestural or physical cues combined with vocalizations, while the older child or the child with mild disabilities uses verbalizations combined with gestures.

Jenny was quite effective at sending her mother cues of how she was feeling and what she wanted. She grimaced and looked away when not happy with the toy presented to her. She vocalized and used direct gaze to indicate a desire for an object.

The child's activity level is examined in relation to the percentage of time the child spends interacting with the parent. What amount of activity is directed toward interaction with the parent? A child might be occupied with a toy without interacting with the parent at all. Close proximity or efforts at communication on the part of either parent or child does not guarantee mutual or reciprocal interaction.

The team also examines the frequency of child-initiated versus parent-initiated interactions. Activities that are initiated by the child demonstrate the child's ability to actively influence the environment. However, when the parent is the initiator of activities, the child becomes a responder, following the parent's lead and interests. A balance in initiation of interaction fosters the child's development and mutuality of interaction.

Elizabeth, a 3½-year-old child with Down syndrome, was observed playing with her father. He presented a small musical toy to Elizabeth, pushed on the keys, and then told her to do the same. Elizabeth looked at him, then picked up a doll and hugged it. Her father then put blocks in front of Elizabeth and told her to stack them up like he did. Elizabeth threw the blocks instead. These unsuccessful interactions continued through a series of toys.

Elizabeth's is a common interaction pattern in children with disabilities. Even if Elizabeth had responded in the way her father wanted, she was not initiating the interactions. To become an effective communicator and learner, Elizabeth needs to be able to initiate and maintain interactions.

Maintenance of interactions, or turn-taking, is another target of observation. Mahoney and Powell (1986) have identified reducing directiveness and increasing turn-taking as key areas for intervention. During the play session, the team ascertains how many turns the child can maintain.

During Elizabeth's play session, turn sequences were limited. Her father initiated a turn, and Elizabeth responded with an unexpected behavior. Her father repeated the behavior again, and Elizabeth responded with a behavior that terminated the sequence. He then initiated a new activity and the cycle repeated itself.

Three-year-old Mark sat with his mother putting together a puzzle. Mark took a piece and said, "Where does this go?" His mother replied, "Oh, I don't know. Think about it." As a result of his cerebral palsy, Mark struggled with the placement of the piece but finally succeeded, with a little verbal prompting and encouragement from his mom. He then picked up the next piece and the cycle began again.

This example presents a picture quite different from that of Elizabeth. Here, Mark verbally initiated interactions with his mother. Although he knew the placement of the pieces, he continued to question and comment. Give-and-take characterized the activity with the puzzle. Mark's mother did not "take a turn" at putting in a puzzle piece, but they choreographed a delightful game with Mark in the lead and his mother responding.

During the session with the parent or parents, the team has the opportunity to observe each parent directing and managing the child's behavior. The child's reaction to limit-setting by the parent and the facilitator can then be compared.

When Elizabeth was observed in interaction with her father, for example, her behavior was the same regardless of what her father said or how he said it; she was virtually oblivious to his wishes. Her behavior was similar with the facilitator, revealing that the response pattern was not limited to her father (a fact that was comforting to him).

Knowing the interaction characteristics of the child can assist the team in working with the family and in working directly with the child. *For Jenny, whose positive responses could be read as negative, the team saw that Jenny's mother had learned to interpret Jenny's responses accurately. She was able to adjust her activity based on the cues she was getting from Jenny. The information gained was helpful to the team members working with Jenny.*

Elizabeth was also giving cues to her father, but he was not as perceptive in reading them. Elizabeth was using both physical and vocal cues to indicate that she was not happy with the activities presented. Elizabeth's father was frustrated by her lack of cooperation and needed help in reading Elizabeth's cues, adjusting to the type of input she preferred, and modifying his activities to meet her needs. He also needed reassurance that many of Elizabeth's behaviors were frustrating to others as well.

The Parent—Child Interaction

After looking at the child's characteristics, dyadic interactions are easier to understand. It is difficult to separate what is taking place with the child from what is taking place with the parent. As this is meant to be a child-focused assessment, however, examining the child's contribution to interactions is vital. Looking at the parent and child together enables the team to make supportive recommendations to the parents to strengthen interactions.

Brazelton et al. (1975) and Mahoney and Powell (1986) discuss the importance of mutual involvement and *affective synchrony,* or the regulation of content, timing, and intensity of emotional expression. Observations of mutuality include noting similarity of focus and content, such as whether the child and parent are attending to the same activity, object, or person. The team should determine if parent and child seem to have the same "agenda" for their play and if they are playing at the same developmental level. As the cycles of engagement, play, and disengagement occur, the timing of the shifts of attention can be examined. The extent to which there is a balance in turn-taking, or reciprocity (Gottman, 1978; Walker, 1982), with the child and parent both having an opportunity to equally engage in the interaction, is also important. Observations can also be made regarding whether a similar level of intensity of affect within the interactions exists.

The sequence of play behaviors is also important. Parent—child interactions are usually characterized by a sequence of interactions that are repeated with variations and extensions (Brazelton et al., 1975; Stein, Beebe, Jaffee, & Bennett, 1977; Stern, 1977, 1985). The patterns are predictable to each partner, thus promoting the continuation of the play. With children who have disabilities, this pattern may break down. Cue-giving and cue-reading may be difficult for one or both parties in the interaction. The team watches the sequence of interactions to discern whether themes are repeated often enough for the child with disabilities to "catch on." Also, team members should examine whether parent and child are anticipating each other's actions, and whether the parent is able to modify the activity to match the capabilities of the child. Different patterns of interaction are evident with different children.

Jenny's mother was adept at matching Jenny's developmental level. She was able to slow the pace to allow time for Jenny to motorically respond, and she modified her affective intensity to lessen Jenny's increased tone. She watched for a response from Jenny, anticipating her responses and modifying her next action in order to get a slightly different response. During the assessment, Jenny and her mother appeared to be in harmony.

The interaction between Elizabeth and her father was more asynchronous. Although they frequently had a mutual focus of attention, the content, timing, level of play, and balance in turn-taking contrasted sharply. Elizabeth's developmental level was lower than her father's expectations. Neither was reading the other's cues and anticipating responses, and their play lacked continuity, sequence, and mutuality. The result was unpleasant for both parent and child.

Mark's mother focused on the same content as her child. She let him problem-solve at his own level. She matched his level of enthusiasm, and she took a verbal "turn" after each comment or action made by her son. The theme of "find a piece, figure out where it goes, place it, and reward the accomplishment" was repeated. There was no modification or expansion of the activity, but Mark and his mother seemed to enjoy the interaction.

Information from observation of the characteristics of the child and the parent—child interactions are combined to develop recommendations for intervention.

No specific recommendations were made for Jenny's mom with regard to interaction. Instead, the team took notes on the successful methods of engagement used by the mother, so that those methods could be incorporated into their intervention strategies.

Mark's mother was given suggestions for incorporating expansions and variations into her interactions, and encouraged to continue the interactions that worked for her and Mark.

Elizabeth's father needed acknowledgment of his feelings of frustration and helplessness and assistance in making his interactions with his daughter more pleasurable. One of the team members met with him to watch the tape of his interactions with Elizabeth. The father noted that Elizabeth never did what he wanted her to do, that she seemed to enjoy manipulating and throwing, and that he wanted to be able to interact with her without feeling so frustrated. The team member agreed that it was difficult to interact with a child who always followed her own agenda. Instead of identifying all of the interaction concerns for the father, the team member elected to identify two considerations. The first was matching Elizabeth's developmental level, and the second was imitating Elizabeth to allow her to initiate activities and encourage turn-taking. The team member modeled interactions with Elizabeth several times, focusing on imitating Elizabeth's manipulation and exploration of toys. After incorporating the ideas at home, her father noted that the interactions with Elizabeth lasted longer and seemed to be more pleasurable for both of them. The team then continued to support him by identifying other methods for improving interactions with Elizabeth.

Characteristics of the Child in Relation to the Parent While Not in Direct Interaction

The child is not in direct contact with the parent for the majority of the play session; most interactions take place with the facilitator. The team also has an opportunity to observe the child's reaction to the absence of the parent. The observation of dependency and attachment behaviors will vary, depending on the age of the child (Emde & Harmon, 1982, 1984; Foley, 1985; Mahler, Pine, & Bergman, 1975). In the child under 2 years of age, the observations of the child's need for proximity to the parent and reaction to separation can reveal the child's level of emotional dependency (Ainsworth, Blehar, Waters, & Wall, 1978; Foley, 1985).

Ainsworth et al. (1978) found that children from 10 to 24 months of age characteristically behaved in one of three ways. The first group, called *securely attached,* showed distress at separation, and pleasure and proximity-seeking upon being reunited with the parent. The second group showed distress at absence, sought contact with the parent upon reunion, and then angrily rejected comfort when it was offered. Ainsworth and her colleagues called this group *insecurely attached.* The third group was not concerned by the parent's absence and avoided the parent upon reunion. This group was considered *avoidantly attached.* As discussed further in Chapter 11, secure attachment appears to be associated with positive developmental outcomes, and is therefore important in assessment.

By the age of 3 years, most children have gained a sufficient degree of memory, language ability, and independence that the need for proximity and anxiety at separation are not critical issues (Gaensbauer & Harmon, 1982). For children over 3 years old, however, the observation of strong emotional response to parental separation can have clinical importance. By 3 years of age, the child should be able to initiate activities and play comfortably alone (Foley, 1985). Independence is also demonstrated as the 4-year-old begins to choose friends and establish a wider social world beyond the family.

This ability stems from the child's growing awareness of his or her own "personness" (individuality) or differences. The child becomes aware of the ability to make decisions, to control the environment, and to act on his or her desires (Rothbart, 1984). The child can remember his or her mother and father and their continued presence, even when they are not physically present.

Indicators that children differentiate and understand that they are unique, independent people can be observed in play. As infants acquire language skills, they will be able to identify and name people in their environments, and then name themselves. They will be able to identify their own possessions with the ubiquitous "mine" (Cohen & Gross, 1979). Between 2 and 3, they are able to identify their own and others' feelings, noting happiness, anger, sadness, and other clearly portrayed emotions (Brooks-Gunn & Lewis, 1978). Also at this time, they will identify sexual differences and know their own genders (Hutt, 1978). By 4, they can talk about the concrete characteristics of others (hair color, height, age, and clothing) and by 6, they can talk about subtle, abstract characteristics, such as sharing and selfishness (Rogers, 1978).

Children use various means to maintain contact with their parent(s). Observations to make during the TPBA play session include the amount and type of signaling or sensory cuing the child gives the parent, and whether visual "checking-in" or physical contact with the parent is necessary for the child's satisfaction. In addition, the team should observe vocal or verbal interactions that the child (or parent) initiates. The child may also move in order to maintain physical proximity to the parent, thus enabling the child to feel comfortable with the facilitator and others who are present. How often the child uses proximity-seeking or other "checking-in" behaviors should also be noted. Some children do not look toward or approach the parent, while others constantly need to use the parent for what Mahler et al. (1975) call *emotional refueling*.

Different children demand varying amounts of the parent's attention. Sometimes a look is enough; and at other times the parent needs to intermittently hold or hug the child, or actually join the play session for the child to feel comfortable. All of these behaviors can be observed by the team. During the play session, an opportunity may arise to observe the child's reactions to strange or fearful situations. The child may demonstrate a fearful or surprised response if a new team member enters the room, if the peer who is brought in becomes belligerent with the child, or if a toy reacts in an unpredictable way (topples over, or makes a loud noise). The team observes how the child handles the situation, noting whether he or she remains secure, or needs to have parent support to deal with additional stress. In addition, if the child is fatigued at any point in the session, he or she may turn to the parent for support.

Much can be learned by watching the child's interactions when the parent is present, but valuable inferences can also be made by watching the child's response to the parent's absence. This aspect of the session is conducted with children after they are mobile or mature enough to have formed secure attachments, usually after 10 months of age (Lamb & Campos, 1982). At some point in the session, usually while the child is playing with the parent, the parent is asked to leave the room. The parent announces to the child that he or she is leaving for a few minutes and will be back soon. The child under 2 years of age may demonstrate various reactions: some children may continue to play as before; some may indicate uneasiness by looking frequently at the door or fussing; some may go to the door and attempt to follow the parent; and others may cry and not want to continue playing. The verbal child may talk to himself or herself, saying, "Mommy be right back," thus using self-consolation. Others may move closer to or away from the facilitator. The mechanisms that the child uses to adjust to the parent's absence are also important to observe.

Responses when the parent returns are also important. Some children may physically or verbally greet the parent, or glance in the parent's direction, then return to play. Others may be oblivious to the fact that the parent has returned. Again, the responses may vary depending on the age as well as the emotional security of the child (Ainsworth et al., 1978; Emde & Harmon, 1982). If the child is young, or if the team has learned from the parent that the child exhibits an intense negative reaction to separation, this aspect of the session should be delayed until the end of the TPBA. Otherwise, rapport may be difficult to reestablish.

During the play session, the child may use language that indicates his or her knowledge of self and others, gestures or words to indicate awareness of emotions in others, and labels to indicate possession or characteristics of others. The facilitator may also prompt this by probing at various times. If the child is drawing a picture of people, for example, the facilitator might ask, "Tell me about this guy. What kind of person is he?" Observers may also have an opportunity to note the child's use of reference to gender and sexual identification.

☞ Transdisciplinary play-based assessment offers only a cursory look at attachment, separation, and individuation behaviors. Observations serve only as a screening to determine if further evaluation is desired. There can be no immediate recommendations for intervention as a result of observations of *indirect* interaction between parent and child.

It should be noted, however, that the child who has extreme anxiety with separation from the parent may experience great difficulty with a center-based program in which the parent is not present. Some preschool children are not secure enough emotionally to separate from their parent for long periods of time. They spend their time at preschool engaged in unrelenting sobbing, preventing them from learning or interacting positively with others. For these children, a further evaluation of attachment and separation issues is needed, along with alternatives for providing services. A home-based program or a center-based program with the mother may be a more appropriate alternative, until the child has developed a stronger perception of self and others, and sense of trust in various environments.

Knowledge of self and others may be addressed through activities that encourage the child to differentiate his or her individuality. Activities in front of a mirror, such as putting on make-up, dressing in funny clothes, or tactile games with different parts of the body, are all ways of helping the child to notice and recognize his or her characteristics compared to those of others. Exaggerated expression of emotions may help the child to correlate affect with actions of self and others. The establishment of a consistent, supportive environment that encourages exploration and experimentation both at home and at school is also important.

SOCIAL INTERACTIONS WITH THE FACILITATOR

The Child in Interaction with the Facilitator

Just as the child learns to differentiate self from others, so, too, does he or she learn to differentiate one person from another. As infants develop, they distinguish between mother and father and other significant people. Differentiation is based not only on distinctions in appearances, but also on affects and unique interaction patterns (Stern, 1985).

Research has shown that mothers and fathers interact differently with a baby. Fathers tend to play more vigorously, for shorter periods of time, and they tend to use physically stimulating types of interaction. Fathers seem to respond to the infant's vocalizations with vocalizations, whereas mothers tend to respond to vocalizations with touching. Fathers' interactions are more unpredictable, allowing the child to experience peaks of excitement; mothers play more quietly and for longer periods of time (Lamb & Campos, 1982). Both types of interaction allow the child to experience a range of emotions. These different styles also are the child's first exposure to social differentiation, or learning to respond and interact with different people in different ways (Bricker, 1986). By 6 months of age, most babies can differentiate strangers.

In most cases, the facilitator is a stranger to the child. Contrasts between the child's interactions with the parent(s) and the facilitator can provide significant information. For this reason, observations of child–facilitator interactions parallel those of the parent and child. This is done intentionally, so that a direct comparison can be made.

How does the child react differently to the facilitator's interactions? Qualitative and quantitative differences should be noted. Changes in affect, language, play, or other behaviors may be seen. Discrepancies are particularly meaningful when parents or teachers report incongruities between behaviors at home and those at school; these differences may result from, among other things, the child's comfort level with unfamiliar adults, the child's emotional security, or variations in interaction patterns.

The child's overall comfort level with the facilitator and other adults who are observing can be noted. The child may be cautious or fearful, affectionate, comfortable, or oblivious, and may relate differently with specific people (e.g., males or females). Such observations may serve as a red flag for further evaluation or may provide enough information to serve as a beginning point for intervention. Children with autism, for example, may appear to be unaware of adults in the room. Children who have been sexually abused may sometimes be overly seductive or indiscriminately affectionate.

Children may react differently to emotions and affect expressed by the facilitator, and to various forms of input from the facilitator. A child may give various cues to the faciliator, and use the facilitator to get needs met. Some children physically gesture or move the adult toward the desired goal. Others verbally indicate or instruct the adult.

The degree of activity versus inactivity with the facilitator and the percentage of time spent in direct interaction can be compared to those with the parent. Observations can be made about the frequency of child-initiated interactions with the facilitator, and the type of interactions that are initiated. Does the child initiate interaction with manipulatives, like Legos, or representational toys, like telephones? How long are interaction sequences?

At some point during the session, observations of the child's reaction to authority can be made. Limits can be set on the use of a toy, an activity the child is enjoying can be cut short, or specific instructions can be given for how to do a task. The child may be compliant, or perhaps even overly compliant, never asserting his or her own desires. Or the child may instead be oblivious to adults' attempts to control, proceeding with his or her own agenda and ignoring the facilitator's attempts to provide guidance. Active physical resistance may also be seen, including hitting or throwing a tantrum. (Attempts at control should be made only at the end of the session, if possible, as this contradicts the nondirective philosophy of TPBA, and may jeopardize rapport.)

The interaction patterns observed between the child and facilitator may vary during the session, depending on the activity in which they are engaged. The child may initiate, take turns, verbalize, and interact positively in one situation, and be withdrawn or self-absorbed in another. Opportunities are presented for exploratory, manipulative, or constructive play; representational or dramatic play; motor activities; and tactile stimulation. The child may have varying skill levels in each area, may need adult intervention or support at different levels, and may display contrasting interaction patterns with each activity. All areas need to be compared to the child's interactions with the parent and peer.

☞   The child's interaction patterns with the facilitator during the session have direct implications for his or her intervention program. In particular, these observations may lead to recommendations regarding: 1) the level and type of adult supports necessary in different circumstances, 2) activities that encourage the child to initiate and maintain social interactions, and 3) sequences for activities to keep the child's level of interaction at optimal levels.

Elizabeth displayed the same cues with the facilitator as she did with her father. Her interaction patterns were quite different, however, with the facilitator; she initiated activities more fre-

quently and was more responsive to the facilitator. This was primarily due to the differences in interaction patterns established by the facilitator.

The Facilitator–Child Interaction

The facilitator, if well trained, is able to incorporate the techniques of matching the child's developmental level, play content, timing, and intensity. To the degree that these interaction patterns differ from those of the parents, discrepancies may be seen in initiation of interaction or activities, turn-taking, and affective responses. The facilitator's use of repetition, imitation, and expansion may affect the length of play sequences, and the quality and degree of communication.

☞   If parent and facilitator interaction styles are similar, the responses of the child may be parallel. When the child is uncomfortable with the unfamiliar adult, resulting interactions may be negatively affected. If the child achieves a comfortable rapport with the facilitator, the facilitation techniques should result in optimal play behaviors. Disparities between parent–child interaction and facilitator–child interaction may result from contrasting patterns of behavior.

Elizabeth's play appeared quite different with the facilitator than with her father. When the facilitator imitated Elizabeth's actions on the toy, Elizabeth looked at her, smiled, and repeated her actions. After several repetitions, the facilitator expanded or modified the activity. Elizabeth threw the blocks and the facilitator imitated her several times. The facilitator then introduced a can and modeled throwing the blocks into the can and dumping them out. Elizabeth laughed and tried to imitate the facilitator. This interaction style was incorporated throughout the play session, and Elizabeth demonstrated a wider range of her abilities. Her vocalizations increased and her affect became more positive.

The facilitator incorporates the technique of matching the child's level, play interests, timing, and intensity. The facilitator must be creative to encourage the child to initiate desired activities.

The team discovered that Elizabeth responded to modeling and imitation when her attention was captured, and that she was motivated by initiating the activity. Elizabeth needed a careful transition from area to area, as she exhibited perseveration. The techniques used in facilitating the TPBA were also good approaches to intervention with Elizabeth. Her parents were able to see the difference in her behavior, the assessment process served as a basis for discussion of facilitating interaction with Elizabeth.

SOCIAL INTERACTIONS WITH PEERS

Interactions with Peers in Dyad

Children behave differently with other children than they do with parents and other adults (Eckerman, Whatley, & Kutz, 1975; Hartup, 1978, 1983). Interaction with play material occurs more often. There is less fussing, more joint use of play materials, more give and take, and more struggles. Eckerman et al. (1975) reported that infants ages 10 to 12 months move from social play with the parent to play with objects and peers. By 2 years of age, peer social play predominates. Between 12 months and 2 years, the child's play with peers changes dramatically. Mueller and Lucas (1975) identify stages through which the child progresses. In the first stage, contacts with peers center around an object. The second stage reveals simple actions and responses between children. In the third stage, interactions between two children become longer and more sophisticated, until true role sharing and turn-taking is evident in the fourth stage. The play of the 2-year-old is, however, still characterized by intense watchfulness of the peer, parallel, or side-by-side, noninteractive play, and an almost compulsive desire to imitate (Jennings & Curry, 1982).

Imitative behaviors increase in older children (Hartup, 1978). By age 3, children are very aware of each other and will make verbal efforts to maintain social interaction. By 4 years of age, children are capable of engaging in complex interactions with their peers (Jennings & Suwalsky, 1982). With the preschool-age child, there is little seeking or expression of affection, while there is increased rough-and-tumble play, talking, and laughing (Charlesworth & Hartup, 1967; Heathers, 1955).

Parten (1932) identified social participation categories that appeared to be developmentally sequenced; however, later research has established that the child does not abandon lower-level play skills, but incorporates them when appropriate (Yawkey & Pelligrini, 1984). The categories identified by Parten included unoccupied behavior, solitary independent play, onlooker, parallel activity, associative play, and cooperative or organized play. The child is engaged in *unoccupied behavior* when not playing or interacting with others. In *solitary play,* the child plays alone and without concern for the activities of those around him or her. When the child watches the play of other children, he or she is engaged in *onlooker behavior.* In *parallel play,* the child plays beside rather than with other children, usually with similar toys and materials. Actual play with other children, such as sharing toys and talking about the play activities, even though the play agendas of the children may be different, is called *associative play. Cooperative play,* in contrast, is goal-oriented, with children playing in an organized fashion toward a common end (Parten, 1932).

Group play becomes more important in the child over 3 years of age. By age 4, the child can play group interactive activities. Several children may act out sequences in dramatic play scenarios, such as fighting a fire, saving residents of a house, and taking them to the hospital. The characters each have roles and interact in appropriate ways (Watson & Fischer, 1980). Between 5 and 6 years of age, children have developed the cognitive understanding and social skills to play group games with rules (Cohen & Gross, 1979; Garvey, 1977).

The fact that children behave differently with peers makes observation of child–peer interaction a significant aspect of the TPBA. Selection of the peer can make a difference. Doyle, Connolly, and Rivest (1980) found that peers who were familiar with each other engaged in more frequent social interactions, sustained their play longer, and played more constructively. Guralnick and Groom (1987) studied children with mild disabilities paired with children without disabilities who were younger but at the same developmental level, and children who did not have disabilities and the same age or older, with other peers with mild disabilities. Their findings revealed that children with mild disabilities had substantially improved peer interactions when paired with older children without disabilities. Limited social interactions were observed when children with mild delays were matched with other children with mild delays. It has also been found that children prefer same-sex peers as playmates (Brooks-Gunn & Lewis, 1978).

Although these findings need to be confirmed through further research, the implications for TPBA are that play with a familiar, slightly older (several months older, according to the Guralnick and Groom study) child who does not have disabilities will increase the child's play interactions. This pairing should allow the team to observe a broader range and higher-level of play skills, but if such a peer is unavailable, another peer may be used, preferably a familiar child, who if he or she has a disability, has slightly higher abilities. Siblings are not recommended. Although they may be included in the TPBA, and will provide valuable information on family interaction, behaviors with siblings will undoubtedly be different with a peer.

The peer can be brought into the playroom at any time during the play session, but it is recommended that this occur after the child becomes comfortable with the facilitator. The facilitator can then serve as a support for the child and encourage peer interaction. Alternately, if the child is having difficulty relating to the facilitator, the peer may be brought in after parent–child observations have been made. The team must make a judgment about the best time to introduce the peer.

Peer interaction is best arranged in a play area that promotes interaction. For younger children, the manipulative area with blocks, trucks, and so on can stimulate interaction. The motor area may also provide opportunities for social turn-taking with balls, spin boards, slides, and other materials. For older children, the house area with telephones and dishes or the block area with trucks and cars can provide the stimulus for social give-and-take. The peer may also be reintroduced into the playroom at the end of the play session for a snack, which provides another opportunity to observe social interaction.

When the peer enters the playroom where the child is playing, the facilitator can indicate that the peer is going to play with the child for a while. The team notes if and how the child acknowledges the presence of the peer. The child may simply look up and return to his or her play, vocalize or verbalize toward the peer, or approach the peer and initiate interaction. As the peer becomes involved in play, the child's reactions are observed. Parten's (1932) social participation categories are useful here. The team can observe whether the child primarily watches the peer in onlooker behavior or plays alone without regard for the peer. The child might also play in parallel fashion, with similar toys, but not with the child. Associative play may be demonstrated, where the children play in a common play setting, but with separate goals; they may both be in the play house interacting, but they are involved in different activities. They may also play cooperatively, with common goals, such as building a block road together for their cars.

Some children will take the lead and initiate an interaction, some will pick up on the other child's activities through imitation, and others will interact if the peer initiates an interchange. If interactions do take place, the quality of behaviors can be observed. What kinds of prosocial behaviors are observed? The children may exhibit turn-taking with toys, sharing of toys or food, or one helping the other child when he or she is having trouble with a toy. If the peer demonstrates emotions, the team members need to watch the child's reaction.

If conflict arises during the course of play, the team can note the child's responses, who initiated the conflict, and how the child attempts to resolve the conflict. Some children will immediately acquiesce, while others will assertively persist to get their needs met. The means of conflict resolution, whether physical or verbal, needs to be observed as well.

Finally, the child's play with the peer usually differs from his or her play with the parent and facilitator, both quantitatively and qualitatively. For instance, the child may initiate interaction more frequently, and communication may be heard more often. The team can also observe whether the child demonstrates a higher or lower level of skills with the peer, variation in the length of play sequences, and whether the child demonstrates a different affect. Distinctions in interaction patterns can be analyzed to determine the characteristics that are contributing to more positive social skills.

If peer interaction appears to be a problem area, the facilitator may want to include the peer in additional activities to enable further interactions to take place. Observations of peer interactions give the team knowledge about the child's emotional and social developmental level. They also provide insight into needs for programming. The staff will want to design activities to foster the child's emotional development and social interaction.

Comparison of social skills across persons will enable the team to see which interpersonal situations foster social interactions. *In the play interactions with both her mother and the facilitator, Laura demonstrated little positive affect. She rarely smiled, paid little attention to the adults who were attempting to play with her, and followed her own agenda. In contrast, her interactions with Mary, who was more verbal and slightly higher developmentally, were quite different. She observed Mary carefully, initiated an interaction by serving her "coffee," and laughed when Mary drank the "coffee." The team discovered that Laura was capable of higher-level social interactions. Peers were an avenue for intervention with Laura. The team recommended that Laura be paired with an enthusiastic peer who was slightly higher in functioning level for both play and classroom activities. A suggestion was made that the teacher model appropriate interactions with the peer for Laura. In that way Laura would initiate activities, imitate the peer's higher-level skills and behaviors, and increase her social interactions.*

Relation to Peers in Group

For assessing a child over the age of 3, observation in a group situation can be useful. The child may be seen outside of the evaluation session in a preschool or day care group. Whenever this is an option, the additional observation time can yield valuable information about the child's social skills. Observation of both structured and unstructured times are useful.

The child's awareness of and interaction with the group are observed. As with the peer, the child will probably engage in isolated, onlooker, parallel, associative, or cooperative play. Varying levels of initiation and maintenance of interaction will also be seen. Some will observe and imitate behaviors of the other children and follow their lead or suggestion. Still other children are leaders themselves, and tend to not only initiate activities, but also organize the behaviors of others.

Children also vary in relation to how much adult support they need to stay involved in a structured group activity. Some will need constant adult attention. They may need to sit right next to a staff person, either to keep the adult's attention or in order for the adult to be able to control the child's behavior. The amount of reinforcement and verbal or physical support the child needs to pay attention to the activity, to respond appropriately, and to maintain appropriate behavior is an important part of the team's observations.

Children are very perceptive about their peers. They tend to associate with other children for particular reasons. Likewise, they tend to avoid other children for specific reasons. Observations should be made of the responses of other children in the group to the child being assessed in TPBA. Do they seek interaction with him or her? If so, what type? Some children are sought out as targets for others' aggressions, some are seen as people who need help or assistance, and some are sought out for their skills (Rogers, 1978). Still others seem to mix well with almost everyone. They are sought out because they are fun to be with. By noting which children approach the target child, what patterns emerge in relation to this child's role in the group, and how the child responds to the approach and engagement efforts of others, the team members can gain valuable information.

Observations can also be made regarding which children the target child seeks out, and in what ways the child engages others: through prosocial or antisocial behaviors and vocal or physical means. In addition, particular activities may elicit the child's imitation, turn-taking, and verbal exchanges. Some children will engage other children in dramatic play, in motor activities, or in constructive play, while they prefer to do other activities alone. The team needs to observe the child's patterns of interaction and isolation, and determine with whom the child exhibits the most social interaction (an adult in the classroom or a particular child).

The TPBA play session allows the child to be in a one-to-one play situation. For many children with disabilities, this is an optimal situation, because the behaviors the child exhibits in the classroom may be completely different. Knowing what the child is like in a group can assist the team in making practical, functional recommendations.

Zach appeared social and cooperative in the play-based session. His skills appeared to be approximately at age level. When observed in the classroom, however, Zach lacked focus, wandered around the room, and could not attend in a group. He followed the teacher around and associated with his peers only when they approached him, which was infrequently. Directions needed to be given to Zach on an individual basis, and frequently had to be repeated several times. Observations of Zach in a group setting led the team to request further evaluation of Zach's auditory processing skills. This evaluation did, indeed, reveal that Zach was having difficulty isolating sounds in his environment. In a one-to-one situation, Zach did not have to deal with as much interference and was better able to focus. In the noisy classroom environment or in a group setting with more than one person talking, Zach was at a loss. Final recommendations included changing the setting and structure of Zach's learning environment, providing auditory training, and beginning to help Zach develop social skills while paired with individual peers.

This example illustrates the importance of looking at the whole child and the significance of seeing the child in different environments. *Zach had, in fact, been evaluated by a psychotherapist based on the teacher's concerns about his behavior. This therapist had diagnosed Zach as having "deviations in maturational patterns" and recommended psychotherapy. Observations revealed that Zach was having social-emotional difficulties, but they seemed to be related to the consequences of his auditory processing problems. Zach felt insecure and resisted group encounters as a means of coping with his deficits. Zach is a child who needs the transdisciplinary approach both in assessment and intervention.*

DRAMATIC PLAY IN RELATION TO EMOTIONAL DEVELOPMENT

If a child is referred for TPBA because social and emotional problems are the primary concern, the psychologist would be the facilitator of choice. He or she may choose to analyze the content of play from a different perspective than would an educator. The psychologist will assess internal conflict as reflected in themes in the child's play. Cursory guidelines are offered to assist in observation of play in relation to emotional problems. If a psychologist is not a member of the transdisciplinary team, other team members may analyze the play to determine the need for a referral for further psychological evaluation. As with all areas of transdisciplinary play-based assessment, the evaluators should document and describe all behaviors carefully, without resorting to pathological labels.

Depending on the theoretical orientation of the psychologist, different approaches to play can be taken. Dodds (1987) notes that *ego-psychoanalytic theorists* examine the child's play for evidence of "psychosocial development, predominant modality, sexual and aggressive drive level, guilt, object relations and range, and strength and modulation of defenses" (p. 39). The *phenomenological theorists* "attempt to understand the child's level of self-awareness and experiences and the degree of his/her sensitivity to these experiences" (p. 40). The *behavioral theorists* will probably not find the play assessment as helpful as observing "the child in real-life situations in order to discover the environmental stimuli and reinforcers of the target behavior" (p. 40). These different perspectives influence the interaction style of the psychologist, as well as his or her interpretation.

The section that follows is not meant to embrace any one theoretical perspective, but rather provide a more eclectic view of the child's emotional life and view of self. The psychologist on the team may want to emphasize one aspect more than others, or add to these guidelines.

Structure of Play

One of the characteristics that many children with emotional disturbances exhibit is illogical or dysfluent thought processes. This is seen in dramatic play, when the sequence of ideas appears fragmented or disjointed.

Kelly (age 6) was a child who had lived in several foster homes. He was placed in foster care by court order, due to incidences of child abuse by his parents. When observed playing with a toy soldier, he changed the identification of the doll with which he was playing several times. The soldier started out as "Kelly," and then became "mean monster," and then "my friend." The actions of the character also showed no continuity. As the identity of the character shifted, the actions of the doll changed from a doll fighting, to a monster eating someone, to a doll being put to sleep.

Depending on the age of the child, an understanding of the relationship of past, present, and future should be demonstrated. *Kelly confused time. He spoke of what he was going to do at his grandmother's this afternoon, when he been to visit his grandmother in Texas the week before. His focus on his grandmother also showed rigid thought patterns; regardless of the topic of discussion, Kelly shifted the subject to his grandmother.*

Content of Play

The content of the child's play is another crucial element to examine. Again, depending on the psychologist's theoretical perspective, he or she will interpret this content differently. Themes that appear in children's play include dependency, loss, power or control issues, fear or anxiety in relation to specific areas, and poor or inflated self-concept. These are themes that emerge in all children's play. In the play of children with emotional disabilities, an emphasis or predominant concern with one or more of these themes is observed. Their play will seem unbalanced, and may lack spontaneity and exuberance commonly seen in children's play. Their unhappiness, anger, or concern may also be reflected in their affect.

Kelly appeared to be a very angry child; his play demonstrated a desire for power and control that masked a deeper fear and anxiety about issues in his life. Superimposed on this was a dependency on his grandmother, the one stable, loving person in his life.

The child's ability to recognize and separate fantasy from reality is another important factor in play. Play is fantasy and is the means by which children make the world into anything they want. Problems arise when the child finds this fantasy world so satisfying that he or she chooses not to enter the real world.

Kelly appeared to shift between his fantasy world and reality. Once he began to play in earnest with his toys, he became so engrossed that it was difficult to get him back to the present reality. He demonstrated a high degree of confusion concerning the boundaries between reality and fantasy.

Awareness of Self and Others

While observing the child, it is possible to determine whether or not the child is capable of joint referencing, or sharing a topic of attenion. The TPBA team needs to observe whether the child is able to incorporate the adult or another child into the play with shared goals. (This will be seen only after the child has reached a developmental level appropriate for cooperative play.) It is also important to understand whether the child has the ability to see another person's point of view, or can predict the consequences of actions.

Children with emotional disturbances frequently have difficulty with the expression and modulation of emotions. They may not be able to label their own emotions or recognize emotions in others, and they may demonstrate poor impulse control.

Kelly had very poor impulse control. If a toy was broken or unavailable when he wanted it, he immediately had a tantrum, throwing chairs and toys around the room. He seemed unaware of the consequences of his actions, and could not understand why the facilitator seemed upset with him.

☞ Children with problems as severe as Kelly's in the previous examples will need further evaluation.

Kelly will need individual therapy. There were, however, recommendations that could be made for the team that would be working with him. During play, Kelly benefited from interacting with an adult who could help him develop continuity and sequence in his play, and help him identify and interpret the feelings and actions he was incorporating into his play. The intervention team was told to help Kelly learn to identify what was real and what was not. They needed to help him see the consequences of his actions, both for himself and others. A behavioral program was also recommended, to reward him for controlling his tantrums and other outbursts.

HUMOR AND SOCIAL CONVENTIONS

Sense of Humor

Recent research has shown that the child's sense of humor can tell us much about his or her level of cognitive development (Cicchetti & Sroufe, 1976; McGhee, 1977, 1979) and social awareness. The young infant finds tactile input and movement of his or her body amusing. Later, that infant enjoys things that adults do to entertain him or her, such as making strange noises, making faces, and moving in unexpected ways. Still later, he or she can find objects amusing when they behave in expected or unexpected ways. As the child develops language, atypical words may become humorous, and the child may experiment with changing words and using words in nontraditional (or even culturally unacceptable) ways. Making jokes or using words in new ways that are humorous to self and friends may also occur (Garvey, 1977). In addition, the child also begins to be able to analyze situations and finds incongruous situations humorous.

McGhee (1977, 1979) distinguished four stages of humor development. In the first stage (early in the second year) the child finds incongruous actions toward objects humorous. Laughter based on the inappropriateness of the action "reflects the pleasure derived from creating in fantasy play a set of conditions known to be at odds with reality" (McGhee, 1979, p. 67). A child in this first stage may laugh at the adult pretending to drink from a hat. In stage two (late in the second year), the child laughs at incongruous labeling of objects and events (calling a nose an ear). The third stage exhibits greater conceptual understanding, as the child of about age 3 gains a better understanding of characteristics of things. Humor at this stage relates to incongruous elements of a concept (a cow that barks) or distortions of familiar sights and sounds (rhyming words or nonsense words). The fourth stage, understanding multiple meanings of words, does not occur until about 7 years of age. The child needs to have acquired the cognitive correlates to understand humor at each of these stages. Humor, therefore, reveals both social and cognitive development.

When observing the play session, the team should note the times during which the child is seen smiling or laughing. The facilitator may set up situations that might be perceived as funny, depending on the child's age (knocking down blocks, wearing a pan for a hat, putting a box of cereal in the oven, or telling a joke). In addition, noting information such as the initiator of the humorous event, the level of cognitive understanding required to perceive the event as funny, and the social role of the child in the humorous event will be helpful in TPBA.

For children with physical disabilities who are unable to verbalize or act on their environment in the same ways that other children do, observation of humor can provide valuable information about social cognition. The same is true of children with language impairments.

Some children may have a distorted view of reality. These children may find humor in situations that no one else perceives as funny. One child, for example, while placing a miniature doll on the stove laughed, "My brother's melting, my brother's melting." This type of "humor" needs further investigation. This particular child had emotional problems that were evident in his play themes, in his sense of what was funny, and in his interactions. Sense of humor links cognitive, language, and social-emotional development, and is therefore an important component of the TPBA.

Awareness of Social Conventions

Each society has social conventions governing how individuals should behave in various situations. Greetings and goodbyes when arriving and leaving, "please" and "thank-you" at the table, and "excuse me" or "I'm sorry" when making an error are examples of social conventions. During the play session, the team should be aware of the child's use of and response to these social conventions. Use of such customs indicates social awareness, and, even if used in a rote manner, affects the child's social functioning.

Children may also exhibit maladaptive, unusual, or even bizarre behaviors. Ritualized behaviors, such as hand-flapping, eye-poking, constant jumping, and rocking, are some of the obvious behaviors sometimes seen in children with special needs. Eccentric habits such as smelling things, picking at strings, and rubbing textures are also noteworthy, and may relate to cognitive, sensory, or emotional deficits. Further environmental and/or developmental evaluation may be required.

Children who exhibit extreme forms of unacceptable behavior directed toward others, such as hitting or spitting, may also need further evaluation. An occasional tantrum in a 2-year-old is developmentally appropriate, but constant kicking and screaming by a 6-year-old is not. A further discussion with parents and teachers concerning the behaviors is needed. Staff will want to investigate the *pattern* of these behaviors, as well as the environmental circumstances surrounding the behaviors, to determine possible causes and recommend intervention approaches.

☞   Awareness of social conventions is included in most curricula, whether formally or informally. This area can be incorporated naturally and functionally into the day. For children who have maladaptive or socially unacceptable behaviors, a behavioral program in conjunction with a functional curriculum is suggested.

Summary

Assessment of social skills and emotional problems is best accomplished with input from a qualified child psychologist. The addition of this individual to the play-based assessment team is highly recommended. Follow-up evaluations with the child and other family members will frequently be necessary. The play-based assessment can provide team members with valuable information from which to proceed, but is not to be used to determine a diagnostic label.

REFERENCES

Affleck, G., McGrade, B.J., McQueeney, M., & Allen, D. (1982). Promise of relationship-focused intervention in developmental disabilities. *Journal of Special Education, 16,* 413–430.

Ainsworth, M.D., Blehar, M.C., Waters, E., & Wall, S. (1978). *Patterns of attachment.* Hillsdale, NJ: Lawrence Erlbaum Associates.

Bell, R.Q. (1968). A reinterpretation of the direct effects of studies of socialization. *Psychological Review, 75,* 84–95.

Brazelton, T., Tronick, E., Adamson, L., Als, H., & Wise, S. (1975). Early mother–infant reciprocity. In *Parent-Infant Interaction, Ciba Foundation Symposium 33.* Amsterdam: Associated Scientific Publishers.

Bricker, D.D. (1986). *Early education of at-risk and handicapped infants, toddlers, and preschool children.* Glenview, IL: Scott, Foresman.

Brockman, L.M., Morgan, G.A., & Harmon, R.J. (1988). Mastery motivation and developmental delay. In T. Wachs & R. Sheehan (Eds.), *Assessment of young developmentally disabled children.* New York: Plenum.

Brooks-Gunn, J., & Lewis, M. (1978). Early social knowledge: The development of knowledge about others. In H. McGurk (Ed.), *Issues in childhood social development* (pp. 79–106). London: Methuen.

Bruner, J.S. (1977). Early social interaction and language acquisitions. In H.R. Schaffer (Ed.), *Studies in mother-infant interaction* (pp. 271–290). New York: Academic Press.

Buss, A.H., & Plomin, R. (1975). *A temperament theory of personality development.* New York: John Wiley & Sons.

Carey, W.B., & McDevitt, S.C. (1978). Revision of the infant temperament questionnaire. *Pediatrics, 61,* 735–739.

Charlesworth, R., & Hartup, W.W. (1967). Positive social reinforcement in the nursery school peer group. *Child Development, 3*(2), 146–158.

Cicchetti, D., & Sroufe, L.A. (1976). The relationship between affective and cognitive development in Down's syndrome infants. *Child Development, 47*(4), 920–929.

Cohen, M.A., & Gross, P.J. (1979). *The developmental resource: Behavioral sequences for assessment and planning* (Vol. 2). New York: Grune & Stratton.

Comfort, M. (1988). Assessing parent–child interaction. In D.B. Bailey, Jr., & R.J. Simeonsson (Eds.), *Family assessment in early intervention* (pp. 65–94). Columbus, OH: Charles E. Merrill.

Cunningham, C., Reuler, E., Blackwell, J., & Deck, J. (1981). Behavioral and linguistic developments in the interactions of normal and retarded children with their mothers. *Child Development, 52,* 62–70.

Dodds, J.B. (1987). *A child psychotherapy primer.* New York: Human Sciences Press.

Doyle, A., Connolly, J., & Rivest, L. (1980). The effect of playmate familiarity on the social interactions of young children. *Child Development, 51,* 217–223.

Eckerman, C.O., Whatley, J.L., & Kutz, S.L. (1975). The growth of social play with peers during the second year of life. *Developmental Psychology, 11*(1), 42–49.

Emde, R.N., Gaensbauer, T., & Harmon, R.J. (1981). Using our emotions: Some principles for appraising emotional development and intervention. In M. Lewis & L. Taft (Eds.), *Developmental disabilities in preschool children* (pp. 409–424). New York: Spectrum Publications, Medical and Scientific Books.

Emde, R.N., & Harmon, R.J. (Eds.). (1982). *The development of attachment.* New York: Plenum.

Emde, R.N., & Harmon, R.J. (Eds.) (1984). *Continuities and discontinuities in development.* New York: Plenum.

Emde, R., Katz, E., & Thorpe, J. (1978). Emotional expression in infancy: II Early deviations in Down's syndrome. In M. Lewis & L. Rosenblum (Eds.), *The developmental of affect* (pp. 351–360). New York: Plenum.

Field, T. (1979). Interaction patterns of high-risk and normal infants. In T. Field, A. Sostek, S. Goldberg, & H.H. Shuman (Eds.), *Infants born at-risk.* New York: Spectrum Publications.

Field, T. (1983). High-risk infants "have less fun" during early interactions. *Topics in Early Childhood Special Education, 3,* 77–87.

Foley, G. (1985). Emotional development of children with handicaps. *Journal of Children in Contemporary Society, 17*(4), 57–73.

Foley, G., & Hobin, M. (1981). *The attachment-separation-individuation (A-S-I) scales* (Revised). Reading, PA: Family Centered Resource Project.

Gaensbauer, T.J., & Harmon, R.J. (1981). Clinical assessment in infancy utilizing structured playroom situations. *Journal of the American Academy of Child Psychiatry, 20,* 264–280.

Gaensbauer, T.J., & Harmon, R.J. (1982). Attachment behavior in abused/neglected and premature infants: Implications for the concept of attachment. In R.N. Emde & R.J. Harmon (Eds.), *The development of attachment and affiliative systems* (pp. 263–279). New York: Plenum.

Gaiter, J.L., Morgan, G.A., Jennings, K.D., Harmon, R.J., & Yarrow, L.J. (1982). Variety of cognitively-oriented caregiver activities: Relationships to cognitive and motivational functioning at 1 and 3½ years of age. *Journal of Genetic Psychology, 141,* 49–56.

Garvey, C. (1977). *Play.* Cambridge, MA: Harvard University Press.

Goldberg, S. (1977). Social competency in infancy: A model of parent–child interaction. *Merrill-Palmer Quarterly, 23,* 163–177.

Goldsmith, H.H., & Campos, J.J. (1982). Toward a theory of temperament. In R.N. Emde & R.J. Harmon (Eds.), *The development of attachment and affiliative systems* (pp. 161–193). New York: Plenum.

Gottman, J. (1979). *Marital interaction: Experimental investigations.* New York: Academic Press.

Guralnick, M.J., & Groom, J.M. (1987). Dyadic peer interactions of mildly delayed and nonhandicapped preschool children. *American Journal of Mental Deficiency, 92*(2), 178–193.

Hanson, M.J. (1984). Parent–infant interaction. In M.J. Hanson (Ed.), *Atypical infant development* (pp. 179–206). Baltimore: University Park Press.

Hanzlik, J., & Stevenson, M. (1986). Interaction of mothers who are mentally retarded, retarded with cerebral palsy, or nonretarded. *American Journal of Mental Deficiency, 90,* 513–520.

Harmon, R.J., Morgan, G.A., & Glicken, A.D. (1984). Continuities and discontinuities in affective and cognitive motivational development. *International Journal of Child Abuse and Neglect, 8,* 157–167.

Harter, S. (1977). The effect of social reinforcement and task difficulty level on the pleasure derived by normal and retarded children from cognitive challenge and mastery. *Journal of Experimental Child Psychology, 24,* 476–494.

Harter, S. (1978). Effectance motivation reconsidered: Toward a developmental model. *Human Development, 21,* 34–64.

Harter, S. (1981). A model of intrinsic motivation in children: Individual differences and developmental change. In A. Collins (Ed.), *Minnesota Symposium on Child Psychology, 14* (pp. 251–255). Hillsdale, NJ: Lawrence Erlbaum Associates.

Hartup, W.W. (1978). Children and their friends. In H. McGurk (Ed.), *Issues in childhood social development* (pp. 130–170). London: Methuen.

Hartup, W.W. (1983). Peer relations. In E.M. Hetherington (Ed.), *Handbook of child psychology*. (pp. 103–196). New York: John Wiley & Sons.

Heathers, G. (1955). Emotional dependence and independence in nursery school play. *Journal of Genetic Psychology, 87*(1), 37–57.

Hunt, J.M. (1965). Intrinsic motivation and its role in psychological development. In D. Levin (Ed.), *Nebraska Symposium on Motivation*. Lincoln: University of Nebraska Press.

Hutt, C. (1978). Sex-role differentiation in social development. In H. McGurk (Ed.), *Issues in childhood social development* (pp. 171–202). London: Methuen.

Jennings, K., & Curry, N.E. (1982). *Toddler social play*. Paper presented at the annual conference of the Association for Anthropological Study of Play, London, Ontario, April, 1982.

Jennings, K.D., Harmon, R.J., Morgan, G.H., Gaiter, J.L., & Yarrow, L.J. (1979). Exploratory play as an index of mastery motivation: Relationships to persistence, cognitive functioning, and environmental measures. *Developmental Psychology, 15*(4), 386–394.

Jennings, K., & Suwalsky, J.T.D. (1982). Reciprocity in the dyadic play of three-year-old children. In J. Loy (Ed.), *The paradoxes of play* (pp. 130–140). West Point, NY: Leisure Press.

Jones, O. (1978). A comparative study of mother-child communication with Down's syndrome and normal infants. In H. Schaffer & J. Dunn (Eds.), *The first year of life: Psychological and medical implications of early experience* (pp. 175–195). New York: John Wiley & Sons.

Kagan, J. (1988). *Temperamental contributions to social behavior*. Presented as a distinguished scientific award addressed to the American Psychological Association. August, 16, Atlanta, Georgia.

Keogh, B.K. (1982a). Children's temperament and teacher's decisions. In M. Rutter (Ed.), *Temperamental differences in infants and young children*. London: Ciba Foundation.

Keogh, B.K. (1982b), Temperament: An individual difference of importance in intervention programs. *Topics in Early Childhood Special Education, 2*(2), 25–31.

Keogh, B.K. (1986). Temperament and schooling: Meaning of "goodness of fit?" In J.V. Lerner & R.M. Lerner (Eds.), *Temperament and social interaction infancy and childhood; New dimensions for child development, 31*. San Francisco: Jossey-Bass.

Keogh, B.K., Pullis, M.E., & Cadwell, J. (1980). *Revised parent temperament questionnaire*. Unpublished report, Project REACH, University of California, Los Angeles.

Kusmierek, A., Cunningham, K., Fox-Gleason, M., & Lorenzini, D. (1985). *South Metropolitan Association birth to three transdisciplinary assessment guide*. Flassmoor, IL: South Metropolitan Association for Low-Incidence Handicapped.

Lamb, M.E., & Campos, J.J. (1982). *Development in infancy: An introduction*. New York: Random House.

Mahler, M., Pine, F., & Bergman, A. (1975). *The psychological birth of the infant*. New York: Basic Books.

Mahoney, G., & Powell, A. (1986). *The transactional intervention program: A child-centered approach to developmental intervention with young handicapped children*. Farmington, CT: Pediatric Research and Training Center.

McGhee, P.E. (1977). A model of the origins and early development of incongruity-based humor. In A.J. Chapman & H.C. Foot (Eds.), *It's a funny thing, humor*. Oxford, England: Pergamon.

McGhee, P.E. (1979). *Humor: Its origin and development*. San Francisco: Freeman.

Morgan, G.A., & Harmon, R.J. (1984). Developmental transformations in mastery motivation. In R.N. Emde & R.J. Harmon (Eds.), *Continuities and discontinuities in development*. New York: Plenum.

Morgan, G.A., Harmon, R.J., Pipp, S., & Jennings, K.D. (1983). *Assessing infants' perceptions of mastery motivation: Utility of MOMM questionnaire*. Unpublished manuscript, Colorado State University, Fort Collins.

Mueller, E., & Lucas, T. (1975). A developmental analysis of peer interaction among toddlers. In M. Lewis & L.A. Rosenblum (Eds.), *Friendship and peer relations* (pp. 223–257). New York: John Wiley & Sons.

Parten, M.B. (1932). Social participation among preschool children. *Journal of Abnormal and Social Psychology, 27*, 243–269.

Persson-Blennow, I., & McNeil, T.F. (1979). A questionnaire for measurement of temperament in six-month old infants: Development and standardization. *Journal of Child Psychology and Psychiatry, 20,* 1–13.

Piaget, J. (1936). *The origins of intelligence in children.* New York: International Universities Press.

Pullis, M., & Cadwell, J. (1985). Temperament as a factor in the assessment of children educationally at risk. *Journal of Special Education 19*(1), 91–102.

Ramey, C.T., Farran, D.C., & Campbell, F.A. (1979). Predicting IQ from mother–child interactions. *Child Development, 50,* 804–814.

Rheingold, H.L. (1977). A comparative psychology of development. In H.W. Stevenson, E.H. Hess, & H.L. Rheingold (Eds.), *Early behavior: Comparative and developmental approaches* (pp. 279–293). New York: John Wiley & Sons.

Rogers, C. (1978). The child's perception of other people. In H. McGurk (Ed.), *Issues in childhood social development* (pp. 107–129). London: Methuen.

Rothbart, M.K. (1984). Social development. In M.J. Hanson (Ed.), *Atypical infant development* (pp. 569–578). Baltimore: University Park Press.

Rothbart, M.K., & Derryberry, D. (1981). Development of individual differences in temperament. In M.E. Lamb & A.L. Brown (Eds.), *Advances in developmental psychology, 1* (pp. 207–236). Hillsdale, NJ: Lawrence Erlbaum Associates.

Scarr, S. (1981). Testing for children. *American Psychologist, 36,* 1159–1166.

Stern, D. (1985). *The interpersonal world of the infant.* New York: Basic Books.

Stern, D.N. (1977). *The first relationship: Infant and mother.* Cambridge, MA: Harvard University Press.

Stein, D., Beebe, B., Jaffe, J., & Bennett, S. (1977). The infant's stimulus world during social interaction: A study of caregiver behaviors with particular reference to repetition and timing. In H. Schaffer (Ed.), *Studies in mother–infant interaction* (pp. 177–202). London: Academic Press.

Thomas, A., & Chess, S. (1977). *Temperament and development.* New York: Brunner/Mazel.

Thomas, A., Chess, S., & Birch, H.G. (1968). *Temperament and behavior disorders in children.* New York: New York University Press.

Thomas, A., Chess, S., Birch, H.G., Herzig, M.E., & Korn, S. (1963). *Behavioral individuality in early childhood.* New York: New York University Press.

Tronick, E.Z., & Gianino, A. (1986). Interactive mismatch and repair: Challenges to the coping infant. *Zero to Three, 6*(3), 1–6.

Walker, J. (1982). Social interactions and handicapped infants. In D.D. Bricker (Ed.), *Intervention with at-risk and handicapped infants: From research to practice* (pp. 217–232). Baltimore: University Park Press.

Watson, M.W., & Fischer, K.W. (1980). Development of social roles in elicited and spontaneous behavior in the preschool years. *Developmental Psychology, 16,* 483–494.

Wedell-Monig, J., & Lumley, J. (1980). Child deafness and mother–child interaction. *Child Development, 51,* 766–774.

White, R.W. (1959). Motivation reconsidered: The concept of competence. *Psychological Review, 66,* 297–323.

Yarrow, L.J., Klein, R., Lomanaco, S., & Morgan, G. (1975). Cognitive and motivational development in early childhood. In B.Z. Friedlander, G.M. Sterritt, & G.E. Kirk (Eds.), *Exceptional infant 3: Assessment and intervention.* New York: Brunner/Mazel.

Yarrow, L.J., Morgan, G., Jennings, K.D., Harmon, R.J., & Gaiter, J.L. (1982). Infants persistence at tasks: Relationships to cognitive functioning and early experience. *Infant Behavior and Development, 5,* 131–141.

Yawkey, T.D., & Pelligrini, A.D. (Eds.). (1984). *Child's play: Developmental and applied.* Hillsdale, NJ: Lawrence Erlbaum Associates.

7

Observation Guidelines for Social-Emotional Development

I. Temperament
    A. Activity level
        1. How motorically active is the child during the session?
        2. Are there specific times during the session when the child is particularly active?
            a. Beginning, middle, or end
            b. During specific activities
    B. Adaptability
        1. What is the child's *initial* response to new stimuli (persons, situations, and toys)?
            a. Shy, timid, fearful, cautious
            b. Sociable, eager, willing
            c. Aggressive, bold, fearless
        2. How does the child demonstrate his or her interest or withdrawal?
            a. Smiling, verbalizing, touching
            b. Crying, ignoring and moving away, seeking security
        3. How long does it take the child to adjust to new situations, persons, objects, and so forth?
        4. How does the child adjust to new or altered situations after an initially shy or fearful response?
            a. Self-initiation (slowly warms up, talks to self)
            b. Uses adult or parent as a base of security (needs encouragement and reinforcement to get involved)
            c. Continues to resist and stay uninvolved
    C. Reactivity
        1. How intense does the stimuli presented to the child need to be in order to evoke a discernible response?
        2. What type of stimulation is needed to interest the child?
            a. Visual, vocal, tactile, combination
            b. Object, social
        3. What level of affect and energy are displayed in response to persons, situations, or objects?
        4. What response mode is commonly used?
        5. What is the child's response to frustration?
II. Mastery Motivation
    A. Purposeful activity
        1. What behavior demonstrates purposeful activity?
        2. How does the child explore complex objects?

B.   Goal-directed behaviors
1.   What goal-directed behaviors are observed?
2.   How does the child respond to challenging objects or situations?
  a.   Looking
  b.   Exploring
  c.   Appropriate use
  d.   Persistent, task-directed
3.   How often does the child repeat successfully completed, challenging tasks?
4.   How persistent is the child in goal-directed behavior?
  a.   With cause-effect toys
  b.   With combinatorial tasks
  c.   With means-end behavior
5.   Given a choice between an easy and more challenging task, which does the child select? (Examine if the child is over 3½ years old.)
6.   How does the child demonstrate self-initiation in problem-solving?
  a.   How frequently is assistance requested?
  b.   How does the child organize problem-solving?

III.   Social Interactions with Parent
A.   Characteristics of child in interaction with the parent
1.   What level of affect is displayed by the child in interactions with the parent? Does the child appear to find the interactions pleasurable?
2.   How does the child react to the emotions expressed by the parent?
3.   How does the child respond to vocal, tactile, or kinesthetic stimulation by the parent?
4.   What type of cues does the child give the parent (vocal, tactile, kinesthetic)? How easily are these cues interpreted?
5.   What percentage of the time is the child active versus inactive in the play time with the parent? What amount of activity is directed toward interaction with the parent?
6.   How frequently does the child initiate an interchange with the parent?
7.   How many interactive behaviors is the child capable of maintaining?
8.   How does the child react to parental requests, limit-setting, or control?
B.   Characteristics of the parent-child interaction
1.   Describe the level of mutual involvement that is demonstrated.
  a.   To what degree is there continuity of content in the play?
  b.   To what degree is there synchrony of timing in the interactions?
  c.   To what degree is there similarity in the level of intensity in the interactions?
  d.   To what degree is there equality of turn-taking?
2.   To what degree do the interactions demonstrate a sequence of behaviors with a beginning, middle, and end?
  a.   To what degree are themes repeated with variation or expansion?
  b.   To what degree do parent and child anticipate the actions of each other?
  c.   To what degree does the parent modify sequences to match the capabilities of the child?
3.   How do the parent and child indicate their enjoyment of the interactions?
C.   Characteristics of the child in relation to the parent while not in direct interaction (i.e., while interacting with the play facilitator)
1.   What type and amount of sensory cues does the child give to the parent in order to

maintain emotional contact (visual "checking in," seeking physical contact, talking to the parent, or none)?

2. How much does the child seek proximity with the parent while playing with the facilitator?
3. Do the child's reactions to the parent change during the play session? What behaviors does he or she exhibit when he or she is proud of an accomplishment, or when anxious or fatigued?
4. How does the child react to parental separation or absence? What type and amount of response is seen?
5. What mechanisms does the child use to cope with the parent's absence?
6. How does the child react to the parent's return?
7. How aware is the child of self and others?
   a. Identification of self and others
   b. Identification of emotions in self and others
   c. Use of pronouns (I, you, me, mine)
   d. Identification of gender
   e. Use of adjectives to label concrete (brown hair) or abstract (nice person) personal characteristics

IV. Social Interactions with Facilitator
   A. Characteristics of child in interaction with the facilitator
      1. What level of affect is displayed by the child in interactions with the facilitator? Does the child appear to find the interactions pleasurable?
      2. How does the child react to the emotions expressed by the facilitator?
      3. How does the child respond to vocal, tactile, or kinesthetic stimulation by the facilitator?
      4. What type of cues does the child give the facilitator (vocal, tactile, kinesthetic)? How easily are these cues interpreted?
      5. What percentage of the time is the child active versus inactive in the play time with the facilitator? What amount of activity is directed toward interaction with the facilitator?
      6. How frequently does the child initiate an interchange with the facilitator?
      7. How many interactive behaviors is the child capable of maintaining with the facilitator?
      8. How does the child react to requests, limit-setting, or control by the facilitator?
   B. Characteristics of the facilitator-child interaction
      1. In general, how does the child relate to the facilitator (e.g., oblivious, cautious, anxious, fearful, comfortable, affectionate)?
      2. How do the facilitation techniques of matching the child's content, timing, and intensity affect the child's:
         a. Initiation of interactions or activities
         b. Turn-taking
         c. Affect
      3. To what degree do repetition and expansion of themes affect the child's play
         a. Length of sequences
         b. Quality and degree of communication
         c. Initiation of interaction on the part of the child
         d. Affect

V. Characteristics of dramatic play in relation to emotional development
    A. Structure of play
        1. To what degree is there continuity and logical sequence versus fragmented thought presented in the child's play?
        2. To what degree is there a linkage or recognition of past, present, and future?
        3. To what extent does the child's play demonstrate rigid or inflexible thought patterns?
    B. Content of play
        1. What are the dominant themes of the child's play?
            a. Dependency
            b. Loss
            c. Power/control
            d. Fear/anxiety
            e. Self-image
        2. Does the child recognize the boundaries between reality and fantasy?
    C. Awareness of self and others in dramatic play
        1. Is the child capable of joint referencing or sharing joint "topics" of attention?
        2. Does the child have the ability to see another's point of view?
        3. Is the child able to incorporate the adult into the play with shared goals?
        4. Is the child capable of making judgments about the consequences of actions?
        5. Is the child capable of recognizing and labeling emotions?
        6. Is the child capable of expressing and modulating his or her emotions?
        7. To what extent does the child demonstrate impulse control?
VI. Humor and Social Conventions
    A. Does the child demonstrate a sense of humor with smiling or laughter directed at appropriate events in the environment?
        1. Physical events in the environment involving self and others
        2. Physical events in the environment involving objects
        3. Physical events in the environment involving others
        4. Verbal jokes from self, parent, adult, child
            a. Involving labeling ambiguities
            b. Involving conceptual ambiguities
    B. Does the child show awareness of socially acceptable behaviors in specific contexts?
        1. Greetings
        2. Sharing, helping, and so forth
        3. Behaviors around eating, toileting
        4. Respect for adult authority
    C. Does the child exhibit maladaptive or socially inappropriate behaviors?
        1. "Self-stimulating" or self-abusive behaviors
        2. Eccentric habits or rituals
        3. Unacceptable behaviors directed toward others
VII. Social Interactions with Peers
    A. Interactions with peers in dyad
        1. How does the child acknowledge the presence of a peer?
            a. Ignoring, withdrawing, unaware
            b. Looking at, watching
            c. Touching, gesturing
            d. Vocalizing toward, talking with the peer
        2. What level of play does the child exhibit?
            a. Unoccupied—not involved in play

      b.   Isolated—primarily plays alone, oblivious to others

      c.   Onlooker—primarily watches the other child

      d.   Parallel play—plays with same or similar toys, but not together

      e.   Associative play—plays with peer in common play setting

      f.   Cooperative play—engages other child in play with similar goals and expectations

      g.   Games with rules—engages in games with preestablished rules and roles

3. What role does the child play in the dyad?

      a.   Plays no role

      b.   Follows lead of other child

      c.   Initiates and directs play of the other

4. What types of prosocial behaviors does the child display?

      a.   Taking turns with a toy or object

      b.   Sharing toys, food, and so forth

      c.   Helping other child to accomplish a goal

      d.   Responding to feelings of other children

5. How does the child handle conflict?

      a.   Assertiveness versus acquiescence

      b.   Use of physical means

      c.   Use of verbal (positive/negative) means

6. How does the child's play with peers differ from his or her play with parent and facilitator?

      a.   Qualitatively

      b.   Quantitatively

B. Interactions with peers in group (can be observed in classroom)

  1. How aware is the child of being in a group experience?

      a.   Oblivious of the group

      b.   Watches others in group

      c.   Participates in group—imitates others or follows their lead

      d.   Participates in group—initiates group activities

  2. How much adult support does the child need to be able to maintain group involvement?

      a.   Demands individual attention

      b.   Needs occasional reinforcement and encouragement

      c.   Waits for turn in group without adult support

      d.   Operates independently without awareness of group expectations

  3. How do others in the group respond to him or her?

  4. How much does the child seek social interaction? In what ways does he or she try to engage others?

  5. During what type of activities does the child exhibit the most social interaction (turn-taking, imitation, verbal exchange)?

      a.   Exploratory

      b.   Manipulative or constructive

      c.   Representational or dramatic play

      d.   Motor

      e.   Tactile/social

  6. With whom does the child exhibit the most social interaction?

7

Age Ranges

Mastery Motivation

6 mo. +	Demonstrates exploration and curiosity in investigation of complex object that is not too challenging cognitively or motorically
9 mo. +	Practices skill repeatedly and is successful on: 1) cause-and-effect toys 2) combinatorial tasks (putting pegs in holes) 3) means-ends tasks requiring getting a toy from behind a barrier
12 mo. +	Smiles at mastery of self-generated goal
15 mo. +	Is persistent in completing multipart tasks: 1) combinatorial tasks (form board, shape sorter) 2) means-ends tasks (lock board, cash register)
24 mo. +	Recognizes adult standards and corrects self
36 mo. +	Prefers challenging tasks when given a choice between relatively easy and difficult tasks

Adapted from Kusmierek, Cunningham, Fox-Gleason, & Lorenzini, 1985; Morgan & Harmon, 1984.

Attachment, Separation, and Individuation

5–8 mo.	Shows active differentiation of strangers
6–8 mo.	Recognizes self in mirror
7–8 mo.	Shows special dependence on mother—wants food, attention, stimulation, and approval from her, even when others are available As long as child sees parent, he or she plays contentedly. As he or she leaves the room, child cries and tries to follow
8–10 mo.	Shows mild to severe anxiety at separation
10–12 mo.	Shy period passes, eager to go out into the world
12 mo. +	Distinguishes self from others Reacts sharply to separation from parent Reacts to emotions expressed by parents and others
12–15 mo.	Uses mother for emotional "refueling"
15–18 mo.	Moves away from parent as home base into widening world Brings toys to share with parent
18–24 mo.	Demands proximity of familiar adult Alternates between clinging and resistance to familiar adult Refers to self by name Conscious of own acts as they are related to adult approval or disapproval
24–30 mo.	Shy with strangers, especially adults; may hide against parent when introduced to strange adults

(continued)

Attachment, Separation, and Individuation *(continued)*

	Makes constant demands of parent's attention
	Clings tightly to parent in affection, fatigue, and fear
30–36 mo.	Recognizes self in photograph
	Understands needs of other persons
36–48 mo.	Can answer whether he or she is a boy or girl
	Separates from parent without crying
	Joins other children in play
48–60 mo.	Can explore neighborhood unattended
	Strong sense of family and home, quotes parents as authorities

Adapted from Cohen & Gross, 1979; Emde, Gaensbauer, & Harmon, 1981; Foley & Hobin, 1981.

Development of Humor

4–12 mo.	Child smiles, later laughs at physical games and anticipated actions of objects
12–18 mo.	Child laughs at incongruous events (wearing a bowl as a hat)
12 mo. +	Child laughs at events that deviate sharply from everyday experiences
18–24 mo.	Child laughs at incongruous labeling of objects and events (calling a nose an ear)
24–36 mo.	Child laughs at combinations of incongruous events and use of words (milking a dog)
36–60 mo.	Child laughs at concrete, perceptually incongruent events, and distortions of familiar sights and sounds (rhyming and nonsense words)
60–72 mo.	Child laughs at multiple meanings of words

Adapted from McGhee, 1979.

Social Relations with Peers

6–8 mo.	Infant-to-infant interactions increase
9–12 mo.	Responds differently to children and adults
12 mo. +	Begins to prefer interactions with peers
12–15 mo.	Contacts with peer center around an object
15–18 mo.	Simple actions and contingent responses between peers
18–24 mo.	Spends most group time in solitary activity, watching other children
	Interactive sequences become longer until role-sharing and turn-taking are evident
24 mo. +	Intense watchfulness of peer
	Child imitates peer
	Child watches, points at, takes toys of other child
24–30 mo.	Parallel, noninteractive play predominates
24–48 mo.	Aggression increases, then declines (but at no time exceeds positive or neutral interactions)
30–36 mo.	Plays well with two or three children in a group
	Associative play predominates
36 mo. +	Plays spontaneously with other children in complicated verbal communication
	Increased rough-and-tumble play
36–48 mo.	Begins cooperative play
	Group play replaces parallel play
48 mo. +	Prefers playing with other children to playing alone, unless engrossed in a project

(continued)

Social Relations with Peers *(continued)*

48–60 mo.   Peer interactions characterized by talking, smiling, laughing, playing
              Begins group games with simple rules
              Shows concern and sympathy for others in group

60–72 mo.   Understands rules of fair play
              Likes competitive games

Adapted from Cohen & Gross, 1979; Hartup, 1978; Mueller & Lucas, 1975.

| Social-Emotional Observation Worksheet |

Name of child: _____ Date of birth: _____ Age: _____

Name of observer: _____ Discipline or job title: _____ Date of assessment: _____

On the following pages, note specific behaviors that document the child's abilities in the social-emotional categories. Qualitative comments should also be made. The format provided here follows that of the Observation Guidelines for Social-Emotional Development in **Transdisciplinary Play-Based Assessment.** *It may be helpful to refer to the guidelines while completing this form.*

I. Temperament

    A. Activity level

        1. Motor activity:

        2. Specific times that are particularly active

            a. Beginning, middle, or end:

            b. During specific activities:

    B. Adaptability

        1. Initial response to stimuli

            a. Persons:

            b. Situations:

            c. Toys:

        2. Demonstration of interest or withdrawal *(circle one)*:

            a. Smiling, verbalizing, touching

            b. Crying, ignoring or moving away, seeking security

        3. Adjustment time:

        4. Adjustment time after initially shy or fearful response *(circle one)*:

            a. Self-initiation   b. Adult as base of security   c. Resists; stays uninvolved

    C. Reactivity

        1. Intensity of stimuli for discernible response:

        2. Type of stimulation needed to interest child *(circle those that apply)*:

            a. Visual, vocal, tactile, combination

            b. Object, social

         3. Level of affect and energy:

        4. Common response mode:

        5. Response to frustration:

(continued)

II. Mastery Motivation

A. Purposeful activity
   1. Behavioral demonstration:

   2. Exploration of complex objects:

B. Goal-directed behaviors
   1. Behaviors observed:

   2. Response to challenging objects or situations *(circle those that apply)*:
      a. Looking   c. Appropriate use
      b. Exploring   d. Persistence, task directedness
   3. Repetition of completed, challenging task? *(yes or no)*
   4. Persistence in goal-directed behavior
      a. With cause-and-effect toys:

      b. With combinatorial tasks:

      c. With means–end behavior:

   5. Selection of easy or challenging task:
   6. Demonstration of self-initiation in problem-solving
      a. Frequency of requests for assistance:

      b. Problem-solving organization:

III. Social Interactions with Parent

A. Characteristics of child
   1. Level of affect:

   2. Reaction to the parent's emotions:

(continued)

Name of child: _____ Date of birth: _____ Age: _____

Name of observer: _____ Discipline or job title: _____ Date of assessment: _____

3. Response to parent's vocal, tactile, or kinesthetic stimulation:

4. Type and ease of interpretation of cues given by child:

5. Active versus inactive time:

6. Frequency of initiation of interchange:

7. Number of interactive behaviors child maintains:

8. Reaction to parent's requests, limit-setting, or control:

B. Characteristics of parent–child interaction
   1. Level of mutual involvement
      a. Continuity of content:

      b. Synchrony of timing:

      c. Similarity in level of intensity:

      d. Equality in turn-taking:

   2. Sequence of behaviors demonstrated:

      a. Themes repeated with variation or expansion:

      b. Anticipation of others' actions:

      c. Parent modification of sequences to match child's capabilities:

(continued)

3. Indication of enjoyment:

C. Characteristics of child in relation to parent while not in direct interaction
   1. Type and amount of sensory cues child gives to maintain emotional contact:

   2. Seeking of proximity to parent:

   3. Change in child's reactions to parent:

   4. Reaction to parental separation or absence:

   5. Mechanisms used to cope with parent's absence:

   6. Reaction to parent's return:

   7. Awareness of self and others *(circle those that apply)*:
     a. Identification of self and others
     b. Identification of emotions in self and others
     c. Use of pronouns
     d. Identification of gender
     e. Use of adjectives to label concrete or abstract

IV. Social Interactions with Facilitator

A. Characteristics of child
   1. Level of affect:

   2. Reaction to the facilitator's emotions:

   3. Response to facilitator's vocal, tactile, or kinesthetic stimulation:

   4. Type and ease of interpretation of cues given by child:

   5. Active versus inactive time:

(continued)

Social-Emotional Observation Worksheet

Name of child: _____ Date of birth: _____ Age: _____

Name of observer: _____ Discipline or job title: _____ Date of assessment: _____

6. Initiation of interchange:

7. Number of interactive behaviors child maintains:

8. Reaction to facilitator's requests, limit-setting, or control:

B. Characteristics of facilitator–child interaction
   1. How child relates to facilitator:

   2. Effect of facilitation techniques of matching child's content, timing, and intensity on:

      a. Initiation:

      b. Turn-taking:

      c. Affect:

   3. Affect of repetition and expansion of themes on:
      a. Sequence length:

      b. Quality and degree of communication:

      c. Child's initiation of interaction:

      d. Affect:

V. Characteristics of Dramatic Play in Relation to Emotional Development

A. Structure of play
   1. Continuity and logical sequence versus fragmented thought:

   2. Recognition of past, present, and future:

(continued)

    3. Rigid or inflexible thought patterns:

B. Content of play
    1. Dominant themes *(circle those that apply)*:
        a. Dependency   d. Fear/anxiety
        b. Loss   e. Self-image
        c. Power/control
    Examples:

    2. Recognition of boundaries between reality and fantasy:

C. Awareness of self and others in dramatic play
    1. Joint referencing:

    2. Seeing another's point of view:

    3. Incorporation of adult into play with shared goals:

    4. Making judgments about consequences:l

    5. Recognizing and labeling emotions:

    6. Expressing and modulating emotions:

    7. Demonstrating impulse control:

VI. Humor and Social Conventions

A. Smiling and laughter directed at appropriate events?
    1. Physical events involving self and others? *(yes or no)*
    2. Physical events involving objects? *(yes or no)*
    3. Physical events involving others? *(yes or no)*
    4. Verbal jokes from self, parent, adult, child *(circle those that apply)*:
        a. Labeling ambiguities
        b. Conceptual ambiguities
    Examples:

(continued)

Name of child: _____ Date of birth: _____ Age: _____

Name of observer: _____ Discipline or job title: _____ Date of assessment: _____

B. Awareness of socially acceptable behaviors in specific contexts?

1. Greetings? *(yes or no)*
2. Sharing, helping? *(yes or no)*
3. Behaviors around eating, toileting? *(yes or no)*
4. Respect for adult authority? *(yes or no)*

Examples:

C. Maladaptive or socially inappropriate behaviors?

1. Self-stimulating or self-abusive behaviors? *(yes or no)*
2. Eccentric habits or rituals? *(yes or no)*
3. Unacceptable behaviors directed toward others? *(yes or no)*

Examples:

VII. Social Interactions with Peers

A. In dyad

1. Acknowledgment of peer *(circle those that apply)*:
   a. Ignoring, withdrawing, unaware
   b. Looking at, watching
   c. Touching, gesturing
   d. Vocalizing toward, talking with peer

   Examples:

2. Level of play *(circle those that apply)*:
   a. Unoccupied
   b. Isolated play
   c. Onlooker play
   d. Parallel play
   e. Associative play
   f. Cooperative play
   g. Games with rules

   Examples:

3. Role of child in dyad *(circle those that apply)*:
   a. No role
   b. Follows other child's lead
   c. Initiates and directs

   Examples:

4. Prosocial behaviors *(circle those that apply)*:
   a. Takes turns
   b. Shares
   c. Helps other child accomplish goal
   d. Responds to other child's feelings

   Examples:

5. Handling of conflict *(circle those that apply)*:
   a. Assertiveness versus acquiescence
   b. Physical means
   c. Verbal means

   Examples:

(continued)

6. Differences between play with peers and play with adults
   a. Qualitative:
   b. Quantitative:
   Examples:

B. Interactions with peers in group
   1. Awareness of being in group experience *(circle those that apply)*:
      a. Oblivious
      b. Watches others
      c. Imitates others
      d. Initiates activities
      Examples:

   2. Adult support needed to maintain group involvement *(circle one)*:
      a. Demands attention
      b. Occasional reinforcement and encouragement
      c. Waits for turn without adult support
      d. Operates independently without group awareness
      Examples:

   3. Response of others to child:

   4. Social interaction and engagement of others:

   5. Type of activities with most social interaction *(circle those that apply)*:
      a. Exploratory
      b. Manipulative or constructive
      c. Representational or dramatic
      d. Motor
      e. Tactile/social
      Examples:

   6. With whom does child exhibit most social interaction?

Additional Comments

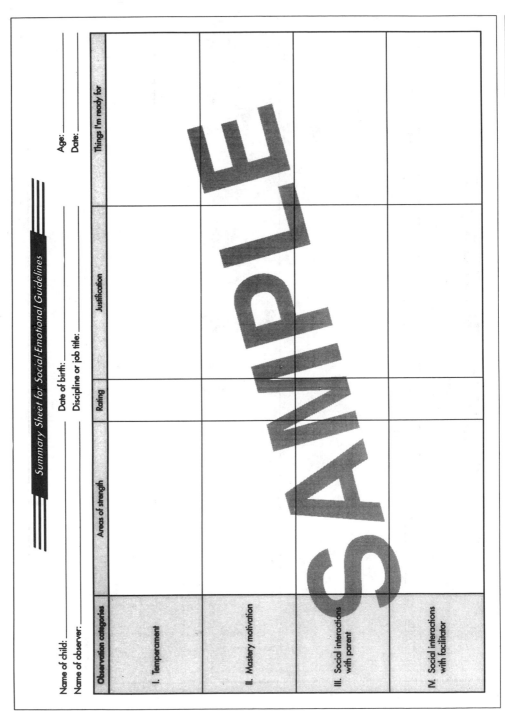

Summary Sheet for Social-Emotional Guidelines

Name of child: _____
Name of observer: _____

Date of birth: _____
Discipline or job title: _____

Age: _____
Date: _____

Observation categories	Areas of strength	Rating	Justification	Things I'm ready for
I. Temperament				
II. Mastery motivation				
III. Social interactions with parent				
IV. Social interactions with facilitator				

(continued)

Summary Sheet for Social-Emotional Guidelines

Name of child: _____

Name of observer: _____

Date of birth: _____

Discipline or job title: _____

Age: _____

Date: _____

Observation categories	Areas of strength	Rating	Justification	Things I'm ready for
V. Characteristics of dramatic play				
VI. Humor and social conventions				
VII. Social interactions with peers				

SAMPLE

Observation of Communication and Language Development

Kim Dickson, Toni W. Linder, and Paula Hudson

Transdisciplinary play-based assessment is a particularly suitable format for the assessment of the communication abilities of young children. Communication is most easily expressed in the natural, functional environment of play.

Communication is the process of exchanging ideas, information, and feelings. Speech and language are encompassed within the broader meaning of communication. Speech refers to verbal means of communication, and language refers to a rule-governed system for representing concepts through symbols, which can be verbal or nonverbal. The emphasis in transdisciplinary play-based assessment is to analyze the child's total communication system, including content, method, attitudes and emotions, gestures, body posture and movement, physical distance, quality, quantity, and effectiveness of communication. Many of these aspects are addressed in other chapters and guidelines in more depth, and need to be integrated with knowledge gained from the communication guidelines. Transdisciplinary discussion is, therefore, critical if a complete picture of the child's communication abilities is to be obtained.

Observation of communication is divided into the following areas: 1) modalities, or methods of communicating; 2) components of language, including pragmatics, phonology, syntax, and semantics; 3) receptive language skills; and 4) oral motor skills. Observations of specific concerns related to hearing, voice quality, cognitive, social-emotional, and sensorimotor development are also addressed. Each section of the guidelines is presented with a brief literature review, descriptions of TPBA observations, and implications for intervention. Age ranges are provided, when possible, indicating approximate age levels at which various language skills typically appear.

The major categories of communication are not mutually exclusive, but are dynamically interwoven. Children may be in a transition phase from one level of complexity to another, while simultaneously refining previously learned verbal and nonverbal behaviors. Age tables are offered to enable observers to determine *approximate* ranges of abilities. As with the other areas of development, when TPBA does not yield sufficient information, further evaluation using a standardized instrument or other assessment may be needed.

When evaluating a child's speech production, a tape-recorded sample is highly recommended. The videotape of the TPBA play session will frequently provide the needed documentation of language. Videotapes provide the additional benefit of enabling the team to observe nonverbal behaviors, as well as the context in which communication took place. An audiotape may also be used, if incorporated so as not to distract the child. Either recording allows the speech-language pathologist on the team to transcribe a sample of the child's speech for analysis.

Facilitating Communication   The play-based setting provides an optimal opportunity to observe a child's language. The child should find motivating toys and events awaiting him or her within the playroom. (Use of the parent inventory will assist in determining appropriate toys.) The facilitator must be able to effectively engage the child in interaction and elicit different aspects of language. The TPBA process allows for both naturalistic observation of the child, where the observers note the child's spontaneous communication, and structured, elicited interaction. Roberts and Crais (1989) offer suggestions for interaction with children that are useful in the transdisciplinary play-based assessment process:

1. Limit your own talking, especially questions. Pause often to encourage the child to initiate communication and take a turn.
2. Watch for and encourage any mode of communication demonstrated by the child (eye gaze, point, shrug, word, etc.).
3. Parallel play with the child, mimicking her actions. Play animatedly with object or toy and occasionally comment on an object or action.
4. Place a few items within eye gaze but out of reach; partially hide a few objects as well. If necessary, point to or comment on objects to encourage a comment or request by the child.
5. Let the child choose objects and/or activities, particularly in the beginning (and

The play setting allows the team to observe not only the child's specific use of components of language, but also the qualitative and social aspects of the child's communication.

throughout the interaction if possible). Be prepared to watch and interact/comment when the child shows interest.

6. Include parent or another child to help break the ice. Stay in the background and slowly get into the interaction.
7. Begin interaction with activities that require little or no talking, and gradually move into more verbal tasks.
8. Be genuine in your questions, and stay away from asking what is obvious to both you and the child.
9. Follow the child's lead in the interaction by maintaining the child's focus on particular topics and meanings.
10. Show warmth and positive regard for the child, and value his comments. (p. 351)

These recommendations are important for the facilitator to follow with all children. As was noted in Chapter 4, depending on the child, any one of the team members may be called upon to be the facilitator. Each team member must, therefore, be familiar with these techniques for facilitating communication.

MODALITIES OF COMMUNICATION

The primary mode of communication used by a child varies depending upon the functioning level of the child and possible disabilities. Argyle and Ingham (1972) found that very young children use gaze and proximity to regulate turn exchanges within given interactions. Infants and young children may use eye gaze, gestures, physical manipulation, and vocalization before and after verbalizations are produced. Children with limited oral language skills may continue to employ these prelinguistic communication skills; by combining other methods with the child's prelanguage skills, new forms of communication can be devised for such children. Eye gaze is used with symbol or picture boards, physical manipulation is used to control a computer, and gesture is incorporated into sign language.

Studies of infants have contributed to understanding the richness of infant vocalizations of speech and nonspeech sounds (Oller, 1978; Rosenwinkle, 1983; Stark, 1978). Analysis of the context of the vocalization also aids in interpreting the child's meaning. Children who were once viewed as incapable of developing language are now communicating through a combination of primitive and technologically advanced methods.

Evaluation of the forms used within a child's communication system is important for successful intervention. The team observes the frequency with which various forms of communication are used. The child may primarily use one form or a combination of methods. A child with physical impairments, for example, may primarily use eye gaze and vocalization. Another child may use verbalization and gaze at objects, but avoid eye contact with people. A child with articulation problems may rely heavily on gestures in combination with verbalizations. The team needs to assess the primary and supplemental communication modes that are used by the child, as well as those that are available but not being optimally utilized by the child. Analysis of the expectations being placed on the child during interactions with others is also relevant.

During a play session, 4-year-old Leslie used vocalizations and physical manipulations to communicate. Her parents and teacher were frustrated about her inability to use words to communicate. Leslie's use of eye gaze, gesture, and physical manipulation were good. Vocalizations were limited to vowel sounds, and the consonants "b" and "d." Most objects were labeled by combining these consonants with a vowel.

Nicole, who had been in a preschool program for children with disabilities, used a combination of eye contact, physical manipulation, and several signs to communicate. When she wanted an object, for example, she would point and sign "more." Her use of signs indicated a beginning understanding of one-to-one correspondence between a word and a symbol.

☞   Recognition of the child's forms of communication is the first step in developing intervention approaches that are compatible with cognitive and motor abilities. For Leslie and Nicole, the suggestion was made to encourage and reinforce the communication systems they were spontaneously using.

Leslie's parents and teacher were helped to see the consistent patterns that she used, so that they could better "read" her cues and interpret her vocalizations. Leslie also needed to develop systematic communication that could be interpreted by others. She demonstrated the physical and cognitive ability to begin to use signs or pictures paired with vocalizations. Further therapy to develop both speech and language was desired, but consistent, predictable communication was needed immediately. Discussions with Leslie's parents indicated a preference for a communication board and work on simple labeling games on the computer.

The recommendations for Nicole included reinforcing her communication behaviors and encouraging the further development of her use of sign language through modeling new, functional signs both at home and at school. A sequence of important words was developed with the parents, to be practiced at school as well as at home.

Quantity of Communicative Acts

Morehead and Ingram (1973) suggested that the language of a child with a linguistic disorder parallels typical development, but demonstrates slower onset of acquisition of structure, and less frequent and less creative use of language. The number of studies discussing the frequency of communicative acts demonstrated by a child is limited. Bates, Begnigni, Bretherton, Camaioni, and Volterra (1977) report that the amount of nonverbal behavior (pointing, giving, and showing) the child generates in early communication is a prognostic indicator of how highly communicative the child will be in a later stage.

The amount of communication the child uses may also be an indicator of problems in other areas. The child with motor disabilities may find it so difficult to speak that language attempts are minimal. Infrequent communication may also be an indicator of social-emotional concerns. A child who is highly withdrawn, for example, may choose not to communicate unless absolutely necessary. The child may have speech and language capabilities that are typical, but the frequency of communicative interaction is reduced. Duration or length of communication is also important. MacDonald (1978) characterized communication as fleeting, consistent, intermittent, or perseverative. Duration of communication has implication for both the quantity and quality of communication.

Measurement of the *quantity* of communication acts is accomplished by observing the frequency of the child's attempts at communication during an hour. The team needs to observe how often the child attempts to communicate (using the previously discussed modes of communication), as well as the duration of those attempts.

Two-year-old Ben demonstrated infrequent communicative interactions; he played quietly with the facilitator, did not comment spontaneously, and responded only when asked a question. His responses revealed age-appropriate language patterns and vocabulary. Ben's history of neglect and other play observations revealed social and emotional issues that appeared to be affecting the frequency of his communication.

The TPBA team also needs to note when the child demonstrates the greatest frequency of communication. *Michael, a nonverbal child with autism, showed increased vocalizations dur-*

☞ Indicates discussion of implications for intervention. Readers will see this symbol throughout each of the guidelines chapters.

ing motor activities. He also demonstrated increased gestures and eye contact with the facilitator during these activities.

☞   *For Ben, the infrequency of his communication acts had implications for assessment and intervention in the social-emotional area. Recommendations were made to provide a safe, secure, emotionally supportive environment for him. Ben had learned that communication did not result in getting needs met; therefore, recommendations were made to create situations throughout the day to enable him to receive immediate feedback and gratification. The teacher was also asked to comment on Ben's activities frequently. It was also suggested that she share her thoughts and feelings with him, in an effort to elicit similar responses from him.*

    For Michael, recommendations were made to increase movement activities as a motivating factor for communication, and to accept and respect his prelanguage forms as communication. Suggestions were also made to imitate and expand his vocalizations. Michael was also beginning to use gestures, and this form of communication was to be encouraged. Several common signs were identified ("want," "drink," and "cookie") to be paired with verbalizations. Any vocal or gestural approximation of a word was to be reinforced.

PRAGMATICS

Bates (1976a) defined pragmatics as "rules governing the uses of language in context" (p. 420). Pragmatics includes the social aspects of communication. Assessment of young children has traditionally focused on the form and content of language. Recent theories, however, describe pragmatics as an overall organizing principle of language, as the need to communicate precedes selection of form and content (Bates, 1976b; Bloom & Lahey, 1978; Ervin-Tripp, 1971; Grice, 1975; Ress & Wollner, 1981).

    Within TPBA, several aspects of pragmatics are examined. The stage of intentionality demonstrated and the functions and meaning expressed are interrelated, and are therefore considered together. Discourse skills are another important aspect of pragmatics. And echolalia, or repetitive language, is included in the discussion of pragmatics, because many children with disabilities use this as a form of communication to impart meaning.

Communicative Intent

Researchers and practitioners now accept the idea that infant language begins long before the first word, with the intention to communicate. Bates, Camaioni, and Volterra (1975), as well as other researchers, suggested a progression in the development of communicative intentions as the child moves from prelinguistic to multiword communication. She and her colleagues defined a three-stage sequence in the development of intentionality.

    The first stage, the *perlocutionary stage*, is seen from birth to approximately 8 months of age. In early infancy, the baby's sounds and movements are primarily reflexive, with the parent interpreting these behaviors to have certain meanings. The baby cries, and the parent determines that he or she is hungry or uncomfortable (wet diaper, etc.). As motor control develops, the infant acquires an increased ability to look at, reach for, and manipulate objects. However, behaviors are for the child's benefit, and not directed communicatively toward others. The child will also "show" himself or herself to others in peekaboo games (Owens, 1988).

    By 8–9 months of age, the infant begins to consistently use a number of nonverbal behaviors that carry an intent to communicate. These behaviors mark the onset of the illocutionary stage. The infant will show or give objects to the adult or point toward a desired object; a full range of gestures and vocalizations are used to communicate a variety of intentions.

The ~~locutionary stage~~ parallels the ~~emergence of the use of words to communicate~~ ~~intentions previously expressed nonverbally.~~ Words are used first with gestures, and are closely tied to the context of the situation. Words gradually become less context-bound throughout the preschool years. With the onset of reading, true decontextualization is seen (Bates et al., 1979).

Meaning

Several authors (Coggins & Carpenter, 1981; Dore, 1974; Prutting, 1979; Roth & Spekman, 1984) have developed categories to describe the meaning children generate at different stages and age levels. Identification of the child's intent and means of expression of intent provides important information about the child's cognitive and communicative understanding. Age ranges for categories of communicative intentions provide examples of each at the prelinguistic, one-word, and multiword stages appear following the Observation Guidelines.

Functions

Along with intention, the young child's early language demonstrates several other pragmatic functions. Halliday (1975) describes these pragmatic functions as:

1. Instrumental—to satisfy the child's needs or desires ("I want cookie.")
2. Regulatory—to control the behavior of others ("No hit.")
3. Interactional—to define or participate in social interaction ("Mommy and Alex go.")
4. Personal—to express personal opinions or feelings ("Me mad.")
5. Imaginative—to engage in fantasy ("Pretend I'm the mommy.")
6. Heuristic—to seek information ("What's that?")
7. Informative—to provide information ("See my red shirt.")

Halliday found that simple forms of these functions develop by the age of 2 years. Intentions are separate from grammatical structure. One structure may convey several intentions; conversely, one intention may be expressed in different grammatical forms.

During the play session, observers should note behaviors that occur both verbally and nonverbally. When behaviors occur nonverbally, the professional must use personal judgment regarding the intent of the child, which is usually determined through analysis of the context of the situation. The level of intention that is demonstrated by the child's behaviors and vocalizations should be noted. The functions for which the child uses communication, and the meaning that is implied in those communications, are also important observations for team members to make.

Three-year-old Sandy uses gestures and vocalizations in combination to express intentions, demonstrating communication at the illocutionary stage. During the session, Sandy's behaviors fulfilled several functions and expressed numerous meanings. He used gestures and vocalization for primarily instrumental reasons (he grunted and pointed to the plastic hot dogs—requesting an object). He also exhibited regulatory functions (when he stopped the facilitator from spinning a top—protesting), heuristic functions (when he handed the lock box to the facilitator to open for him—requesting information), and informative functions (when the facilitator asked him where his daddy was—answering). At different times, grunting and a gesture were also used to comment on an object (when he found a toy buried in the sand table and handed it to the facilitator), and to request action (when he wanted the facilitator to lift him up onto the climbing gym).

The speech-language pathologist can decide whether to report on the child's language functions, the meanings, or both. Functions are more global and encompass several meanings, so if the child is at least at the one-word stage, implied meanings are important to document.

When identifying the level of intent, function, or meaning of an utterance, gesture, or vocalization, descriptions of the child's behaviors and the context in which the behavior was observed must be included. For example: the child demonstrated a request by extending his hand toward the play telephone and making the vocalization "uh." Description of specific gestures and vocalizations, combined with the context in which they were observed, allows the team to obtain a more comprehensive picture of how the child uses his or her communication system. Alternative interpretations can also be discussed, particularly if the child has idiosyncratic movements, gestures, or sounds; parents are particularly helpful in identifying the intent of the child's idiosyncratic behaviors.

Analysis of the range and frequency of intentions indicated by the child may also yield relevant information. *Morgan, for example, seemed to be a relatively verbal child, but her use of language was limited. Analysis of her intentions revealed that she primarily used words to greet, request, and protest.* These patterns are important to identify, because they have implications for treatment.

One of the goals of intervention is to increase the child's ability to make his or her intentions understood. This can occur by expanding the range of communicative functions and by clarifying or making the existing methods more precise. *Sandy, whose vocal repertoire consisted mostly of grunts, used that one sound for a variety of purposes. He needed to enlarge his means of expressing intentions. Recommendations were made to increase his discrete vocalizations in combination with a symbol system, such as a communication board, which would offer him a broader range of options for expressing his intentions.*

For Morgan, who had words with which to express intentions, recommendations were made to encourage her to use these words for a greater range of intentions. The team suggested that situations be devised that required Morgan to comment and question. Setting up problem situations, for example, in which her chair was missing from the table, or a pitcher was on the table with no glasses, might encourage Morgan to comment and question. Modeling of a variety of pragmatic functions was also recommended. Morgan's parents helped identify situations at home that would encourage Morgan to expand her pragmatic repertoire.

Discourse

When evaluating a child's communication strategies, an additional pragmatic area of interest involves the child's ability to initiate and maintain discourse. Discourse involves the child's ability to take turns and move from one topic to another in a conversation. Although research in the area of conversational skills is relatively new, several researchers have investigated the concept of discourse extensively. Despite the fact that discourse appears to require verbalizations, young preverbal children demonstrate readiness skills for later conversational abilities.

Early nonverbal interchanges between a child and his or her caregivers form the foundation for later conversational abilities. The young infant engages in reciprocal interaction with the parent through mutual eye gaze, vocal imitation, and physical interchanges (Argyle & Ingram, 1972; Bruner, 1977). Alternating vocalizations between adult and child (Stern, Jaffe, Beebe, & Bennett, 1975) also provide a basis for turn-taking.

As noted above, the prelinguistic child can initiate a topic by getting the listener's attention and identifying a topic. As the child acquires words, he or she is able to provide more information so that the listener can determine the semantic relations, or meaning, among the words (Keenan & Schieffelin, 1976). In order to maintain a topic, the child must learn to take turns in the exchange of comments. This ability usually occurs within the second year of life, and increases as the child matures and can add greater amounts of information to the dialogue (Bloom, Rocissano, & Hood, 1976).

The child's discourse skills include his or her ability to extend a conversation. The ability to maintain topics progresses from the capability of expanding short simple sequences to maintaining a topic over adjoining successive utterances. Bloom et al. (1976) found, when evaluating topic maintenance, that around 3½ years of age the child acquires an ability to maintain a variety of topics over several sequences. This occurs as a result of the child's increased fund of knowledge and advanced linguistic structures. They noted that, at this stage, the child's conversation skills more closely resemble that of an adult.

The content of discourse relates to topic maintenance. Some children with disabilities may exhibit appropriate linguistic skills, but be unable to maintain a topic. Other children may demonstrate preoccupation with certain topics in their discourse. These topics range from subjects commonly experienced by the child to subjects with emotionally charged content. As was discussed in the chapter on social-emotional development, children with psychological disorders exhibit preoccupations with specific fantasy or real themes.

Revision is another discourse strategy that assists the child in topic maintenance. Keenan (1975) found, in the study of her twin sons (2 years and 9 months of age), the use of two revision strategies. The first device was identified as *focus operation* where part of the previous utterance is repeated in the subsequent utterance (e.g., mother says, "Johnny, get your shoes," and Johnny says, "Get shoes?"). The second strategy was identified as *substitution,* where part of the utterance is repeated but altered in some way (Mother says, "Johnny, get your shoes," and Johnny says, "My shoes?"). The predominant device used by a child changes developmentally, with focus operations appearing first and substitution operations emphasized later.

Three other behaviors are used by children to maintain dialogue. *Clarifications,* or asking for a repetition or additional information, is commonly used. The child who repeatedly asks, "What?" keeps the interaction going (and also drives parents crazy). A second behavior is extensions. The child adds some piece of information ("See the dog?" "Ooh, big dog"). Questioning is a third discourse behavior. For many children with disabilities, questioning, in the absence of other conversational strategies, becomes a means of continuing a conversation. The child may ask one question after another, without following up with comments. Excessive questioning can limit dialogue. For some children, use of the questioning technique is a defense mechanism that enables them to avoid sharing personal information. Excessive questioning on the part of an adult in conversation with a child limits the child's initiation of discourse.

As the child develops discourse skills and incorporates different strategies into turn-taking, he or she must also learn the rules for when to take a turn, how to take a turn, and how long a turn should be, as well as when not to take a turn. These rules are sophisticated nuances of conversation, with which many adults still have difficulty.

Another higher-level discourse ability is role-taking. The child must learn to monitor the listener in order to determine what is being understood. Four-year-old children have been found to modify their speech as a function of the age of the listener (Gordon & Ervin-Tripp, 1984; Leonard, Bolders, & Miller, 1976). They use shorter, simpler utterances when talking to 2-year-olds, as compared with talking to adults. In addition to monitoring the listener, the child must also self-monitor, to determine what aspects of the conversation are being understood (DeHart & Maratsos, 1984). The ability to monitor the self and the listener is not well developed in the preschool-age child.

During the play session, the team observes the child's level of discourse skills. The team should note whether the child is able to initiate an interaction, either verbally or non-verbally, and what behaviors are used to initiate an interaction. Other important observations include the techniques that the child employs to maintain a topic, and descriptions of strategies, such as revisions, clarifications, extensions, topic changing, and questioning. What prelinguistic or linguistic behaviors does the child exhibit in turn-taking? For the child with severe disabilities, early infant behaviors may be seen. These social interchanges should also be described because they will lay the foundation for higher-level interaction.

Four-year-old Rosalie, a child with severe disabilities, had discourse skills that were limited by her physical restrictions. Rosalie could maintain discourse if the responses required of her were limited to one word. Her lack of breath control and difficulty with articulation precluded actual conversation. When observed in interaction with her mother, she initiated interaction by looking at a doll. Her mother then picked up the doll and asked, "Would you like to hold it, Rosalie?" Rosalie nodded and grunted. Her mother put the doll into her arms and Rosalie smiled. Her mother commented, "That's a nice doll, isn't it?" Rosalie nodded and looked at the baby bottle. "Should we feed her?" Mother asked. Rosalie nodded. Mother held the bottle up to the doll's mouth, and Rosalie said, "Mmm." This sequence of interaction continued through several more turns, before Rosalie changed the topic of conversation by looking at another toy. Analysis reveals that Rosalie is capable of initiating and maintaining a topic with adult support. She is capable of extending the interaction and changing the topic of conversation. However, she is limited in the means she employs in her discourse.

Derrick, a 3-year-old child with mild cerebral palsy, controlled the conversation with an overabundance of questions. As he played, he asked one question after another, appearing uninterested in the facilitator's response to his questions. "What color is this chair? What program is he watching? Where should he go in?" He already knew the answers to most of the questions; questioning was used by Derrick as a turn in the conversation pattern.

☞   Discourse skills, although difficult to quantify, provide useful information. First, these skills reflect the appropriateness of a child's communication style. Second, these skills reflect the child's desire to participate in a given interaction. *Rosalie demonstrated both a desire to communicate and an ability to take turns. However, she needed to expand vocalizations and alternative means of communication.*

Derrick also had the desire to maintain interaction. He needed to incorporate variations in his turn-taking. Recommendations were made to help Derrick monitor his questions and comments, in order for him to understand what subject matter would be of interest to his listener. If he asked a question to which he already knew the answer, the question was reversed and the teacher or his parent reminded Derrick that he knew the answer. They would then help him think of a comment or question that added or requested new information. The team also suggested that adults model alternative communication patterns for Derrick.

Echolalia

Echolalia is defined as the immediate or delayed repetition of a word or group of words just spoken by another person. In the young child's early development, imitation is a normal pattern that serves multiple purposes. Imitation increases the child's performance ability beyond that which he or she is spontaneously capable of generating. In addition, imitation provides an opportunity for the child to practice new constructions and gain an understanding of how and what those constructions communicate (Clark, 1973). During imitation sequences, the child is also practicing turn-taking (McDonald & Gillette, 1982). With many children who have disabilities, however, imitation may become a means of discourse.

In the past, echolalia has been considered a nonfunctional or undesirable symptom of children with autism. Prizant and Duchan (1981) analyzed two specific forms of echolalia (immediate and delayed) to determine if these forms of communication serve any purpose for the speaker. Results indicated that immediate and delayed echolalia can assist the child in continuing an interaction and provide the speaker with additional time to process the spoken information. Echolalia can be an exact replication, or it can be mitigated (containing minor changes in structure from the original model); a combination of *both* exact and mitigated echolalia may also occur. The area of echolalia is addressed within the communication guidelines because many children with special needs will demonstrate some form of echolalic behavior that serves functional purposes for them.

In TPBA, the examination of echolalia focuses upon the function that echolalia has in the child's speech. Whether the imitation is developmentally appropriate, and whether it is used to continue the interaction, are two important considerations. *For example, Dan, age 3 years, would echo the facilitator and glance at her simultaneously. He apparently wanted to continue the interchange.*

Some children use echolalia to enhance comprehension, with the repetition acting as a verbal mediator for processing information. *During the play session, Dan would repeat a phrase before beginning an activity. The facilitator said, "I'm combing my doll's hair." Dan repeated, "I'm combing my doll's hair," and then proceeded to get his doll and comb.*

Another consideration is whether the child uses echolalia in a way that is successful pragmatically. *Alex, age 4 and diagnosed with mild autism, would frequently use utterances in which the form was inappropriate but the emotional/pragmatic context was correct. Upon being strongly pressed for his attention when he was inattentive, Alex said "Be back after these messages."*

Alex's statement is an example of delayed echolalia. Most striking, however, is the appropriate pragmatic context. The team should note the child's imitations, the context of the imitation, and its consequence for the child or the interaction.

☞ When echolalic speech is part of a child's language, every attempt should be made to evaluate these speech patterns according to their function in the child's repertoire. The desire to communicate should be reinforced. Determination of the length of rote memory demonstrated in the child's repetitions, as well as syntactic structures reproduced, provides direction to intervention. Development of spontaneous language should emphasize vocabulary, syntactic structures, and sentence length, within a child's scope of reproduction. Expectation for spontaneous language should begin with one word and then expand to more than one word.

For Dan, recommendations were made to give him choices. If he repeated the question, the teacher was told to model a response, then leave a blank for Dan to fill in. "What do you want, the ball or the car?" "I want the car." "I want the ---." During Dan's TPBA play session, the facilitator would say, "I am combing my doll's ---."

If highly motivating toys are used and wait time is extended, the child will eventually provide a response. The "close" technique described above can be extended as the child begins to provide spontaneous language.

PHONOLOGY: SOUND PRODUCTION PATTERNS

Phonemes or Speech Sounds

Preverbal behavior refers to sounds made by children prior to their first recognizable word. During the first year of age, infants produce a variety of speech-like and non–speech-like sounds. Many researchers (Bates, 1976a, 1976b, 1976c; Oller, 1978; Stark, 1978) have identified preverbal behaviors as precursors to future communication development. Stark

(1978) found a progression in the development of infant sounds in children between 2 and 88 weeks of age. She found that the sounds infants made at 2 weeks of age were regrouped into more sophisticated sounds over time.

Vocalizations in the first year of life are strongly influenced by simultaneous motor development. If a child's motor development is impaired, affecting head and neck control, vocalizations may also be affected. As the result of low muscle tone, for example, children with Down syndrome have decreased breath control, resulting in vocalizations that are shorter in length and are qualitatively different from typical children.

From 6 months to 1 year of age, vocalizations include several forms of babbling. By the ninth or tenth month, these vocalizations become smooth and regular in rhythm. As babbling develops, the infant's vocalizations begin to include various consonant–vowel combinations (such as didadubo). The final stage of preverbal vocalizations includes *jargoning*, which emerges around 12 months of age. Jargoning joins consonant–vowel combinations with a variety of intonation patterns and inflections that sound very similar to adult conversational speech.

Throughout the play session, notation should be made of the sounds produced by the child. Preverbal sounds, speech sounds, babbling, jargon, and actual words are documented. With many children who have disabilities, vocalizations are the primary means of communication. The information communicated via these vocalizations varies considerably. *Three-year-old Peter relied primarily on a grunting sound to communicate. He requested, denied, called attention to, greeted, and made choices—all with one vocalization. Conversely, another child who used several different vocalizations was observed to primarily request and deny.* The size of vocal repertoire does not always reflect the child's communication expertise. However, the larger the repertoire, the greater the opportunity for fostering consistent communication patterns.

When facilitating a child's play, vocalizations should receive the same respect as verbalizations. When a child holds a baby doll in his or her arms and vocalizes, the facilitator is encouraged to imitate the vocalizations first, and then to provide the appropriate label (e.g., baby) during the interaction. Imitation of the child's sounds stimulates vocalization. In addition, interpretation of the child's intent, with the shortest possible verbalization, enhances comprehension. By providing the label, one-to-one correspondence between the word and the object is also encouraged.

Analyzing vocalizations provides information about the child's prelanguage skills during the first year of life. Particularly for the minimally verbal child, whose vocalizations can predominate beyond the first year of life, understanding and appreciating the complexity of vocalizations can provide insight into programming. Once the patterns are analyzed, program plans follow a developmental approach, as outlined in *Targeting Intelligible Speech* (Hodson & Paden, 1983). An understanding of the normal sequence of phonological acquisition aids the team in developing appropriate activities to stimulate the production of developmentally appropriate sounds. The child, for instance, who was noted to produce only the consonants /b/ and /d/, was ready to work on other frontal sounds, such as /t/, /s/, and /l/. Activities were recommended that incorporated those sounds in a playful way to stimulate imitation. Playing with trains to make "toot-toot" sounds and singing "la la" to favorite songs are examples of recommended activities.

Phonological Processes or Errors

Phonology deals with the sound system of language. Prior to the use of words, the child has experimented with all of the sounds the human is capable of making. As imitation and reinforcement of culturally relevant sounds occurs, the child's noises come to sound increasingly like those of his or her caregivers. Babbling and jargoning allow for the practice of these sounds.

Early in the child's speech development, his or her first words are monosyllabic, usually consisting of consonant–vowel (CV) or vowel–consonant (VC) patterns. Patterns of CVCV reduplications (dada, mama) are also present (Lewis, 1951). First consonants are those made with the lips and teeth toward the front of the mouth (/b/, /d/). Fricatives (those sounds made at the front of the mouth, and emitting air, such as /f/, /v/, /s/, /z/) may also be heard. Vowel sounds heard in first words include /a/, /i/, and /u/. The sequence of the development of phonology and syllable structure differs greatly for each individual child (Owens, 1988). By the time the child has approximately 25 words, he or she demonstrates an emerging phonological system, or understanding of how sounds in the infant's cultural environment are combined (Hodson, 1983). Invariably, however, as the child begins to create words, he or she makes phonological errors. Known sound patterns are substituted for others not yet mastered, or complex sounds are omitted or altered. These errors result from patterns of simplification that children use when learning words.

Not all words that are understood are attempted (Owens, 1988). The child appears to select the words he or she produces. How these words are selected is not totally understood (Farwell, 1976; Ferguson, 1978). As the child learns new words, he or she applies a personal system of phonological rules.

The most common phonological errors made by children have been analyzed, described, and outlined by Ingram (1976). For the purposes of this chapter, these errors have been simplified into three categories, based on the work of Ingram (1976).

Deletions are noted when the child omits sounds from words. Common deletions include: deletions of the final consonant ("ca" for "cat"), deletion of unstressed syllables ("nana" for "banana"), deletion of a sound in a consonant cluster ("top" for "stop"), and deletion of a sound within the word ("ba-oon" for "balloon").

The child may also make *assimilation* errors, in which one sound in the word becomes similar to another sound in the word. Examples include: an end sound becoming like a front sound ("dod" for "dog"), a front sound becoming like an end sound ("gog" for "dog"), and one syllable sounding like another ("wawa" for "water").

The third category of phonological errors is *substitutions*. Common errors include: substitution of initial sounds ("dis" for "this," "dun" for "gun," "tan" for "can"), substitution of final sounds ("sin" for "sing," "horsie" for "horse"), substitution of /l/ and /r/ with /j/ or /w/ ("wabbit" for "rabbit"), and substitution of vowel sounds ("fawa" for "flower"). Combinations of errors can also occur, making analysis of errors difficult. Research suggests that these processes are prevalent in children under 2 years of age and disappear between 3 and 4 years of age (Dyson & Paden, 1983).

The preschool-age child is developing the phonological rules that govern sound distribution and sequencing. Such a child is learning which sounds can be put together, which sounds can appear in different parts of the word, and which sounds should be stressed (Ingram, 1976; Oller, 1974). The young child with disabilities may exhibit problems with phonological processes and phonological rules far longer than the typical child.

Intelligibility Level

Phonological errors affect the degree to which a child's language is understood. Compton (1970) and Oller (1973) were among the first to demonstrate that children whose speech is highly unintelligible have phonological systems that are as structured and regular as do children whose speech is developing in typical fashion. The phonological system of a child with language impairments may be unique to the individual, making deciphering the child's language a perplexing task. Parents and persons familiar with the child may become accustomed to the child's idiosyncratic patterns, and thus are able to interpret the child's language. Similarly, cultural or dialectical variability influences intelligibility. It is therefore important to include parents on the assessment team, and, if possible, professionals of a similar cultural background.

Another aspect of speech intelligibility is the concept of pitch and prosody patterns. For example, in a question, the voice pitch is usually raised at the end of the phrase. Many times with children with unintelligible speech, pitch can assist in the understanding of the utterance.

It is important to note that lack of intelligibility due to the child's individual phonological system differs from dysfluency or articulation problems. Children who stutter are dysfluent primarily as a result of sound and syllable repetitions, word repetitions, phrase repetitions, broken words, and prolonged sounds (Bloodstein, 1981; Johnson and Associates, 1959). There is, unfortunately, a lack of normative data relating to the dysfluencies of preschool children (Bloodstein, 1981). If observed, this behavior may be noted on the summary sheet under the category of "Other." Similarly, a child who demonstrates inability to formulate sounds due to oral motor dysfunction will probably demonstrate difficulties in eating and drinking, which can be documented in the corresponding section. In both instances, further assessment will be required.

The child's phonological system and intelligibility are determined through documentation of the child's language during the session, and through analysis of the videotape after the session. Assistance may be obtained from the parents in deciphering words that are intelligible to them but not to the team. The speech-language pathologist may then be able to break the child's individual phonological code. Patterns of deletions, assimilations, or substitutions are determined in order to identify specific areas for intervention.

During a play session, Glenna commented, "I da dum i da do" (a unique rendition of, "I have gum in my mouth"). This was interpreted through context (she pointed to her mouth) and through her mother's interpretation. Analysis revealed a variety of substitutions and deletions. Glenna was substituting sounds made at the front of the mouth for sounds made in other articulatory positions. The /d/ sound was substituted, for instance, for /g/, /m/. Deletions of back sounds (/v/, /n/, /th/) and alterations of sounds (/a/ for /ai/, and /o/ for /ou/) also occurred.

The speech-language pathologist, the facilitator (in some instances, this may be the same person), other observers, and parents determine the intelligibility of the child's speech. The team can observe the percentage of the child's utterances that were intelligible to the facilitator, to observers, and to the parents, and whether knowledge of the context of the child's actions improved the intelligibility (e.g, Glenna pointing to the gum in her mouth). Inflection patterns or intonation may also improve intelligibility. Documentation should be made of utterances understood by the parents.

In Glenna's play session, the parent facilitator asked the mother to interpret Glenna's comments. She wrote Glenna's statements down, to be shared with the speech-language pathologist at a later time. The speech-language pathologist also had the benefit of the videotape. The mother's interpretations could then be matched with actual phonology and the context of play, in order to obtain an accurate picture of Glenna's speech sounds and meaning.

Intelligibility findings are recorded in percentage form. *Glenna's speech was 70% intelligible in a known context; however, in an unknown context, intelligibility was reduced to 30%. Glenna's mother was able to interpret 60% of her utterances. These percentages are based on the overall utterance number.*

If a child's speech is highly unintelligible, it is recommended that a complete phonological assessment be done. Structured assessments may assist in a detailed analysis. (See, for example, *The Assessment of Phonological Process* [Hodson, 1981]).

☞   For children with phonological difficulties, the goal is to acquire new sound patterns that the child is capable of utilizing in speech production. *For Glenna, who was using limited and primitive sound patterns, one goal was to expand her repertoire of beginning sounds. Recommendations were made to incorporate words beginning with bilabial sounds (/p/, /b/, /m/). These sounds are among the earliest to develop. Common words, such as "baby," "box," "potty," were targeted for inclusion in play and home routines. Rapid motor practice of sounds in play would help her to practice these sounds, including making boat sounds, imitating popcorn popping, making boom-boom noises with falling objects. The suggestion was also made to help Glenna focus on the speaker, because the sounds she needed to learn can be visually observed, thus facilitating production. Final sounds, which develop later and are more complex, were only to be emphasized after successful initial sound production.*

Phonological goals are approached in a developmental sequence, working from the skills that the child already exhibits to gradually add more complex sounds. Generalization across a variety of words is also important in planning an intervention program.

SEMANTIC AND SYNTACTIC UNDERSTANDING

Semantics refers to the rules for establishing the meaning of words, individually and in combination. *Syntax* refers to the rule system for combining words or symbols into meaningful phrases and sentences, including the parts of speech, word order, and sentence structure. This section of the chapter addresses the knowledge level expressed by words, the parts of speech employed, the semantic relation exhibited in the child's speech, the type of sentences used by the child, the morphological markers used, and the mean length of utterance. Due to the interrelationship of the subcategories within semantics and syntax, observations and implications are described at the end of the section, rather than for each subcategory.

Knowledge Level

Semantics is closely related to the previously discussed area of pragmatics. In TPBA, the knowledge level represented by the child's use of words and the semantic relations expressed are analyzed. A child's first words are usually approximations of adult words and refer to a particular object or situations. Referential nouns account for 60%–65% of the child's first words (Benedict, 1979; Nelson, 1973; Schwartz & Leonard, 1984), with animals, foods, and toys being most often represented.

By 18 months of age, the child has a lexicon of approximately 50 words. In addition to referential nouns, the child has action words (verbs, such as *go*) and verblike words (*up*, *down*), modifiers (*your*, *mine*), personal-social words (*please*, *thank you*), and functional words (*this*, *that*) (Nelson, 1973).

The child's words demonstrate his or her conceptualization of the world. As experiences with persons, objects, and events increase, the words used are generalized to mean more than a specific referent. The child begins to extend meanings of words to include various people or objects with specific attributes; for example, a cup is now any cup, not just his or her cup. Overgeneralization also occurs, as the child includes items that share common perceptual characteristics into the word category; "Daddy" may mean all men, and "hat" may mean all things that can be placed on a head (Clark, 1973).

Verbs and other categories demonstrate the child's understanding of the relationship between objects and events. The attainment of the cognitive skills of object permanence, object constancy, and causality are needed in order for the child to be able to express relational meanings (Sinclair, 1970; Werner & Kaplan, 1963). Relational categories include statements pertaining to existence, nonexistence, disappearance, action, location, possession, and characteristics of objects, persons, or situations (Owens, 1988). As the child matures, his or her language reflects a growing categorical understanding, or an ability to group concepts.

A final stage of concept development involves the ability to think more abstractly, as represented by the child's ability to talk about language. Bloom and Lahey (1978) term this ability *metalinguistic knowledge*.

The above categories demonstrate the relationship between cognitive and semantic development. One of the age ranges at the end of the chapter summarizes these semantic-knowledge levels, with approximate ages for the initiation of each stage. There is considerable overlap between levels, with each level retaining the abilities attained in the previous stages.

Semantic Relations

The child's increasing cognitive ability is also reflected in the relationship of words expressed. As previously discussed, the child's prelinguistic and one-word utterances carry communicative intentions. As multiword combinations are formed, more complex semantic relations are expressed. Retherford, Schwartz, and Chapman (1981) identify 21 semantic categories found in early language. See Table 8.1 for a comparison of the semantic relations expressed in prelinguistic, one-word, and multiword combinations.

Syntactic development can be analyzed as the child begins to combine words into two- and three-word utterances. The parts of speech that the child uses can be identified in combination with an analysis of semantic relations. Nouns, verbs, adjectives, prepositions, and negatives all appear during the second year of age. Adverbs and conjunctions are seen in the third and fourth years.

Basic sentence structure (subject clause + verb clause) and basic sentence forms, including declaratives, imperatives, negatives, and questions, are acquired between 18 months and 3 years of age. Children begin to use compound sentences, two independent clauses joined by a conjunction ("I ate my cookie and washed my hands") between 2 and 2 ½ years of age. Complex sentence structure, an independent and a dependent clause ("I took the book that was on the table"), appears between 2 and 3 years of age (Trantham & Pedersen, 1976). Complex sentences become increasingly sophisticated into the school-age years.

Morphological Markers

Syntactic complexity can also be analyzed by examining morphological structure. A morpheme is the smallest meaningful unit of language. For example, adding the letter /s/ to a word to make it plural changes the meaning of the basic word. The word "chairs" thus consists of two morphemes. Brown (1973) suggested that there are five stages in the growth of language that correspond to an increase in the child's mean length of utterance (MLU), as measured in morphemes (see Table 8.2; Miller, 1982). Brown also identified 14 grammatical morphemes that occur in young children's speech. The age of mastery of these morphemes ranges from 19 to 50 months. See the age ranges for a description of these morphemes, and a suggested sequence of acquisition. Brown attributes the order of acquisition to increasing semantic-syntactic complexity.

In the stages that Brown (1973) discussed, Stage I identifies children's earliest attempts

Table 8.1.   Semantic relations expressed in prelinguistic, one-word, and multiword utterances

General relationship	Function/meaning	Child Behavior		
		Prelinguistic	One word	Multiword
Agent	States the individual performing the action	Throws ball to teacher and smiles proudly	Thows ball and says, "Me"	"Me throw"
Action	Requests action	Holds hands up to be picked up	"Up," to indicate pick me up	"Up Mommy"
Object	Comments on the object of action	Points to ball being pushed	"Ball," as ball is pushed	"Ball go"
Recurrence	Requests/comments on repetition of activity/object	Drinks milk and holds up empty bottle	"More," to indicate more milk	"Me more milk"
Nonexistence	Comments on nonexistence/ disappearance of object or person	Points to missing wheel on car	"Wheel," while pointing to car	"No wheel"
Cessation	Comments on cessation of activity	Points to top that stopped spinning	"Stop," to indicate top is no longer spinning	"Top stop"
Rejection	Protests/comments on undesired action or something forbidden	Turns head away from food	"No," in response to peas	"No peas"
Location	Comments on spatial location	Holds truck and points to box	"Box," while pointing to toy box	"Put box"
Possession	Comments on possession of object	Reaches for own shoes among others' shoes and points	"Mine," while getting own shoes	"My shoes"
Agent action[a]	Comments on agent and action			"Boy hit"
Action object[a]	Comments on action and object			"Kick ball"
Agent action object[a]	Comments on agent, action, and object			"Mommy throw ball"
Action object location[a]	Comments on agent, action, and location			"Put ball chair"

[a]These are more commonly used examples of relational combinations; many possibilities exist.

Source: Roberts, J., & Crais, E. (1989). Assessing communication skills. In D. Bailey & M. Wolery (Eds.), *Assessing infants and preschoolers with handicaps*. Columbus, OH: Merrill Publishing Co. Reprinted with permission.

at utterances, as described previously, as single words. At age 19 months, mostly nouns, verbs, and adjectives are used. Among the first grammatical morphemes indicating Stage II, at approximately 2–2½ years of age, are the present progressive (*me playing*), preposition (*in, on*), and plural regular (*-s, -es*) morphemes.

During Brown's Stage III, ages 2½–3, children begin using past irregular (*she came, we*

Table 8.2.   Predicting chronological age from mean length of utterance

Brown's stage	MLU	Predicted chronological age[a]	Predicted age ± 1 SD middle 68%
Early Stage I	1.01	19.1	16.4–21.8
	1.50	23.0	18.5–27.5
Late Stage I	1.60	23.8	19.3–28.3
	2.00	26.9	21.5–32.3
Stage II	2.10	27.7	22.3–33.1
	2.50	30.8	23.9–37.7
Stage III	2.60	31.6	24.7–38.5
	3.00	34.8	28.0–41.6
Early Stage IV	3.10	35.6	28.8–42.4
	3.50	38.7	30.8–46.6
Late Stage IV/	3.60	39.5	31.6–47.4
Early Stage V	4.00	42.6	36.7–48.5
Late Stage V	4.10	43.4	37.5–49.3
	4.50	46.6	40.3–52.9
Post Stage V	4.60	47.3	41.0–53.6
	5.10	51.3	46.9–59.7
	5.60	55.2	46.8–63.6
	6.00	58.3	49.9–66.7

Source: Bailey, D., & Wolery, M. (Eds.). (1989). *Assessing infants and preschoolers with handicaps.* Columbus, OH: Merrill Publishing Co. (As adapted from Miller, 1981.) Reprinted with permission.

[a]Age is predicted from the equation: Age (in months) $= 11.199 + 7.857$ (MLU). Computed from obtained standard deviations.

went). In Stages IV and V, from ages 3–4, children begin using articles (*a dog, the truck*), past regular (*he walked*), third person regular (*s,* as in *she runs*), and contractible copula (*here's my coat*). In post Stage V, from ages 4–4½, contractible auxiliary (*they're playing*), uncontractible copula (*who's here? I am*), uncontractible auxiliary (*who was playing? I was*), and irregular third person singular (*she has, he does*) are seen (Bellugi & Brown, 1964; Brown, 1973; deVilliers & deVilliers, 1973; Miller, 1981).

Mean Length of Utterance

The mean length of utterance (MLU) has been found to be a reliable predictor of the child's syntactic abilities. The MLU corresponds to chronological age as well as the stages of linguistic development, as described by Brown (1973). MLU is computed by dividing the number of morphemes in a sample by the total number of utterances in the sample. Brown noted that the MLU increased predictably each year up to about 4 years of age.

When the child's use of morphemes is beyond 4.5, content and sentence structure are more appropriate indices of language development.

During the play session, syntactic and semantic abilities may be informally documented. A sufficient language sample, however, is essential for comprehensive analysis. The facilitator needs to provide opportunities for the child to demonstrate the various aspects of language.

While playing with the dollhouse and barn in the playroom, 3-year-old Alex placed a doll on a horse and rode him into the barn. Alex said, "Horse eat." The facilitator placed a doll on a cow and said "My horse is hungry, too." Alex responded, "No horse," took the cow away, and handed the facilitator a horse, stating "you horse." The facilitator then said, "My horse is hungry, too." Alex pointed to the barn and said, "More food." The facilitator directed her horse into the barn. Alex brought his horse out of the barn, stating, "All gone."

In this short interaction, Alex used words to demonstrate referential, extended, and relational understanding. He also demonstrated beginning categorical understanding, by removing the cow from the category of horses. He used words demonstrating semantic relations, including recurrence, nonexistence, rejection, possession, and agent action, but he employed no morphological markers. The mean length of his utterances was 2.0. Although his play revealed higher-level conceptualization, Alex's language was delayed approximately 1 year in MLU, and 18 months in syntactic development.

☞   Syntax skills have often been identified as a need on the IEPs of children with language disorders. The recent emphasis on pragmatic skills, however, has shifted the focus from obtaining syntactically correct utterances to producing pragmatically successful communication. Once the child's intentions are clear, the child's semantic relations are expressed, and the child has progressed to multiword utterances, then syntactic abilities can be addressed.

The child must be exposed to a variety of situations that allow his or her knowledge base to expand. The development of relational and categorical knowledge is assisted through organizing items in a classroom (toys in one area, books in another area, and dress-up clothes in another). Grouping items within an activity is also important, so that children can perceptually relate characteristics and functions.

One important aspect of early syntactic development is that the child employs various strategies that produce errors. These errors demonstrate that the child has generalized specific rules regarding the use of certain words. Allowing children to make these errors is important, as is modeling appropriate forms and providing many opportunities for generalization of rules across words and situations.

Alex was demonstrating semantic understanding of various meanings, but was employing only simple words, such as "eat," "more," and "all gone." He needs to expand his vocabulary and show more variety in his two-word combinations; therefore, expanding his semantic relations and lengthening his utterances to 3–4 words became goals for Alex.

For Alex, it was recommended that action words (i.e., "come," "go," "in," "out") be incorporated into his play and combined with various agents and objects. Emphasis was to be placed on developing sequences of agent–action–object ("Horse go barn") or other similar two- to three-word semantic sequences. Activities involving action with cars, trucks, animals, and people, and activities in which Alex moved through the actions himself ("Alex throw ball") were suggested.

The child will talk about experiences in his or her world. For example, a child with limited mobility will probably not use many action words, or a child with limited sight might demonstrate limited use of attribute words. The focus in intervention should be to provide the child with the experiences necessary for gaining the knowledge pertaining to certain words. For example, a child who demonstrates a fondness for movement activities will more readily recognize the effectiveness of action words when paired with a movement activity. Hopper and Naremore (1973), in their chapter entitled "How Children Learn to Communicate," provide tactical tips for devising a syntactic program that follows a developmental progression.

COMPREHENSION

Receptive language, or language comprehension, is usually determined through directing the child to respond to behaviors, pictures, or questions. During the TPBA play session, the "examiner" is an observer and facilitator. The goal is to follow the child's lead in a natural environment. Directing and questioning is kept to a minimum, to prevent the environment from seeming test-like. Receptive understanding is determined through observation of semantics and cognitive behaviors that reflect a child's perceptions.

Observation of only the child's language usage can be deceptive. Historically, receptive language development has been thought to precede expressive language. Thus, any statement used by the child must be comprehended by the child. Recent research has shown that children do use words and structures that are beyond their comprehension, by remembering and repeating words and phrases within an appropriate context. Children with disabilities may also demonstrate this pattern. Leonard et al. (1976) suggest that to receive credit for a language structure, a child should demonstrate the ability to use the structure in several situations.

A second obstacle to using the child's expressed language as an indicator of receptive language is that the child will not use all of the language he or she knows within the TPBA play session. For these reasons, the speech-language pathologist may want to pursue further formal evaluation of vocabulary, semantic, and syntactic comprehension.

Although limitations exist, a great deal of information related to the child's language comprehension can be gained from TPBA. The facilitator needs to be adept at creating an environment that allows the child maximum opportunities to demonstrate as many skills as possible.

Language comprehension skills are also outlined in the age ranges. When combined with information obtained from the previous sections relating to the child's expressive language, the speech-language pathologist will have baseline data to determine whether or not further evaluation is needed.

There is a strong correlation between the development of cognitive abilities and the comprehension and production of language. For example, comprehension of *when, how,* and *why* questions develops after comprehension of *what, where,* and *who* questions. The child must understand cause, manner, and time in order to respond appropriately to the former (Piaget, 1926). Children will frequently respond to questions without understanding the question; they will respond to one of the semantic features contained within the question. For example, the child might respond to, "When are you going to eat?" with the answer, "A cookie," responding to the verb in the question (Owens, 1988). Listening to a child's response can give clues to comprehension. Causal questions are particularly difficult to understand, because they require the child to do reverse-order thinking. To answer why an event happened, the child has to think about what occurred prior to the event. This is difficult for most preschoolers.

Sequence of Question Comprehension

Yes/No Questions	1) Rising intonation at the end of declarative sentence
	2) Reversing the subject of sentence and the auxiliary verb (Is Mommy going?)
Wh- Questions	1) Inverting subject and auxiliary as well as correctly placing the wh- word at the beginning
	2) What, where, who acquired first
	3) When, how, why acquired later

(Ervin-Tripp, 1970; Tyack & Ingram, 1977)

Temporal terms (*before, after*), relational terms (*more/less, same/different*) and locational terms (*behind, in front of*) are all closely related to the child's cognitive development. Prepositions usually follow a progression from those related to self to those outside of self. Clark (1973) found that spatial terms develop in a progression from vertical (*up, down*) to horizontal-frontal, then to horizontal-lateral. In addition, specific terms may be understood prior to others as a result of environmental experiences. As it is not possible to assess the child's comprehension of every term, sampling is used. For purposes of program development, sampling provides sufficient information to provide direction for intervention.

Analysis of comprehension is done through observation of the child's physical and verbal responses during the play session. Observing the videotape after the session is also helpful. (The guidelines suggest general areas for observation.) The speech-language pathologist must record the exact terms, semantic relations, and sentence structure comprehended by the child.

The first area relates to sounds that the child hears and with which he or she associates meaning; the team notes the child's responses. In addition to referencing sounds, an early prerequisite to comprehension is visual joint-referencing to an object or event. The adult or child will initiate visual regard to the object. As both are looking at the object, the adult will usually comment on the referent object. The child will later comprehend the label attached to the object or event.

The team should note any evidence that the child comprehends routines. For example, the young child will demonstrate understanding of meaning by lifting a cup to the lips, or playing peekaboo when the facilitator covers his or her eyes. The child may also demonstrate comprehension without contextual cues; as mother rises to leave, the child picks up his or her coat.

Examine the semantic relations previously discussed, such as two-word or multiword expressions that the child comprehends. (The facilitator says, "Comb hair," and the child picks up the comb and combs the doll's hair, demonstrating comprehension of action-object relations.)

Although questions are kept to a minimum, the questions to which the child responds are important. During the parent–child observations, the team may be able to observe responses to questions, because parents frequently use a question format with their child. The team can also observe the child's use of questions with the facilitator, parents, and peer.

In one session, 5-year-old Betsy remarked to a peer, "I'm going to call my boyfriend. Do you want to call yours?" She picked up the phone and said, "When can you come over?" She used questions throughout the session, exhibiting comprehension of most interrogatory forms.

Commands are difficult to insert into the TPBA play session without becoming directive. Again, opportunities to observe response to commands may be seen with parents or peers. Retention and comprehension of one-step, two-step, and multistep commands are observed.

When playing in the water table with her mother, 3-year-old Sally was told to "Get the towel and the lotion for the baby." At a later time, her mother said, "The baby's wet. Go get her a diaper. Then give her a bottle." In both instances, without contextual cues, Sally was able to remember only one step of the command. She understood all of the components, as demonstrated by her behaviors in play with the towel, lotion, diaper, and bottle. In the first instance, Sally retrieved the lotion and applied it to the baby in the water. In the second instance, she got the baby's diaper. She appeared to focus on and retain the part of the command that held the most interest to her.

What level of prepositions does the child understand? While playing, the facilitator can comment on the location of objects: "I need the truck. It's in the box." The same is true for temporal and relational terms. The facilitator needs to incorporate terms into the play situations, such as, "Let's wash before we eat." "I need that bigger block. It's behind you." "Could I have the tall glass?"

Analysis of the parent inventory prior to the play session will assist the facilitator in selecting terms that he or she would like to incorporate into the session. If the approximate developmental level of the child is known in advance, the facilitator can use appropriate syntactic and semantic structures and vocabulary to ensure comprehension. For instance, for the child who functions on a lower level, the child emphasis might be on prelinguistic comprehension and comprehension of simple referents.

☞   Prior to intervening with any child, a complete audiological evaluation is recommended. However, based on the information that is obtained, intervention goals should reflect the developmental progression with which children learn certain information. For example, if a child demonstrated an understanding of the prepositions *up* and *down,* which reflects the vertical progression that Clark (1973) discussed, a goal stating that "Jimmy will demonstrate an understanding of *in* and *on*" would be appropriate.

ORAL MOTOR DEVELOPMENT

Oral motor development is important for the accurate production of speech sounds. Accurate eating and drinking skills also depend on oral motor abilities. Precise oral motor skills depend on the development of head, neck, lip, tongue, and jaw control, and the ability to swallow. Head and neck control develop in the first 6 months of life. By age 6 months, the child is able to sit unsupported with head in midline, and can voluntarily move his or her head from side to side and up and down. During this time, the child has also developed a coordinated suck and swallow, with good lip closure around a nipple. Small amounts of baby food may be taken on a spoon, but a parent does the work of getting the food off of the spoon, by pressing the spoon up against the upper lip and gum while the spoon is being removed. The child may then thrust the tongue forward, along with much of what has gone in. As the child gains voluntary control over the lips and tongue, the ability to actively participate in the acquisition and retention of food increases (Morris, 1982).

By 1 year of age, the child's jaw and lips will meet the cup; the teeth or tongue may be used as a stabilizer for support. The lips can seal around the cup to permit drinking. At the same time, the child can now bite and release with an up-and-down movement of the jaw. By age 18 months, he or she can monitor the suck and swallow of fluids, so that coughing and choking are now infrequent. When food is presented to the mouth of the 18-month-old, the jaws can move in a diagonal rotary pattern and the tongue can move from side to side to locate food.

Between 18 and 24 months of age, the child can inhibit breathing while swallowing, drink 1 ounce of liquid from a cup without pausing, and close the lips to retain fluid when the cup is removed. When food is presented, a rotary chewing pattern is used, and the tongue has more ability to move food around. The lips can move independently of the jaw, allowing the child to retrieve food from the lips. Food and saliva then remain in the mouth while chewing.

The 24-month-old can maneuver tongue and lips and coordinate suck and swallow to be able to drink from a straw. Playing with the food by moving it around with the tongue and sticking the tongue out to expose the food are fun games at this age. Between 24 and 36 months of age, the child can use the tongue to remove food from the lips. By 3 years of age, the child can manage most types of food and drink neatly (Morris, 1982).

Obviously, oral motor difficulties will influence the child's ability to produce sounds or sounds in sequence. Depending on the degree of impairment, oral motor problems may influence speech production in minor ways, or they may preclude the development of normal language patterns. For example, children with severe cerebral palsy may exhibit oral motor impairments that are of such an extreme nature that alternative forms of communication are needed.

At the end of the play session, a snack is served. The child, parents, and peer (if still available) are asked to join the facilitator at a small table. A pitcher of juice, glasses, and finger food, such as raisins, peanut butter and crackers, or pieces of fruit, may be served. For developmentally younger children, a bottle and/or baby food may be appropriate.

The snacktime serves multiple purposes. Observations of the child's eating skills serves as an initial screening for oral motor problems. Children who demonstrate problems with eating and drinking should receive a complete oral motor evaluation at a later time.

The snack also provides an opportunity to observe further social interactions between the child and his or her parents and the peer. Initiations and maintenance of dialogue, use of social conventions (e.g., "please" and "thank you"), and prosocial behaviors (e.g., sharing) may be observed.

Preparation and consumption of the snack also allows the team to observe fine motor and adaptive skills. The child may be asked to pour the juice, spread peanut butter on the crackers, distribute napkins, or give the same number of raisins to everyone. (The last two provide opportunities for the child to exhibit one-to-one correspondence, as well.)

While the child is eating and drinking, the speech-language pathologist and the occupational therapist will observe the child's control of head and neck, lips, jaw, and tongue. Depending on the age of the child, different degrees of control will be expected (see age ranges). The amount of food or liquid retained and lost, the child's awareness of food on the lips and face, the amount of choking, and extraneous movements such as tongue thrusting should all be noted.

During snacktime, Sarah, who was 2½ years old, stuffed the crackers into her mouth and sat with her cheek pockets full. She was unable to monitor the amount of food in her mouth and could not move it around with her tongue. She had peanut butter around her mouth, but seemed unaware of its presence. She also chewed with her mouth open, losing some of its contents. When drinking, lip closure around the cup was poor, resulting in loss of liquid.

Children who have difficulty with control of the oral musculature, breathing, and/or swallowing will also have difficulty producing many of the sounds necessary for speech. The lip seal, for instance, is necessary for making plosive sounds, such as /p/, and continuant sounds, such as /m/. Tongue control is necessary for precision in making points of articulation. For example, the tongue must be pulled back in the mouth to make guttural sounds such as /g/ and /k/. Children with oral motor difficulties will need remedial help to enable them to develop the control essential for eating, drinking, and speaking accurately.

Sarah demonstrated low tone and poor control of lips, jaw, and tongue. She also appeared to be insensitive to tactile input to the mouth and face area. This was also reflected in her speech, which was virtually unintelligible. Recommendations were made to increase Sarah's tactile sensitivity by providing input to the mouth at various times of the day, including before eating. Sarah's mother was to brush Sarah's teeth using various stimulating toothbrushes, and to wipe her face before, during, and after eating and drinking. Both her mother and father would play kissing games requiring Sarah to "pucker up," and imitation games, in which Sarah could try to imitate their funny movements of the tongue and face. Sarah was also to be seen in private therapy with the speech-language therapist, who would conduct activities with her to increase her tongue mobility, increase her breath control, and improve her bite and jaw movement. The teacher was provided with similar suggestions for the classroom.

RELATION TO OTHER AREAS OF DEVELOPMENT

Examinations of other domains in relation to language is critical, since problems with hearing, voice quality, cognitive, social-emotional, or motor development can affect language production and comprehension. This section is not meant to be a comprehensive description of each domain in relation to language, but rather offers suggestions to consider when analyzing the data from the assessment. The reader is referred to the chapters relating to other domains for in-depth descriptions of observation and implications.

Hearing is not directly assessed in the TPBA, but indicators of hearing deficits, such of lack of response to sounds or voices, may be observed. All children should be screened for hearing problems prior to the TPBA play session if possible. Audiological information should be included in the full assessment prior to the development of the child's program plan.

Voice quality is another area in which the child may exhibit deviations that are atypical and worthy of further evaluation. The child may demonstrate unusual pitch or loudness of voice; atypical variations of voice quality, including breathiness, harshness, or hoarseness; problems with resonation, including hypernasality (excessive nasal resonance) or hyponasality (lack of nasal resonance); or difficulty with endurance for speech. These problems may be indicative of organic involvement, requiring evaluation of the structural and functional integrity of the laryngeal mechanism; respiratory issues relating to respiratory patterns, muscle coordination, or respiratory efficiency; or hypertension (Prater & Swift, 1984). Concerns about the child's voice quality will need to be referred for further evaluation by appropriate professionals.

Cognition

The relationship of language to cognition has been noted throughout this chapter, but two specific areas are worthy of further discussion. Imitation skill and cognitive prerequisites to language are areas having implication for diagnosis and treatment.

Imitation   Symbolic functioning builds upon the base of imitation skills (Bates, Benigni, Bretherton, Camaioni, & Volterra, 1979; Piaget, 1952). As the child imitates the motor and vocal behaviors of others, he or she internalizes these behaviors, and is later able to represent them independently without a model. The child first imitates behaviors within his or her own repertoire (ages 4–8 months), and then imitates novel behaviors (ages 8–12 months). By ages 12 to 18 months, the child is a skilled imitator, and deferred imitation (later in time) is seen.

Physical imitation is not necessary for facial and vocal imitation, although a correlation exists. Bates and Snyder (1987) found a strong correlation between naming and the emergence of recognitory gestures and deferred imitation. Although disagreement exists about the role of imitation in language development, it appears that imitation is an important device for the acquisition of words, morphology, and syntactic-semantic structures (Bloom, Hood, & Lightbown, 1974; MacWhinney, 1976). After the age of 2, as language becomes more complex, imitation appears to be used less as a learning strategy. Children appear to imitate language aspects that they are in the process of learning. This allows the child to practice language features while they are stabilizing. What the child is imitating may therefore reflect his or her developmental level.

For children with disabilities, as with children who use imitation as a primary means of communication, imitation may have diagnostic implications. Some children may be unable to imitate, indicating oral motor problems that will influence the production of language. Imitation of the various aspects of language should be seen in a child just prior to spontaneous usage.

TPBA observation of imitation abilities includes imitation of gestures (see Chapter 6), oral motor acts (kissing, blowing, sucking), and speech and nonspeech sounds. Once the child acquires referential understanding, imitation will include word approximations, and finally, words. The analysis of the child's ability to imitate words, word combinations, sentences, and morphological markers will also provide guidance for intervention. Actions, sounds, words, and structures that the child can imitate can be incorporated into the intervention program. By providing opportunities for spontaneous use and generalization, the skills will be acquired more quickly.

Cognitive Prerequisites   Many of the cognitive skills that develop in the first year of life are thought to influence the development of language (Bates et al., 1977, 1979; Bowerman, 1974; Piaget, 1926). Development of object permanence, means–end behavior, functional use of objects, and object classification appear to precede both physical and verbal symbolic behavior. The reader is referred to Chapter 6 for a review of the development of these skills. Children with sensory, physical, or cognitive impairments may demonstrate delays in these abilities. Analysis of communication skills should therefore include an analysis of cognitive understanding.

Social-Emotional Development

Many of the pragmatic skills described in this chapter are indicators of social interaction skills. Children with emotional problems may reveal pragmatic difficulties (Bates, 1976c). Timing of communication, turn-taking skills, knowing when to initiate or terminate a conversation, and role-taking skills may be difficult for a child with emotional problems; the child's topic of conversation may also be inappropriate. The child may only be able to communicate well with certain individuals. For children who display these pragmatic difficulties, the speech-language pathologist may want to compare notes with the team psychologist. Joint analysis may provide a more complete picture of the child's skills and deficits.

Sensorimotor Development

Children who have difficulty with sensorimotor skills may also exhibit problems with several of the areas of communication. Children with visual-motor problems may have difficulty with joint referencing of objects early in development, affecting prelinguistic communication. Later in development, visual-motor problems can affect the development of written symbolic skills needed for reading and writing.

Difficulty with muscle tone, either hypertonia or hypotonia, can affect postural control and stability. Head control and diaphragm control affect the breath available for speech. Breath, in turn, affects the sounds produced and the length of the sequence of verbalizations.

Reflexes that have not been integrated at the appropriate time may also influence communication. An asymmetric tonic neck reflex (the "fencer's position"), for example, may preclude the child from looking at referent objects or the speaker. Other reflexes may also impact the child's ability to communicate. See Chapter 9 for further discussion of reflexes.

Fine motor skills, although not directly related to speech (except through oral motor skills), are important for children for whom an alternative form of communication is necessary. Fine motor skills are needed for sign language and certain types of communication boards or computers. Although alterations of systems are possible, knowledge of the child's fine motor abilities is necessary to select an appropriate augmentative system. Motor planning is also a necessary component for oral language and sign language. Articulation problems may reflect problems with the ability to formulate movements required to produce specific words. Discussion with an occupational or physical therapist is recommended when motor planning problems are evident.

Summary

Communication is closely intertwined with, and provides much of the basis for, the continuing development of cognitive and social skills. Effective assessment of language production and the pragmatics of language can occur through the transdisciplinary play-based assessment model. Comprehension of language is more difficult to assess in this format, but adequate information is obtained for determining the need for further evaluation. Assessment information from other domains of development should be combined with data from communication observations to obtain a more complete picture of the child's abilities.

REFERENCES

Argyle, M., & Ingham, R. (1972). Gaze, mutual gaze and proximity. *Semiotica, 4,* 32–49.

Bates, E. (1976a). Pragmatics and sociolinguistics in child language. In M. Moorehead & A.E. Morehead (Eds.), *Language deficiency in children: Selected readings* (pp. 411–463). Baltimore: University Park Press.

Bates, E. (1976b). *Language and context: The acquisition of pragmatics.* New York: Academic Press.

Bates, E. (1976c). *Pragmatics and sociolinguistics in child language.* Baltimore: University Park Press.

Bates, E., Benigni, L., Bretherton, I., Camaioni, L., & Volterra, V. (1977). From gesture to the first word: On cognitive and social prerequisites. In M. Lewis & L. Rosenblum (Eds.), *Interaction, conversation, and the development of language.* New York: John Wiley & Sons.

Bates, E., Benigni, L., Bretherton, I., Camaioni, L., & Volterra, V. (1979). *The emergence of symbols: Cognition and communication in infancy.* New York: Academic Press.

Bates, E., Camaioni, L., & Volterra, V. (1975). The acquisition of performatives prior to speech. *Merrill Palmer Quarterly, 21*(3), 205–226.

Bates, E., & Snyder, L. (1987). The cognitive hypothesis in language development. In I. Uzgiris & J. Hunt (Eds.), *Infant performance and experience: New findings with the ordinal scale.* Urbana: University of Illinois Press.

Bellugi, U., & Brown, R. (1964). The acquisition of language. *Monographs of the Society for Research in Child Development, 29*(92), 1–192.

Bernthal, J., & Bankson, N. (1981). *Articulation disorders.* Englewood Cliffs, NJ: Prentice-Hall.

Benedict, H. (1979). Early lexical development: Comprehension and production. *Journal of Child Language, 6,* 183–200.

Bloodstein, O. (1981). *A handbook on stuttering.* Chicago: National Easter Seal Society.

Bloom, L., Hood, L., & Lightbown, P. (1974). Imitation in language development: If, when and why. *Cognitive Psychology, 6,* 380–420.

Bloom, L., & Lahey, M. (1978). *Language development and language disorders.* New York: John Wiley & Sons.

Bloom, L., Rocissano, L., & Hood, L. (1976). Adult–child discourse: Development interaction between information processing and linguistic interaction. *Cognitive Psychology, 8,* 521–552.

Bowerman, M. (1974). Discussion summary—Development of concepts underlying language. In R. Schiefelbusch & L. Lloyd (Eds.), *Language perspectives—Acquisition, retardation, and intervention.* Baltimore: University Park Press.

Brown, R. (1973). *A first language: The early stages.* Cambridge: Harvard University Press.

Bruner, J. (1977). Early social interaction and language acquisition. In R. Schaffer (Ed.), *Studies in mother–infant interaction.* New York: Academic Press.

Bzoch, K., & League, R. (1970). *Receptive-Expressive Emergent Language Scale.* Baltimore: University Park Press.

Clark, E. (1973). What's in a word? On the child's acquisition of semantics in his first language. In T. Moore (Ed.), *Cognitive development and the acquisition of language.* New York: Academic Press.

Clark, T.C., Morgan, A.L., & Wilson-Vlotman, C. (1984). *The INSITE model: A model for home intervention for multiply handicapped sensory impaired infants.* Logan, UT: The SKI*HI Institute.

Coggins, T.E., & Carpenter, R.L. (1981). The Communication Intention Inventory: A system for observing and coding children's early intentional communication. *Applied Psycholinguistics, 2,* 235–251.

Compton, A.J. (1970). Generative studies of children's phonological disorders. *Journal of Speech and Hearing Disorders, 35,* 315–339.

DeHart, G., & Maratsos, M. (1984). Children's acquisition of presuppositional usages. In R. Schiefelbusch & J. Pickar (Eds.), *The acquisition of communicative competence.* Baltimore: University Park Press.

deVilliers, J. & deVilliers, P. (1973). Development of the use of word order in comprehension. *Journal of Psycholinguistic Research, 2,* 331–341.

Dore, J. (1974). A pragmatic description of early language development. *Journal of Child Language, 2,* 21–40.

Dyson, A. & Paden, E.P. (1983). Some phonological acquisition strategies used by two-year-olds. *Journal of Child Communication Disorders, 7,* 6–18.

Eisenberg, A., Murkoff, H., & Hathaway, S. (1989). *What to expect the first year of life.* New York, NY: Workman Publishing Company, Inc.

Ervin-Tripp, S. (1970). Discourse agreement: How children answer questions. In J. Hayes (Ed.), *Cognition and the development of language.* New York: John Wiley & Sons.

Ervin-Tripp, S. (1971). Social backgrounds and verbal skills. In R. Huxley & E. Ingram (Eds.), *Language acquisition models and methods.* New York: Academic Press.

Farwell, C. (1976). *Some ways to learn about fricatives.* Paper presented to the 8th Child Language Research Forum, Stanford University, Palo Alto, California.

Ferguson, C. (1978). Learning to pronounce: The earliest stages of phonological development in the child. In F. Minifie & L. Lloyd (Eds.), *Communicative and cognitive abilities—Early behavioral assessment.* Baltimore: University Park Press.

Gordon, D., & Ervin-Tripp, S. (1984). The structure of children's requests. In R. Schiefelbusch & J. Pickar (Eds.), *The acquisition of communicative competence.* Baltimore: University Park Press.

Grice, H. (1975). Logic and conversation. In D. Davidson & G. Harmon (Eds.), *The logic of grammar.* Encina, CA: Dickenson Press.

Halliday, M. (1975). *Learning how to mean: Explorations in the development of language.* New York: Arnold.

Hodson, B.W. (1981). *The assessment of phonological process.* Danville, IL: Interstate Printers and Publishers.

Hodson, B.W. (1983). *Targeting intelligible speech.* San Diego, CA: College Hill Press.

Hodson, B., & Paden, E. (1981). Phonological processes which characterize unintelligible and intelligible speech in early childhood. *Journal of Speech and Hearing Disorders, 46,* 369–373.

Hodson, B.W., & Paden, E. (1983). *Targeting intelligible speech: A phonological approach to remediation.* San Diego: College Hill Press.

Hopper, R., & Naremore, R.C. (1973). *Children's speech.* New York: Harper & Row.

Ingram, D. (1976). *Phonological disability in children.* London: Arnold.

Johnson, W., and Associates. (1959). *The onset of stuttering.* Minneapolis: University of Minnesota.

Keenan, E. (1975). Evolving discourse—The next step. *Papers and Reports on Child Language Development, 10,* 80–87.

Keenan, E., & Schieffelin, B. (1976). Topic as a discourse notion: A study of topic in the conversation of children and adults. In C. Li (Ed.), *Subject and topic: A new typology of language.* New York: Academic Press.

Leonard, L., Bolders, J.G., & Miller, J.A. (1976). An examination of the semantic relations reflected in the language usage of normal and language disordered children. *Journal of Speech and Hearing Research, 19,* 371–392.

Lewis, M. (1951). *Infant speech: A study of the beginnings of language.* New York: Humanities Press.

MacDonald, J.D. (1978). *Environmental language inventory.* Columbus, OH: Charles E. Merrill.

MacWhinney, B. (1976). Hungarian research on the acquisition of morphology and syntax. *Journal of Child Language, 3,* 397–410.

McDonald, J., & Gillette, Y. (1982). Ecological communication assessment. *Assessment of language through conversation.* Columbus: Nisonger Center Ohio State University.

Miller, J. (1981). *Assessing language production in children.* Austin, TX: PRO-ED.

Morris, S.E. (1982). *The normal acquisition of oral/feeding skills.* New York: Therapeutic Media, Inc.

Morehead, D., & Ingram, D. (1973). The development of base syntax in normal and linguistically deviant children. *Journal of Speech and Hearing Research, 16,* 330–352.

Nelson, K. (1973). Structure and strategy in learning to talk. *Monographs of the Society for Research in Child Development, 69*, 409–415.

Oller, D. (1973). The effect of position in utterance on segment duration in English. *Journal of the Acoustical Society of America, 14*, 1235–1247.

Oller, D. (1974). Simplification as the goal of phonological processes in child speech. *Language Learning, 24*, 299–303.

Oller, D.K. (1978). Infant vocalization and the development of speech. *Allied Health and Behavioral Sciences Journal, 1*(4).

Owens, R.E. (1988). *Language development: An introduction.* Columbus, OH: Charles E. Merrill.

Pendergrast, K., Dickey, S.E., Selman, J.W., & Soder, A. (1969). *Photo articulation test.* Danville, IL: The Interstate Printers and Publishers, Inc.

Piaget, J. (1926). *Language and thought of the child.* London: Routledge & Kegan Paul.

Piaget, J. (1952). *The origins of intelligence in children.* New York: International Universities Press.

Prater, R.J., & Swift, R.W. (1984). *Manual of voice therapy.* Boston: Brown and Company.

Prizant, B.M., & Duchan, J.F. (1981). The function of immediate echolalia in autistic children. *Journal of Speech and Hearing Disorder, 46* 241–249.

Prutting, C. (1979). Process/Pra,ses/n: The action of moving forward progressively from one point to another on the way to completion. *Journal of Speech and Hearing Disorders, 44*, 3–30.

Ress, N., & Wollner, S. (1981). *An outline of children's pragmatic abilities.* Paper presented at the American Speech-Language-Hearing Association annual convention, Detroit.

Retherford, K., Schwartz, B., & Chapman, R. (1981). Semantic roles and residual grammatical categories in mother and child speech: Who tunes into whom? *Journal of Child Language, 8*(3), 583–608.

Roberts, J.E., & Crais, E.R., (1989). Assessing communication skills. In D.B. Bailey and M. Wolery (Eds.), *Assessing infants and preschoolers with handicaps.* Columbus, OH: Charles E. Merrill.

Rosenwinkle, P. (1983). *The development of prepositions in young children.* Unpublished document. Champagne-Urbana: University of Illinois Speech and Hearing Science.

Roth, F., & Spekman, N. (1981). *Preschool children's comprehension and production of directive forms.* Paper presented at the American Speech-Language-Hearing Association annual convention, Detroit.

Roth, F., & Spekman, N. (1984). Assessing the pragmatic abilities of children: Part 1. Organizational framework and assessment parameters. *Journal of Speech and Hearing Disorders, 49*, 2–11.

Schwartz, R., & Leonard, L. (1984). Words, objects, and actions in early lexical acquisition. *Journal of Speech and Hearing Research, 27*, 119–127.

Sinclair, H. (1970). The transition from sensorimotor to symbolic activity. *Interchange, 1*, 119–126.

Stark, R.E. (1978). Features of infant sounds: The emergence of cooing. *Journal of Child Language, 5*(3), 379–390.

Stern, D., Jaffe, J., Beebe, B., & Bennett, S. (1975). Vocalizing in unison and in alternation: Two modes of communication within the mother–infant dyad. In D. Aaronson & R. Rieber (Eds.), *Developmental psycholinguistic and communication disorders.* New York: New York Academy of Science.

Trantham, C.R., & Pedersen, J. (1976). *Normal language development.* Baltimore: Williams & Wilkins.

Tyack, D., & Ingram, D. (1977). Children's production and comprehension of questions. *Journal of Child Language, 4*, 211–224.

Weiss, C., & Lillywhite, H. (1981). *Communicative disorders: Prevention and early intervention.* St. Louis: C.V. Mosby Company.

Werner, H., & Kaplan, B. (1963). *Symbol formation: An organismic development approach to language and the expression of thought.* New York: John Wiley & Sons.

8

Observation Guidelines for Communication and Language Development

I. Modalities of Communication
    A. What is the primary method of communication used by the child?
        1. Eye gaze
        2. Gesture
        3. Physical manipulation
        4. Vocalization (nonspeech, e.g., grunts)
        5. Sign language
            a. Idiosyncratic
            b. Formal
        6. Verbalization
        7. Augmentation (e.g., symbol board)
    B. What supplemental forms are used in communication?
    C. What is the frequency of communication acts?
II. Pragmatics
    A. What pragmatic stage or level of intention is demonstrated by the child?
        1. Perlocutionary stage—lack of specific intent on the part of the infant, but behaviors are interpreted by the parent or caregiver
        2. Illocutionary stage—use of conventional gestures or vocalizations to communicate intentions
        3. Locutionary stage—use of words to show intent
    B. What meaning is implied by the child's gestures, vocalizations, and verbalizations?
        1. Seeking attention
        2. Requesting object
        3. Requesting action
        4. Requesting information
        5. Protesting
        6. Commenting on an object
        7. Greeting
        8. Answering
        9. Acknowledging other's speech
        10. Other
    C. What functions does the child's communication fulfill?
        1. Instrumental (to satisfy needs or desires)
        2. Regulatory (to control the behavior of others)

       3. Interactional (to define or participate in social interchange)
       4. Personal (to express personal opinions or feelings)
       5. Imaginative (to engage in fantasy)
       6. Heuristic (to obtain information)
       7. Informative (to provide information)

   D. What discourse skills does the child demonstrate (typically and optimally)?
       1. Attending to speaker
       2. Initiating conversation
       3. Turn-taking
       4. Maintaining a topic
       5. Volunteering/changing a topic
       6. Responding to requests for clarification
       7. Questioning

   E. Does the child demonstrate echolalia in communication?
       1. Timing
          a. Immediate
          b. Delayed
       2. Echolalia
          a. Exact
          b. Mitigated (changed)
       3. Function
          a. To continue interaction
          b. To demonstrate comprehension
       4. Degree of pragmatic success

III. Phonology: Sound Production Patterns
   A. What phonemes or speech sounds are produced by the child?
       1. Preverbal sounds
       2. Speech sounds
       3. Babbling—consonant–vowel combinations
       4. Jargon—speech sounds combined into patterns with cultural intonations
       5. Words

   B. Phonological processes or errors
       1. Deletions
          a. Consonants
          b. Syllables
          c. Sounds
       2. Assimilations (one sound becomes similar to another in the same word)
       3. Substitutions
          a. Initial sounds
          b. Final sounds
          c. For liquids, /l/ and /r/
          d. Vowels

   C. Intelligibility level—percentage of verbalizations understood
       1. In known context
       2. In unknown context
       3. By familiar person or family member
       4. Appropriateness of intonation
       5. Dysfluencies or stuttering

IV. Semantic and Syntactic Understanding
   A. What cognitive level of understanding is demonstrated in the child's language?
      1. Referential (specific objects)
      2. Extended (more than one object)
      3. Relational (relations between objects)
      4. Categorical (discrimination and classification)
      5. Metalinguistic (talking about language)
   B. What types of words are used?
      1. Nouns
      2. Verbs
      3. Adjectives
      4. Adverbs
      5. Prepositions
      6. Negatives
      7. Conjunctions
   C. What semantic relations are expressed in the child's language?
      1. Agent (*baby*)
      2. Action (*drink*)
      3. Object (*cup*)
      4. Recurrence (*more*)
      5. Nonexistence (*all gone*)
      6. Cessation (*stop*)
      7. Rejection (*no*)
      8. Location (*up*)
      9. Possession (*mine*)
      10. Agent–action (*baby drink*)
      11. Action–object (*drink juice*)
      12. Agent–action–object (*baby drink juice*)
      13. Action–object–location (*throw ball up*)
      14. Other
   D. What type of sentences are used by the child?
      1. Structure
         a. Declarative
         b. Imperative
         c. Negative
         d. Questions
      2. Level of complexity
         a. Simple
         b. Compound
         c. Complex
   E. What morphological markers does the child use?
      1. Present progressive (*-ing*)
      2. Prepositions (*in, on*)
      3. Regular and irregular past tense (*-ed, came*)
      4. Possessives (*'s*)
      5. Contractible and uncontractible copula (*dog's little; he is*—in response to question, "*Who is happy?*")
      6. Regular and irregular third person (*jumps, does*)

      7. Contractible and uncontractible auxiliary (*Mommy's drinking*; *he is*—in response to question, *"Who is combing his hair?"*)

  F. What is the child's mean length of utterance?

V. Comprehension of Language

  A. What early comprehension is demonstrated?
     1. What is the child's reaction to sounds?
     2. Does the child exhibit joint referencing with an adult?
       a. With visual regard
       b. With verbal cue
       c. With physical cue
     3. Does the child respond to common routines or statements?
       a. With contextual cues
       b. Without contextual cues

  B. What comprehension of language forms is demonstrated?
     1. To which semantic relations does the child respond?
     2. To which questions does the child respond?
       a. Yes/no questions
       b. Simple "wh" questions (*where, what, who*)
       c. Advanced "wh" questions (*which, when, why, how*)
     3. What commands can the child follow?
       a. Complexity (one-step, multistep)
       b. With/without contextual cues
     4. What prepositions can the child understand?
       a. Simple (*in, on*)
       b. Advanced (*next to, behind, in front of*)
     5. What temporal terms does the child understand?
     6. What relational terms does the child understand?

VI. Oral Motor Development

  A. What cup drinking skills does the child demonstrate?
     1. Is the head aligned with the body?
       a. Midline
       b. Head extension or retraction
     2. What degree of lip control is seen?
       a. Degree of lip seal when cup to lips
       b. Ease with which jaw and lips meet cup
       c. Lip control when cup removed from mouth
     3. What degree of tongue control is seen?
       a. Degree of tongue protrusion under cup
       b. Lack of tongue thrust forward
     4. How does the child coordinate suck/swallow?
       a. Sequence of suck/swallow
       b. Amount child can drink without pause
       c. Can inhibit breathing while swallowing
       d. Frequency of coughing and choking

  B. How adept is the child at chewing and swallowing solids?
     1. Can the child sustain and control a bite?
     2. What jaw movement is observed?
       a. Bite release
       b. Rotary pattern—diagonal

        c.   Rotary pattern—circular

    3.   To what degree does the tongue assist in moving food from side to side?

    4.   What degree of lip control is seen?

        a.   Movement is independent of jaw

        b.   Mouth closure

        c.   Amount of food loss or salivation while chewing

VII.   Observations Related to Other Areas

    A.   Hearing

    B.   Voice quality

    C.   Cognitive development

        1.   What level of imitation is indicated in the child's language?

           a.   Motor acts

           b.   Oral motor acts

           c.   Speech and nonspeech sounds

           d.   Word approximations

           e.   Words (one-syllable, two-syllable, multisyllable)

           f.   Word combinations (two-word, three-word, etc.)

           g.   Complete sentences

           h.   Morphological markers

        2.   What cognitive prerequisites to language are evident?

           a.   Object permanence (ability to represent objects and events not perceptually present)

           b.   Means-ends behaviors (actions to achieve a goal)

           c.   Functional object use and object classification (perception of relationships)

           d.   Symbolic behavior (ability to internalize and reproduce information)

    D.   Social-emotional development

        1.   See pragmatic skills related to social interaction (Observation Guidelines, Chapter 7)

        2.   Are topics of communication appropriate?

        3.   Does the child communicate in a similar manner with all partners?

    E.   Sensorimotor development

        1.   Visual-motor skills

        2.   Muscle tone and postural control

        3.   Reflexes

        4.   Fine motor skills

        5.   Motor planning

8

Age Ranges

Development of Intentionality

Age (Months)	Stage	Characteristics
0–8 (approx.)	Perlocutionary	Child cries, coos, and makes movements; intention inferred by adult
8–12	Illocutionary	Emergence of intention to communicate Demonstrates understanding of objects' purpose Displays full range of gestures
12+	Locutionary	Words accompany or replace gestures to express communicative functions previously expressed in gestures alone or gestures plus vocalization

Adapted from Owens, 1988.

Communicative Intentions Expressed in Prelinguistic, One-Word, and Multiword Utterances

Intention	Definitions	Prelinguistic	One Word	Multiword
Attention seeking 12–18 mo.	Solicits attention to self or aspects of the environment: has no other intent.	Child tugs on his or her mom's skirt.	"Mommy" as she tugs on skirt.	"You know what?"
Request objects 13–17 mo.	Demands desired tangible object: includes requesting consumable and nonconsumable objects.	Child points to a dog he or she wants.	"Dog."	"Give me dog."
Request action 13–17 mo.	Commands another to carry out an action: includes requesting assistance and other actions involving another person or between another person and an object.	Child puts adult's hand on jar while looking at the adult.	"Open," while giving jar to adult.	"Mama, open bottle."

(continued)

Communicative Intentions *(continued)*

Intention	Definitions	Prelinguistic	One Word	Multiword
Request information 24 mo.	Finds out something about an object or event: includes "wh-" questions and other utterances having the intonation contour of an interrogative.	Child points to shoe, and with intonation of question, says "uh?"	"Shoe?" while pointing to shoe box.	"Where shoe?"
Protest 13–17 mo.	Commands another to cease an undesired action: includes resisting another's action and rejection of object that is offered.	Child pushes the adult's hand away when an undesired food item is offered.	"No," in response.	"No peas, Mama."
Comment on object 13–17 mo.	Directs another's attention to an object: pointing showing, describing, informing, and interactive labeling.	Child holds up toy car toward the adult and smiles while looking at the adult.	"Car," said while pointing.	"My car."
Comment on action 12–18 mo.	Calls listener to the movement of some object or action of others or self.	Laughs and looks at adult while adult falls down.	"Down" as adult falls.	"Bobbie fall down."
Greeting 13–17 mo.	Communicates salutation and offers conversation rituals: "hi," "bye," "please," and "thank you."	Child waves as mother leaves.	"Bye."	"Bye, Mom."
Answering 9–18 mo.	Responds to request for information.	Child points to his or her nose to answer the question "Where's your nose?"	Child says "nose" in response to "Where's your nose?"	"Here my nose."
Acknowledgment of other's speech 9–18 mo.	Acts or utterances used to indicate that the other's utterance was received, not in response to a question; includes repetition of an utterance.	Child acknowledges another's speech by turning head and smiling.	Child says "yea" when favorite song is mentioned.	"My song."
Other 9–18 mo.	Tease, warn, alarm, exclaim, or convey humor.	Child giggles as he or she takes a turn in a tickle routine.	Child says "no" as he or she sticks out tummy.	"No tickle me."

Adapted from Coggins & Carpenter, 1981; Dore, 1974; and Roth & Spekman, 1984.

Discourse Skills

Age	Discourse Skills	Content
By 1 year	Initiates a topic by combination of glances, vocalizations	Limited to topics that are physically present
	Maintains one or two turns	
	One-half utterances on topic, extended topic maintenance in routines	
2–3 years	Can introduce topic	Topic does not have to be physically present
	Engages in short dialogue of a few turns	Uses attention-getting words, rising intonation (*more, what, mine*)
	Adult scaffolds or structures conversation (give child choices)	Provides descriptive detail
	Repetition used to remain on topic	Can comprehend and use "I," "you," "he," and polite form "please"; responds to partner
3–4 years	Can engage in dialogue beyond a few turns	Action is a common topic Verbs "go" and "do" predominate
	More aware of social aspects of discourse	Uses direct requests (*May I, Could you*)
	Acknowledges partner's turn, can determine how much information listener needs	
4–5 years	Modifies language when talking to younger child	Discusses state, feelings, emotions, attitudes
	Increased awareness of listener's role and understanding	Verbs "be" and "do" predominate
		Indirect requests increase
5–6 years	Can sustain topic through a dozen turns	Uses most varieties of English sentences
	Conversation much like adults'	

Articulation Test Profile Showing Age Level at Which 75 Percent or More of Subjects Correctly Produced Given Phonemes from PAT*

Articulation Behaviors

Age			
24 mo.	t-	m-	ɛ (s<u>e</u>nt)
	n-	-m	a (f<u>a</u>ther)
	-n	h-	i (f<u>ee</u>t)
	k-	au	e (v<u>a</u>cation)
	g-	u	ʌ (<u>u</u>p)
	p-	æ (c<u>a</u>t)	ʊ (b<u>oo</u>t)
	-p	ɔ (f<u>a</u>ll)	o (<u>o</u>bey)
	b-	ə (sof<u>a</u>)	ɪ (b<u>i</u>n)
		ai	oi (o<u>i</u>l)
28 mo.	-s	-k	-ŋ (<u>ng</u>)
	d-	f-	j- (<u>y</u>ell)
	-d	-f	
32 mo.	-t	-b	ɝ (b<u>ir</u>d)
	-r	w-	
36 mo.	s-	-g	ɚ (crack<u>ers</u>)
	-l		

(continued)

Articulation Behaviors   *(continued)*

40 mo.	-'ʃ(di<u>sh</u>) l-	bl- r- br-		tr- -v	
44 mo.	ʃ-(<u>sh</u>oe) t-	-tʃ(<u>ch</u>oke) fl-			
48 mo.	sp- st-	kl- ð- (<u>th</u>eir)		-ð (smoo<u>th</u>) -ʒ (mea<u>s</u>ure)	
48 mo. +	z- -z	θ- (<u>th</u>umb) -θ (ba<u>th</u>)	hw- (<u>wh</u>at) ju	-ʤ (bu<u>dge</u>) ʤ- (<u>j</u>oy)	

Adapted from Pendergast, Dickey, Selman, & Soder, 1969.

*Symbols are from the International Phonetic Alphabet. Examples are provided for unusual sounds. The hyphen indicates the position of the word.

Semantic-Knowledge Levels Reflected in Words

Referential Knowledge
9–15 months

A particular word represents a specific item (e.g., "bankie" refers to the child's blanket only).

Extended Knowledge
15–18 months

A word represents various kinds of objects (e.g., "chair" can mean several types of chairs).

Relational Knowledge
18 months +

A word understood to relate to itself or something else. Categories of relational words include:

Reflexive relational (mark existence, nonexistence, disappearance, and recurrence: "this," "all gone," "more").

Action relational (movement implied: "up," "down," "bye-bye," "do").

Location relational (direction or spatial relationship—where object is located).

Possessional relational (object associated with a person: "mine").

Categorical Knowledge
2 years +

The semantic category of words demonstrating the awareness of common aspects among objects (e.g., the word "toys").

Metalinguistic Knowledge
4–5 years

The ability to think about language and comment on it as well as produce and comprehend it (e.g., the child states that "ball" begins with a 'b').

Adapted from Bloom & Lahey, 1978.

Brown's 14 Morphemes

Age of Mastery[1] (in months)	Morpheme	Example
19–28 mo.	Present progressive -ing (no auxiliary verb)	"Mommy driving."
27–30 mo.	In	"Ball in cup."
27–30 mo.	On	"Doggie on sofa."

(continued)

Brown's 14 Morphemes   *(continued)*

24–33 mo.	Regular plural -s	"Kitties eat my ice cream."
		Forms: /s/, /z/, and /ɪz/
		    Cats (/kæts/)
		    Dogs (/dogz/)
		    Classes (/klæsɪz/), wishes (/wɪʃɪz/)

25–46 mo.	Irregular past	"Came," "fell," "broke," "sat," "went"
26–40 mo.	Possessives	"Mommy's balloon broke." Forms: /s/, /z/, and /ɪz/ as in regular plural
27–39 mo.	Uncontractible copula (verb to be as main verb)	"He is." (response to "Who's sick?")
28–46 mo.	Articles	"I see a kitty." "I throw the ball to Daddy."

26–48 mo.	Regular past -ed	"Mommy pulled the wagon."
		Forms: /d/, /t/, ɪd/
		    Pulled (/puld/)
		    Walked (/wc̄kt/)
		    Glided (/g l aɪ d ɪ d/)

26–46 mo.	Regular third person -s	"Kathy hits." Forms: /s/, /z/, and /ɪz/ as in regular plural
28–50 mo.	Irregular third person	"Does," "has"
29–48 mo.	Uncontractible auxiliary	"He is." (response to "Who's wearing your hat?")
29–49 mo.	Contractible copula	"Man's big." "Man is big."
30–50 mo.	Contractible auxiliary	"Daddy's drinking juice." "Daddy is drinking juice."

---

[1]Used correctly 90% of the time in obligatory contexts.
Source: Brown, 1973; Miller, 1981; Owens, 1988.

Language Comprehension

3–6 mo.	Responds to sound frequencies Anticipates routines when sees familiar objects (bottle) Responds to sound frequencies within varying environment
6–9 mo.	Responds to own name Recognizes words like "bye-bye," "mama" Looks, stops, or withdraws in response to "no" Recognizes family members' names Responds with appropriate gestures (e.g., "up") and familiar routines Appears to listen to conversations of others Stops activity when name called Recognizes names of familiar objects
9–12 mo.	Looks at objects that mother looks at Identifies individuals in their own environment Appears to understand simple commands or requests ("Give me _____," "Where's the _____?") Responds to music with body movement
12–18 mo.	Responds to facial expressions of emotion Will look for and find objects not in view Recognizes names of various body parts
18–24 mo.	Comprehends action words Follows simple 1-step commands

(continued)

Language Comprehension   *(continued)*

	Identifies familiar objects from a group
	Identifies pictures
	Understands complex sentences
	Uses prepositions *in* and *on*
18–30 mo.	Can carry out 2- to 3-step directions
18 mo. +	Comprehends numbers (see one-to-one correspondence)
24–36 mo.	Understands possessives such as "mine," "yours," and "his"
	Uses preposition *under*
	Understands words through function (what you eat with)
	Understands common verbs
	Understands common adjectives
24 mo. +	Understands prepositions
36–40 mo.	Uses preposition *next to*
36–48 mo.	Follows complex multistep commands
	Uses prepositions *behind, in front of*
	Wants explanation of "why," "how"
	Can follow 3-step commands given in a complex sentence
48–60 mo.	Temporal terms before and after
	Uses prepositions *above, below, at the bottom*
60 mo. +	Locational prepositions in temporal expressions such as "in a week"
	Locative directions in reference to the body (*left* and *right*)

Adapted from Bzoch & League, 1970; Clark, Morgan, & Wilson-Vlotman, 1984; Owens, 1988.

Oral/Motor Skills

	(Early Infant Feeding)
0–4 mo.	Oral reflexes (suck/swallow, rooting, gag)
	Suckling (tongue moves up and down, in and out)
	Loses liquid from sides of mouth, incomplete lip closure
4–6 mo.	Cup drinking introduced, tongue may thrust
	Mouth opens for spoon
	Tongue thrusts when spoon withdrawn, food ejected
6–12 mo.	Jaw moves up and down
	True suck, stable jaw
	Tongue lateralization begins
	Upper lip comes down well on spoon
	(Cup Drinking Skills)
12–18 mo.	Lip seal intact when cup to lips
	Jaw and lip meet cup easily, may bite edge of cup (stability or fun)
	Tongue may or may not protrude under cup (a cupper tongue position expected)
	No tongue thrust forward
	No head extension (thrust forward accompanies swallow)
	Infrequent coughing/choking
18–24 mo.	Lip control when cup removed from mouth
	Does sequence of suckle-swallow
	Drinks 1 ounce from cup without pause
	Can inhibit breathing while swallowing
	(Chewing/Swallowing Solids)
12–18 mo.	Sustained, controlled bite
	Jaw movement: bite release
	rotary pattern—diagonal
	rotary pattern—circular

(continued)

Oral/Motor Skills   *(continued)*

18–24 mo.	Tongue lateralizes when food is at side of mouth
	Lips move independently of jaw (18–24 mo.)
	Chews with lips closed
	No loss of food or saliva while chewing
18–24 mo.	Chews with mouth closed
24–36 mo.	Cheeks assist in holding food
	Can easily transfer food from one side of the mouth to other
36 mo.	Child has all basic movement components of oral motor function

Adapted from Hall, Cirrillo, Reed, & Hylton, 1987; Morris, 1982.

(This section was developed by Sandy Patrick, M.S., CCC/SLP. She is a speech-language pathologist with Family Connections and the University of Colorado, Department of Communication Disorders and Speech Sciences/In REAL Project.)

Development of Speech/Sound Production

Birth	Cry, burp, cough, sneeze, and hiccup
1–3 months	Cooing and throaty gurgles
	Sounds such as a, e, o, and u are heard
2–4 months	May produce consonants such as k, g, or h
	Laughs out loud
3–5 months	Squealing
3–6 months	Two-syllable, one-consonant sound strings are produced (a-ga, a-ba, a-da) repetitively
4–6 months	Growling
	Yelling, not associated with distress
	Inhalation/exhalation sequences
	Variation in vocal pitch
	Consonants produced may include b, m, w, d, n, r
6–7 months	Makes a wet razzing sound
6–8 months	Babbling begins to occur, for example, sing-song strings of consonants (da-da-da-da) and word-like double consonants (da-da, ma-ma, ba-ba)
7–13 months	Says Mama and Dada indiscriminately
	May produce vc, cvc syllables occasionally
	Intonation patterns include rising pattern for "yes/no" questions and rising/falling of declarative sentences
10–14 months	Says Mama or Dada discriminately
10–18 months	Jargon-like speech and nonreduplicated babbling
	Child's speech sounds like a foreign language with adult-like intonation
18 months	Child will produce up to 21 different consonant and vowel sounds. Jargon and echolalia are present
24 months	Child will produce up to 25 different phonemes
	Jargon and echolalia are almost gone

Adapted from Bankson & Bernthal, 1981; Eisenberg, Murkoff, & Hathaway, 1989; Weiss & Lillywhite, 1981.

Communication and Language
Observation Worksheets

These worksheets are easiest to complete while watching the videotape of the session. The tape can be stopped after an activity, so that the pragmatic section can be marked. This worksheet is helpful if baseline data are needed, if patterns are not obvious to the observer, if certain aspects of pragmatics need more specific analysis, or if the child is nonverbal.

If the child is verbal, the observer may want to concentrate on taking a language sample[1] (on the first page) during the TPBA play session and use the pragmatic analysis form when reviewing the video. For the verbal child, the remaining sections can be completed from the language sample and other nonverbal observations.

For the nonverbal child, the language sample and semantic and syntactic sections may be omitted. Any eye gaze, gesture, vocalization or other form of communication should be documented under the sections indicating the functions and meaning implied by the child's nonverbal communication.

Oral motor observations are noted for all children.

[1]Tanya Paleski, M.S., CCC-SLP, is gratefully acknowledged for developing the format of the Language Sample portion of the Communication and Language Observation Worksheet.

Communication and Language Observation Worksheet

Name of child: _____ Date of birth: _____ Age: _____

Name of observer: _____ Discipline or job title: _____ Date of assessment: _____

On the following pages, note specific behaviors that document the child's abilities in the Communication and Language categories. Qualitative comments should also be made. The format provided here follows that of the Observation Guidelines for Communication and Language Development in **Transdisciplinary Play-Based Assessment.** It may be helpful to refer to the guidelines while completing this form.

Language Sample

Sample 20% of each phase of the TPBA play session. This section may be completed during observation of the session and/or the videotape.

Child	Facilitator	Parent	Peer(s)	Behaviors (of child and interactors)	Eye gaze	Gesture	Physical manipulation	Vocalization	Verbalization	Sign language	Augmentation

(continued)

				Communication and Language Observation Worksheet							

Child	Facilitator	Parent	Peer(s)	Behaviors (of child and interactors)	Eye gaze	Gesture	Physical manipulation	Vocalization	Verbalization	Sign language	Augmentation

SAMPLE

(continued)

Communication and Language Observation Worksheet

Name of child: _____ Date of birth: _____ Age: _____

Name of observer: _____ Discipline or job title: _____ Date of assessment: _____

Child	Facilitator	Parent	Peer(s)	Behaviors (of child and interactors)	Eye gaze	Gesture	Physical manipulation	Vocalization	Verbalization	Sign language	Augmentation

(continued)

				Communication and Language Observation Worksheet								
Child	Facilitator	Parent	Peer(s)	Behaviors (of child and interactors)	Eye gaze	Gesture	Physical manipulation	Vocalization	Verbalization	Sign language	Augmentation

SAMPLE

(continued)

Communication and Language Observation Worksheet

Name of child: _____   Date of birth: _____   Age: _____

Name of observer: _____   Discipline or job title: _____   Date of assessment: _____

I. Modalities of Communication

A. Primary method (circle one):
1. Eye gaze
2. Gesture
3. Physical manipulation
4. Vocalization
5. Sign language
   a. Idiosyncratic? (yes or no)
   b. Formal? (yes or no)
6. Verbalization
7. Augmentation

B. Supplemental forms used in communication:

C. Frequency of communication acts:

II. Pragmatics

A. Stage or level of intention (circle one):
1. Perlocutionary   2. Illocutionary   3. Locutionary

Examples:

B. Meaning implied by gestures, vocalizations, and verbalizations (circle those that apply):
1. Seeking attention   6. Commenting on object
2. Requesting object   7. Greeting
3. Requesting action   8. Answering
4. Requesting information   9. Acknowledging other's speech
5. Protesting   10. Other:

Examples:

C. Functions fulfilled (circle those that apply):
1. Instrumental   5. Imaginative
2. Regulatory   6. Heuristic
3. Interactional   7. Informative
4. Personal

Examples:

D. Discourse skills demonstrated (typically and optimally) (circle those that apply):
1. Attending to speaker   5. Volunteering/changing topic
2. Initiating conversation   6. Responding to requests for clarification
3. Turn-taking   7. Questioning
4. Maintaining topic

Examples:

(continued)

E. Echolalia? *(yes or no)*

    1. Timing *(circle one)*:
        a. Immediate   b. Delayed

    2. Echolalia *(circle one)*:
        a. Exact act   b. Mitigated

    3. Function *(circle one)*:
        a. Continue interaction   b. Demonstrate comprehension

    4. Degree of pragmatic success:

Examples:

III. Phonology: Sound Production Patterns

A. Phonemes produced *(circle those that apply)*:

    1. Preverbal sounds   4. Jargon
    2. Speech sounds   5. Words
    3. Babbling
    Examples:

B. Phonological processes or errors

    1. Deletions *(circle those that apply)*:
        a. Consonants   b. Syllables   c. Sounds
    Examples:

    2. Assimilations? *(yes or no)*
    Examples:

    3. Substitutions *(circle those that apply)*:
        a. Initial sounds   c. Liquids
        b. Final sounds   d. Vowels
    Examples:

C. Intelligibility level
    1. In known context:

    2. In unknown context:

    3. By familiar person:

    4. Appropriateness of intonation? *(yes or no)*
    5. Dysfluencies or stuttering? *(yes or no)*

(continued)

Name of child: _____ Date of birth: _____ Age: _____

Name of observer: _____ Discipline or job title: _____ Date of assessment: _____

IV. Semantic and Syntactic Understanding

A. Cognitive level of understanding *(circle those that apply)*:

1. Referential
2. Extended
3. Relational

4. Categorical
5. Metalinguistic

Examples:

B. Types of words used *(circle those that apply)*:

1. Nouns
2. Verbs
3. Adjectives
4. Adverbs

5. Prepositions
6. Negatives
7. Conjunctions

Examples:

C. Semantic relations *(circle those that apply)*:

1. Agent
2. Action
3. Object
4. Recurrence
5. Nonexistence
6. Cessation
7. Rejection

8. Location
9. Possession
10. Agent–action
11. Action–object
12. Agent–action–object
13. Action–object–location
14. Other:

Examples:

D. Sentences

1. Structure *(circle those that apply)*:

   a. Declarative
   b. Imperative

   c. Negative
   d. Questions

   Examples:

2. Level of complexity *(circle one)*:

   a. Simple   b. Compound   c. Complex

   Examples:

E. Morphological markers *(circle those that apply)*:

1. Present progressive
2. Prepositions
3. Regular and irregular past tense
4. Possessives

5. Contractible and uncontractible copula
6. Regular and irregular third person
7. Contractible and uncontractible auxiliary

Examples:

F. Mean length of utterance *(see Table 8.2 in Transdisciplinary Play-Based Assessment)*:

(continued)

V.   Comprehension of Language

A. Early comprehension

1. Reaction to sounds:

2. Joint referencing with adult? *(yes or no)*
    a. With visual regard? *(yes or no)*
    b. With verbal cue? *(yes or no)*
    c. With physical cue? *(yes or no)*
    Examples:

3. Response to common routines or statements? *(yes or no)*
    a. With contextual cues? *(yes or no)*
    b. Without contextual cues? *(yes or no)*
    Examples:

B. Comprehension of language forms

1. Response to semantic relations:

2. Response to questions *(circle those that apply)*:
    a. Yes/no questions   b. Simple "wh-" questions   c. Advanced "wh-" questions
    Examples:

3. Commands followed *(circle those that apply)*:
    a. Complex   b. With contextual cues   c. Without contextual cues
    Examples:

4. Prepositions understood *(circle those that apply)*:
    a. Simple   b. Advanced
    Examples:

5. Temporal terms understood:

6. Relational terms understood:

VI.   Oral Motor Development

A. Cup-drinking skills

1. Head aligned with body? *(yes or no)*
    a. Midline *(yes or no)*
    b. Head extension or retraction? *(yes or no)*

(continued)

Name of child: _____ Date of birth: _____ Age: _____

Name of observer: _____ Discipline or job title: _____ Date of assessment: _____

2. Lip control

   a. Degree of lip seal:

   b. Ease with which jaw and lips meet cup:

   c. Lip control when cup removed:

3. Amount of tongue control

   a. Tongue protrusion under cup:

   b. Lack of tongue thrust forward? *(yes or no)*

4. Coordinated suck/swallow? *(yes or no)*

   a. Sequence:

   b. Amount child can drink without pause:

   c. Inhibited breathing while swallowing? *(yes or no)*

   d. Frequency of coughing and choking:

B. Adept at chewing and swallowing solids? *(yes or no)*

   1. Sustaining and controlling a bite? *(yes or no)*

   2. Jaw movement? *(circle those that apply)*:

      a. Bite release   b. Diagonal rotary pattern   c. Circular rotary pattern

   3. Tongue assistance in moving food? *(yes or no)*

   4. Lip control

      a. Movement independent of jaw? *(yes or no)*

      b. Mouth closure? *(yes or no)*

      c. Food loss or salivation while chewing? *(yes or no)*

VII. Observations Related to Other Areas

A. Hearing:

B. Voice quality:

C. Cognitive development

   1. Level of imitation indicated by child's language *(circle those that apply)*:

      a. Motor acts   e. Words

      b. Oral motor acts   f. Word combinations

      c. Speech and non-   g. Complete sentences
         speech sounds   h. Morphological markers:

      d. Word approximations

(continued)

2. Cognitive prerequisites to language *(circle those that apply)*:
   a. Object permanence
   b. Means–end behaviors
   c. Functional object use and object classification
   d. Symbolic behavior

D. Social-emotional development
   1. Social interaction:

   2. Topics appropriate? *(yes or no)*
   3. Similarity of communication with different partners:

E. Sensorimotor development
   1. Visual-motor skills:

   2. Muscle tone and postural control:

   3. Reflexes:

   4. Fine motor skills:

   5. Motor planning:

Additional Comments

SAMPLE

Summary Sheet for Communication and Language Guidelines

Name of child: _____   Date of birth: _____   Age: _____

Name of observer: _____   Discipline or job title: _____   Date: _____

Observation categories	Areas of strength	Rating	Justification	Things I'm ready for
I. Communication modalities				
II. Pragmatics A. Stages				
B. Range of meaning				
C. Functions				
D. Discourse skills				
E. Imitation/echolalia				

SAMPLE

214

Summary Sheet for Communication and Language Guidelines

Name of child: _____   Date of birth: _____   Age: _____

Name of observer: _____   Discipline or job title: _____   Date: _____

Observation categories	Areas of strength	Rating	Justification	Things I'm ready for
III. Phonology: Sound production system				
IV. Semantic and syntactic understanding in verbal expression				
V. Comprehension of language				
VI. Oral motor				
VII. Other concerns (identify):				

SAMPLE

215

9

Observation of Sensorimotor Development

Susan Hall

During the course of child development, sound sensorimotor function enhances attachment (Greenspan & Greenspan, 1985), exploration of the environment (Connolly, 1975; Piaget, 1954), and early vocalizations and sound play (Morris, 1987). Physical and occupational therapists, therefore, play a significant role in the life of a young child who has a motor delay. Despite the importance of movement to many aspects of life, motor skills are often neglected in play assessments. This chapter provides the framework for observing sensory and motor behaviors during the TPBA play session. This evaluation is not intended to be diagnostic. Its usefulness lies in determining sensorimotor strengths and needs.

The TPBA approach to assessment is unique because it looks at the child's ability to perform milestone skills, such as sitting and walking, while also noting the quality of the child's performance, such as whether the child is able to freely turn the upper body while in the sitting position. Observation Guidelines, consisting of a series of questions that assist the observer in organizing information from the play session, follow this chapter. Physical and occupational therapists may use their expertise in motor development to expand these guidelines. Ideally, therapists are present during the assessment process and responsible for analyzing and interpreting motor behaviors. However, in the absence of a therapist, other professionals may gather enough information about a child's motor skills to advocate, when necessary, for a referral to a therapist.

A number of people helped to move the sensorimotor chapter from a fledgling to a "real" manuscript. Without these folks the dream would never have become a reality. My husband and children, Rick, Mindy, and Kristina, patiently tolerated the frequent absences needed to bring this chapter to fruition. Their resilience and unconditional love provided the impetus to continue. My parents, Lionel and Burnett Brenneman, assisted with much-needed child care and permitted me to temporarily move in and monopolize their computer.

Eleanor Westcott, mentor and friend, kindled my initial interest in movement and provided input and guidance during the initial phases of this project. I am saddened that she was unable to see the final product; she will be greatly missed. Two friends and colleagues, Gordon Williamson and Nancy Graham, literally sustained me through this endeavor. These two individuals generously shared their time and expertise. The sensorimotor chapter reflects their support, their knowledge, and their gifted methods of constructively challenging my thinking. Philippa Campbell provided valuable assistance in modifying the outline and helping me focus the content. Ann Grady, Marge Adams, Denise Carrico, and Lisa Ross read versions of the outline and manuscript, contributing to clarity and content. Last, though not least, Toni W. Linder's vision encouraged me to broaden my perspective.

This chapter follows the organization of the guidelines. Major categories from the outline include:

I. General Appearance of Movement
II. Muscle Tone/Strength/Endurance
III. Reactivity to Sensory Input
IV. Stationary Positions Used for Play
V. Mobility in Play
VI. Other Developmental Achievements
VII. Prehension and Manipulation
VIII. Motor Planning

Each section of the guidelines is presented by briefly reviewing typical motor development, and is followed by a discussion of how to observe sensorimotor behaviors in play. Unlike traditional motor assessments, during TPBA observations of the child's movements are made while the child plays with the facilitator. For this reason, examples are given to assist the therapist in transferring familiar motor skill observations to the play environment. *Approximate* age ranges for some motor skills are provided at the end of the chapter and may be used as a general guideline for determining developmental delay. These age tables should not be rigidly followed, since there is great variability in normal development (McGraw, 1966; Touwen, 1971). Implications for intervention are briefly discussed.

Three general opportunities exist to observe the child's movements during the play session:

1. When the child plays with toys in a stationary position (e.g., sitting or lying on the floor)
2. When the child is moving from one area to another
3. When the child chooses to play with the gross motor equipment

The play area is set up ahead of time to invite sensorimotor exploration. The child's interactions with objects and people provide opportunities to watch movement and the effect of these movements on other areas of development. Planning potential activities that challenge higher-level skills is important. For example, indoor jungle gyms, mini trampolines, and large cardboard boxes may entice the older child to engage in motor games. Many of the play areas can be structured to observe sensorimotor skills. Materials in the kitchen area, for example, may elicit grasping skills, object manipulation, and sensory responses. Dishes, clay, pretend food, whipping cream, cookie cutters, and stackable measuring cups could be included in this area. Reviewing the guidelines prior to a session will familiarize the team with the types of sensory and movement activities that are desired.

Having the child remove some clothing or change into a pair of shorts will enhance observations of movement patterns. Information about adaptive skills, differential responses to touch, and motor planning may also be gained during undressing. Following a warm-up period, undressing can be built into the play session at the water table. The facilitator must, however, respond sensitively to the child. If undressing is met with resistance, or if the child's history makes undressing inappropriate, the assessment can be done without this intrusion.

GENERAL APPEARANCE OF MOVEMENT

Motor and sensory dysfunction can occur in conjunction with a variety of disabilities. Atypical motor development may be present in children with cerebral palsy, chromosomal abnormalities, spina bifida, emotional disturbance, congenital abnormalities, hearing impairment, or peripheral nerve injuries. Some children will demonstrate delays in acquiring motor milestones. Others may demonstrate delays but also use abnormal patterns of movement. Some preschoolers may be able to perform age-appropriate skills, yet with movements that are clumsy and awkward. Such a preschooler may be reluctant to attempt challenging motor skills. These different types of motor problems need to be considered, since each leads to different types and styles of intervention.

Initial questions in the guidelines are designed to assist the observer in noting the child's physical appearance and general motor activity.

Physical Appearance

The team members need to note anything unusual about the child's body that might affect movement, such as: 1) genetic abnormalities; 2) discrepancies in limb length, size, or shape; and 3) a disproportionate appearance between the head, trunk, and limbs. Physical growth of the infant and young child influence the child's ability to perform motor skills (Espenschade & Eckert, 1980). Expectations for performing certain tasks may change for a child who is small for his or her chronological age. Team members need to determine whether the child's height and weight are age-appropriate. Plotting these physical characteristics on a growth chart helps to eliminate subjective judgments and individual biases.

Motor Activity

There is some overlap between the general characteristics of the child's movements discussed in this section and activity level discussed in Chapter 6. The frequency of the child's movements may influence the team's perception of temperament.

One consideration is whether the child is able to move from one play area to another independently, and how this is accomplished. The child who crawls or walks from one area to another presents a different picture from the child who runs from area to area. It is also important to note how often the child moves around the room, and how often the child adjusts his or her position while playing in one place. The team should be aware of the child who moves more or less than a typical child. Some children will play in one place and infrequently shift positions. In contrast, there are also children who cannot seem to sit still. These children may wander from area to area or constantly wiggle while sitting on the floor or in a chair.

What positions are used for play? *Sally, a typical 2-year-old, was observed getting up from the floor several times to engage her mother. When playing on the floor with the facilitator, she frequently shifted her weight and used a variety of positions. She played in a sitting position, with her legs bent to the right or left side, with both legs in front of her, with her heels tucked under her bottom, and with her bottom resting between bent legs. She leaned forward, supporting herself on one arm in sitting. She planted one foot flat on the floor while the other leg remained bent. She crawled on her hands and knees to get a toy that was out of reach, and spent some time upright on her knees. These observations point out Sally's capacity to use diverse positions. She also frequently adjusted her body in these positions.*

Although most children demonstrate a preference for one or two positions, a variety of movements are possible. In addition, there may be some positions or motor activities that the child avoids; these should be noted as well.

☞ Sole observations of the general appearance of the child's movements will not lead to the development of appropriate intervention strategies. These observations are meant to be combined with the rest of the guidelines, and should be noted throughout the session.

☞ indicates discussion of implications for intervention. Readers will see this symbol throughout each of the guidelines chapters.

MUSCLE TONE/STRENGTH/ENDURANCE

Muscle Tone

Muscle tone is the amount of tension in muscles at rest. This resting tension permits the muscles to contract quickly, allowing a coordinated motor response (Bobath, 1971a). Muscle tone may be influenced by a variety of factors, including fatigue, alertness, activity level, body position, body temperature, the child's level of excitation, and the amount of effort being used (Ingram, 1966; Scherzer & Tscharnuter, 1982).

Movement abilities can be limited by several different types of atypical muscle tone. Muscle tone that is lower than normal is referred to as *hypotonia*. In contrast, *hypertonia* refers to muscles that have more tone than normal. The term *fluctuating tone* is used when tone appears to alternate between hypotonia and hypertonia. Muscle tone also varies along a continuum. Normal tone represents the midrange of the continuum, with severe hypotonia on one end and severe hypertonia at the other. The severity of the child's atypical tone affects the degree to which motor skills are limited. The child with markedly atypical tone may be unable to move independently. The child with borderline tonal problems may appear clumsy and awkward during play.

Movement during the first 4–6 months of life is partially influenced by early appearing, primitive reflexes. When development proceeds normally, these reflexes become integrated. The influence of the reflex is over-ridden by voluntary control. When there is damage to the central nervous system, these primitive reflexes may not integrate as they should. Such retained neonatal reflexes are often present in the child with atypical muscle tone. Formal reflex tests consist of the presentation of a different stimulus for each primitive reflex. This type of examination is beyond the scope of the play-based model, and is also incompatible with the child-directed nature of this model. Observations of naturalistic movement, however, will often reveal the influence of retained reflexes.

The guidelines provide questions that identify a few features of normal and unusual muscle tone. The child should be referred for further evaluation if there is not a therapist on the team and any of the unusual features of muscle tone are noted.

Features of Normal Muscle Tone

If muscle tone is normal throughout the body, the child is able to assume a variety of positions (developmentally appropriate for his or her age). Body parts on the right and left side of the body will look alike and move in similar ways. Movements will also appear smooth, steady, and coordinated when the child is changing positions.

Common Features of Unusual Muscle Tone

The first category in this section helps the observer look for clues that would indicate low tone. These observations should be noted in as many different positions as possible. The child may have difficulty holding the head up in a variety of positions, or may slump in upright positions. Children with low tone will often spread their legs wide in various positions and movements; thus, a broad base of support should be noted. When muscle tone is low, the child has difficulty supporting the body in different positions and remaining upright against gravity. In order to compensate for this difficulty, the child may lock the joints or lean against a support to remain upright. The child may use "w" sitting, with the buttocks resting between bent hips and knees and the feet behind the body. "W" sitting gives the child a broad base of support, providing a more stable position.

Two-year-old Nate was referred for a play-based evaluation. His mother's primary concern was his inability to talk, since he seemed to understand language. Nate had a "flat affect" and his mouth was usually open. Although he had begun walking at 15 months of age, his walking pattern (at 2 years of age) looked like that of a typical 1-year-old. His feet were widely spread and he appeared to waddle when walking; he was unable to run or jump. His positioning for play lacked variety. He stayed mainly in a wide-based ring sit. Rising to stand was slow and appeared to take effort. Ball skills and stair climbing were age-appropriate, and Nate enthusiastically attempted all obstacle course activities. During these gross motor activities, however, his balance reactions were sluggish and movements were slow. The facilitator played a rough-and-tumble game with Nate on her lap. During this time, she noticed that his body felt "mushy" and his limbs seemed to dangle loosely. Further consultation with a physical therapist confirmed the facilitator's impression that Nate had low tone. Since low tone can impede speech development as well as motor skills, activities were designed to build tone prior to and during language intervention.

In contrast, the child with high tone presents a different picture during play. The arms or legs may appear to be stiff. Movement is often slow, laborious, and restricted. When the child does move, the body gets stiffer. As the child struggles to overcome the resistance of tight muscles he or she may use abnormal movement patterns. Abnormal movement patterns are the child's way of adapting to the lack of voluntary control in some muscles. These compensations become habits that the child practices and may lead to changes in the muscles and joints, thus causing deformity. Fisting, balance problems, and walking on the toes may also be evident in the child with high tone. High tone should be suspected when there is a movement discrepancy between limbs on the right and left sides of the body.

Fluctuating tone is difficult to identify through visual observation alone. The child's movements may appear exaggerated, uncontrolled, clumsy, or awkward.

Terry frequently staggered when walking. Her movements were generally clumsy during gross motor activities. She spent a significant amount of time standing while playing in the kitchen area. She fell to the floor when she tried to bend over to put her "cake" in the oven, and often stumbled when trying to turn around in the small space between the stove and the table. At one point, she appeared to trip just prior to falling, but there was nothing in her path. Fluctuating tone was confirmed when the therapist employed therapeutic techniques to handle Terry at the end of the session.

Finally, the team members should observe whether any pattern of tone can be detected. Differences between the right and left sides of the body, and between the arms and the legs, should be noted.

The therapist will often want to handle the child to confirm visual observations of muscle tone. This may be done at the end of the play session or later, in a follow-up evaluation. The decision to include additional physical evaluation by the therapist at the end of a session depends on the child's level of fatigue and resistance to being controlled. Due to the nondirective nature of TPBA, the child often has difficulty "shifting gears" and relinquishing control of his or her movements to an adult.

Children with atypical muscle tone require a variety of intervention strategies. Therapeutic activities aim at managing muscle tone within the context of facilitating desired patterns of movement. Sensory input and appropriate support for a movement may be provided through the use of "key points of control" (Bobath & Bobath, 1972). The therapist places his or her hands on specific body parts, such as the trunk, hips, or shoulders, and guides the child's movements. External assistance from the therapist is kept to a minimum, however, so that the child learns to control the body independently.

In addition to individual therapy, use of the same movement patterns in the child's daily life is essential. Parents, teachers, and other caregivers should be provided with information regarding the best ways to encourage more functional movements. For an infant, strategies are needed that can be used during bathing, dressing, feeding, and carrying the child. Inquiries should be made about the type of baby equipment used at home. Positioning in infant seats, walkers, jumpers, and chest carriers can influence muscle tone. It is important to consider these items when planning home intervention for the child with atypical muscle tone.

For preschoolers, information should be provided to the teacher regarding the best positions to use during classroom activities. Techniques can also be used to modify muscle tone prior to an activity. Therapeutic input, including regular consultation, training, and assistance in implementing motor goals, will help the classroom staff encourage appropriate movement. Physical and occupational therapists should also work closely with other team members, such as the speech-language therapist. Appropriate handling and positioning affect the muscles used for feeding, breathing, vocalization, and sound production (Morris, 1987).

Adaptive equipment may be needed for some children. Equipment can improve a child's position, increase independent functioning, or help with caregiving routines. A special chair, an adapted eating utensil, and an electronic communication board are examples of adaptive equipment. A number of resources are available that discuss appropriate positioning, physical handling, and adaptations for the child with a motor dysfunction (Connor, Williamson, & Siepp, 1978; Finnie, 1975, Hanson & Harris, 1986; Musselwhite, 1986; Scherzer & Tscharnuter, 1982).

In addition to therapeutic and adaptive intervention strategies, a variety of medical interventions may be used when children have atypical muscle tone. Katz (1988) provides a good overview of different medical approaches used to deal with spasticity.

Strength and Endurance

Strength is not equivalent to muscle tone, although it is difficult to distinguish the two when observing a child in play. Strength is the capacity of a muscle to exert pressure against resistance (Singer, 1968). Impairments in strength may result from neuromuscular disease (e.g., muscular dystrophy), paresis, infectious disease, a metabolic disturbance, malnutrition, or general weakness (Touwen, 1979).

Endurance refers to the child's ability to maintain motor activity. Limitations in repeating an activity may result when muscles fatigue or cardiovascular endurance is diminished. The child who fatigues quickly when engaged in motor activities may have difficulty matching the pace of same-age peers. Children with a history of cardiac and/or respiratory difficulties are more likely to exhibit low endurance.

Clues to the child's strength and endurance may be obtained in play by observing his or her ability to perform repetitions of movements. A child with weakness may have age-appropriate coordination yet demonstrate deteriorating performance when repeating a skill, such as jumping forward. Weakness may also be revealed when the child tries to lift or push heavy objects. Rising from squatting to standing, carrying a bucket of water to fill the water table, and lifting a telephone book from a shelf are examples of activities that may reveal weakness. Hand weakness may be noted when the child tries to use a stapler in the office area, dough in the kitchen area, or snap-together beads in the manipulation area.

The facilitator should be cognizant of any signs of physiological distress. Skin changes (e.g., mottling, clamminess, a change in temperature or color) and breathing difficulties (e.g., shortness of breath, arrhythmical breathing, rapid shallow breathing) are a signal to the facilitator that the activities during play need to be modified.

☞   An important issue when intervening with children who demonstrate either strength or endurance problems is the need for communication with the child's physician. The therapist and teacher need to understand the child's physical limitations and be aware of any precautions that should be taken when the child is engaged in motor activities. The appropriateness of an exercise program is determined by the underlying cause of the problem. In degenerative disorders, further deterioration of motor skills occurs. The intervention team should seek information about the typical course of the disease and plan priorities accordingly.

If an undiagnosed child has symptoms of deteriorating motor skills, a prompt referral to a physician is critical. Certain types of neuromuscular disease, such as Duchenne muscular dystrophy, Rett syndrome, and spinal muscle atrophy, are genetic. An accurate and speedy diagnosis has implications not only for the child but also for the parents. Genetic counseling permits the parents to make informed family planning choices.

REACTIVITY TO SENSORY INPUT

During infancy, the typical child uses his or her senses and movements to explore the environment and discover the impact that his or her actions have on the world. One of the child's major tasks during the first 3 months of life is to learn to take in sensory information while remaining calm and organized (Greenspan & Greenspan, 1985). The body receives sensory information through a variety of receptors in the eyes, ears, skin, muscles, and joints. Sensory information is used to help shape motor responses to the environment (Scherzer & Tscharnuter, 1982; Touwen, 1976). Sensory impairments or delays may alter motor development (Touwen, 1976) and social interaction (Greenspan & Greenspan, 1985).

Early sensory regulation serves as the foundation for perceptual skills that emerge over time, such as discriminating an object's orientation (spatial relations) and attending to what is important (figure ground). The play-based assessment often provides observational suggestions that a perceptual problem is emerging. A referral for additional assessment would thus be indicated.

The Observation Guidelines identify two key questions for noting a child's responses to touch, movement, auditory, and visual input during play. For each sensory system, the team should note: 1) whether the child is responsive to input, and 2) whether the child seems to experience pleasure with the specified input.

Providing a variety of tactile materials provides opportunities to note the child's responses to self-directed touch. The team can observe whether the child seeks out shaving cream on a mirror, Play-Doh in the kitchen area, boxes of Styrofoam peanuts or shredded paper, finger paints near an easel, or feathery boas in a dress-up box. When encountering these materials, the child may derive pleasure from these play experiences or become distressed. The child with diminished touch perception may require a high level of input prior to a response. In contrast, another child may be hypersensitive to tactile input, becoming distraught and irritable (Ayres, 1979). It is also important to note the child's reaction to being touched. The facilitator can gently pat the child's shoulder from behind or stroke the child's arm or neck during the play session. Light, unanticipated touch on bare skin is more likely to elicit an adverse response than deep pressure.

Receptors in the inner ear and in the muscles, tendons, and joints supply the child with information about his or her movements and body in space. The child may be resistant to opportunities for movement activities, or continuously seek equipment that provides movement experiences. Barrels, rocking horses, swings, slides, climbing apparatus, and riding toys may all entice the child to practice movement.

A child with excessive sensitivity to movement may be startled when jostled. This child may be unwilling to attempt obstacle course items involving an unsteady surface. Being playfully lifted in the air may frighten the child. Offering to swing the child in a blanket or helping him or her to jump from a table may also elicit negative reactions.

Movement for 18-month-old Katie was pleasurable and motivating. Katie had a diagnosis of developmental delay. She was able to pull to a standing position using furniture and could walk with one hand held. During the play session, she demonstrated a strong preference for movement activities. She crawled in and out of a barrel, crawled up and over low stairs, and climbed on top of a large foam block. She pushed a weighted cart around the room and squealed with delight when the facilitator gave her a fast ride in the cart. Each time she was successful with a difficult movement activity she would sit up, laugh, and clap for herself.

The child's attentiveness and response to auditory stimuli is also important. Does the child respond to sounds? Unique responses to various sounds may be noted. *Tara demonstrated minimal responses to voices. When a musical switch-activated toy was started, however, she became distressed; she cried and sought her mother. Throughout the play session, this response was noted with louder noises.*

Chris, during his play session, appeared oblivious to all auditory input. He did not attend to voices, noisy toys, or frequent loudspeaker announcements.

Similarly, the way that the child responds to visual input is also important. Experiencing pleasure when visual input is provided is a precursor to social eye contact. The child may demonstrate a differential response to assorted types of materials, being more attentive to brightly colored or shiny objects.

Melissa, a young child with a congenital visual impairment, preferred large, brightly colored toys during the session. She was also inclined to choose toys that moved or made a sound. When the facilitator tried to shine a small flashlight on tinsel, Melissa took the light and shone it directly into her own eyes.

Observing the child's responses to a variety of sensory input has direct implications for intervention. Opportunities to experience sensory input should be provided for the child. However, the interventionist should pay close attention to the child's responses. Some children may benefit from strategies that incorporate more than one type of sensory information. For other children, it may be more desirable to limit or modify input from certain senses. Both the type and intensity of sensory activities can be varied. Recommendations may also be made to the classroom teacher regarding how to attend to the child's cues and modify sensory input during activities.

Jacob, a 5-year-old with autism, illustrates the value of observing reactivity to sensory input. For approximately the first hour of the play session, he wandered aimlessly, made little eye contact with the facilitator, and explored most toys through mouthing. He repeatedly put shaving cream in his mouth, yet did not appear to want it on his hands. Jacob finally wandered into the gross motor area, where an obstacle course had been previously set up. He ran up and down a ramp, spent some time on a rocking board, and engaged in a tickling session with the faciitator. To help him make the transition back to other types of actvities, the facilitator then began to slowly rock him on her lap. Following these more vigorous movements and tactile activities, he was observed to imitate the facilitator and permit her to come closer to him. He also engaged her in close, sustained eye contact. Recommendations were made to precede cognitive activities with movement and tactile input, whenever possible. Jacob's occupational therapist provided the teacher with information about the type and intensity of sensory input that should be used.

STATIONARY POSITIONS USED FOR PLAY

Motor skills are generally acquired in a predictable sequence. Control occurs first while lying on the abdomen (prone), then back-lying (supine), then sitting, then on hands and knees, and finally, standing. Although the sequence is fairly constant, children may master these skills at a different rate. As the child's nervous system matures, muscle control develops and the child overcomes the forces of gravity. The child must first move against gravity, such as when lifting the head in prone, then hold this new position. When the child is able to steadily hold a new position, it becomes possible to move in and out of this position (Campbell, 1989; Gilfoyle, Grady, & Moore; 1981). Specific movements that the child practices in one position are later adapted to the next position in the sequence (Gilfoyle et al., 1981).

Muscle contractions permit the development of movement against gravity, holding a position against gravity, moving within a position, and changing from one position to the next (Gilfoyle et al., 1981). In normal development, muscle activity is balanced on all sides of the joints. The ability to maintain this postural control to move between positions depends, in part, on the child's capacity to shift body weight in all directions. All movements begin with a weight shift (Bly, 1983). The balance of muscle activity around a joint enhances the development of weight shifts. Weight shifts stimulate the development of rotation that enables performance of skilled, coordinated movements. Atypical muscle tone often affects a group of muscles on only one side of a joint. Thus, balanced muscle function is not present.

Specific aspects of motor skill performance have been discussed by many researchers and clinicians (Ayres, 1973; Bly, 1983; Bobath & Bobath, 1975; Boehme, 1988; Connor et al., 1978; Erhardt, 1982; Espenschade & Eckert, 1980; Gilfoyle, Grady, & Moore, 1981; McGraw, 1966; Scherzer & Tscharnuter, 1982; Wickstrom, 1983). These sources and many others were compiled in developing the Observation Guidelines, and to provide a review of normal development for the following sections of the chapter.

Each stationary position that a child may choose in play is discussed in the next section. The team should note which positions the child can maintain alone, which positions the child can maintain with support, and which positions are impossible for the child. Observing the child in as many positions as possible provides information about the impact of motor skills on function.

The nondirective nature of TPBA permits the team to easily observe spontaneous positions. As mentioned in Chapter 5, if the child's primary area of concern is motor development, the physical or occupational therapist should be the facilitator. When the child's primary concern is not in the motor area, the motor therapist still provides ongoing input to the play facilitator. The therapist may make suggestions about how to prompt the child to move into different positions.

Alysha was able to sit alone but was wobbly and reluctant to move in and out of sitting. The motor therapist, facilitating this session, pretended to go to sleep when playing with the baby doll. Alysha imitated this behavior, permitting observation of her ability to move out of sitting. After lying on the floor, Alysha began to play on her stomach, permitting observation of motor skills in prone. Watching Alysha play in the prone position revealed that she was also having difficulty steadying her head and reaching in positions other than sitting.

Stomach-Lying (Prone)

The full-term newborn lies on his or her stomach in a curled-up position. As the infant struggles to lift the head, muscles in the back of the neck and down the spine develop. This development of extension causes the baby's body to unfold, and the baby becomes more stretched out. The baby, however, is not able to control the head well because extensor activity has not been counterbalanced by the muscles on the front of the neck and chest (flexors). By 3 to 4 months of age, the baby can hold his or her head up in midline (center of the body). The flexors are developing, balancing the activity of the extensors along the back. The baby is now able to prop on the forearms and can gaze down at the hands. By 5–6 months of age, the child can shift upper body weight onto one forearm and reach forward for a toy. Over time, extension progresses down the spine to the pelvis and hip area. The pelvis and hips flatten against the floor and the child's legs come together. By 7–8 months of age, the baby can move freely in the prone position, and variations of the position become evident.

Observations of the child's motor skills in the prone position are guided by a normal developmental sequence. The child's ability to hold the head and trunk up against gravity is essential to the development of movement skills. As the child shifts body weight in prone, he or she develops control of the neck, trunk, shoulder, and hip muscles. The baby learns to adapt the head and trunk position to keep from falling. These unconscious, automatic adjustments are the result of righting reactions. Righting reactions stimulate the head to remain in a position in which the face is vertical and the mouth is horizontal. These reactions also stimulate body parts to stay aligned with each other. Righting reactions will later stimulate the trunk to remain upright in higher positions, such as sitting and standing, and are eventually modified and incorporated into a more mature balance response (equilibrium reactions). The child must be able to automatically and consistently control the body to master functional movements, such as rolling.

A newborn begins to lift the head in an uncontrolled bobbing motion. After head lifting is possible and righting reactions have begun to develop, the team should observe the child's ability to function in prone. It is important to observe if flexion has balanced extension, permitting the child to prop on the forearms and then gaze at the hands. Later, the child is able to shift the weight onto one forearm, in order to reach forward with the other hand for a toy. The team should also be aware of whether movement in the prone position is controlled well enough to permit the child to play with a toy. Noting how widely the legs are spread and how flat the pelvis is against the floor provides information about the development of extension through the body. When the pelvis is not flat against the floor, the child will have difficulty lifting the head and chest to interact with toys.

Four-year-old Brice had meningitis as an infant, and subsequently developed motor difficulties. He was unable to sit alone, but could drag himself forward with his arms and prop on his forearms in a prone position. When he was 3 years old, Brice's intervention plan had targeted reaching in prone as an objective. He had not yet accomplished this objective. Carefully analyzing alignment in the prone position revealed the problem. Brice's pelvis was not flat against the floor, and his legs were widely spread apart. His teacher had been trying to assist reaching by guiding movement from his shoulder. With adequate positioning of the pelvis and legs, Brice began to reach in prone without a physical prompt.

☞ Children with motor problems may need a variety of intervention strategies to help them achieve their maximum potential. Specific intervention strategies are related to the nature of the motor problem. The child who has typical muscle tone and movement patterns but demonstrates delays in motor milestones may benefit from practicing the motor skills that are delayed. In contrast, if the child demonstrates atypical tone and movements, the practice of skills will not address the qualitative aspects of motor performance that may ultimately affect function. Intervention goals for the child with motor dysfunction should include altering muscle tone, preventing the use of high tone for functional motor skills, preventing the use of abnormal movements, facilitating the development of coordinated patterns of functional movement, preventing deformities, and remediating any delays in performance (Campbell, 1989).

Brice receives individual therapy. His therapist uses physical handling procedures and movements that activate the flexors, particularly the abdominals. These handling techniques also encourage normal patterns of movement. Intervention goals are accomplished by prompting weight shifts in prone, sitting, and four-point (hands and knees) positions. As Brice begins to control the movements, the hand support from his therapist will fade, permitting Brice to manage the move-ments more independently. If Brice struggles, reverting to undesirable movement strategies, the therapist reapplies her support and guidance at key points on his body. Careful attention is given to head and trunk alignment as his balance is challenged, thus facilitating righting reactions. Provid-ing Brice with the opportunity to feel normal patterns of movement increases the likelihood that he will functionally use these patterns (Bobath, 1971b). Brice's therapeutic goals are incorporated in home and classroom activities, through consultation with his family and other members of his early intervention team. Instructions regarding optimal positions and movement for daily caregiv-ing activities and play expand the opportunities for Brice to experience the sensations of normal movement.

Back-Lying (Supine)

When lying on his or her back, the newborn's head is turned to one side. Just as in the prone position, flexor control has not yet developed. By ages 3–4 months, however, the head is held in midline and is tipped so the chin rests on the chest. The hands come together at midline, first on the child's chest and, later, in space above the chest. As control of the abdominals and hip muscles improves, the baby's legs come together. By 5–6 months of age, the baby has conquered gravity. This control is evident as the baby brings the feet to the mouth and plays with the feet above the body. Improved flexor control also permits the baby to reach with one or both hands to secure a desired toy. By 7 or 8 months of age, the baby's equilibrium reactions in the supine position are present. Because of these equilibrium reactions, the baby can independently get from supine into sitting and into a hands-and-knees position.

The team's attention is directed first to the head and trunk, and then to the arms and legs. Finally, the interaction between the arms and legs is noted. The team will want to know if the child can maintain the head in midline and then turn it to both sides. Poor develop-ment of the muscles on the front side of the neck and chest may prevent the chin from tucking, and the child will have difficulty bringing the hands together over the chest and in space. Therefore, information about whether the child can bring the hands together on the chest or reach above the chest is important.

Christopher, an 8-month-old infant with Down syndrome, was motivated to move and ex-plore his environment. In the prone position, he was able to prop on forearms, and he tried to shift his weight to reach for toys. He was able to roll, but did so by arching his back and locking his elbow and knee joints. In the supine position, Christopher had difficulty moving his body against gravity, and his chin was not tucked on his chest. These limitations restricted his interactions with people and objects, and prevented hand gazing in the supine position (frogged). His legs were also widely spread, with the hips and knees bent (frogged) in the supine position, often seen in children with low muscle tone. His body sunk into the floor, and most of the time his arms lay on the floor next to his shoulders.

☞ *The qualitative aspects of Christopher's movements became targets for intervention. Inter-vention goals included activating flexor control, facilitating normal movement patterns, and im-proving righting reactions. The implementation of these goals was accomplished through a variety of positions and movements. During his early intervention program, the physical therapist showed the teacher how to use positions that would promote intentional and functional movements. For example, Christopher was positioned in a semireclining position on his back, against a wedge, and small towel squares were placed under his shoulder blades and buttocks. Sandbags were placed alongside the upper thighs to keep the legs closer together. This position was used for brief periods of time, enabling Christopher to actively engage both objects and people. He was able to reach for toys that were suspended in front of him, encouraging the coordination of reach and vision. He was able to participate in face-to-face interactions with his mother, encouraging mutual turn-taking skills necessary for language development. He was also able to actively experience a variety of textures on a flannel board placed in front of him, preparing his hands for the future development of manipulation skills.*

Sitting

The ability to sit is important from an educational standpoint. Children with severe motor limitations may need an adapted wheelchair to sit upright in the classroom. Even with adaptations, however, the child who is able to hold his or her head up will be better oriented to receive input from the environment.

An infant is frequently held by an adult in a sitting position. Although a full-term newborn can be supported in sitting, the back is rounded, lacking extension, and the head flops forward. Being supported in sitting provides the baby with an opportunity to practice using muscles that will eventually hold the body upright. By 5–6 months of age, head and trunk control have improved, and the baby can use the hands and arms to prop in a sitting position. The balance between flexion and extension, which began to develop in the prone and supine positions, continues to develop in sitting. Extensor muscles along the baby's back strengthen, and the back becomes straighter. Development of flexor muscles on the front of the body counterbalances the backward pull of the extensor muscles. By ages 7–8 months, control of opposing muscle groups on both sides of the trunk enable the baby to sit alone. The arms can now be used to play with toys. However, sitting balance is initially precarious. Protective responses develop and the baby is able to catch him- or herself with the arms when falling. Increased trunk control and balance also permit the baby to turn the upper body, while the lower body remains stationary. As control improves, the legs move closer together. By 11–12 months of age, trunk control and balance reactions are fully developed. The baby can then use a variety of sitting positions and move in and out of sitting.

First, team members need to determine whether the child sits alone, or needs to be held in sitting, and the amount of support that is needed. The child may be able to sit by propping on the arms, or sitting alone may be possible. In each of these sitting situations, the child may or may not be able to control the head or maintain a straight back. Head control is evident when the head is held up and can be turned from side to side. A rounded, low back (rather than straight) results in an awkward head and neck position and restricted shoulder movement. Vocalization, visual range, and hand use are also limited by a rounded back. The position of the legs, either widely spread or maintained more closely together, is also important. A wide base of support blocks the ability to change positions.

If the child can sit alone, it is important to observe the ability to bring the hands together in front of the body. In addition, the child's use of the arms and hands to play with toys is noteworthy. Behaviors that indicate the presence of adequate trunk control and balance reactions should be recorded, such as whether the child turns the upper body while keeping the lower body stationary. Using the arms for support when reaching out for toys restricts a child's play. Using the arms to protect against a fall to the front, both sides, and the back is an important functional skill; however, excessive use of the arms for protection also restricts movement and play. A wide base of support, excessive use of the arms for support, and increased frequency of protective responses reflect immature balance reactions. It is also important to note the child's ability to cross the center of the body when reaching.

The videotape can be used to confirm the types of sitting positions used and the frequency of each. Sitting positions that may be noted in play include: 1) long sit (both legs straight out to the front), 2) heel sit (feet tucked under the buttocks), 3) side sit (both legs bent to one side of the body), 4) tailor sit (cross-leg sitting), 5) "W" sit (buttocks resting between bent hips and knees, feet behind the body), and 6) chair sitting. Normally developing children use the "W" sit. These children, however, also use a variety of other positions. In the child with unusual muscle tone, the "W" sit may be undesirable, since it can contribute to joint problems and deformity. This position also tends to block weight shifting, thus becoming an obstacle to movement (Scherzer & Tscharnuter, 1982). Noting the older child's ability to sit in a chair will provide information that the therapist can use to assist the teacher. Sitting on the narrow base of a small chair and reaching out enables the child to participate in table activities at school.

Jacob, a 4-year-old with spastic diplegia, demonstrated age-level cognitive and language skills. His motor development, however, was significantly delayed. His primary means of moving from place to place was to creep on his hands and knees. His preferred position for play was "W" sitting. He was unable to tuck his chin in the sitting position, limiting interaction with toys on the floor below him. An attempt to turn and look at the facilitator, who was slightly behind him, was accomplished with head-turning only; he could not turn the upper body. In addition, his trunk was slumped. When reaching for a toy that was beyond arm length, he needed to place the nonreaching hand on the floor for support. His head and trunk did not remain upright when he reached to the side for a toy, demonstrating immature righting and equilibrium responses. Jacob was unable to long sit because of muscle tightness in the buttocks and legs. He had to use his arms to support himself in long sit and keep his legs pressed tightly together.

☞   *Jacob needs a program of intervention that will: 1) reduce muscle tone in his arms and legs while improving tone in his trunk, 2) encourage a balance between flexor and extensor muscles, 3) facilitate movements that will minimize the use of abnormal compensatory strategies and encourage control of the trunk and limbs, 4) facilitate mature equilibrium responses, and 5) prevent deformities (permanent muscle shortening and orthopedic changes).*

Jacob's educational program should include therapeutic support in the classroom to ensure that therapeutic goals translate into functional activities. The therapist and teacher chose more suitable positions than "W" sitting for Jacob to use in the classroom. The therapist also showed the teacher how to guide movement from the hips and shoulders to help Jacob change his sitting position. During circle time, Jacob was provided with a low bench to sit on, minimizing the amount of time spent in "W" sitting.

Hands and Knees

Some children may briefly play on their hands and knees. However, this position is most often used to move from one place to another. Therefore, a more extensive discussion on this position appears in the section on mobility.

Two questions are provided for the child who remains stationary in a hands-and-knees position to play. The first is related to the development of righting reactions. Thus, is the child able to hold the head up when playing on hands and knees? Second, can the child shift body weight to one side and reach for a toy?

Standing

The development of standing is similar to the development of sitting. The baby is first held in the standing position, then stands by holding onto a support, then stands alone without support, and finally, moves with control in standing (Campbell, 1989). When held in a standing position, with the feet touching the supporting surface, the full-term newborn is able to bear weight on the legs. As head and trunk control improve, the baby's back straightens and he or she needs less support. Between 5 and 10 months of age, the baby begins to stand by holding onto a low table. Initially, this skill is accomplished by pressing down with the arms onto the supporting surface, but dependency on the arms for support decreases with increasing trunk control. The legs are widely spread in this initial stage, with the toes turned outward. Between 9 and 13 months of age, standing alone without support is possible. A "high guard" position of the arms (arms held high at side of shoulders, with elbows bent) and widely spread legs stabilize the baby in this newly discovered position (Bobath & Bobath, 1962). The final phase in the development of standing occurs when the child begins to walk. Later, the child will get in and out of standing without using external supports.

Whether the child is able to stand with support or without support, and how much support is needed to maintain the upright position are characteristics to be observed by the team. In the standing position, the child may or may not hold his or her head and trunk upright. It is also helpful to note the position of the arms. The child will not be able to use the arms for play if they are still needed for balance. In addition, if a wide base of support is used in standing, it blocks the ability to shift weight, just as it did in sitting. Coordinated movement in a standing position is possible only after the legs have moved closer together.

☞   The presence of delayed motor skills versus atypical movement needs to be addressed to determine appropriate targets for intervention. Difficulties in standing may occur because of unusual muscle tone and an imbalance between flexor and extensor muscle groups. Intervention goals may include modifying muscle tone to support desired movement patterns, encouraging use of both sides of the body, and activating righting and equilibrium responses. These goals can be accomplished using movement in a variety of positions.

MOBILITY IN PLAY

Movements in Prone and Supine Positions

Rolling is the first strategy that a child uses to get from one place to another in the environment. The ability to roll occurs first from the stomach to the back, and then from the back to the stomach. Rolling begins as an "accident." The baby shifts his or her weight onto one forearm while propping in prone, and falls over to the side. Or, while lying on his or her back, the baby may bring the hands to the knees, and fall to his or her side (Bly, 1983). During initial rolling efforts, the baby "log rolls," with the body moving as a total unit. By 6 months of age, the baby is able to roll with control from prone to supine and supine to prone. Instead of rolling like a log, the baby's trunk rotates, or twists, during rolling.

Attempts to move forward on the stomach begin with the child's pushing and pulling efforts during arm propping. At about 7 months of age, the baby may pivot in a circle in the prone position. At about the same time, the baby is able to shift the weight onto one side of the body, moving the other side of the body forward. Forward movement on the stomach is referred to as *crawling*; forward progression on hands and knees is referred to as *creeping*.

The observer should note whether the child rolls from prone to supine and from supine to prone, and whether the body appears rigid during rolling, with the hips and shoulders staying in line with each other. In contrast, the trunk may twist so that the hips and shoulders do not move as a unit. Smooth and controlled rolling is dependent on the development of balanced flexor and extensor activity. It is important to observe whether the child's rolling pattern appears graceful and coordinated, or whether there is excessive arching of the back. The child may be able to roll toward both the left and right sides, and control the rolling movement, stopping at any point in the sequence. When the child can control the movement, he or she will be able to use more varied positions in play. The child may play in side-lying, propping up on one forearm with the top leg bent so that the foot is flat on the floor, while the bottom leg is straight. The final item for this section is to record whether the child is able to move forward in prone.

Wendy, a bright-eyed 2-year-old with spastic quadriplegia, was motivated to explore her environment. Although movement posed some difficulties, she rolled and used belly-crawling to get from one area of the play session to another. When rolling, however, her body was stiff and she arched her back. During belly-crawling, the legs became stiffer and were pressed tightly together. All of her movements were slow and laborious.

☞   Therapeutic goals again depend on the factors influencing the child's motor difficulties, such as muscle tone. Observing the child's motor performance during a variety of positions and movements helps the therapist determine how well the child is overcoming the forces of gravity.

In addition to the therapeutic intervention provided for Wendy, her mother was shown some strategies that would help Wendy feel the sensations of desired movement patterns. Wendy's mother usually picked Wendy up from the floor by grasping her underneath the shoulders and lifting her straight into the air, but this method of lifting Wendy resulted in increased stiffness throughout her body. The therapist showed Wendy's mother how to prompt a roll to the side, encouraging more active use of flexion. From this side-lying position, she then assisted Wendy into a side-sitting position. The therapist demonstrated how she could use her hands on Wendy's shoulders and pelvis to encourage the desired movements. The therapist then placed her hands on top of Wendy's mother's hands to help her guide Wendy's movements. This process was repeated until Wendy's mother felt comfortable trying the movement alone. Even when Wendy's mother does this only part of the time, it provides the experience of a normal movement sequence.

Movements in Sitting

By 11–12 months of age, improved control in floor-sitting positions permits the baby to move freely. Pivoting around in a circle and scooting on the buttocks are both sitting movements that occur in normal development (McGraw, 1966). In addition to these methods of locomotion, the child is able to get in and out of a sitting position.

The guidelines remind the team to look for pivoting in a circle and scooting on the buttocks. It is also important to note the child's ability to move in and out of sitting alone, such as moving from prone to sitting and from sitting to the prone position, or into a hands-and-knees position and back to sitting.

Movement in the Hands-and-Knees Position

The child's first attempts to assume a hands-and-knees position occur when the baby pushes straight back with the arms from a prone position. When the hands-and-knees position is initially assumed, the legs are widely separated. Early movement consists of a front to back rocking motion, which prepares the baby to control weight shifts in this position (Scherzer & Tscharnuter, 1982). Creeping occurs when the baby is able to shift weight to one side, allowing the arm and leg on the unweighted side to move forward. Increased trunk control and trunk rotation eventually enable the baby to creep with a reciprocal pattern. The arm and leg on opposite sides of the body move forward at the same time. The child learns over time to move in and out of the hands-and-knees position. The child may drop straight back between the thighs into heel or "W" sitting, or lower the buttocks into side-sitting. To move from sitting into a hands-and-knees position, the child reverses the pattern.

Noteworthy observations on the guidelines are based on the normal developmental acquisition of motor skills in the hand-and-knees position. Movements in the hands-and-knees position, such as rocking back and forth or creeping forward, provide clues about the level of control present in this position. A less mature pattern may be used, in which the arm and leg on the same side of the body move forward together, or the arm and leg on opposite sides of the body may move forward together. It is also important to note whether the child can move from hands and knees into sitting, and whether this is accomplished by dropping back between the thighs or by lowering the bottom to one side.

Matthew, an 18-month-old with spastic hemiplegia, was able to sit and creep independently. He could also get in and out of these positions. His preferred positions in floor play were heel sitting and lying on his involved side. In heel sitting, he never completely shifted his weight onto the affected side of his body, and his foot on that side remained tucked under his bottom. In addition, he did not have good control of the neck and trunk muscles on that side. When sitting, therefore, he could not keep his head up or in the center. When creeping, the legs were widely spread, he never fully shifted his weight onto the involved side, and his arms and legs did not move forward in an alternating pattern. To get in and out of sitting, he dropped his bottom down between the thighs or rose straight up onto his hands and knees.

☞   Qualitative aspects of the child's movements become the focus of intervention. To help the child reach his or her fullest potential, therapeutic goals should be incorporated into functional activities. Matthew has atypical muscle tone that is interfering with the development of more advanced movement patterns.

Matthew's therapist works on decreasing tone on his affected side and activating his trunk muscles. She also encourages more symmetrical alignment. Weight shifts onto his affected side are facilitated in sitting positions, in standing positions, and during transitions from sitting to the hands-and-knees position. Matthew is encouraged to move from the hands-and-knees position to sitting, and vice versa, in both directions (right and left). Matthew's therapist works with his mother and his early intervention teacher, providing them with strategies that will decrease the high tone on his right side and encourage him to use both hands during play. Feeding problems have been a concern for Matthew's mother. The therapist, therefore, has worked with her to determine the best positions for mealtime. Matthew's lack of trunk rotation may be the most obvious movement problem to the untrained observer. An imbalance between flexion and extension, poor weight shifting, and immature righting and balance reactions also need to be addressed in his intervention program. All aspects of Matthew's movement intervention program should be incorporated into functional skills.

Movements in Standing

Between 5 and 6 months of age, a baby being held in a standing position will begin to bounce up and down. This action is the first notable voluntary movement in standing. Between ages 6 and 12 months, the baby pulls up to standing at furniture. Movement in this new position begins as the baby repeats the bouncing action that was practiced earlier. He or she may also lift one foot, then the other, in a stomping action. The ability to pull to a standing position develops before the ability to get down from standing. An infant may pull to a stand, then cry in desperation when stuck. If not rescued, fatigue or poor balance usually cause the child to fall onto the buttocks. With improved muscular control, the child can lower him- or herself to the floor. Between 9 and 12 months of age, the baby begins to move sideways around furniture (cruising).

Many different movements may be observed in standing. For example, the child may bounce up and down when held in standing. It is important to note that children with high tone should not be encouraged to bounce in standing, since it increases muscle tone.

Nicole's father told the team that Nicole always wanted to stand and was very strong. During the parent–child portion of the play session, he held her in standing on his lap. Nicole's body and limbs stiffened, her legs pressed together and she rose up on her toes. As her father began to bounce her up and down in this position, her body became stiffer. Her face expressed distress during this activity.

The child's first independent steps may occur anytime between 9 and 18 months of age. Early attempts to walk alone are awkward. The legs are widely spread and the arms are held in a "high guard" position. Step length is short. As control improves, the arms lower to the side, the legs come closer together, and step length increases. After the arms have lowered, they begin to swing. Initially, the right arm will swing with the right leg and the left arm will swing with the left leg. Later, the arm will swing with the leg on the opposite side of the body.

An item from the guidelines to consider is the child's ability to pull up on furniture and cruise around furniture. If the child is walking alone, the position of the arms and legs provide clues about the maturity of the pattern. As walking alone is mastered, the child becomes able to freely move in and out of standing without using external supports.

Another category for observation is that of running skills. Running can be viewed as an extension of walking. This skill, however, requires more coordination and better balance. When the child begins to run, the pattern will resemble that of the early walker (Burnett & Johnson, 1971). The arms are in "high guard" and the steps are short. The "fast walk" used by the early runner becomes true running when both feet are off the floor momentarily. The arms lower and swing with the legs. The legs bend more during the action, and stride length increases. As control and coordination improve, the child will be able to change direction, run on varied surfaces, avoid obstacles in his or her path, and stop quickly. Running may be stiff and awkward or coordinated. It is important to note whether there is a moment when both feet are off the ground, as well as other specific characteristics of the child's running. It is also important to observe the kinds of surfaces that the child can run on, and whether particular surfaces seem to present a greater challenge.

Jacob, a 3-year-old with spastic diplegia, was just beginning to take a few steps alone. He was motivated to try this new skill, and seemed pleased when he was successful. Jacob's pattern of movement, however, did not resemble that of a typical early walker. He had difficulty keeping his head up, and his balance was poor. His legs were too close together, failing to provide him with a stable base of support. The arms were held in an atypical "high guard" position; the hands were tightly fisted, his elbows were excessively bent, and his shoulders were scrunched up next to his ears.

Jacob's family reported that they would like Jacob to be able to walk alone. He receives a 45-minute individual therapy session once a week, just prior to his preschool class. His therapist also spends 2 hours a week in his classroom, helping the educational team carry out program goals for Jacob and four other children with physical disabilities. Jacob's intervention plan included a goal for independent walking, since this was a priority for the family. To incorporate this goal into a functional activity, Jacob would hold onto two upright poles and walk from the bus to the classroom. Jacob held onto these head-high poles at the level of his shoulders, alternately planting each one in front of him as he progressed forward. He also used these poles to walk from the classroom to the bathroom. The therapist showed the classroom team how to properly use the poles, marking them for appropriate hand placement. She also showed the team how to hold Jacob at the hips to help him move forward.

OTHER DEVELOPMENTAL ACHIEVEMENTS

Jumping

Running is the beginning of jumping skills, as the child reaches the point when both feet are off the ground. Greater strength, however, is needed to push the body off the ground. Balance must be sufficient to adjust the body in flight and accommodate the sudden end of motion upon landing (Espenschade & Eckert, 1980). Jumping can be defined as "a motor skill in which the body is propelled into the air by a thrust from one or both legs and then lands on one or both feet" (Wickstrom, 1983, p. 65). This general description of jumping would include variations such as hopping and leaping. Jumping down from a surface, such as a bottom step, develops before the child can jump up from the ground (Wickstrom, 1983). Similarly, jumping with both feet together, progressing forward in a jump, and jumping over obstacles require increasing skill (Wickstrom, 1983). The "high guard" position of the arms, seen earlier in walking and running, recurs when the child is learning to jump. With practice, the arms lower to the sides and begin to assist the jumping effort. The child will also prepare for the jump by crouching. Hopping is a more difficult and refined form of jumping. Because the child must stand on one foot, better control of balance is required (Espenschade & Eckert, 1980).

Team members need to look at what movements demonstrate the child's ability to project the body in space, such as whether the child jumps down from a bottom step or up from the floor. In addition, looking at the position of the arms and body helps determine the maturity of the pattern. Finally, any variations of jumping that the child can perform, such as hopping, skipping, galloping, and leaping, should be noted.

Sheila was almost 3 years old at the time that the play-based evaluation was done. She and the facilitator had been interacting in the motor area for about 15 minutes. The facilitator began to model jumping, saying, "Look at me—I'm a bunny." Throughout the session, Sheila had demonstrated an ability to imitate the facilitator. She watched the facilitator jumping and began to alternately stomp her feet. She was unable to get a lift-off. The facilitator then went to the stairs and modeled jumping from the bottom step. Sheila followed, stepped onto the bottom step using the rail, and turned around. Still holding the rail, she stepped forward off the step, unable to project her body into the air.

☞   *In some cases, muscle tone and immature balance reactions affect a child's performance on motor skills. Sheila's motor delays, however, were related to a congenital heart defect. Although the heart problem had been corrected at the time of this evaluation, she had a history of multiple hospitalizations and surgeries. Following the final corrective surgery, there were no physical limitations for Sheila. She was weak, however, and her endurance was poor. Despite her motor delays, Sheila was integrated into a typical preschool setting following the play-based assessment. Her imitation skills prompted her to copy the vigorous activities of her peers. Thus, she experienced more practice with motor skills.*

In Sheila's case, communication between her physician and intervention team was essential. This communication ensured that the most appropriate placement and activities were provided for Sheila. The team needed to know the current status of Sheila's medical condition before encouraging motor activities during the play-based session. This information also helped the team to look at her strengths and needs and make appropriate placement recommendations. Follow-up to the evaluation included consultation and recommendations to the staff in her new preschool setting.

Climbing

Crawling up stairs begins at about the time a child starts to creep and pull up to a standing position. Espenschade and Eckert (1980) summarize the expected sequence for the development of stair climbing in standing:

1. Climbing up is mastered before climbing down.
2. Walking with support is possible before climbing alone.

3. Shorter flights of stairs and lower steps are possible before longer flights and higher steps.
4. Stair climbing begins by taking one step at a time (marking time by placing first one foot and then the other on the step).
5. Alternating feet, placing only one foot on each step, is possible when strength, balance, and coordination improve.

(Adapted)

If portable stairs are available, they can be placed in the gross motor area. Some children will choose to try climbing stairs on their own. Other children may be enticed by placing a desired toy at the top of the stairs. If the child does navigate the stairs, the team can note the level of the child's performance, including whether the child creeps or walks up and down the stairs, whether a rail or adult support is needed, and whether the child places both feet on each step (marking time) or alternates the feet on the steps. In addition, the length and size of steps that can be managed, and any other types of climbing skills that are demonstrated (jungle gym or ladder) should be noted.

☞ *Briana, a 2-year-old with Down syndrome, was observed creeping up the stairs. Her legs were widely spread, and she locked her elbow joints. Her mother had expressed concern that Briana would fall, since she was unable to climb back down after she reached the top. She had tried several times to crawl down head first. Briana was motivated to explore her environment, and she frequently sought the stairs at home. Because Briana's mother had expressed a concern for Briana's safety, the therapist spent some time guiding Briana down the stairs. The therapist also*

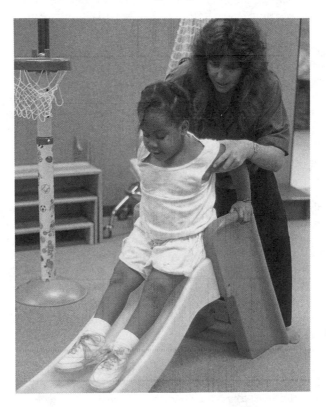

After observing how the child moves spontaneously, the facilitator may use positioning or adaptive techniques to observe the level of movement attainable with environmental support.

showed Briana's mother how to guide Briana's movements in the same way; Briana quickly learned how to get down the stairs. In this instance, the practice of a motor skill was important for the child's safety. The quality of Briana's movements was not the primary focus of concern.

Ball Skills

Throwing   The child's ability to throw a ball can be described in terms of the distance thrown, the size of the ball thrown, and the accuracy of aim during throwing. Small balls are thrown before large balls, and distance and accuracy increase with age (Espenschade & Eckert, 1980). The child may use one or both hands when throwing. A preference for overhand throwing is often seen in the early years (Wickstrom, 1983).

Throwing begins in infancy, when objects are released with a crude flinging motion (Espenschade & Eckert, 1980). Later, early efforts to throw in standing are accomplished with a lack of body movement and firmly planted feet (Wild, 1938). As the child develops, arm movements become more efficient and the trunk rotates. Finally, the feet move to assist the throwing action. Initially, the foot on the same side of the body steps forward with the throwing arm. Later, the foot on the opposite side of the throwing arm steps forward, increasing the force of the throwing action (Wild, 1938).

Catching   Catching develops after throwing. A successful catch depends on a number of factors, including: 1) the size of the ball, 2) how the ball is thrown, 3) how far the ball has traveled, 4) the speed of the ball, 5) the catcher's arm and body movements, and 6) the child's perception of time and space.

A baby sitting on the floor is able to grab or trap a rolling ball. In standing, the child learns to chase, stop, and control a rolling ball. At about 2 years of age, the child will chase a ball that has bounced off his or her chest. Later, the child holds the arms straight out in front of the body and traps the ball against the chest. Eventually, the child catches the ball with the hands only. In a mature catching pattern, the position of the feet is adjusted, improving success.

Kicking   The child as young as 18 months of age may be able to kick a ball forward while standing. This is accomplished by walking or running into the ball. Kicking with a swinging leg requires shifting body weight onto one leg. Since balance reactions are not fully developed in the young child, he or she cannot swing the leg for a true kick while standing. As the child develops, kicking becomes more efficient. The body becomes involved in the movement, and the kicking leg bends more.

Balls of various sizes should be provided in the play session. Most children seem to enjoy playing with balls, and can easily be prompted to play a ball game. These games can be useful to look at throwing, catching, and kicking skills. Turn-taking and interaction skills, important for language and social development, can also be observed.

Questions on the guidelines are divided into throwing, catching, and kicking. For each skill, it is important to note the size of the ball used in addition to the other characteristics listed in the guidelines. The use of the hands, arms, and feet provides clues about the maturity of the child's ball skills.

☞   Success with ball skills depends on a variety of factors. Poor balance reactions, atypical muscle tone, poor visual responses, and poor body awareness are examples of underlying difficulties that may hamper the development of ball skills. For some children, these underlying difficulties need to be addressed to improve these skills. For other children, experience may improve these skills.

Five-year-old Stacey did not enjoy playing catch. As the ball approached, she demonstrated a strong visual startle, flinched, and closed her eyes while turning away from the ball. Before the ball reached her, she placed her hands in front of her face to protect herself. The facilitator noticed

Stacey's anxiety and started rolling the ball on the floor. When Stacey realized the ball was not going to hit her in the face, she began to participate in the game; after a couple of trials, she was able to follow and entrap the ball as it came toward her.

Modifying ball games is a strategy that can be used during intervention. Starting by rolling the ball is less threatening to the young child. The child can experience success without fear of the ball hitting him or her in the face. In addition, visually tracking a rolling ball is easier than tracking an airborne ball. The activity can be expanded after the child can maintain visual regard of a rolling ball. The interventionist may then want to try tossing a large, soft ball to the child from a short distance (one foot).

PREHENSION AND MANIPULATION

Prehension refers to the position of the hand when holding an object without changing contact with the object (Kamakura, Matsuo, Ischi, Mitsuboshi, & Miura, 1980). More generally, prehension is often used to describe reach, grasp, and release skills. In the typical child, prehension is fully developed by 15 months of age (Erhardt, 1982). Manipulation is more global, including prehension and the child's ability to handle objects after they have been seized. Thus, the term *manipulative prehension* is used (Gilfoyle et al., 1981). Coordination and a variety of new fine motor skills continue to develop throughout life. A child's unique style of demonstrating fine motor skills also affects mature hand function. Primitive reflexes, visual skills, tactile exploration, and posture and movement strategies all contribute to the development of fine motor skills (Field, 1977; Gilfoyle et al., 1981; Twitchell, 1965; White, Castle, & Held, 1964).

Muscle Tone and Strength

Adequate muscle tone is just as essential to coordinated fine motor behaviors as it is to coordinated total body movements. Muscle tone permits the muscles to remain ready to contract. This readiness state contributes to smooth and coordinated manipulation skills. Retained primitive reflexes that interfere with gross motor skills may also interfere with fine motor skills. A retained grasp reflex, for example, prevents the child from separating the fingers during manipulation tasks. Adequate strength in the arm and hand muscles permits the child to play with resistive toys.

Each time the child plays with objects, the team should look at how muscle tone and/or strength may be affecting fine motor skills. The guidelines provide examples of some behaviors that may indicate atypical muscle function. Because fine motor tasks require greater precision, they may be more stressful to the child. Atypical muscle tone, therefore, may be revealed during fine motor tasks even though it was not apparent during gross motor tasks. Associated reactions may be present in the child with high tone (Bobath, 1971a). These reactions result in an increase in tone in parts of the body that are not involved in the activity, such as the opposite arm getting stiff while one hand plays with a toy.

Jamie, a 5-year-old with a diagnosis of developmental delay, provides an example of associated reactions. In the office area of the playroom, she was trying to cut out a shape with scissors. Each time she tried to cut, the holding hand would tear the paper. When the cutting hand began to open and close on the scissors, flexor tone in the holding hand and arm increased. The more frustrated Jamie became, the tighter the holding hand gripped the paper.

The child who demonstrates excessive tongue movements, a protruding tongue, increased drooling, an open mouth, or tightly pursed lips when concentrating may also have atypical muscle tone. Noting the general posture of the hands, open or closed, also provides clues about muscle tone.

In addition, the child's ability to play with resistive toys (e.g., pop beads), lift heavy objects, and perform resistive adaptive activities (e.g., pulling off tube socks or zipping a zipper) provide information about the child's strength, and should be noted. Fatigue with repetition of a fine motor activity provides clues about muscular endurance.

Head and Trunk Control during Prehension and Manipulation

Classic studies of motor development suggested that control of the trunk and shoulders (proximal control) is present before hand skills (distal control). More recent research has demonstrated that distal control may not be dependent upon proximal control (Loria, 1980). The child who lacks the stable base that results from proximal control, however, will not be as free to reach out into the environment.

Righting and equilibrium responses enable the child to remain upright while playing with objects. If these automatic reactions are immature, the child will experience difficulty staying erect and reaching away from the body. Thus, it is important to note whether the child is able to keep his or her head and trunk upright when playing with objects, and whether the child uses his or her arms for support when reaching for toys.

A drooping head and trunk during fine motor activities may be an indication that the activity is stressful for the child. The interventionist may want to modify the activity so that the child is more successful. If the child has low tone, an activity that builds tone may help to prepare the child. Changing the amount of body support may also improve performance during fine motor activities. Sitting behind a child on the floor, moving the child from a chair to the floor or moving from the floor to a chair, or providing a different type of chair are examples of changing support. Finally, the activity itself may need to be modified for a child who has difficulty holding the head and trunk erect during manipulation.

Reaching Skills

Reaching begins when the baby plays on his or her stomach and back. Random, swiping movements activate muscles and increase range of motion in the arms. Control of elbow and wrist motions develops before voluntary forearm rotation (supination and pronation). Forearm rotation begins to develop when the baby shifts weight while propping on forearms in prone (Boehme, 1988). This ability to supinate and pronate the forearm is later used to adjust the orientation of the hand when reaching. Thus, the hand adjusts to the vertical or horizontal direction of an object. In addition, visual skills are closely linked to accurate reaching. Before the child actually reaches for an object, he or she visually pays attention to the object. The child may then begin to alternate his or her gaze between the hand and the object. Eventually, the child will attend to an object, and directly reach for the object while maintaining visual attention. When reaching becomes fully coordinated with vision, the child will be able to look at the object, then look away while accurately reaching.

Reaching skills may be noted in a variety of positions, including prone, supine, sitting, and standing. For infants who are still playing on their stomach or back, it may be helpful to hang toys from a batting bar or suspend an exciting mobile. If the child can be supported in sitting, placing toys on a low bench may improve visual attention to objects and encourage reaching. In addition, placing toys on different sides of the child will permit the team to look at a broader range of reaching skills.

Accuracy of the child's reach provides clues about shoulder control. The team can watch for over-reaching, reaching the target directly, or using a wide, sweeping motion to seize an object. Visual skills are also important to note when observing the child's ability to reach for objects; the child may look before reaching, watch the hand or the object while reaching, or look away while contacting the object. In addition, the team should observe whether the child is able to direct the hand and arm so that they are oriented to an object's position. Accommodating the hand to an object's size and position is closely linked to motor control and visual awareness of an object's features. Adjusting the hand requires adequate forearm rotation and the ability to modulate hand opening prior to reaching.

Grasping Skills

The development of grasp is characterized by a shift from crude raking to fine control of the index finger and thumb (Landreth, 1958). Visual regard of objects and tactile input to the hands both play an important role in the development of prehension (Gilfoyle et al., 1981). In the prone position, the baby begins to "scratch" the surface when the palmar grasp reflex decreases. This scratching provides tactile input to the hands and activates the muscles of the hands. Later, the child is able to "rake" a small object into the palm. Attempts to rake objects into the hand are followed by crude clutching. The baby seizes an object by trapping it between the fingers and the palm. Refinement of prehension occurs when parts of the hands begin to perform separate functions (Rosenbloom & Horton, 1971). The thumb becomes more active, objects move away from the palm toward the fingertips, and the fingers can be isolated. The type of grasp and the number of objects that can be held depend on the size of the child's hand and the individual features of the object (McGraw, 1966).

Historically, researchers and clinicians have used a variety of terminology to describe grasping patterns (Erhardt, 1982; Halverson, 1931; Rosenbloom & Horton, 1971; Touwen, 1971). Use of terminology to describe grasp and pinch patterns is inconsistent, even among occupational therapists (Smith & Benge, 1985). The team should adopt a standard set of terms that provide consistency between therapists and across multiple evaluations of the same child. Erhardt (1982) provides drawings and descriptors of common prehension terminology.

In the Observation Guidelines, grasping patterns are described by the actions of the hand and fingers, such as whether the total hand or fist is being used, whether the thumb is involved, and the specific actions of the fingers. The development of pinch, or a pincer grasp, indicates the development of more mature prehension. As this pattern matures, thumb control improves. The thumb may trap an object against the side of the index finger, the pads of the thumb and index finger may come in contact, or the very tips of the index finger and thumb may come in contact. It is also important to note the types and number of objects that a child can grasp.

Daryl, a 4-year-old with spastic quadriplegia, was able to crudely grasp an object in his fist. The thumb was not involved in his grasp, and he could not isolate a finger to poke or point. He was also unable to orient his hand to an object's direction. Picking up small objects, such as Cheerios, was impossible for Daryl. Daryl's cognitive skills were much higher than his motor skills. Thus, he frequently became frustrated in play because he could not participate with his peers in a dramatic play sequence.

☞ Children need to experience success when they play. If the development of grasping skills is not compatible with the child's cognitive skills, then toys may be adapted to improve success. Technology has provided a multitude of adaptations that permit young children with motor difficulties to play. Computers and switch-activated toys enable children with severe motor challenges to experience success. The child's occupational therapist may adapt commercial toys and adaptive tools by creating a handle, or building up an existing handle with modeling materials. Terry-cloth mitts and Velcro can also be used to help a child hold a toy. Musselwhite (1986) describes a variety of play adaptations for the child with physical disabilities (see Linder, 1993).

When the teacher and physical or occupational therapist work closely together, many classroom activities can be modified for the child with motor limitations. *Daryl, described above, was ready to discriminate and identify a variety of shapes. His teacher wanted him to try a complex shape sorter. He could not hold the sorter in one hand, however, while placing the pieces with the other hand. He was also unable to orient the pieces correctly if someone else held the sorter. The occupational therapist suggested that a cookie sheet filled with flattened clay be substituted for the sorter. The teacher pressed the shapes into the clay for Daryl. The cookie sheet was placed on a tray in front of Daryl. Using a crude grasp, he could approximate the location of the shape. Thus, Daryl was able to discriminate and match shapes successfully.* This is only one example of how a toy can be adapted for a child.

Releasing Skills

Purposeful grasp of an object develops before purposeful release. A baby begins to experience release when playing with the hands together in front of the body and then letting go. Release of an object occurs first with assistance, and later with control in space. When the baby begins to mouth objects, the mouth provides the assistance for release. Transfers from hand to hand are initially accomplished with assistance from the receiving hand. As the object is transferred, there is a period of time when both hands are holding the object and the taking hand assists the release by pulling. As control improves, the holding hand will release as the taking hand comes in contact with the object. Similarly, release onto a surface or into a container initially requires assistance. The child releases by pressing the object down onto the surface, or by resting the wrist on the edge of the container. Mature release occurs when the child can smoothly release in the space above a surface or container.

During play, the maturity of the child's release is noted by three different observations, including whether: 1) the child is able to release by transferring objects from one hand to the other (it is important to note the child's ability to perform this transfer in both directions), 2) the child needs to support the arm on a surface or press down with an object, and 3) the child is able to smoothly release objects in free space. The child with poor control of release may fling an object, exaggerate finger opening, or pull an object out of the hand. These compensations restrict the child's ability to place objects where he or she wants them.

Bilateral Development

A baby initially reaches for and grasps objects with both hands together. As development continues, the child alternates between using both hands together and preferring one hand or the other (Espenschade & Eckert, 1980; Gesell & Ames, 1947; Gilfoyle et al., 1981). The normal alternating preference for one hand and then the other is important to consider when assessing a young child (Belmont & Birch, 1963). By the age of 5, the child will begin to use one hand predominantly (DeGangi, Berk, & Larsen, 1980; Scherzer & Tscharnuter, 1982; Tan, 1985). Even when dominance is well established, the nondominant hand should be readily used to assist the dominant hand. In addition, strong dominance prior to 15 months of age may indicate impairment in the hand that is not being used (Erhardt, 1982). "Handedness" is normally affected by cultural factors. Some tasks, such as writing and self-feeding, lend themselves to using a preferred hand (Espenschade & Eckert, 1980).

Bringing both hands together is necessary for the two hands to interact with each other, and should be noted as part of midline development. Another skill that contributes to midline development is the child's ability to reach across the front of the body to get a toy on the other side. Play is usually restricted when the child manipulates toys on the left side with the left hand and toys on the right side with the right hand. Some of the guidelines questions examine the development of dominance. It is important to note whether there is no difference between the two hands versus a strong preference for one hand. And if a preference exists, it is important to note whether the nonpreferred hand is also readily used. Toys that encourage two-handed manipulation will help the team look at the interaction between the two hands. A jack-in-the-box or See-n-Say, for example, require the child to stabilize the toy with one hand while manipulating with the other. Drawing or writing also requires the child to hold the paper with one hand while using a tool in the other.

Shelley, a 9-month-old, was evaluated using transdisciplinary play-based assessment. A variety of age-appropriate cognitive skills were observed. For example, she was able to find a toy that was put in a cup, then hidden under a bucket. Mouthing objects had been replaced by banging on objects. However, she was not able to throw objects, and she did not bang two objects together spontaneously. The therapist noticed that Shelley's left arm appeared tense, and that she was unable to put her full weight on her left arm when crawling. Following the assessment, the team met together to discuss their observations. The teacher thought that Shelley had some possible cognitive delays. As the team discussed their findings, however, they realized that most of Shelley's limitations in cognitive skills involved a higher level of motor control than was needed for her successful cognitive skills. Shelley was unable to use both sides of the body together and demonstrated poor object release.

☞ Atypical muscle tone, poor trunk responses, poor body awareness, and retained primitive reflexes are examples of factors that may affect bilateral development. These underlying factors need to be addressed in intervention for the young child. *Identification of Shelley's motor difficulties in play prompted a referral to a neurologist. Shelley had mild hemiplegia that had not been diagnosed prior to this session. Once Shelley was diagnosed, her intervention goals were clarified.*

Manipulative Prehension

Variety of movement in the hands is necessary for higher-level manipulation skills. Sufficient muscle development and adequate range of motion contribute to fine motor control. The ability to separate the fingers and to move the fingers in different directions permits the child to expand object use. Boehme (1988) describes three manipulation patterns. When the fingers and thumb move in an opposite direction, the child becomes capable of managing more difficult object manipulations, such as turning the mechanism on a wind-up toy. Reorienting small objects within the hand, such as a puzzle piece, requires the child to sequence movements within one hand, and tasks such as cutting with scissors require the child to hold an object in one part of the hand while moving another part of the hand.

During normal development, there is maximum involvement of the body when the young child is learning to control a tool for writing. Control eventually progresses down the arm, until isolated movements of the hand and fingers are achieved (Boehme, 1988; Landreth, 1958; Rosenbloom & Horton, 1971). Mature handwriting illustrates complex manipulation skills. First the tool is picked up, then reoriented in the hand to obtain an adequate grasp. When the child is actually writing, the little-finger side of the hand rests on the paper while the thumb side of the hand moves the tool (Rosenbloom & Horton, 1971).

When a child is learning to color within a confined space, he or she initially uses all vertical strokes. Later, the child adapts to coloring by turning the body or the paper. The child then begins to use horizontal strokes in coloring. Finally, the child combines strokes in all directions to accomplish the task (Komich, 1987).

Drawing skills are closely linked with conceptual development (Kaufman & Kaufman, 1977). Chapter 6 discusses the representational aspects of drawing.

Toys that provide opportunities for a variety of hand movements should be provided during the session. Poker chips, for example, can be provided in the dramatic play area as pretend money, allowing the team to observe the way the child holds and repositions the chips. In addition, observations of coloring skills may be possible if the child chooses to play in an office or art area. A child who seems uninterested will often follow the facilitator's lead if these skills are modeled. When coloring or writing, the team should note the child's control of his or her body and the tool, such as the presence of total body movement. Improving control would be indicated by less movement in the joints closer to the body. Other examples of higher-level tool use may be demonstrated, such as using scissors, turning the key on a shape sorter, unscrewing a jar lid in the kitchen area, and turning the knob on a wind-up toy.

When a child experiences difficulty with manipulative activities, a variety of intervention strategies may be used to resolve the difficulty. The child may need to be prepared for the activity by altering muscle tone, inhibiting high tone, or building low tone. Weight-bearing activities may be indicated to improve shoulder stability, develop range in the arms, or encourage development of the muscles in the hands. With an older child, a large easel or blackboard may help develop shoulder control. Drawing in a thin layer of clay, using a larger tool, or using an adapted tool may improve handwriting skills. Splints or inhibitive casts may be used as an adjunct to therapy, maximizing the child's function. Modification of materials or activities may enable the child to experience success with fine motor tasks.

Cognitive, perceptual, and fine motor skills are closely linked. It is important to determine which of these abilities presents the greatest challenge for the child.

Four-year-old Carla, for example, identified colors by pointing. She was unable to hold a crayon, however, and could not color a picture with her peers. She grasped and released objects in a clumsy manner. The therapist and the teacher developed an art activity for Carla. A piece of paper was covered with a layer of glue. She was able to pick up precut squares of tissue paper and drop them onto the piece of paper. With this adapted activity, Carla could choose and identify colors. She was able to visually experience blends of color when different pieces of tissue paper fell on top of each other. At the end of the activity, the teacher wrote the title of Carla's picture on her drawing, enabling Carla to represent something with her drawing. Carla also had a set of rubber alphabet stamps. She would grasp the "c" and stamp her "name" on her picture. With these modifications, Carla could participate with her peers when they colored a picture. She was also able to work on age-appropriate cognitive and perceptual concepts, even though her motor skills were significantly delayed.

MOTOR PLANNING

Conscious attention is required when learning a new task. With practice, familiar motor skills become automatic. When first learning to manipulate scissors, for example, the child watches the hands and the scissor blades closely. The child must concentrate on each snip. In contrast, an adult seamstress cuts along a pattern edge automatically, and her thoughts may shift to how she is going to sew the seam she is cutting at the moment. Controlling the scissors no longer requires motor planning. Motor planning (praxis) is the ability to plan and carry out purposeful, coordinated movements (Paget & Bracken, 1983). Ayres (1979) describes motor planning as the "bridge" between the intellect and the muscles. "The brain tells the muscles what to do, but the sensations from the body enable the brain to do the telling" (Ayres, 1979, p. 94). Meaning is attached to sensory input and the child uses this information to carry out fine and gross motor acts (Weeks & Ewer-Jones, 1983).

Motor planning problems can affect muscles in the arms, legs, lips, and tongue. As a result, motor skills may be awkward and delayed. The child may demonstrate difficulty with adaptive tasks, and frustration tolerance may be low. Motor planning problems may exist in the presence of normal muscle tone and age-appropriate cognitive abilities. Tasks requiring a sequence of movements are particularly difficult for the child with poor motor planning. In normal daily life, many motor acts are carried out simultaneously. When a person lifts a telephone receiver with one hand, for example, the other hand may begin dialing. The caller may also be rising from a chair, or slipping shoes off at the same time. If the caller had a motor planning problem, each of these steps would demand undivided concentration. TPBA may identify the child whose interactions with toys are immature and inefficient.

The child's awareness of his or her own body and how it relates to surrounding objects is closely linked to motor planning. Efficient motor functioning requires an accurate awareness of the position of body parts in space, and the movement capabilities of these parts. The child must also have an accurate sense of an object's orientation in space. As he or she picks up a tool, such as a screwdriver, touch receptors in the palm relay a message to the brain. The brain then directs the muscles in the wrist and fingers to orient the tool in the hand. However, the child with a motor planning problem may be unable to orient the tool in the hand or on the screw. Excessive visual monitoring of the hands allows some success, but the action may be slow and/or conducted with errors.

When a child demonstrates motor delays and there is no evidence of neurological or cognitive deficits, praxis should be considered. The first item on the guidelines looks at the child's ability to imitate movements. The child with motor planning problems may not be able to perform a task spontaneously, but can imitate a demonstration. Activities for this item could include gross and fine motor tasks, and imitation of gestures. When the child moves to the obstacle course, the team can note the child's ability to move the body through space, moving up, on, through, around, under, and into the gross motor equipment. An inability to change direction during movement and excessive visual monitoring of motor tasks may indicate poor body awareness.

The final item on the guidelines looks at the child's ability to sequence movements to accomplish a goal. *Three-year-old Paige had a diagnosis of development delay. Muscle tone was normal, and primitive reflexes were well integrated. She demonstrated delays in functional fine and gross motor skills, yet cognitive, language, and social skills were age-appropriate. She had great difficulty sequencing motor skills into multiple step actions. She had normal fine motor coordination, but could not seem to figure out how to accomplish new tasks. In the art area, for example, she could not make a paper chain with a stapler. She had the neat pincer grasp needed to hold the paper. Her grasp and strength were adequate to use a stapler. She was able to staple and fold, but could not seem to put the actions together to make the chain. Attempts to create this project required intense concentration. Her actions were slow and her verbalizations ceased as she struggled with the project.*

Dressing and undressing may also provide an opportunity to look at praxis. Dressing requires a higher level of motor planning than undressing. Motor planning during dressing can be observed by noting the child's ability to sequence the task.

Ayres (1979) suggested that the child with a motor planning problem has poorly developed tactile and body awareness. A sensory approach to intervention, therefore, is often indicated for this child. Materials are provided for the child to self-direct sensory experiences. Observations of the type of sensory input the child strongly prefers will help the team select appropriate materials. For example, opportunities can be provided in the classroom for the child to experience movement and deep pressure. During the early childhood years, the child learns how to manage gravity. Motor challenges permit the child to test how far he or she can go without getting hurt. The child has an inner drive and motivation to master motor skills. Intervention is not limited to providing more stimulation. The child needs to actively participate in sensory and movement experiences and respond adaptively.

SUMMARY

Sensorimotor Observation Worksheets are provided to record observations. These worksheets follow the format of the guidelines, and are offered only as a suggestion. The section on stationary play positions and mobility in play appear one below the other. During play, observations of mobility in a particular position usually occur simultaneously with observations of the static position.

In summary, a framework has been provided for assessing both qualitative and quantitative aspects of sensorimotor development. Observations during play enable the therapist to plan a functional intervention program for the young child. Sensorimotor development blends with cognitive, language, and social development. Consideration of all developmental areas, therefore, is essential to assess strengths and needs effectively and determine their priority.

REFERENCES

Ayres, A.J. (1973). *Sensory integration and learning disorders.* Los Angeles: Western Psychological Services.

Ayres, A.J. (1979). *Sensory integration and the child.* Los Angeles: Western Psychological Services.

Belmont, L., & Birch, H.G. (1963). Lateral dominance and right–left awareness in normal children. *Child Development, 34,* 257–270.

Bly, L. (1983). *The components of normal movement during the first year of life and abnormal motor development.* Oak Park, Illinois: The Neuro-Developmental Treatment Association (P.O. Box 70, Oak Park, Illinois 60303).

Bobath, B. (1971a). *Abnormal postural reflex activity caused by brain lesions* (2nd ed.). London: William Heinemann Medical Books Limited.

Bobath, B. (1971b). Motor development, its effect on general development, and application to the treatment of cerebral palsy. *Physiotherapy, 57,* 526–532.

Bobath, B., & Bobath, K. (1962). An analysis of the development of standing and walking patterns in patients with cerebral palsy. *Physiotherapy, 48,* 144–153.

Bobath, B., & Bobath, K. (1975). *Motor development in the different types of cerebral palsy.* London: William Heinemann Medical Books.

Bobath, K., & Bobath, B. (1972). Diagnosis and assessment of cerebral palsy. In P.H. Pearson & C.E. Williams (Eds.), *Physical therapy services in the developmental disabilities* (pp. 31–185). Springfield, IL: Charles C Thomas.

Boehme, R. (1988). *Improving upper body control: An approach to assessment and treatment of tonal dysfunction.* Tucson, AZ: Therapy Skill Builders, a division of Communication Skill Builders.

Burnett, C.N., & Johnson, E.W. (1971). Development of gait in childhood: Part II. *Developmental Medicine and Child Neurology, 13,* 207–215.

Campbell, P.H. (1989). Posture and movement. In C. Tingey (Ed.), *Implementing early intervention* (pp. 189–208). Baltimore: Paul H. Brookes Publishing Co.

Chandler, L. (1979). Gross and fine motor development. In M.A. Cohen & P.J. Gross (Eds.), *The developmental resource: Behavioral sequences for assessment & program planning* (Vol. 1) (pp. 119–153). New York: Grune & Stratton.

Connolly, K. (1975). Movement, action and skill. In K.S. Holt (Ed.), *Movement and child development* (pp. 102–110). *Clinics in Developmental Medicine, #55.* Philadelphia, PA: J.B. Lippincott.

Connor, F.P., Williamson, G.G., & Siepp, J.M. (Eds.). (1978). *Program guide for infants and toddlers with neuromotor and other developmental disabilities.* New York: Teachers College Press.

Degangi, G.A., Berk, R.A., & Larsen, L.A. (1980). The measurement of vestibular-based function in pre-school children. *American Journal of Occupational Therapy, 34,* 452–459.

Erhardt, R.P. (1982). *Developmental hand dysfunction: Theory, assessment, treatment.* Laurel, MD: Ramsco.

Espenschade, A.S., & Eckert, H.M. (1980). *Motor development* (2nd ed.). Columbus, OH: Charles E. Merrill.

Field, J. (1977). Coordination of vision and prehension in young infants. *Child Development, 48,* 97–103.

Finnie, N.R. (1975). *Handling the young cerebral palsied child at home* (2nd ed.). New York: E.P. Dutton.

Folio, M.R., & Fewell, R.R. (1983). *Peabody Developmental Motor Scales and Activity Cards.* Allen, TX: DLM Teaching Resources.

Furono, S., O'Reilly, K., Hosaka, C., Zeisloft, B., & Allman, T. (1984). *Hawaii Early Learning Profile.* Palo Alto, CA: VORT.

Gesell, A., & Ames, L.B. (1947). The development of handedness. *Journal of Genetic Psychology, 70,* 155–175.

Gilfoyle, E.M., Grady, A.P., & Moore, J.C. (1981). *Children adapt.* Thorofare, NJ: Charles B. Slack.

Greenspan, S., & Greenspan, N.T. (1985). *First feelings.* New York: Viking Penguin.

Halverson, H.M. (1931). An experimental study of prehension in infants by means of systematic cinema records. *Genetic Psychological Monographs, 10,* 107–286.

Hanson, M.J., & Harris, S.R. (1986). *Teaching the young child with motor delays: A guide for parents and professionals.* Austin, Texas: PRO-ED.

Hellebrandt, F.A., Rarick, G.L., Glassow, R., & Carns, M.L. (1961). Physiological analysis of basic motor skills: I. Growth and development of jumping. *American Journal of Physical Medicine, 40,* 14–25.

Ingram, T.T.S. (1966). Spasticity in cerebral palsy. *Clinical Orthopedics, 46,* 23–26.

Kamakura, N., Matsuo, M., Ischi, H., Mitsuboshi, F., & Miura, Y. (1980). Patterns of static prehension in normal hands. *American Journal of Occupational Therapy, 34,* 437–445.

Katz, R.T. (1988). Management of spasticity. *American Journal of Physical Medicine and Rehabilitation, 67(3),* 108–116.

Kaufman, A.S., & Kaufman, N.L. (1977). *Clinical evaluation of young children with the McCarthy scales.* New York: Grune & Stratton.

Komich, P. (1987, February). *Fine motor and perceptual foundations for handwriting.* Lecture presented for Sensorimotor Development Course at the University of Denver, Denver, CO.

Landreth, C. (1958). *The psychology of early childhood.* New York: Alfred A. Knopf.

Loria, C. (1980). Relationship of proximal and distal function in motor development. *Physical Therapy, 60(2),* 167–172.

McGraw, M.B., (1966). *The neuromuscular maturation of the human infant.* New York: Hafner.

Morris, S.E. (1987). Therapy for the child with cerebral palsy: Interacting frameworks. *Seminars in Speech and Language, 8(1),* 71–86.

Musselwhite, C.R. (1986). *Adaptive play for special needs children: Strategies to enhance communication and learning.* San Diego, CA: College-Hill Press.

Newborg, J., Stock, J.R., Wnek, L., Guidibaldi, J., & Svinicki, J. (1984). *Battelle Developmental Inventory.* Allen, TX: DLM Teaching Resources.

Paget, K.D., & Bracken, B.A. (Eds.). (1983). *The psychoeducational assessment of preschool children.* New York: Grune & Stratton.

Piaget, J. (1954). *Origins of intelligence.* New York: Basic Books.

Rosenbloom, L., & Horton, M.E. (1971). The maturation of fine prehension in young children. *Developmental Medicine and Child Neurology, 13,* 3–8.

Scherzer, A.L., & Tscharnuter, I. (1982). *Early diagnosis and therapy in cerebral palsy: A primer on infant developmental problems.* New York: Marcel Dekker.

Singer, R.N. (1968). *Motor learning and human performance: An application to physical education skills.* London: The Macmillan Company.

Smith, R.O., & Benge, M.W. (1985). Pinch and grasp strength: Standardization of terminology. *American Journal of Occupational Therapy, 39,* 531–535.

Tan, L.E. (1985). Laterality and motor skills in four-year-olds. *Child Development, 56,* 119–124.

Touwen, B.C.L. (1971). A study on the development of some motor phenomena in infancy. *Developmental Medicine and Child Neurology, 13,* 435–446.

Touwen, B. (1976). *Neurological development in infancy. Clinics in Developmental Medicine,* #58. Philadelphia, PA: J.B. Lippincott.

Touwen, B.C.L. (1979). *Examination of the child with minor neurological dysfunction* (2nd ed.). *Clinics in Developmental Medicine, #*71, Philadelphia, PA: J.B. Lippincott.

Twitchell, T.E. (1965). The automatic grasping responses of infants. *Neuropsychologia, 3,* 247–259.

Weeks, Z.R., & Ewer-Jones, B. (1983). Assessment of perceptual-motor and fine motor functioning. In K.D. Paget & B.A. Bracken (Eds.), *The psychoeducational assessment of preschool children* (pp. 261–294). New York: Grune & Stratton.

White, B.L., Castle, P., & Held, R. (1964). Observations on the development of visually directed reaching. *Child Development, 25,* 349–364.

Wickstrom, R.L. (1983). *Fundamental motor patterns* (3rd ed.). Philadelphia: Lea & Febiger.

Wild, M.R. (1938). The behavior pattern of throwing and some observations concerning its course of development in children. *Research Quarterly, 9*(3), 20–24.

9

Observation Guidelines for Sensorimotor Development

I. General Appearance of Movement
  A. Physical appearance
    1. Is there anything unusual about the child's body?
    2. When plotted on a chart, are the child's height and weight appropriate for age?
  B. Motor activity
    1. Is the child able to get from one play area to another alone?
    2. What is the child's primary means of moving during play (crawling, walking, running, etc.)?
    3. Does the child appear to move more often or less than other children?
    4. What positions does the child choose for play?
    5. How often does the child use each position for play?
    6. Are there any motor skills that the child seems to avoid?
II. Muscle Tone/Strength/Endurance
  A. Features of normal muscle tone
    1. Do body parts on the right and left side look and move the same?
    2. Does the child assume a wide variety of positions?
    3. Does the child look coordinated when moving from one position to another?
  B. Common features of unusual muscle tone
    1. What behaviors indicate the presence of low tone?
      a. Does the child have difficulty holding the head up?
      b. Is the child's posture slumped?
      c. Is there a wide base of support?
      d. Is there a tendency to lock joints?
      e. Is there a tendency to lean against supports?
      f. Is there a tendency to "W" sit?
    2. What behaviors indicate the presence of high tone?
      a. When the child moves, does the body get stiffer?
      b. At rest, do the arms or legs appear to be stiff?
      c. Is there fisting in one or both hands?
      d. Does the child stand or walk on the toes?
      e. Does the child have balance problems?
    3. What behaviors suggest the presence of fluctuating tone?
    4. Can any pattern of unusual tone be detected?
      a. Does one side of the body appear to be stiffer than the other?
      b. Do the legs appear to be stiffer than the arms?

C.   Strength and endurance
1.   Does the child get tired if a motor activity is performed over and over?
2.   Are there indicators of decreased cardiovascular function?
a.   Skin changes?
b.   Blue lips and fingernails?
c.   Breathing difficulty?

III.   Reactivity to Sensory Input
A.   Touch
1.   Does the child respond to tactile stimuli?
2.   Does the child seem to have a pleasurable reaction to tactile input?
B.   Movement
1.   Does the child respond to movement?
2.   Does the child seem to have a pleasurable reaction to movement?
C.   Auditory
1.   Does the child respond to auditory stimuli?
2.   Does the child seem to have a pleasurable reaction to auditory stimuli?
D.   Visual
1.   Does the child respond to visual stimuli?
2.   Does the child seem to have a pleasurable reaction to visual stimuli?

IV.   Stationary Positions Used for Play
A.   Prone (lying on the abdomen)
1.   Is the child able to raise the head in prone?
2.   Can the child prop on the forearms?
3.   Can the child bring the hands together and look at them while propped on the forearms?
4.   Can the child reach for a toy and play with it while lying on the stomach?
5.   Are the legs widely spread apart or close together?
B.   Supine (lying on the back)
1.   Can the child maintain the head in midline and turn it to both sides?
2.   Does the child bring the hands together on the chest?
3.   Does the child reach above the chest for objects? (with one or both hands?)
4.   Are the legs together or apart?
5.   Can the child play with the feet (e.g., put the hands on the knees, play with the feet, bring the feet to the mouth)?
C.   Sitting
1.   Does the child need to be held in sitting?
2.   How much support does the child need when held in sitting?
3.   Is the child able to hold the head up?
4.   Is the child able to freely turn the head? (to both sides, up and down?)
5.   Is the back rounded or straight?
6.   Is the child able to sit by propping on the arms?
7.   Does the child sit independently without support?
8.   Can the child bring the hands together in front of the body?
9.   Can the child use the arms and hands to play with toys in sitting?
10.   Does the child turn the upper body to reach for or watch objects, keeping the lower body stationary?
11.   Is the child able to cross the center of the body with the arms when reaching for a toy?

12. Does the child use the arms to catch him- or herself when falling (forward, sideways, backward)?
13. Are the legs spread widely apart or maintained more closely together?
14. How many different sitting positions are used?
15. When sitting in a chair, does the child's body droop forward?
16. Does the child's bottom slide forward in a chair?

D. Hands and knees
1. Can the child hold the head up when playing on hands and knees?
2. Can the child reach for a toy while on hands and knees?

E. Standing
1. Does the child need to be held to stand?
2. How much support is needed when held in standing?
3. Can the child hold the head up in standing?
4. Does the child stand alone at a low table or support, steadying by leaning against the table?
5. Can the child stand without support, and for how long?
6. How far apart are the legs when standing?
7. Are the arms in "high guard"?
8. Do both sides of the body appear to function equally well?

V. Mobility in Play
A. Movements in prone and supine
1. In stomach-lying, can the child roll onto the side or over to the back?
2. In back-lying, can the child roll onto the side or over to the stomach?
3. Does the body appear rigid during rolling ("log roll")?
4. Does the trunk twist during rolling, so that the hips and shoulders do not move as a unit?
5. Does the child's body arch backward during rolling?
6. Does the child roll toward both the left and right?
7. Can the child control rolling, stopping at any point in the sequence?
8. Is the child able to move forward while lying on the stomach?

B. Movements in sitting
1. Does the child pivot in a circle in sitting?
2. Does the child scoot on his or her bottom in sitting?
3. Does the child move in and out of sitting alone?
   a. From stomach to sitting and sitting to stomach?
   b. From sitting to hands and knees and vice versa?
   c. To both sides (to the right and to the left)?

C. Movements in the hands-and-knees position
1. Does the child rock back and forth while on hands and knees?
2. Does the child move forward while on hands and knees?
3. How mature is the child's creeping pattern?
   a. Do the arm and leg on the same side of the body move forward simultaneously?
   b. Do the arm and leg on the opposite side of the body move forward simultaneously?
4. How does the child move from hands and knees to sitting?
   a. Does the bottom drop straight back, between the thighs?
   b. Does the bottom drop to one side, into side-sitting?

    c. Does the child move in both directions (to the right and to the left)?

   5. Can the child rise from hands and knees up into kneeling?

 D. Movements in standing

   1. Does the child bounce up and down when held in standing?

   2. Is the child able to pull up to standing by holding onto furniture?

   3. When pulling up, do both legs push together or does the child plant one foot and come up through half-kneel?

   4. Can the child walk sideways while holding onto furniture?

   5. Does the child demonstrate the ability to walk without support?

    a. Are the arms in "high guard" or down by the child's side?

    b. How far apart are the legs?

   6. Is the child able to rise to standing from the floor, without the use of furniture? (Does the child need to place the hands on the floor for support when rising to standing?)

   7. Can the child squat in play?

   8. Is the child able to lower to the floor from standing?

   9. Is the child able to run?

    a. Is there a moment when both feet are off the ground?

    b. Are the arms in "high guard"?

    c. Does running appear stiff and awkward, or coordinated?

    d. Can the child stop quickly, avoid obstacles, and change directions?

    e. Can the child run on varied surfaces (grass, gravel, tile)?

VI. Other Developmental Achievements

 A. Jumping

   1. What movements demonstrate the child's ability to project the body in space?

    a. Does the child jump down from a bottom step?

    b. Does the child jump up from the floor?

    c. Are the arms in "high guard" during jumping?

    d. Does the child crouch in preparation for jumping?

   2. What variations of jumping are observed (hopping, skipping, galloping, leaping)?

 B. Climbing

   1. What method does the child use to climb stairs?

    a. Does he or she creep on hands and knees or hands and feet?

    b. If upright, is a rail or adult support needed?

    c. Does the child place both feet on each step (marking time) or alternate feet?

   2. What size and length of stairs can the child manage?

   3. What other types of climbing are demonstrated (onto a foam block, up a ladder, on a jungle gym)?

 C. Ball skills

   1. Throwing

    a. What size balls is the child able to throw?

    b. Do the feet remain firmly planted?

    c. Does the foot on the same side of the body as the throwing arm step forward as the ball is thrown?

    d. Does the foot on the opposite side of the body step forward as the ball is thrown?

   2. Catching

    a. What size balls is the child able to catch?

          b.   Can the child trap a ball that has been rolled to him or her?

          c.   From a straight elbow position, do the elbows bend and trap the ball against the chest?

          d.   Can the child catch the ball with the hands, without making contact with other parts of the body?

          e.   Does the child change the placement of the feet in preparation for the catch?

     3.   Kicking

          a.   Does the child walk into the ball in an attempt to kick it?

          b.   Does the kicking leg actually swing in preparation for and follow through on the kick?

VII.   Prehension and Manipulation

    A.   Muscle tone and strength

       1.   Muscle tone

          a.   Does the opposite arm get stiff while one hand plays with a toy?

          b.   Does the tongue move or come out of the mouth when the child is concentrating?

          c.   Is the mouth open or closed when the child is concentrating?

          d.   Are the hands generally open or closed?

       2.   Strength

          a.   What is the child's ability to lift heavy objects?

          b.   Is the child able to pull apart and push together resistive toys?

          c.   Is the child able to pull up a zipper or pull off tube socks?

          d.   Does the child demonstrate fatigue with increasing repetitions of the same activity?

    B.   Head and trunk control during prehension and manipulation

       1.   Is the child able to keep the head and trunk upright when playing with objects?

       2.   Does the child use the arms for support when reaching?

    C.   Reaching skills

       1.   Accuracy of reach

          a.   Does the child over-reach?

          b.   Does the child go directly to the target, or use wide, sweeping motions or corralling of the object?

       2.   Visual guidance of reach

          a.   Does the child look before reaching?

          b.   Does he or she watch the hand or the object while reaching?

          c.   Does he or she look away while contacting the object?

       3.   Is the child able to position the hand and arm, accommodating them to an object's orientation?

    D.   Grasping skills

       1.   Is the total hand or fist being used?

       2.   Is the thumb involved?

       3.   What are the actions of the fingers?

          a.   Do all the fingers move as a unit?

          b.   Is the child able to point or poke with one finger?

       4.   What is the grasping action of the thumb and index?

          a.   Mostly at the side of the index

          b.   Pads of the index and thumb contact

          c.   Very tips of the index and thumb contact

      5. Is the child able to grasp more than one object at a time?

E. Releasing skills
1. Is the child able to release objects by transferring them from one hand to the other (left to right and right to left)?
2. In order to release with one hand alone, does the child need to support the arm on a surface or press down with the object?
3. Is the child able to smoothly release objects in free space?

F. Bilateral development
1. Is the child able to bring both hands together in front of the body?
2. Can the child reach across the front of the body to get a toy on the other side?
3. Is there a preference for one hand?
    a. No difference?
    b. Strong dominance?
4. If there is a preference, is the nonpreferred hand also readily used (i.e., to stabilize a toy)?

G. Manipulative prehension
1. When holding an object in one hand, is the child able to reposition it within the hand?
2. What is the quality of the child's motor control when coloring?
3. Does the child attempt to color within a confined space?
4. What other examples of higher-level tool use are demonstrated (scissors, turning key on a shape sorter, unscrewing lids)?

VIII. Motor Planning
1. What behaviors are demonstrated that indicate the child's awareness of the body in space?
    a. Can the child perform a motor task following modelling or a demonstration?
    b. Can the child move the body up, on, through, around, under, and into the gross motor equipment?
    c. Can the child change directions in movement?
    d. Is there excessive visual monitoring of movements?
2. What motor activities indicate the child's ability to sequence movements?

9

Age Ranges

Development in Prone

0–2 mo.	Head turns side to side Head lifts momentarily Hips bent with bottom in air
3–4 mo.	Lifts head and sustains in midline Rotates head freely when up Able to bear weight on forearms Able to tuck chin and gaze at hands in forearm prop Attempts to shift weight on forearms, resulting in shoulder collapse
5–6 mo.	Weight shift on forearms and forward reach Weight bearing and weight shifting on extended arms Legs closer together and thighs roll inward toward natural alignment Hips flat on surface Equilibrium reactions present
5–8 mo.	Airplane posturing in prone; chest and thighs lift off surface
7–8 mo.	Increased variety of positions

Adapted from Bly, 1983; Chandler, 1979; Scherzer & Tscharnuter, 1982.

Development in Supine

0–3 mo.	Head held to one side Able to turn head side to side
3–4 mo.	Head held in midline Chin tucked, neck lengthens in back Legs come together Lower back flat against the floor
4–5 mo.	Head lag gone when pulled to sit Hands together in space
5–6 mo.	Lifts head independently Feet to mouth Hands to feet Able to reach for toy with one or both hands Hands predominantly open
7–8 mo.	Equilibrium reactions present

Adapted from Bly, 1983; Chandler, 1979.

Development in Sitting

0–3 mo. (held in sitting)	Head bobs in sitting Back rounded Hips apart, turned out and bent
3–4 mo. (held in sitting)	Head steady Chin tucks, able to gaze at floor Sits with less support Hips bent, shoulders in front of hips
5–6 mo. (supports self in sitting)	Sits alone momentarily Increased extension in back Sits by propping forward on arms Wide base, legs bent Periodic use of "high guard" position Protective responses present when falling to the front
5–10 mo. (sits alone)	Sits alone steadily, initially with wide base of support Able to play with toys in sitting
7–8 mo.	Equilibrium reactions present Able to rotate upper body while lower body remains stationary Protective responses present when falling to the side
8–10 mo.	Sits well without support Legs closer, full upright position, knees straight Increased variety of sitting positions, including "W" sit and side-sit Difficult fine motor tasks may prompt return to wide base of support
10–12 mo.	Protective extension backward, first with bent elbows then straight elbows
11–12 mo.	Trunk control and equilibrium responses fully developed in sitting Further increase in variety of positions possible
18–19 mo.	Seats self in small chair

Adapted from Bly, 1983; Chandler, 1979; Gilfoyle, Grady, & Moore, 1981; Scherzer & Tscharnuter, 1982.

Development in Standing

0–3 mo.	When held in standing, takes some weight on legs
2–3 mo.	When held in standing, legs may give way
3–4 mo.	Bears some weight on legs, must be held proximally Head up in midline, no chin tuck Pelvis and hips behind shoulders Legs apart and turned outward
5–6 mo.	Increased capability to bear weight Decreased support needed, may be held by arms or hands Legs still spread apart and turned outward
5–10 mo.	Stands holding on
9–13 mo.	Stands alone momentarily

Adapted from Bly, 1983; Chandler, 1979.

Mobility in Prone and Supine

3–4 mo.	Rolls prone to side accidentally, due to poor control of weight shift Rolls supine to side

(continued)

Mobility in Prone and Supine   *(continued)*

5–6 mo.	Rolls prone to supine
	Rolls supine to side with right and left leg performing independent movements
	Rolls supine to prone with right and left leg performing independent movements
6–14 mo.	Rolls segmentally with roll initiated by head, shoulder, or hips
7–8 mo.	Pivots in prone
	Crawls forward on belly
	Moves from prone to sit
	Begins to dislike supine and rolls to another position

Adapted from Bly, 1983; Chandler, 1979; Connor, Williamson, & Siepp, 1978; Scherzer & Tscharnuter, 1982.

Mobility in Sitting

6–11 mo.	Gets to sitting from prone
11–12 mo.	Able to move in and out of sitting into other positions
9–18 mo.	Rises from supine by first rolling over to stomach then pushing up into four-point
11–24 mo. +	Rises from supine by first rolling to side then pushing up into sitting
18–19 mo.	Seats self in small chair
5–6 yr.	Some children able to come straight up to sit from supine

Adapted from Bly, 1983; Chandler, 1979; Gilfoyle, Grady, & Moore, 1981; Scherzer & Tscharnuter, 1982.

Mobility in Hands and Knees

7–10 mo.	Reciprocal creep
10–11 mo.	Creeps on hands and feet
11–12 mo.	Creeps well

Adapted from Bly, 1983; Furono, O'Reilly, Hosaka, Zeisloft, & Allman, 1984; Scherzer & Tscharnuter, 1982.

Mobility in Standing

5–6 mo.	Bounces in standing
6–12 mo.	Pulls to stand at furniture
8 mo.	Cruises sideways
	Rotates the trunk over the lower extremities
8–9 mo.	Lower extremities more active in pull to stand
	Pulls to stand through kneeling, then half-kneel
8–18 mo.	Walks with two hands held
9–10 mo.	Cruises around furniture, turning slightly in intended direction
9–13 mo.	Pulls to stand with legs only, no longer needs arms
11 mo.	Walks with one hand held
	Reaches for furniture out of reach in cruising
	Cruises in either direction, no hesitation
9–17 mo.	Takes independent steps, falls easily
10–14 mo.	Walking—stoops and recovers in play
12 mo.	Equilibrium reactions present in standing

(continued)

Mobility in Standing   *(continued)*

15 mo.	Able to start and stop in walking
18 mo.	Seldom falls Runs stiffly, eyes on ground
21 mo.	Squats to play
2–2½ yr.	Runs, whole foot contact; stops and starts
3–4 yr.	Runs around obstacles, turns corners
3½–5 yr.	Walks with a heel-to-toe pattern

Adapted from Bly, 1983; Chandler, 1979.

Jumping

17–21 mo.	Jumps down from step
17 mo.–2½+ yr.	Jumps off floor with both feet
19 mo.–2½+ yr.	Jumps from bottom step
2–5 yr.	Jumps over objects
2½+ yr.	Hops on one foot, few steps
3–5 yr.	Hops on one foot
3–4 yr.	Skips on one foot
5–6 yr.	Gallops, leading with one foot and transferring weight smoothly and evenly
6 yr.	Hops in straight line
6–7 yr.	Skips on alternating feet, maintaining balance

Adapted from Chandler, 1979; Folio & Fewell, 1983; Hellebrandt, Rarick, Glassow, & Carns, 1961.

Development of Climbing

15 mo.	Creeps up stairs
12–23 mo.	Walks up stairs, holding on
13–23 mo.	Walks down stairs, holding on
18 mo.	Climbs into adult chair
18–23 mo.	Creeps backward down stairs
21 mo.	Climbs down from adult chair
2–2½ yr.	Climbs up and down furniture independently
18 mo.–2½+ yr.	Walks up stairs without support, marking time
19 mo.–2½+ yr.	Walks down stairs without support, marking time
23 mo.–3 yr.	Walks up stairs, alternating feet
2½+ yr.	Walks down stairs, alternating feet
2½–3 yr.	Climbs easy nursery apparatus
4–5 yr.	Climbs ladder

Adapted from Chandler, 1979.

Development of Ball Skills

2–5 mo.	Visually tracks ball
9 mo.	Retains or releases without reference to the examiner
9–16 mo.	Plays ball
9–18 mo.	Definite fling of ball
15–18 mo.	Walks into large ball to push it forward
15 mo.–2½ yr.	Throws ball overhead
20–24 mo.	Kicks ball forward
2–2½ yr.	Throws ball in standing without falling
30–35 mo.	Catches ball from straight arm position, trapping ball against chest
3–4 yr.	Catches ball with elbows bent in front of body Throws ball using shoulder and elbow
3–5 yr.	Throws, guiding the course of the ball with the fingers
54–59 mo.	Catches ball with elbows at sides
60–71 mo.	Bounces and catches tennis ball

Adapted from Chandler, 1979; Folio & Fewell, 1983; Scherzer & Tscharnuter, 1982.

Development of Reaching Skills

0–2 mo.	Visual regard of objects
1–3 mo.	Swipes at objects
1–4½ mo.	Alternating glance from hand to object
1–5 mo.	Alternating gaze from one hand to the other
2–6 mo.	Inspects own hands Reaches for, but may not contact object
3½–4½ mo.	Visually directed reaching
3½–6 mo.	Hands oriented to object Rapid reach for object without contact
3½–12 mo.	Circuitous reach, out to side Straight approach in reach
4 mo.	Shoulders come down to natural level Hands together in space Sitting: bilateral backhand approach with wrist turned so thumb is down
5 mo.	Prone: bilateral approach, hands sliding forward Two-handed corraling of object
5–6 mo.	Elbow in front of shoulder joint Developing isolated voluntary control of forearm rotation
6 mo.	Prone: reaches with one hand while weight bearing on other forearm Elbow extended, wrist straight, midway between supination and pronation
7 mo.	Prone: reaches with one hand while weight bearing on other extended arm
7½ mo.	Trunk adapts in reaching by leaning
7–8 mo.	Experiments with forearm rotation by stabilizing against rib cage
8–9 mo.	Unilateral direct approach, reach and grasp single continuous movement
9 mo.	Controls supination with upper arm in any position, if trunk stable
10 mo.	Wrist extended, appropriate finger extension
11–12 mo.	Voluntary supination, upper arm in any position

Adapted from Boehme, 1988; Chandler, 1979; Erhardt, 1982; Espenschade & Eckert, 1980; Gilfoyle, Grady, & Moore, 1981.

Development of Grasp

0–3 mo.	Hands predominantly closed
2–7 mo.	Object is clutched between little and ring fingers and palm
3–3½ mo.	Hands clasped together often
3–7 mo.	Able to hold a small object in each hand
4 mo.	Hands partly open
4–4½ mo.	Hands open in anticipation of contact
4–6 mo.	Hands predominantly open
4–8 mo.	Partial thumb opposition on a cube Attempts to secure minute objects
4–8 mo.	Picks up cube with ease
5–9 mo.	Raking or scooping minute object
6–7 mo.	Object held in palm by fingers and opposed thumb (radial palmar grasp)
6–10 mo.	Picks up minute object with several fingers and thumb
7–12 mo.	Precisely picks up minute object
8 mo.	Minute object held between side of index and thumb (lateral scissors)
8–9 mo.	Object held with opposed thumb and fingertips, space visible between palm and object
9–10 mo.	Small object held between thumb and index, first near middle of index (inferior pincer), later between pads of thumb and index with thumb opposed (pincer)
10 mo.	Pokes with index
12 mo.	Small object held between thumb and index, near tips, thumbs opposed (fine pincer)
12–18 mo.	Crayon held in fist with thumb up
2–3 years	Crayon held with fingers, hand on top of tool, forearm turned so thumb is directed downward (digital pronate)
3½–4 years	Pencil held with mature grasp, but no isolated movements within the hand (static tripod)
4½–6 years	Mature grasp on pencil, fine localized movements present in the hand (dynamic tripod)

Adapted from Chandler, 1979; Erhardt, 1982; Gilfoyle, Grady, & Moore, 1981.

Development of Release

0–1 mo.	No release, grasp reflex strong
1–4 mo.	Involuntary release
4 mo.	Mutual fingering in midline
4–8 mo.	Transfers object hand to hand
5–6 mo.	Two stage transfer, taking hand grasps before releasing hand lets go
6–7 mo.	One stage transfer, taking hand and releasing hand perform actions simultaneously
7–9 mo.	Volitional release
7–10 mo.	Presses down on surface to release
8 mo.	Release above a surface with wrist flexion
9–10 mo.	Release into a container, wrist straight
10–14 mo.	Clumsy release into small container, hand rests on edge of container
12–15 mo.	Precise controlled release into small container, wrist extended

Adapted from Chandler, 1979; Erhardt, 1982.

Development of Manipulative Prehension

18–25 mo.	Separates pop beads
	Snips paper with scissors
18–41 mo.	Strings 3–4 beads
22–30 mo.	Folds paper in half
24–29 mo.	Uses forearm rotation to turn door knob
24–35 mo.	Unbuttons large buttons
28–35 mo.	Snips on line using scissors
30–35 mo.	Cuts paper in half with scissors
30–47 mo.	Buttons one or two buttons alone
36–47 mo.	Holds paper with one hand while writing with the other hand
36–59 mo.	Uses scissors to cut paper on a line
42–47 mo.	Cuts circle with scissors
48–59 mo.	Places paper clips on paper
	Opens small padlock with key
60–71 mo.	Colors within lines

Adapted from Folio & Fewell, 1983; Furono et al., 1984; Newborg, Stock, Wnek, Guidibaldi, & Svinicki, 1984.

Sensorimotor Observation Worksheet

Name of child: _____ Date of birth: _____ Age: _____

Name of observer: _____ Discipline or job title: _____ Date of assessment: _____

On the following pages, note specific behaviors that document the child's abilities in the sensorimotor categories. Qualitative comments should also be made. The format provided here follows that of the Observation Guidelines for Sensorimotor Development in **Transdisciplinary Play-Based Assessment.** *It may be helpful to refer to the guidelines while completing this form.*

I. General Appearance of Movement

  A. Physical appearance
    1. Unusual features:

    2. Height and weight appropriate? *(yes or no)*
  B. Motor activity
    1. Independent transition to new area? *(yes or no)*
    2. Primary means of movement:

    3. Amount of movement compared to others:

    4. Play positions:

    5. Frequency of each position:

    6. Avoided motor skills:

II. Muscle Tone/Strength/Endurance

  A. Features of normal muscle tone
    1. Parallel appearance and movement? *(yes or no)*
    2. Variety of positions? *(yes or no)*
    3. Coordinated when changing position? *(yes or no)*
  B. Common factors of unusual muscle tone
    1. Description of behaviors indicating low tone:

      a. Difficulty holding head up? *(yes or no)*
      b. Slumped posture? *(yes or no)*
      c. Wide base of support? *(yes or no)*
      d. Tendency to lock joints? *(yes or no)*
      e. Tendency to lean against supports? *(yes or no)*
      f. Tendency to "W" sit? *(yes or no)*

(continued)

2. Description of behaviors indicating high tone:

    a. Movement accompanied by stiffening? *(yes or no)*

    b. Stiff arms or legs at rest? *(yes or no)*

    c. Fisting in one or both hands? *(yes or no)*

    d. Standing or walking on toes? *(yes or no)*

    e. Balance problems? *(yes or no)*

3. Behaviors suggesting fluctuating tone:

4. Pattern of unusual tone:

    a. Stiffens on one side? *(yes or no)*   Which side?

    b. Legs stiffer than arms? *(yes or no)*

C. Strength and endurance

1. Tiredness caused by repeated motor activity? *(yes or no)*

2. Decreased cardiovascular function?

    a. Skin changes? *(yes or no)*

    b. Blue lips or fingernails? *(yes or no)*

    c. Breathing difficulty? *(yes or no)*

III. Reactivity to Sensory Input

A. Touch

1. Response to tactile stimuli? *(yes or no)*

2. Pleasurable reaction to tactile input? *(yes or no)*

Examples:

B. Movement

1. Response to movement? *(yes or no)*

2. Pleasurable reaction to movement? *(yes or no)*

Examples:

C. Auditory

1. Response to auditory stimuli? *(yes or no)*

2. Pleasurable reaction to auditory stimuli? *(yes or no)*

Examples:

D. Visual

1. Response to visual stimuli? *(yes or no)*

2. Pleasurable reaction to visual stimuli? *(yes or no)*

Examples:

(continued)

Sensorimotor Observation Worksheet

Name of child: _____   Date of birth: _____   Age: _____

Name of observer: _____   Discipline or job title: _____   Date of assessment: _____

IV.   Stationary Positions Used for Play

A.   Prone

1. Raise head? *(yes or no)*
2. Prop on forearms? *(yes or no)*
3. Bring the hands together and look at them while propped on forearms? *(yes or no)*
4. Reach for a toy and play with it? *(yes or no)*
5. Legs widely spread or close together?

Examples:

B.   Supine

1. Maintain head in midline and turn it to both sides? *(yes or no)*
2. Bring hands together on chest? *(yes or no)*
3. Reach above chest for objects? *(yes or no)*
4. Legs together or apart?
5. Play with the feet? *(yes or no)*

Examples:

C.   Sitting

1. Need to be held in sitting? *(yes or no)*
2. Amount of support needed while sitting:

3. Hold up head? *(yes or no)*
4. Freely turn the head? *(yes or no)*
5. Back rounded or straight?
6. Sit by propping on arms? *(yes or no)*
7. Sit independently without support? *(yes or no)*
8. Bring hands together in front of body? *(yes or no)*
9. Use arms and hands to play with toys in sitting? *(yes or no)*
10. Turn the upper body while keeping the lower body stationary? *(yes or no)*
11. Cross center of body with arms? *(yes or no)*
12. Use arms to catch self when falling? *(yes or no)*
13. Legs spread widely or close together?

14. Sitting positions used:

15. Does body droop in chair? *(yes or no)*
16. Slide forward in a chair? *(yes or no)*

Examples:

(continued)

    D. Hands and knees

        1. Hold head up while on hands and knees? *(yes or no)*

        2. Reach while on hands and knees? *(yes or no)*

        Examples:

    E. Standing

        1. Need to be held to stand? *(yes or no)*

        2. Support needed in standing? *(yes or no)*

        3. Hold the head up in standing? *(yes or no)*

        4. Stand alone at low support? *(yes or no)*

        5. Stand without support? *(yes or no)*   For how long?

        6. Distance between legs when standing:

        7. Arms in "high guard"? *(yes or no)*

        8. Both sides function equally? *(yes or no)*

        Examples:

V. Mobility in Play

    A. In prone and supine

        1. Roll onto side and over onto back in stomach-lying? *(yes or no)*

        2. Roll onto side and over onto stomach in back-lying? *(yes or no)*

        3. Rigid during rolling? *(yes or no)*

        4. Trunk twist during rolling? *(yes or no)*

        5. Body arch backwards during rolling? *(yes or no)*

        6. Roll left and right? *(yes or no)*

        7. Control of rolling? *(yes or no)*

        8. Move forward on the stomach? *(yes or no)*

        Examples:

    B. In sitting

        1. Pivot in a circle in sitting? *(yes or no)*

        2. Scoot in sitting? *(yes or no)*

        3. Move in and out of sitting position alone? *(yes or no)*

           a. Stomach to sitting and sitting to stomach? *(yes or no)*

           b. Sitting into hands and knees and vice versa? *(yes or no)*

           c. To both sides? *(yes or no)*

        Examples:

    C. In hands-and-knees positions

        1. Rocking on hands and knees? *(yes or no)*

        2. Move forward on hands and knees? *(yes or no)*

(continued)

Name of child: _____ Date of birth: _____ Age: _____

Name of observer: _____ Discipline or job title: _____ Date of assessment: _____

3. Maturity of creeping pattern

   a. Simultaneous movement of arm and leg on same side? *(yes or no)*

   b. Simultaneous movement of arm and leg on opposite side? *(yes or no)*

4. Move from hands and knees to sitting *(circle those that apply)*:

   a. Bottom drop straight back, between thighs? *(yes or no)*

   b. Bottom drop to one side, side-sitting? *(yes or no)*

   c. Move in both directions? *(yes or no)*

5. Rise from hands and knees to kneeling? *(yes or no)*

Examples:

D. In standing

1. Bounce when held in standing? *(yes or no)*

2. Pull into standing while holding onto furniture? *(yes or no)*

3. Legs push together when pulling up? *(yes or no)*

4. Walk sideways while holding onto furniture? *(yes or no)*

5. Walk without support? *(yes or no)*

   a. Arms in "high guard" or by sides?

   b. Distance between legs?

6. Rise to standing from floor without the use of furniture? *(yes or no)*

7. Squat in play? *(yes or no)*

8. Lower to the floor from standing? *(yes or no)*

9. Run? *(yes or no)*

   a. Both feet ever off the ground? *(yes or no)*

   b. Arms in "high guard"? *(yes or no)*

   c. Running stiff and awkward, or coordinated?

   d. Stop quickly, avoid obstacles, and change directions? *(yes or no)*

   e. Run on varied surfaces? *(yes or no)*

Examples:

VI. Other Developmental Achievements

A. Jumping

1. Project body in space

   a. Jump from a bottom step? *(yes or no)*

   b. Jump from floor? *(yes or no)*

   c. Arms in "high guard" during jumping? *(yes or no)*

   d. Crouch in preparation for jumping? *(yes or no)*

   Examples:

(continued)

2. Description of jumping variations:

B. Climbing
   1. Method of climbing stairs
      a. Creep on hands and knees or hands and feet?

      b. Rail or adult support needed? *(yes or no)*
      c. Both feet on each step, or alternate feet?
      Examples:

   2. Size and length of stairs child manages:

   3. Other types of climbing:

C. Ball skills
   1. Throwing
      a. Size of balls able to throw:

      b. Feet firmly planted? *(yes or no)*
      c. Does the foot on the same side as the throwing arm step forward as ball is thrown? *(yes or no)*
      d. Does the foot on the opposite side of body step forward as ball is thrown? *(yes or no)*

      Examples:

   2. Catching
      a. Size of balls child is able to catch:

      b. Trap a ball rolled to him or her? *(yes or no)*
      c. Elbows bend and trap ball against the chest from a straight-elbow position? *(yes or no)*
      d. Catch ball with hands? *(yes or no)*
      e. Change placement of feet to catch? *(yes or no)*

      Examples:

   3. Kicking
      a. Walk into ball? *(yes or no)*
      b. Kicking leg swing to kick? *(yes or no)*
   Examples:

VII. Prehension and Manipulation

A. Muscle tone and strength
   1. Muscle tone
      a. Opposite arm stiff while one hand plays with toy? *(yes or no)*

      b. Tongue moves or comes out of the mouth when concentrating? *(yes or no)*

      c. Mouth open or closed when concentrating? *(yes or no)*

      d. Hands generally open or closed?

      Examples:

(continued)

Name of child: _____   Date of birth: _____   Age: _____

Name of observer: _____   Discipline or job title: _____   Date of assessment: _____

  2. Strength
     a. Ability to lift heavy objects:

     b. Pull apart and push together resistive toys? *(yes or no)*
     c. Pull up zipper or pull off tube socks? *(yes or no)*
     d. Fatigue with increasing repetitions of same activity? *(yes or no)*
     Examples:

B. Head and trunk control during prehension and manipulation
     1. Keep head and trunk upright when playing with objects? *(yes or no)*
     2. Use arms for support when reaching? *(yes or no)*
     Examples:

C. Reaching skills
     1. Accuracy of reach
        a. Over-reach? *(yes or no)*
        b. Go directly to target or use wide, sweeping motions?

     2. Visual guidance of reach
        a. Look before reaching? *(yes or no)*
        b. Watch hand or object while reaching? *(yes or no)*
        c. Look away while contacting the object? *(yes or no)*

     3. Position hand and arm to accommodate object's orientation? *(yes or no)*
     Examples:

D. Grasping skills
     1. Total hand or fist? *(yes or no)*
     2. Thumb involved? *(yes or no)*
     3. Actions of fingers
        a. All fingers move as unit? *(yes or no)*
        b. Point or poke with one finger? *(yes or no)*
     4. Grasping action of thumb and index *(circle one)*:
        a. Mostly at side of index
        b. Pads of index and thumb contact
        c. Very tips of index and thumb contact
     5. Grasp more than one object at a time? *(yes or no)*
     Examples:

E. Releasing skills
     1. Release objects by transferring them? *(yes or no)*
     2. Need support arm on a surface or press down with object to release with one hand alone? *(yes or no)*
     3. Smoothly release objects in free space? *(yes or no)*
     Examples:

(continued)

F. Bilateral development
1. Bring both hands together in front of body? *(yes or no)*
2. Reach across front of body? *(yes or no)*
3. Preference for one hand? *(yes or no)*
   a. No difference? *(yes or no)*
   b. Strong dominance? *(yes or no)*
4. Nonpreferred hand readily used? *(yes or no)*
Examples:

G. Manipulative prehension
1. Reposition object in hand? *(yes or no)*
2. Quality of motor control when coloring?
3. Attempt to color in a confined space? *(yes or no)*
4. Higher-level tool use:

Examples:

VIII. Motor Planning

A. Behaviors indicating awareness of body in space
1. Perform motor task following modeling or demonstration? *(yes or no)*
2. Move body up, on, through, around, under, and into gross motor equipment? *(yes or no)*
3. Change directions in movement? *(yes or no)*
4. Excessive visual monitoring of movements? *(yes or no)*
Examples:
B. Description of motor activities indicating child's ability to sequence movements:

Additional Comments

Summary Sheet for Sensorimotor Guidelines

Name of child: _____

Name of observer: _____

Date of birth: _____

Discipline or job title: _____

Age: _____

Date: _____

Observation categories	Areas of strength	Rating	Justification	Things I'm ready for
I. General appearance of movement				
II. Muscle tone/ strength/endurance				
III. Reactivity to sensory input				
IV. Stationary play positions				

SAMPLE

Summary Sheet for Sensorimotor Guidelines

Name of child: _____

Name of observer: _____

Date of birth: _____

Discipline or job title: _____

Age: _____

Date: _____

Observation categories	Areas of strength	Rating	Justification	Things I'm ready for
V. Mobility in play				
VI. Other developmental achievements				
VII. Prehension and manipulation				
VIII. Motor planning				

SAMPLE

269

IV

TPBA and Families

Involving parents in all aspects of the assessment process can help the team to clarify the child's role within the family.

10

Rachel's TPBA

Rachel's TPBA play session takes place in a playroom in the Center. A house area with kitchen and bedroom props is in one corner. A sand-and-water table with cause-and-effect toys and manipulatives is on one side. A table with puzzles, lock boxes, and art supplies, and a block area with miniature dolls, trucks, and a dollhouse are on another side of the room.

Rachel M., who is now 28 months old, has been enrolled in the infant program at the Center for the past 8 months. Her father (Michael M.) was asked to accompany Rachel for a play-based assessment to re-evaluate the appropriateness of her placement. The play session is being conducted in the room where Rachel attends a program with her father twice a week.

Prior to the play session, a pre-assessment planning meeting was held. At this session, the parent inventory that was completed by Mr. M. was reviewed. Rachel's father indicated that Rachel could draw shapes and faces, had a basic knowledge of letters and numbers, and played "house" with her dolls. Play with peers was noted as lacking, but Mr. M. did not identify this as a goal for Rachel. He indicated that she used words to make her wants and needs known. He marked that she could run and climb, but not jump. He noted several goals for Rachel in each developmental area. The team reviewed this information, discussed their observations of Rachel, and determined which toys and materials would be incorporated into the session. They also planned for the inclusion of a peer from the preschool. The physical therapist, Rachel's primary therapist, was selected as the play facilitator. The developmental specialist, who sees Rachel and her father weekly, was chosen as the parent facilitator. The psychologist volunteered to be the videocamera operator. The speech-language therapist agreed to observe and take behavioral notes.

Prior to Rachel's entry into the infant/toddler program at the Center, a developmental and social history was taken. (See Rachel's report, beginning on p. 284.) Her history includes exposure to the drugs her mother took during pregnancy, premature birth, neonatal respiratory problems, early abandonment by her mother, diagnosed motor delays, and ear infections. Rachel's father accompanies her to the Center twice weekly, and has been actively involved in her home program as well. Rachel receives speech-language and physical therapy in a transdisciplinary play-based program. A home visit is made once a month to coordinate the center-based program with Rachel's functional needs at home. Rachel will be 2½ years of age soon and eligible to enter the preschool program. Her father requested a re-evaluation to consider alternatives for preschool for Rachel.

RACHEL'S PLAY SESSION

Rachel first plays with the play facilitator in the house area. Although her face reveals little emotion, she verbalizes while she plays. Michael M. is seated in the corner watching Rachel and talking to her developmental specialist, the parent facilitator. Observing the session, in addition to the other participants, is the speech-language therapist. The psychologist is operating the videocamera several feet away from Rachel.

The parent facilitator is discussing Mr. M.'s current perceptions of Rachel's development with him. Information from the parent inventory is reviewed. Mr. M. states that he is very pleased with Rachel's progress. He feels that she is functioning at or above age level in all areas, with the exception of motor development.

The parent facilitator asks Mr. M. to describe a typical day with Rachel. Mr. M. comments that their day begins at 6:00 A.M., when Rachel runs in to greet him. He says he is trying to get Rachel to stay up longer so she will sleep later. He is currently on the 4:00 P.M. to midnight shift, which he likes, as it allows him to spend days with Rachel. Rachel likes to watch television in the mornings. Mr. M. reports that "Sesame Street" is a big favorite with Rachel. She is learning letters and numbers, and knows all of the characters on the program. Mr. M. says that Rachel plays nicely by herself. There are no other young children in their apartment building, but they occasionally go to a local park to play on the playground equipment. Rachel likes to watch the other children at the park. Mr. M. says that both he and Rachel take a nap during the day, and Rachel is his companion when they go shopping or conduct errands. His present goal for Rachel is to see her enter a regular preschool program.

While the parent facilitator and Mr. M. are watching and talking, Rachel is playing in the house area. Earlier, when Rachel entered the room, she easily separated from her father to join the play facilitator. Rachel is busily moving pots around on the stove. She takes food to the table and feeds the baby, then sits down and feeds herself. The play facilitator comments on what Rachel is doing, telling her, "Baby is hungry." The play facilitator gets another doll and says, "My baby's thirsty." Rachel immediately looks around for milk, searching in the cupboards. One of the cupboard doors falls off, and Rachel tries to put it back. When she is unable to find milk, the play facilitator hands her a pitcher. Rachel pours imaginary liquid into a cup and returns to the table to give her baby a drink. She then goes back to the counter, pours another cup of milk, and gives it to the facilitator's baby.

Play in the house area continues for several minutes, until Rachel takes her baby over to a box with assorted grooming materials in it. She searches out the toothpaste and struggles to get the cap off, finally handing it to the play facilitator and commenting, "Help." The facilitator takes the cap off and Rachel pretends to put paste on a toothbrush and brush her baby's teeth. She repeats the sequence again. The play facilitator imitates Rachel's behavior and then adds another step to the scenario by combing her baby's hair. Rachel watches, searches for a comb, and combs her baby's hair. During this sequence, Rachel is commenting: "Brush teeth." "Comb hair." The play facilitator repeats Rachel's comments and adds a phrase, "Pretty baby." Rachel says, "Pretty."

Rachel then leaves the doll lying on the floor and goes to the sand-and-water table, which has been filled with bird seed. A water wheel, measuring cups, and several miniature figures are on the table. The play facilitator suggests that Rachel take off her shoes and socks, then pants and shirt. The parent facilitator explains to Mr. M. that the team wants to see Rachel's posture and movements without the hindrance of clothing. Rachel struggles with removing the garments, but persists. She bends over and steps on the bottom of the pant leg and tries to extract her leg. She repeats this process several times, and finally falls onto her bottom and pulls them off. "I did it," she states triumphantly.

Rachel then climbs onto a small step and leans against the seed table. She pours bird seed over the water wheel, and experiments with opening and closing a slot on the top of the toy that adjusts the flow of the seed. When she can't get it open, the play facilitator demonstrates how to use a stick to push the slot open. Rachel imitates this process. The facilitator comments on Rachel's actions, and after several minutes models hiding figures under the seed. Rachel is uninterested in this and continues to empty and fill containers. She persists in this task, manipulating the cups and bird seed, for several minutes. The play facilitator watches to see how long Rachel will continue, and whether she will modify the activity. As Rachel is not demonstrating any additional skills at the seed table, the facilitator decides to encourage transition to another activity.

After putting Rachel's shirt back on, the play facilitator takes a small cup of seeds over to the table and pours it into a nesting cup. She then invites Rachel to come see what she has done with it. Rachel stays at the seed table. When the facilitator goes to get her, Rachel throws herself on the floor. Mr. M. remarks that Rachel frequently throws a tantrum when she doesn't get her way. He is concerned about this behavior. Within 30 seconds, Rachel's attention is diverted to the games on the table. She moves to the table, sits down, and begins to nest the cups. After Rachel has finished the cups, the play facilitator pulls out the lock box with different colored shapes, locks, and keys. Rachel immediately starts to name the colors. Mr. M. tells the parent facilitator that he and Rachel watch "Sesame Street" together and play color and shape games. The parent facilitator suggests that this presents an opportunity for Mr. M. and Rachel to play in a familiar task. She approaches the play facilitator and suggests that Mr. M. enter the session.

Mr. M. sits at the table with Rachel and presents shapes to her. "What color is this, Rachel? What shape is this one? What else is this color?" Rachel continues to manipulate the keys and comment on the pieces she is putting in the box. Mr. M. puts several toys in front of Rachel and tells her what to do with each of them. Rachel complies. He then takes out paper and crayons and asks Rachel to draw a face, then letters. Rachel draws a circle. Mr. M. comments that she usually puts in eyes and a mouth. Rachel then draws a vertical line and says "l." Mr. M. asks Rachel to draw several more letters and name some that he has drawn.

The play facilitator then asks Mr. M. to leave the room for a few minutes. Mr. M. tells Rachel he will be right back. She does not look up, but persists in her drawing. Mr. M. returns, announces that he is back and asks, "Did you miss me?" Rachel still does not look up.

The play facilitator draws on a paper next to Rachel. Rachel occasionally looks at the play facilitator's paper. She says "circle" when the facilitator draws a circle. After several minutes, the play facilitator moves over to the dollhouse and asks Mr. M. to join her. Rachel comes over to see what is going on in the dollhouse. Rachel puts one of the dolls in the sink. Her father asks her why she is putting the doll there. He puts another doll in a chair, and Rachel puts that doll in the sink. Mr. M. is somewhat concerned that Rachel isn't playing with the dolls in the "correct" manner. He states that he doesn't know why Rachel keeps putting the dolls in the sink. The play facilitator reassures him that acting out sequences with miniature dolls is a little above Rachel's age level. She introduced it to see how interested Rachel was in a higher level of dramatic play.

The play facilitator suggests that they return to the house area, since that is an area that Rachel seems to like. Rachel joins her father there. They pretend they are eating, then talking on the phone. The play facilitator pretends to use a banana for a phone and says, "It's for Rachel," and hands the banana to Rachel. Rachel registers a look of surprise, then says, "hello" into the banana. Mr. M. asks Rachel a series of questions: "What did you have for breakfast this morning?" "What color are your barrettes?" "What is your last name?" Rachel sits across from him at the little table and responds to his questions. Very little play occurs during this interaction.

Sharon, a peer from the preschool program who is several months older than Rachel, is then brought into the room. Rachel is familiar with Sharon from activities at the Center. Sharon enters the house area; Rachel stands and watches her. Mr. M. returns to sit next to the parent facilitator.

Sharon begins to feed the doll. Rachel glances up briefly, goes to the sink to pour more milk for her doll, and returns to the table to feed the doll. Sharon begins to talk to the facilitator. Rachel watches and continues feeding her doll. No spontaneous verbal inter-change takes place between the two children. The facilitator rings the phone, saying, "It's for Rachel." She hands the phone to Sharon and gestures toward Rachel. Sharon puts the phone to her ear, then hands the phone to Rachel, saying, "It's for Rachel." Rachel takes the phone, says, "Hi," and hangs up. She resumes feeding her doll.

While Sharon is in the room, Rachel's play becomes less focused. She moves from the house area to the seed table, back to the house area, then to the manipulative table, spend-ing only a few seconds in each area. She observes all interactions between Sharon and the play facilitator. The play facilitator says she's thirsty, sets up a tea set in the house area, and invites Rachel to come have tea. Rachel watches, but does not join them. Sharon is returned to her preschool classroom after several minutes. The play facilitator and Rachel leave with her, stopping at the motor area outside the play room.

Rachel again begins to verbalize as the play facilitator engages her in play in the motor area. Rachel awkwardly runs up a ramp, and the play facilitator follows. Rachel gets on a push toy and navigates it using both legs at one time. Rachel sits on a rocking board. The play facilitator suggests it is a boat and sings "Three Little Fishermen" while she rocks the boat. As the boat tips to one side, Rachel catches herself. The play facilitator then suggests they hunt for a lost duck. Rachel staggers as she moves around the room. She crawls through a tunnel (barrel), up over a mountain (up and down steps), and climbs into a duck nest (large foam doughnut), looking for the duck.

Their search for the duck ends back in the play room. Rachel is then asked to put the rest of her clothes back on so that they can all have a snack. With some assistance from her father, she gets her pants on. Shoes and socks are then added by Mr. M. While getting Rachel dressed, Mr. M. plays rough-and-tumble with Rachel, tickling her and tossing her around. Rachel laughs, showing outward pleasure for the first time in the session.

When Rachel is dressed, Mr. M., the play facilitator, and Sharon (who has been brought back to the playroom) all sit around the table and have peanut butter and jam on crackers, and juice. Rachel is given a plastic knife and asked to spread toppings on the crackers. She smiles and says, "Eat crackers, peese." She awkwardly dabs peanut butter or jam on crackers and gives one to her father and the play facilitator. When the play facilitator notes that Sharon needs a cracker, Rachel offers her one too. Rachel smiles at Sharon and offers her another cracker. She pours juice from a small pitcher into the plastic glasses, spilling only a small amount. The play facilitator offers everyone Cheerios. Rachel carefully takes one Cheerio at a time.

After the snack, Rachel and the peer are taken to the preschool room, where they join the class in progress. Mr. M. and the play facilitator accompany them and observe Rachel in class activities for several minutes. Rachel is again quiet, but very observant. She wanders around the room and watches the activities of several of the children. The teacher in the class takes over with Rachel, and involves her in the house area with another child. Her behavior in the preschool class is similar to her behavior in the toddler group that she participates in twice weekly. She seems more interested, however, in observing the behavior of the older, more verbal children.

POST-SESSION MEETING

The play facilitator and Mr. M. return to the conference room to join the rest of the team. Mr. M. is given the parent inventory he completed prior to the session, and each of the other team members have their respective TPBA guidelines and worksheets in front of them. The parent facilitator asks Mr. M. how Rachel's behavior in the play session compares to her typical behavior. He states that Rachel's language and play were similar to what he sees at home, although he feels that she is capable of demonstrating more drawing and pre-academic skills. The team assures him that Rachel performed very well for her age in both of these areas.

The speech-language therapist gives examples from the language and behavior sample she has taken during the session, noting how Rachel's language is in many ways within the normal age range, but in other ways does not reflect her higher-level cognitive skills. She questions whether some of the higher skills related to letters and numbers are perhaps a result of rote practice from watching "Sesame Street." She cited Rachel's average sentence length of two words as being somewhat shorter than would be expected of a child of her age. Mr. M. states that Rachel is capable of longer sentences, but that two words is typical. The speech-language therapist notes that the longer sentences are frequently in imitation of an adult. She suggests that interaction with peers who use longer sentence structures would probably be helpful as well. She states that she would also like to see Rachel initiate conversation more, rather than always responding to questions.

The teacher agrees that Rachel shows varied abilities, saying that Rachel appears to have acquired concepts such as color and shape and is sequencing acts in dramatic play. She also feels that imitation is a strong learning mode for Rachel. She notes that Rachel is still enjoying simple manipulative play, like emptying and filling, and yet is also capable of good problem-solving and higher-level dramatic play, such as using a banana as a telephone. Mr. M. agrees that Rachel learns through imitation. He says she repeats everything she hears on "Sesame Street." The teacher comments that imitation is a first step toward being able to use the new information in a meaningful way.

The psychologist comments on how Rachel used less language when the peer became involved. She notes, however, that although Rachel did not interact directly with the peer, her close observations and interest appear to be a signal of a state of readiness for interaction. Mr. M. states that at the park Rachel will watch children for a long time and then go and play near them. The psychologist indicates that this is a form of parallel play and is an important step to actual joint play. She expresses some concern that Rachel does not exhibit a range of affect, and asks Mr. M. what type of emotions Rachel typically displays. Mr. M. comments that Rachel is usually pretty even-tempered, but that she can get really angry and throw a tantrum when she is asked to do something she doesn't want to do. The psychologist notes that the tantrums of a 2-year-old can be frustrating.

The physical therapist interjects that Rachel's muscle tone is somewhat low, and that low muscle tone can affect facial expressions. The psychologist says she would like to see Rachel use her affect more in communication, as she feels her interactions with peers will improve if the peers are better able to read her facial cues. The physical therapist states that her therapy program should continue to be integrated with play activities so that both tone and affective expression are addressed.

The speech-language therapist indicates that affective expression will also make Rachel's communicative intentions clearer. She also says that the apparent decrease in language use around peers will probably change as Rachel becomes more comfortable in interaction. She feels that Rachel's language will show a rapid spurt when she begins actual communication with and imitation of peers. The psychologist agrees, stating that because Rachel has interacted primarily with adults, peer interaction is now important to her overall development.

Mr. M. asks about Rachel's motor development. The physical therapist talks about Rachel's motivation to try difficult motor tasks, and describes some skills that she is able to accomplish at this time. She notes, however, that Rachel's gross motor skills are still delayed. She indicates that although Rachel has many appropriate skills, the quality of her movements is immature. She cites examples of the way Rachel climbs stairs and her inability to move her body against gravity, such as when she jumps. The therapist also registers some concern about Rachel's inability to monitor the consequences of her movements and anticipate when she is in a precarious or dangerous position. Mr. M. agrees that Rachel is a "real daredevil."

She comments that Rachel is functional with large, simple objects, but has difficulty with age-appropriate materials. She notes that Rachel's fine motor skills are still somewhat immature qualitatively. Rachel's difficulty exploring materials that challenge her cognitive abilities may affect functional skills. She indicates a desire to study the videotape for more precise analysis. She also plans to conduct an additional informal evaluation of Rachel's reaction to sensory input.

The post–play session conference continues for another 30 minutes, with each team member quickly reviewing the guidelines and commenting on their observations. They raise questions concerning the interactive aspects of development, and elicit Mr. M.'s observations. By the end of the session, each team member has identified areas that he or she wants to review on the videotape. The speech-language therapist states that she would like to test Rachel's receptive language, using a formal instrument. She also wants to watch a segment of the tape with Mr. M. to look at the changes in Rachel's language when different approaches, such as commenting, imitating, and questioning, are used with Rachel. A time is scheduled for testing, and Mr. M. agrees to watch portions of the videotape with her following their next visit to the Center. A date and time are also set to hold the program planning meeting, when a more detailed discussion of Rachel's abilities and program needs will be held.

ANALYSIS OF INFORMATION

During the following week, team members review segments of the videotape. The physical therapist watches the tape without the sound, so as to be able to concentrate on Rachel's motor skills. The teacher, who is familiar with Rachel's play from working with her each week, does not feel she needs to watch the tape again to be able to analyze Rachel's cognitive development. The psychologist watches the segments of the tape where Rachel interacts with her father and the peer in order to be able to analyze Rachel's social and emotional development. The speech-language therapist watches segments of the tape with Rachel's father, looking at Rachel's language in various types of interactions. After reviewing the videotape and worksheets, team members examine the guidelines for their area, answer the questions relevant to Rachel's development, and complete the TPBA developmental area Summary Sheets.

TRANSDISCIPLINARY RECOMMENDATIONS

At the end of the week, the professionals on the team meet briefly to review the summary forms and other assessment data prior to the program planning conference. At this time, the team reaches a consensus about the ratings and discusses what Rachel is ready for as implied by the assessment results. The team member responsible for each area leads the respective discussion, with other team members contributing their opinions. Occasionally a rating or area of readiness is changed based on the team discussion. (*The completed developmental area Summary Sheets for Rachel begin on page 296.*) The information from these Summary Sheets, along with other observations from the assessment and from the parents, will be integrated into the TPBI plan.

PROGRAM PLANNING CONFERENCE

At the program planning conference, Mr. M. is given a copy of the parent inventory that he completed prior to the play session, as well as copies of each of the developmental area summary forms. The team considers each developmental area form, identifying Rachel's strengths and the reason a particular rating has been assigned. Examples of Rachel's performance during the TPBA play session are used to support the conclusions reached. Mr. M.'s input is requested throughout the discussion.

All team members agree that Rachel needs to spend more time with children of her own age. Mr. M. states that he had not previously thought that Rachel had social problems, but that now he is concerned about her interactions with peers. The psychologist noted that Rachel has received a great deal of attention from adults, both at home, from her father and with the babysitter, and at the Center, from various professionals. She suggests that Rachel is developmentally ready for more peer interaction. Mr. M. believes that playing with peers without disabilities will promote all areas of Rachel's development.

Mr. M. also notes that, when he watched the videotape with the speech-language therapist, he was shocked to see how many questions he asked Rachel. He says it is interesting to see how much more Rachel says when someone comments on her actions. The speech-language therapist agrees and remarks that, in general, people tend to ask children too many questions.

The teacher comments on Rachel's long attention span and ability to link several activities in play. She notes that Rachel is very persistent in problem-solving. Her classification and discrimination skills are strong, and her drawing ability is above age level. The psychologist interjects that although Rachel's play sequences are appropriate for her age, she would like to see her start taking turns in her play, involving another person in the action. The teacher outlines several types of play that encourage turn-taking, including telephone play and collaborative block building.

The physical therapist remarks that Rachel's object play and manipulation of toys has improved considerably. She cites as an example Rachel's ability to manipulate the keys into the right locks, which she was unable to do at the beginning of the year. She feels that her fine motor skills still need work. She demonstrates how Rachel grasps small objects, and shows Mr. M. how she would like to see Rachel be able to use her arms and hands.

The physical therapist also indicates that the gross motor area is still Rachel's greatest area of need. She describes Rachel's movements in different positions and addresses her awkwardness, immature balance reactions (particularly in standing), and delays in motor milestones.

Information from TPBA can be incorporated into individual objectives, the TPBI plan, and the classroom curriculum.

Mr. M. agrees with the therapist's observations and thinks that therapy is still needed for this area. The physical therapist concurs.

The team then begins to discuss alternatives for meeting Rachel's needs in all areas. The preschool at the Center is an option, but that would mean that Rachel would be placed with many children who have lower-level cognitive and language skills. Mr. M. prefers that Rachel now attend a regular preschool. The team discusses the local preschools and decides to contact one that is close to Rachel's home. The team feels that if the preschool staff are willing to work with them, then Rachel will be able to interact with higher-level peers and have her program modified to meet her individual needs. The team outlines a plan for working with Mr. M. and the local preschool, to be confirmed upon approval of the cooperating preschool staff.

At the end of the conference, a Cumulative Summary Sheet is completed (see p. 308). This Summary Sheet serves as a brief encapsulation for Mr. M. and others, and is meant to be concise and free of jargon. Program plans for Rachel (see p. 304) and her family (see p. 307) are also developed at this time. (These forms address the requirements for an IFSP that were outlined in Chapter 4.) Following the conference, the team members each write their sections of the report, and the psychologist is assigned to assemble the pieces into the final report.

In the report, offered as an appendix to this chapter, the psychologist discusses each area of assessment. Cognitive and language development, which are at age level, are discussed first in the report. Social-emotional development is of some concern and is presented next. Motor development, the primary concern, is addressed last. This sequence ensures that strengths are emphasized, and places the areas of less ability in proximity to the recommendations.

As age ranges vary from skill to skill, and do not take into consideration qualitative aspects of performance, the team incorporates a classification of no delay, mild, moderate, or severe delay for each domain. (If state requirements demand ages, these may be included in the report, based on the age charts provided in Chapters 6–9 or other cited sources.)

FROM ASSESSMENT TO INTERVENTION

Following Rachel's placement in the local preschool, the team meets with the preschool staff to discuss Rachel's needs. The teachers are quite willing to work with Rachel, but indicate a desire for assistance in modifying the curriculum. The intent is not to create a separate program for Rachel, but to incorporate her individual objectives into the regular curriculum. The philosophy of the program is consistent with that of transdisciplinary play-based intervention (Linder, 1993), so the team recommends a modified planning approach.

The preschool is implementing a storybook curriculum that is developmental and center-based. As the teacher discusses her ideas for the unit on *Johnny Appleseed*, the team contributes ideas related to Rachel's needs. Based on a *mapping process* (Figure 10.1), the team and preschool teachers together design a sample unit with modifications for Rachel. The team takes each area of the day and conceives activities related to the storybook theme. They then plan modifications of the activity to incorporate cognitive, language, motor, and social objectives for Rachel (see p. 282, Table 10.1). The preschool teachers note that many of the modifications are appropriate for other children in their class as well. One team member will visit the preschool each week until staff feel comfortable with the program imple-

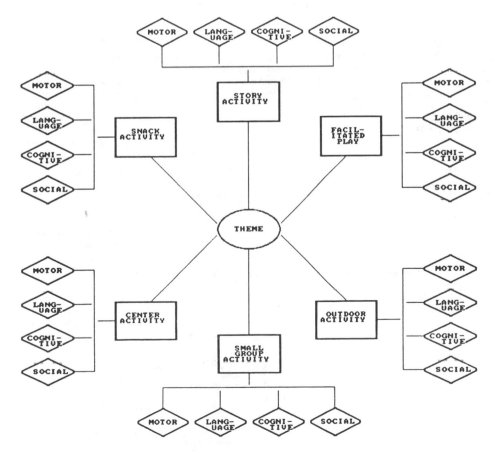

Figure 10.1.   Mapping process for planning a developmental unit.

mentation. The series of activities outlined in Table 10.1, designed to be distributed over a week or more, demonstrates how assessment information is translated into functional activities and strategies. Many more activities or objectives could be included, but these activities are offered to illustrate the planning process. The team offered to develop a TIP sheet for Rachel that could be used across various storybook themes.

As can be seen in Table 10.1, almost every activity can be designed to include objectives for multiple areas of development. The important point is to consciously plan activities with individual children's needs in mind. Rachel does not require totally different activities within the classroom. She needs modifications of activities to enhance her strengths and encourage skills and processes for which she is ready.

Table 10.1.   Storybook curriculum unit on Johnny Appleseed

Activity	Individualization for Rachel	Developmental areas addressed
I. Examine and taste apple juice, apples (red, yellow, green), and applesauce.	Talk about apple, color, shape, using two–three words; pick seeds out of apple and put them in small sack; serve pieces of apple to peer.	*language*—sentence length, semantic structure, vocabulary, prepositions, initiation of topic, turn-taking *cognition*—comparison, classification, identification of parts, problem-solving *fine motor*—bilateral skills *social*—sharing, interaction
II. Read story of Johnny Appleseed. Dress up and act out with props.	Comment on action. Identify missing props. Act out story.	*cognitive*—problem-solving, sequencing *language*—expansion of sentence length, morpheme -ing (digging)
III. Take props and seeds to the playground. Complete obstacle course over a "river," through a "tunnel," up a "mountain," planting seeds.	Rachel pushes and pulls a heavy bag of seeds through the course. Also runs, jumps, and squats (while planting); distributes seeds to peers.	*motor*—tone, stability, equilibrium, transitions *cognitive*—imitation, sequencing, representation *social*—initiation of interaction, turn-taking, dialogue with peer *language*—providing information, using action words, adding -ing, remembering a sequence
IV. Facilitated play. Have a center with props and books available.	Facilitate Rachel's play by imitating, commenting, expanding. Place objects to require position changes. Hide objects to encourage questions.	*cognitive*—representation, sequencing, problem-solving *language*—semantic relations, sentence length, questioning, vocabulary *gross motor*—balance, transitions *social*—initiation of play sequences, parallel play
V. Make applesauce. Use pictures of steps to match objects. Children help make applesauce.	Help Rachel cut up pieces with small plastic knife. Dump pieces into bowl, stir (small bowl, so she will use two hands).	*fine motor*—hand strength, using both hands together *cognitive*—sequencing, representation, cause-and-effect *language*—initiating, questioning, commenting, combining words (action, location), vocabulary
VI. Eat applesauce. Kids prepare snack table. Try warm and cold applesauce. Recall of activity with picture cues.	Setting table, washing hands (soap in two hands), labeling (hot, cold). Make faces for things she likes and doesn't. Help serve other children.	*cognitive*—one-to-one correspondence, sequencing, memory, classification *language*—vocabulary, turn-taking, past tense *fine motor*—use of both hands *social*—sharing, affective expression

The TPBA model is congruent with a play-based curriculum approach. The information gained translates directly into activities for home and school. The team approach results in planning integrated, functional activities that can be used in a variety of different settings. If individual therapy is needed, the therapists can better coordinate what is happening in therapy with what is taking place in the classroom.

The case study and activities presented in this chapter illustrate the value of assessing children through play, writing a comprehensive descriptive report, and planning play-based activities. Daily observation of the child in the play environment also serves as a basis for ongoing evaluation of the child's progress and changing abilities. The transdisciplinary play-based intervention approach (Linder, 1993) provides a logical extension of TPBA into the home, classroom, and community. Assessment, planning, intervention, and re-evaluation thus become part of a cyclical process.

Publisher's Note: As of the fifth printing of this book, in January, 1999, the transdisciplinary play-based assessment and intervention approach has been further expanded to include a transdisciplinary play-based curriculum, called *Read, Play, and Learn!: Storybook Activities for Young Children. Read, Play, and Learn!* provides a teacher's guide and two collections of lesson-plan modules based on popular children's storybooks (Linder, 1999a, 1999b, 1999c). Each module provides creative activities, adapted from the themes of the story, that help children work on skill development while having fun—not just in the core domains covered in depth in TPBA and TPBI but also in the critical area of emerging literacy.

REFERENCES

Linder, T.W. (1993). *Transdisciplinary play-based intervention: Guidelines for developing a meaningful curriculum for young children.* Baltimore: Paul H. Brookes Publishing Co.

Linder, T.W. (1999a). *Read, Play, and Learn!: Storybook activities for young children. Collection 1.* Baltimore: Paul H. Brookes Publishing Co.

Linder, T.W. (1999b). *Read, Play, and Learn!: Storybook activities for young children. Collection 2.* Baltimore: Paul H. Brookes Publishing Co.

Linder, T.W. (1999c). *Read, Play, and Learn!: Storybook activities for young children. Teacher's guide.* Baltimore: Paul H. Brookes Publishing Co.

Appendix

REPORT: RACHEL M.
Name: Rachel M.
Sex: Female
Parent(s): Michael M.
Address: 50 Beehive Lane
Denver, Colorado 80209
Telephone: 111–4321
Examiners: Susan Jones, P.T.
Nancy James, M.A., C.C.C., S.P.
Mary Smith, teacher
Toni Brown, Ed.D.

Date of birth: 7/15/90
Date of testing: 11/29/92
Age at testing: 2 yr., 4 mo., 14 days

Reason for Referral:

Rachel was re-evaluated to assist in the transition from the infant program at Center Pre-school to an appropriate toddler/preschool program.

History:

Developmental and social history were obtained from previous records and from Mr. M. Rachel's mother, Ms. R., was reported by Mr. M. to have been on drugs (marijuana and speed) for the first 4 months of the pregnancy. Ms. R. received no medical care until the seventh month of pregnancy. Rachel was delivered at 36 weeks gestation, after an uneventful labor of 10 hours. Rachel weighed only 5 pounds at birth, and was hospitalized for respiratory problems for 8 days.

Rachel's parents were living together at the time of her birth. Mr. M. and Ms. R. separated when Rachel was 5 months old, and Mr. M. took custody of Rachel. Rachel currently lives with her father and does not see her mother, whose whereabouts are unknown. Mr. M. works evenings as a custodian. A babysitter cares for Rachel while he is working.

Rachel's early years have been marked by several bouts of upper respiratory infections and otitis media. She had tubes placed in her ears at 19 months of age. Her health is monitored by Dr. S. at a local hospital.

Mr. M. reported that Rachel was diagnosed as having gross motor delays. He stated that Rachel's developmental milestones were slightly delayed; she crawled at 11 months, walked at 18 months, and said her first words at 14 months. Mr. M.'s primary concerns are for Rachel's motor development, and he feels that in spite of her delays, Rachel is very bright.

Rachel has been enrolled in the Infant/Toddler Program at the Center since she was 20 months old. Her father has accompanied her to the Center twice weekly, and has been actively involved in her home program as well. Rachel has received a home visit once a month. Rachel will be 2½ years old and eligible to enter the Toddler/Preschool Program in January. Mr. M. wants to consider alternatives for preschool for Rachel.

Method of Assessment:

Rachel was assessed in a TPBA play session at the Center. The TPBA process involves observation of the child in an informal play setting. The preschool classroom at the Center was the site of the assessment. The room contains a house area with kitchen and bedroom props, a sand-and-water table with cause-and-effect toys and manipulatives, and a table with puzzles, lock boxes, and art supplies. In addition, the gym area was used for gross motor observations. It was arranged in an obstacle course, with stairs, barrels, balance boards, therapy balls, and other motor equipment. The play session consisted of observations of Rachel interacting in play with the play facilitator, who was her physical therapist, with her father, and with a peer. Rachel was also observed in a preschool classroom environment.

In addition to the play-based assessment, receptive language was also assessed by the speech-language therapist on a standardized measure, the Sequenced Inventory of Communication Development–R (Hedrick, Prather, & Tobin, 1984).

Informal observations of reactions to sensory input were conducted by the physical therapist.

Mr. M. completed the Parent Inventory of Child Development in Nonschool Environments (Vincent et al., 1986) to document Rachel's level of performance at home.

INTERPRETATION OF ASSESSMENT RESULTS

On the Parent Inventory, Mr. M. reported that Rachel plays alone for 20–30 minutes, answers questions with one- to two-word phrases, recognizes television characters, feeds herself and helps undress herself. Mr. M. indicated that he would like to see Rachel talk in longer sentences, reduce her tantrums, and improve her motor skills.

Cognitive Development:

Categories of Play   Rachel was observed to engage in exploratory, relational, and dramatic play, with approximately equal time spent in each category of play. Slightly more time was spent in exploratory and relational play.

Attention Span   Rachel's longest time playing was spent at the table filled with bird seed. She played there for over 10 minutes, dumping and filling, pouring bird seed over the water wheel, and experimenting with filling different containers. She also demonstrated a long attention span (over 5 minutes) in the house area in representational play, and at the table with manipulatives (over 5 minutes). The shortest amount of time was spent playing with the miniature dollhouse. On the standardized test administered by the speech-language therapist after the play session, when Rachel was not directing the action, her attention was more difficult to maintain.

Rachel appeared to prefer tactile and visual input, commenting frequently on the color of objects. She also seemed to enjoy the bird seed (although she used utensils rather than her hands in most instances). She attended to auditory input, responding to what adults were saying, frequently imitating their words or answering their questions.

Rachel did not need external reinforcement to remain engaged. She continued to play without encouragement, although the presence of the adult provided a form of attention that may have sustained her play for longer periods.

Rachel's attention did not appear to be distracted by nearby activities, sounds, or people. In the one-to-one play situation, Rachel's attention span appeared to be appropriate for her age. Observations of Rachel in her class, however, showed her to be resistant to activities that involved another child. Her attention span with peers is also much shorter; she flits from activity to activity if an adult is not present to interact with her. Personal choice of activity, combined with adult attention, appears to maximize her attention span.

Object Use   Rachel used a variety of behaviors with objects. She stirred, fed a doll, squeezed a toothpaste tube, poured bird seed, pushed and pulled a handle, turned keys, drew with a pencil, and performed other complex schemes appropriate for her age. She also demonstrated generalization of behaviors across objects.

Rachel was observed to link up to eight schemes in a meaningful sequence. She got the toothpaste out of the box, tried to get it open, handed it to the facilitator to open, put the paste on the brush, put the cap back on the tube, brushed the doll's teeth, got more paste on the brush after it fell off, and brushed the doll's teeth again. This was the longest sequence observed. Rachel was also seen to pour imaginary milk from a pitcher into a glass, take it to a baby doll, go back to pour more milk, and take it to feed another baby doll. She also persisted in her sequences with the manipulatives, showing sequences averaging 3–4 steps.

Her use of scheme sequences and interest in experimentation, practice, and manipulation appear age-appropriate. She used schemes differentially with objects and was able, with modeling, to vary her play.

Symbolic/Representational Play   Rachel primarily used real objects in her representation play. However, she imitated the use of a banana for a telephone and pretended there was milk in the empty pitcher. She enjoyed using real toothpaste, combs, and bottles for her dolls.

In her representational play, Rachel directed her actions toward herself and the dolls. She was able to portray a parenting role in feeding and grooming the dolls. She was unable to direct action in the dollhouse, which demands a higher level of representation than expected at her age level.

Imitation   Rachel used imitation as her primary means of interaction. She imitated what she saw (drawing numbers seen on "Sesame Street"), what she heard (words, sentences, and intonation), and the actions of the facilitator. She imitated exploratory behaviors (dumping and filling), relational behaviors (combing the baby's hair), and symbolic behaviors (pouring milk). During the session, her highest level of imitation involved drawing shapes, and her father reported that she can fill in several features of a face. This play was above expectation for her age level. Most of Rachel's imitative behaviors were performed immediately after the model; however, she demonstrated deferred imitation in her drawing.

Rachel did not demonstrate much turn-taking in her imitation. She imitated the facilitator or her father, but then did not wait for the adult to have a turn. Consequently, chains of interactions were short unless the adult interjected a turn.

Problem-Solving   Rachel demonstrated interest in cause-and-effect toys, such as the lock box and the water wheel. Rachel's problem-solving efforts were characterized by repetition of the same approach over and over. When the door fell off the sink, for example, she said, "broke," and tried to push it up several times without success. When trying to remove her pants, she repeatedly tried stepping on the pant leg while standing in the "bear" position.

When Rachel knew the right answer, she used a systematic approach to solve the problem. When her father requested that she pick out specific colored shapes ("Give me the red ball. Give me the blue square."), Rachel responded by visually scanning the options and selecting the right color.

Discrimination/Differentiation   Rachel demonstrated understanding of a variety of concepts. She related objects (plate and spoon, toothpaste and toothbrush, paper and pencil), combined like objects (blocks), and sorted by color and shape. She exhibited spatial matching by putting shapes into a shape sorter. She matched colors on the lock box and stacked cubes by size. She also recognized and labeled the letters "l," "n," "a," and "e," discrimination/classification abilities that are above her age expectancy.

One-to-One Correspondence   Rachel was able to count to 10 by rote and was reported by her father to be able to count much further. She exhibited emerging understanding of one-to-one correspondence with four or five objects. She was observed setting the table before each of two dolls and was able to accurately count up to five Cheerios. These skills are at or above age expectancy.

Sequencing Ability   Rachel's highest level of sequencing skills was noted in dramatic play. She was able to sequence the previously mentioned activity of brushing her teeth. She was not yet combining sequences into stories. She demonstrated time sequence concepts when she responded to her father's question about what color barrettes they had put in her hair "this morning." He reports that she can remember things that happen in previous days and anticipate future events.

Drawing Ability   Rachel drew horizontal and vertical lines, and was able to draw a circle and add eyes and a mouth. She also attempted, at her father's request, to draw an "A." Her father reports that she watches "Sesame Street" every day and is able to draw several letters. Her drawing skills appear to be above age level.

In conclusion, Rachel's cognitive abilities appear to be appropriate or advanced for her age. She was able to sequence schemes in dramatic play; she demonstrated beginning concepts relating to discrimination of shapes, colors, numbers, letters; she demonstrated initial time concepts; and she had beginning drawing skills. Many of these skills resulted, according to her father, from watching "Sesame Street." Her father also spends a lot of time with her, asking her questions about these concepts.

Communication and Language Development:

Modality   Rachel's primary form of communication was verbalization. She interacted with the examiner frequently, although most verbalizations were in response to a model or question presented. Rachel used words, which were occasionally paired with a gesture or eye contact, to communicate.

Pragmatics   The use of words to communicate meaning places Rachel in the locutionary stage of language development, which is appropriate for her age. She appeared motivated to communicate for primarily instrumental reasons (to get her needs met—e.g., "want more"), and to regulate others' behavior (e.g.,"eat that"). Rachel also used words to inform (labeling familiar objects) but did not seek information from other persons.

Rachel's words communicated various intentions. She demonstrated the following pragmatic acts:

greeting (hi, waves)
requesting objects (cup)
requesting action (more milk, turn it, close it, take off)
protesting (Rachel leaves activity, Rachel throws herself back)
commenting on objects (cup, toothbrush, baby)
acknowledging (yeah, favorites, okay, uh-huh)

answering (blue, triangle, square)
closing (bye)

Although Rachel demonstrated a range of intentions, her discourse skills were limited. She infrequently initiated an interaction. When she did initiate a topic, the purpose was to comment on an object ("key"), or make a request for action ("open it"). Turn-taking was limited to one or two turns. Rachel listened and imitated a model but did not offer new information, request information, or change topics. Her discourse skills are slightly delayed for her age.

Rachel used both exact ("comb hair") and mitigated (Dad: "Turn the key"—Rachel: "turn key, open") imitation to prolong interaction. She also used deferred, or delayed, imitation of sentences ("you get to 'Sesame Street'"). These processes are typical for children of her age.

Phonology   Rachel's individual sound system was within the average range. Her speech was 80%–90% intelligible. She demonstrated some deletions of final consonants (do/don't), deletions of syllables (na/banana), substitutions (w/r), reductions of clusters (taɪ/cry), stopping (dump/jump), and fronting (taɪ/cry). All of these processes are considered normal in a child of Rachel's age.

Semantic and Syntactic Understanding   Semantics refers to the child's understanding of the meaning of signs, symbols, and words. Rachel demonstrated referential knowledge (a particular word represents a particular object, such as Daddy), extended knowledge (words represent various kinds of objects, such as toothbrush), relational knowledge (understanding of the relation of words to other words—more, all gone, pour, scoop, some, turn it, up, on, off). Rachel used nouns (baby, bear, triangle), action words (eat, cry, open), adjectives (blue, green), negatives (don't), prepositions (up, down, on, off), and the pronoun *I* (only once).

The meaning imparted by Rachel's utterances, as noted above, demonstrated understanding of the agent, action, object, recurrence, nonexistence, cessation, rejection, location, and possession. Her utterances combined agent-action (baby drink), action-object (comb hair), and action-object-location (pour it on), showing appropriate semantic relations for her age. She is not yet using the present progressive ending (-ing), which usually emerges between 19 and 28 months.

Many of Rachel's longer utterances were made in imitation of a model. Her spontaneous productions, however, were limited to one or two words (mean length of utterance, 1.4), which is somewhat delayed for her age. Imitation appears to be a means for her to practice longer sentence structures.

Comprehension of Language   Receptively, Rachel responded to a variety of sounds and frequencies. Both in the TPBA play session and on the Sequenced Inventory of Communication Development, Rachel demonstrated age-appropriate comprehension. She consistently responded to her name and followed one- to two-step commands. She answered *yes/no* questions and questions beginning with *where, what, who,* and *which.* She understood simple prepositions (in, on, off) and various relational terms, as noted previously in her word production.

Oral Motor   Rachel did not display oral motor difficulties. She was able to keep liquid in her mouth with good lip closure. She showed the ability to bite and chew with both sides of her mouth. Rachel was also able to use her tongue to clean her lips.

Social-Emotional Development:

Temperament   Rachel's activity level appeared in be within the average range. She was able to be active or inactive when appropriate.

Adaptability   Rachel adapted quickly to each situation. She also adapted easily to the shift from the facilitator to her father and back to the facilitator again. She did not need to use an adult or parent as a base of emotional support. The facilitator was familiar to Rachel, and no reaction to the unfamiliar observers was noticed. She appeared to enjoy all the new toys or situations that she chose or that were presented to her. The one exception was in her interaction with peers. Rachel adapted more slowly in the presence of peers.

Reactivity   Rachel demonstrated consistently positive, but low-intensity reactions to stimuli. The range of emotions shown in this session was quite limited. She only laughed once, in reaction to tickling by her father. She was not observed to smile throughout the session. Although little *intense* positive reaction was seen, there was also little negative reaction observed. A negative response was seen when she was asked to move from the seed table into a different activity. She then threw herself backwards onto the floor. The teacher reported that she frequently has a tantrum when she doesn't get her way.

Her temperament characteristics were within the average range, with the exception of her low intensity of responses, which tended to make her affect appear "flat." Tantrums are an expected behavior at her age.

Mastery Motivation   The majority of Rachel's activities were purposeful. With the exception of exploratory play in the seed table, she engaged in goal-oriented activities. When given a complex toy, like the lock box, Rachel was persistent in her efforts to open it. She was persistent in representational, exploratory, and manipulative activities. The hardest task she attempted was manipulation of the key to get the door open on the puzzle box. Rachel's motivational level did not appear to depend on whether the facilitator or her father was interacting with her.

Rachel was not observed to smile, clap, or laugh upon successful completion of a task. Once, as previously noted, she said, "I did it," when she finally got her pants off, but this was without a great deal of expression. Overall, however, Rachel's motivation is high and is a strength for her.

Social Relations with Parent   Rachel's affect with her father was low. She appeared to enjoy the activities with her father, as demonstrated through attention and persistence rather than through positive affect. Rachel responded to her father's questions with appropriate answers. She did not seek or give affection except at the very end of the session, after her father tickled her. She then gave him a hug. Rachel's cues to her father were primarily verbal. She did not seek frequent eye contact.

Rachel was active throughout the play session in interaction with her father. She initiated activities for herself, but did not initiate activities in interaction with her father. Contact was maintained through questions and answers. Turn-taking behavior was seen only once, when he attempted to talk on the phone to her. Rachel, however, spoke to her "Grammy" instead.

During play interactions, Mr. M. and Rachel concentrated on the same objects and themes. Mr. M. directed the play, at times shifting toys or topics while Rachel was still interested in playing with the previous toy. Timing, therefore, was somewhat asynchronous. Rachel primarily responded to her father's requests. There was a lack of expansion and modification of play themes. Neither Rachel nor Mr. M. seemed to anticipate the next phase of the interaction.

Reaction of Child to Parent with Facilitator Present   Rachel was able to function quite well independently. She did not physically "check-in" with her father, and only occasionally looked in his direction. She did not seek him out at any time during the session; however, she was not tired or stressed, so it was not possible to see her reaction under duress.

Rachel did not look up or respond at all when her father left the room or when he re-entered, even though he verbally announced he was leaving and asked, "Did you miss me?" when he came back.

Rachel was aware of self and others. She identified several body parts and possessions. She spoke of her purple barrettes and clothing, identified herself by name, and identified her last name and father's name. She rarely used personal pronouns, such as I or me.

Social Interactions with Facilitator   Rachel's affect with the facilitator was similar to that with her father. Increased affect on the part of the facilitator did not appear to increase Rachel's affective response. Rachel also shared little eye contact with the facilitator. Rachel demonstrated increased initiation of interaction with the facilitator. The facilitator used wait time, set up situations to encourage initiation (with the toothpaste tube), and commented on Rachel's actions. Turn-taking also increased when the facilitator imitated Rachel or modeled an action. The length of scheme sequences was much longer with the facilitator (up to 8) as compared to with her father (2–3). More spontaneous language was also heard during the interactions with the facilitator. Rachel appears to benefit from the facilitative techniques used in the play-based session.

Relation to Peers   Rachel was observed in play with a peer during the session. (The peer was a child, 4 months older than Rachel, who was in the preschool class. Rachel has been involved in activities with her previously.) No spontaneous verbal interchange took place between the two children. Although Rachel was aware of the presence of Sharon, she was contented in parallel play. With the peer in the room, Rachel's play became less focused. Without the one-to-one attention of the facilitator, Rachel moved from toy to toy without sequencing her play. She moved from the house area, to the seed table, back to the house area, over to the manipulative table, and back to the seed table, spending only a few seconds at each.

During the snack at the end of the session, Rachel spontaneously offered the facilitator a cracker. The facilitator commented that Sharon needed a cracker, too. Rachel then handed Sharon a cracker. Rachel appears to be interested in interacting with adults, but is still primarily an observer of peers. Although parallel play is normal for a child of her age, Rachel's response to peers is of some concern. She likes to be the center of attention, and has not yet found that interaction with peers can be as pleasurable as interaction with adults. She seems to function at a lower level, cognitively and socially, when peers are present.

Interaction with Peers in Group   All of the team members have observed Rachel in class. Her behavior with the peer in the play session was similar to her behavior in class, when more peers are present. Her teachers reported that she has very little social interaction. Her behavior in class is characterized by solitary play, with occasional observations of her peers. She has difficulty sitting in a group activity. Tantrum behaviors are primarily seen during group time. If another child is playing with a toy, Rachel wants that toy. She is unable to share her toys or take turns with a peer. Again, much of this behavior is normal for a child of her age. Rachel will need support and gradual introduction into group activities.

Emotional Characteristics of Play   Rachel's predominant themes in dramatic play relate to daily routines and mothering behaviors, both of which are normal for her age. Rachel appears to be developing a concept of self, but is having difficulty incorporating the adult into her play. She does not yet use words to express emotions, such as "happy" or "mad." She also has difficulty demonstrating a range of emotions. She is either complaisant or having a tantrum.

Sense of Humor   Rachel was only observed to laugh once, when her father tickled her, as previously mentioned. This was a fairly intense tactile stimulation. She was not observed to laugh at events in the environment or at her own or others' actions.

Social Conventions   Rachel did greet the facilitator with "hi" at one point in the session. She is reported by her father to use "please" and "thank you," and to eat nicely at the table. She is not yet toilet trained. Rachel did not exhibit any maladaptive or unusual behaviors.

In summary, Rachel exhibited many positive social characteristics. She had an easy temperament, was able to function well when separated from her father, played nicely in parallel play with an adult, conformed to adult guidance, and did not exhibit maladaptive behaviors. Rachel did not, however, initiate interaction unless seeking help. She demonstrated low-level responses and a narrow range of emotional reactions. Temper tantrums are normal for her age.

Sensorimotor Development:

General Appearance of Movement   Rachel's size and body proportions were appropriate for her age. She moved alone from area to area and chose a variety of positions for play. The most frequently chosen positions for play were: 1) standing, and 2) sitting on the floor or a child-sized chair. Each position was assumed without difficulty.

Muscle Tone/Strength/Endurance   Rachel's movements lacked the smooth and controlled quality indicative of normal tone. Gross motor skills generally appeared jerky, awkward, and uncoordinated. She frequently staggered and leaned against supports in standing. During motor tasks, she exhibited increased tone in one arm when manipulating objects with the other hand. Primitive reflexes appeared to be integrated when Rachel's functional movements were observed in play.

Rachel was unable to perform skills that required strength. She could not squeeze the toothpaste tube, pull the latch on the water wheel, or lift her body off the ground for gross motor activities such as jumping.

Reactivity to Sensory Input   Limited opportunities were available to observe Rachel's reactions to tactile materials. She tolerated the seeds in the seed table without difficulty. There were no adverse reactions to the facilitator's touch or to fabrics, carpet, or other surfaces in the play area. She seemed to enjoy a tickling session with her father, laughing as she played with him. This tickling also involved rough-and-tumble play on the floor, as Mr. M. knocked Rachel over. Other movement activities included running, climbing, sliding down a slide, and riding a push toy. Rachel did not demonstrate any fear of movement, and in fact was somewhat careless; she frequently did not see the danger in certain gross motor activities.

A more in-depth informal evaluation of Rachel's reactions to sensory input was conducted following the play-based assessment. Rachel responded appropriately to this broader range of tactile and movement experiences.

Stationary Play Positions   Rachel used a variety of sitting positions during play, including: 1) ring sit (both legs in front with the hips and knees bent), 2) long sit (both legs straight out in front), 3) modified ring sit (both legs in front with one knee bent and one knee straight), and 4) sitting in a child-sized chair. In the modified ring sit, she was able to life one leg off the floor. Her arms were frequently used for support when leaning to the side in sitting.

Automatic reactions are unconscious, automatic adjustments of the head, trunk, and limbs to remain in an upright position. Some components of mature automatic reactions were evident during play. Head and trunk righting responses, for example, were sufficiently developed for Rachel to hold her head and trunk upright in sitting and standing. Rachel's chin, however, frequently rested on her chest. This head position limited her ability to freely turn her head to visually search her environment or interact with the facilitator. In sitting, she was able to catch herself with her arms when falling to the front, the sides, and backwards (protective responses). Equilibrium responses (reactions used to maintain balance), however, were not fully functional. In standing, for example, a change in the surface, a change in direction, or an obstacle in her path often resulted in her staggering to prevent a fall.

Rachel's sitting and standing posture often deteriorated when she manipulated objects. At the seed table, for example, she started out free standing with weight on both legs. As time progressed, she was eventually learning against the table with her tummy, with weight on the right leg only. Her left foot was forward, with the toes gripping the edge of the bench.

Mobility in Play   Rachel was motivated to try difficult motor activities. In positions closer to the floor (back-lying, sitting, and crawling), her movements were more coordinated, controlled, and fluid. In higher positions, such as standing, and during unfamiliar or demanding tasks, her movements were not as smooth and coordinated.

Moving from one position to another was performed with varying degrees of skill. Righting responses were evident when she rolled from her back to her stomach using trunk rotation (the trunk twists and the hips and shoulders do not stay in line with each other). She also demonstrated a nice pattern of movement when changing from a sitting position to a partial hands-and-knees position. When trying to assume a squat from a standing position, however, she was unable to adequately control the movement and "plopped" into sitting. She was unable to rise from a squat position, just as she was unable to maintain a squat position for play. Rachel consistently rose to an upright position from bear-standing (both hands and feet on the floor at the same times with knees straight). When lying on her back, for example, she rolled over to her side, moved into a hands-and-knees position, then stood up from bear-standing.

Rachel crawled reciprocally (right arm moves with left leg and vice versa) up a slide. She was observed to bear-stand while undressing. She could freely separate one leg from another while performing these skills. Rachel was able to run, but her movements were awkward and she frequently appeared on the verge of falling. Her steps were short and plodding during running.

Other Developmental Achievements   Although Rachel's motor skills were qualitatively immature, she was able to perform some expected milestone skills, including navigating her body through a barrel, sliding down the slide, and climbing onto a waist-high foam block. She also was able to maneuver a riding toy without pedals. She encountered difficulty when climbing the stairs. She crawled up and down a small set of steps with both hands and feet on the steps. She attempted to descend the stairs in an upright posture, with one hand held, but lost her balance. She was able to step up onto a small bench with support, placing one foot at a time. Rachel demonstrated that she had the idea of jumping by bouncing up and down. However, she was unable to lift her feet off the floor. She was also unable to jump off a low step. Rachel's stair-climbing and jumping skills were delayed.

Prehension and Manipulation   Rachel was visually attentive to manipulation tasks and seemed to enjoy playing with objects. She was capable of playing with age-appropriate toys without frustration. Close examination of fine motor skills, however, revealed the same lack of graceful and fluid movements that appeared in her performance of total body movements. Although she was capable of age-appropriate manipulation tasks, use of these higher-level skills was fleeting.

Rachel was capable of using full range of motion in her arms and hands. She could bring the arms overhead, out to the side, and forward. The forearm rotated in both directions, turning the thumb up or down. The wrist and finger joints could also move in all directions. Although the ability existed to use a variety of movements, she functionally demonstrated a limited repertoire of movements. She was able to bring both hands together to play with toys in front of her body. She was also able to reach across the front of her body to get a desired toy on the other side. General posturing of her arms during fine motor activities, however, was immature. Her upper arms, for example, were frequently oriented behind the trunk or in line with the trunk. Similarly, she was capable of bringing the thumb around to face the fingers (opposition), yet examination of the hands' resting posture revealed that the thumb was often held at the side of the hand. The ability to accommodate the arm to an object's orientation was demonstrated several times. More frequently, however, she approached objects from the top, lacking a more sophisticated thumb-up position (forearm supination).

Rachel demonstrated a variety of grasping patterns during the play session. Although capable of an age-appropriate grasp, her hands appeared immature for 2 years of age. She picked up Cheerios between the tips of the index finger and thumb with both hands. She also modeled the facilitator's mature grasp on a marker. These types of higher-level skills, however, were observed intermittently. More often, she held objects against the palm of her hand and there was little differentiation of movements between the little finger and thumb sides of the hand. Her hand was frequently directed toward the little-finger side of the hand. She generally used a full-fist grasp on objects (crayon, spoon, bowl). Her little and ring fingers were loosely closed on objects; thus, her grip lacked power.

Rachel was able to release a small Cheerio above a narrow-necked bottle on two occasions. More frequently, release involved downward pressure, through contact with the container or surface. The wrist was often bent down and the joints at the base of the fingers bent back excessively (extension).

Hand dominance is not established (she is too young for this to be a concern), although there appears to be an emerging preference for the right hand during fine motor tasks such as writing and self-feeding. In general, she demonstrated a tendency to manipulate objects on the left with her left hand and objects on the right with her right hand. She was able to stabilize an object with one hand while manipulating with the other hand. Spontaneous assistance from the inactive hand did not occur as frequently as expected. The orientation of her arms and increased muscle tone in her non-active hand (associated reactions) interfered with a smooth, spontaneous assist.

Rachel exhibited the most manipulative control during activities that involved turning the thumb down (forearm pronation), such as pouring from a pitcher, pouring from containers at the seed table, and screwing a toothpaste lid back on the tube. During coloring, the entire arm was involved in the motion. She imitated a horizontal and vertical line, and she drew a circle independently. At one point, she held a marker in her fingertips and performed some nice strokes away from her body.

Other fine motor skills observed included turning the dials on a stove, turning a key on a shape sorter, and isolating her index finger to dial a telephone. She turned puzzle pieces over to look at the bottom, and replace them in the puzzle board. She took a cap off a marker and put it back on. She demonstrated a variety of scooping and pouring activities at the seed table. She stacked rings on a dowel.

Motor Planning   Rachel frequently imitated the facilitator's actions. She was able to plan how to move her body through an obstacle course. She also participated in dressing and undressing. Rachel readily engaged in and enjoyed a variety of sensorimotor activities. There were no behaviors demonstrated in this session that indicated the need for further testing of motor planning.

In summary, Rachel's gross motor skills were delayed. She demonstrated some age-appropriate movement patterns in sitting and on her hands and knees. Quality of movement in standing was immature for a 2-year-old. She exhibited some higher-level milestone skills, such as maneuvering a riding toy and navigating an obstacle course. Other skills should be more refined at this point, such as stair-climbing, jumping in place, running and squatting in play. Fine motor skills were also immature for 2 years of age. She demonstrated higher-level abilities, but these were infrequent and inconsistent. Her general arm posture influenced the ability to use both hands together. Both gross and fine motor skills were poorly controlled in the mid-ranges of the movements. Reactions to sensory input and motor planning abilities were age appropriate, and not a concern at this time.

SUMMARY

Performance Levels:

Cognitively, Rachel appears to be functioning at age level, with some areas slightly above age level. Rachel's expressive language is primarily at a one- to two-word phrase level. In comparison to other children her age, Rachel's language production is primarily within the average range, with some skills showing a slight delay. Language comprehension is at age level. Socially, Rachel is capable of age-appropriate interactions. She does not always exhibit these higher-level skills, however, particularly with peers. Rachel's decreased affect is also influencing her interaction patterns. Motorically, Rachel is moderately delayed in gross motor skills. Fine motor skills are qualitatively immature.

Major Areas of Readiness and Suggested Intervention Strategies:

Motor development is still an area in which Rachel demonstrates less ability. Deficits in this area require intervention in the classroom, with consultation from the physical therapist, and individual physical therapy. Rachel is ready for a variety of gross and fine motor activities that will promote balance, strength, stability, and using both hands together. Therapy goals need to be interfaced with functional activities in the classroom and at home. On the playground, for example, Rachel can experience uneven surfaces, walk barefoot, and climb on playground equipment. The physical therapist will accompany Mr. M. to the park to demonstrate facilitation of motor skills. She will also consult with Rachel's teacher.

Language development is primarily within the expected range. Language will best be encouraged through interaction with peers whose language skills are at or above age level. Suggestions from the speech-language therapist will also be provided to the classroom teacher. Use of the following interventions is recommended: modeling, expanding, commenting, and providing opportunities where Rachel must make requests to get her needs met. Reducing the number of questions that allow for a one-word response is also encouraged. Two-word phrases can be stimulated by pairing Rachel with a peer who uses higher-level language. Reinforcement of the peer's language during an interactive activity will prompt Rachel to expand her language.

Rachel's social skills will also benefit from ongoing interaction with age-level peers. Initial consultation from the psychologist will be provided to the classroom teacher, with follow-up on an as-needed basis. Socially, Rachel needs more opportunity for interactive play with typical peers. This requires setting up situations that encourage give and take. (Ball play, telephones, dressing up, or "painting" peers' faces require interaction. Provision of duplicate objects invites parallel play. Later, reduction of the number of objects available encourages sharing.) All interactions should be reinforced.

Rachel also needs opportunities to *initiate* activities. The teacher can follow Rachel's lead in play situations, then expand on her language, cognitive, and social interactions. Rachel needs time to "develop" a line of play, without shifting too frequently. Low-level turn-taking games with a teacher or peers should be encouraged. Tantrums should be ignored, if possible. She should be invited to join group activities, and reinforced when she participates. The teacher can model exaggerated positive affect when playing, and show enthusiasm and excitement in activities.

Cognitively, Rachel shows no deficits. She can, however, benefit from opportunities to *use* her cognitive skills in functional settings (at the grocery store, helping with dinner, and other home activities). Opportunities can be provided to expand her cognitive schemes through dramatic play (cooking, eating, cleaning-up, washing, dressing for bed, brushing teeth, and going to bed).

In addition to the services provided to Rachel in preschool and through individual therapy, the team will provide parental support and education with regard to Rachel's development and intervention. Ongoing consultation with Mr. M. and Rachel's teachers will be maintained. The type of activities and processes that Rachel is ready for can be integrated into all types of pleasurable activities in the home, school, and community. TPBI is a natural approach for addressing her areas of readiness and specific objectives.

Recommendations:

See the attached forms for the program plan and specific objectives and services for Rachel and her family. These forms fulfill the intent of the law with regard to assessment and demonstrate compliance with various legal requirements. Agencies may have their own forms that fulfill these requirements, or they may want to use or adapt the examples provided. The development of a TPBI plan, including TIP Sheets for home and school, is not discussed here, but is the logical next step in the assessment-intervention cycle. The reader is referred to *Transdisciplinary Play-Based Intervention: Guidelines for Creating a Meaningful Curriculum for Young Children* (Linder, 1993) for a detailed description of the team play-based intervention process.

REFERENCES

Hedrick, D.L., Prather, E.M., & Tobin, A.R. (1984). *Sequenced Inventory of Communication Development–Revised*. Seattle: University of Washington Press.

Linder, T.W. (1993). *Transdisciplinary play-based intervention: Guidelines for developing a meaningful curriculum for young children*. Baltimore: Paul H. Brookes Publishing Co.

Vincent, L., Davis, J., Brown, P., Broome, K., Funkhauser, K., Miller, J., & Grunewald, L. (1986). *The Parent Inventory of Child Development in Nonschool Environments*. Madison: University of Wisconsin, Department of Rehabilitation Psychology and Special Education.

Summary Sheet for Cognitive Guidelines

Name of child: Rachel M.
Name of observer: _____

Date of birth: July 15, 1990
Discipline or job title: _____

Age: 2 years 5 months
Date: December 15, 1992

Observation categories	Areas of strength	Rating	Justification	Things I'm ready for
I. Categories of play	Uses age-appropriate categories	+	Uses exploratory, relational, constructive, and dramatic play	Encourage higher level
II. Attention span	Appropriate in one-to-one	+	Can attend for long periods	Needs to increase in peer situations
III. Early object use	Variety of schemes used	+	Age appropriate	Improve fine motor skills
IV. Symbolic and representational play	Actions directed toward self and dolls	+	Age appropriate	Continue to encourage
V. Gestural imitation	Imitated all types of behavior	+	Age appropriate	Improve turn-taking

Summary Sheet for Cognitive Guidelines

Name of child: _Rachel M._

Name of observer: _____

Date of birth: _July 15, 1990_

Discipline or job title: _____

Age: _2 years, 5 months_

Date: _December 15, 1992_

Observation categories	Areas of strength	Rating	Justification	Things I'm ready for
VI. Problem-solving approaches	Persistence	+	Age appropriate	Encourage seeking alternative solutions
VII. Discrimination/ classification	Recognition of shapes and letters	+	Above age level	Encourage functional categorization
VIII. One-to-one correspondence	One-to-one up to four	+	Above age level	Encourage functional counting
IX. Sequencing ability	Up to eight schemes; initial time concepts	+	Age appropriate in highest ability shown, but not consistent	Facilitate longer play sequences
X. Drawing ability	Beginning face; a few letters	+	Age appropriate	Improve fine motor skills

297

Summary Sheet for Social-Emotional Guidelines

Name of child: _Rachel M._

Name of observer: _____

Date of birth: _July 15, 1990_

Discipline or job title: _____

Age: _2 years, 5 months_

Date: _December 15, 1992_

Observation categories	Areas of strength	Rating	Justification	Things I'm ready for
I. Temperament	Average activity level, adaptable	+	Within average range	Increase range of affective expression
II. Mastery motivation	Purposeful, goal-oriented behavior	+	Self-motivated, persistent	Provide slightly challenging tasks
III. Social interactions with parent	Continuity in play, pleasurable interaction	−	Lacks turn-taking, synchrony and mutuality	Increase R.'s initiation, turn-taking
IV. Social interactions with facilitator	Long interaction sequences	−	Lack of social regard, turn-taking	Increase R.'s turn-taking and attention to play partner

Summary Sheet for Social-Emotional Guidelines

Name of child: _Rachel M._ Date of birth: _July 15, 1990_ Age: _2 years, 5 months_
Name of observer: _____ Discipline or job title: _____ Date: _December 15, 1992_

Observation categories	Areas of strength	Rating	Justification	Things I'm ready for
V. Characteristics of dramatic play	Plays household themes	−	Lacks words of emotion	Encourage affective vocabulary
VI. Humor and social conventions	Laughs at physical stimulation, uses social convention	+	Limited expression of pleasure	Increase exposure to incongruous events; incorporate physical rough and tumble play; Increase social conventions with peers (please, thank you.)
VII. Social interactions with peers	Interest in peer observed	−	Lack of interaction behavior deteriorates in group	Increase response to and turn-taking with peers

Summary Sheet for Communication and Language Guidelines

Name of child: __Rachel M.__   Date of birth: __July 15, 1990__   Age: __2 years 5 months__

Name of observer: _____   Discipline or job title: _____   Date: __December 15, 1992__

Observation categories	Areas of strength	Rating	Justification	Things I'm ready for
I. Communication modalities	Uses words, gestures	+	Age appropriate	Expand current usage and eye contact
II. Pragmatics A. Stages	Locutionary stage	+	Age appropriate	Expand usage.
B. Range of meaning	Uses all communication for a variety of meanings	+	Uses communication for range of intentions	Expand word usage for all meanings
C. Functions	Uses instrumental, regulatory, and interpretive functions	−	Not using full range of functions	Increase interactional, personal, imaginative and heuristic functions
D. Discourse skills	Initiates a topic	−	Limited to one or two turns; doesn't offer new information	Improve turn-taking through extending topic
E. Imitation/ echolalia	Uses imitation to learn	+	Primary mode of learning for R.	Imitation of longer structures

Summary Sheet for Communication and Language Guidelines

Name of child: Rachel M.

Name of observer: _____

Date of birth: July 15, 1990

Discipline or job title: _____

Age: 2 years, 5 months

Date: December 15, 1992

Observation categories	Areas of strength	Rating	Justification	Things I'm ready for
III. Phonology: Sound production system	80% – 90% intelligible	+	Within normal range	Generalization of sounds
IV. Semantic and syntactic understanding in verbal expression	Uses relational and categorical words; adjective negatives; prepositions; uses action-object location	–	Within normal range; lacks early word endings (-ings, -s); longer structures not spontaneous	Expand upper level; Needs activities using action words; increase spontaneous 2-3 word utterances
V. Comprehension of language	Answers simple wh-questions	✓	Extent of vocabulary and semantic comprehension not known	Evaluate receptive language
VI. Oral motor	Eats and drinks well	+	Age-appropriate skills	
VII. Other concerns (identify):				

Summary Sheet for Sensorimotor Guidelines

Name of child: __Rachel M.__   Date of birth: __July 15, 1990__   Age: __2 years, 5 months__

Name of observer: _____   Discipline or job title: _____   Date: __December 15, 1992__

Observation categories	Areas of strength	Rating	Justification	Things I'm ready for
I. General appearance of movement	Physical activity normal; motor activity appropriate	+	Height, weight, and body proportions age-appropriate and adequate for movement	None
II. Muscle tone/strength/endurance	Tone sufficient to support upright positions and walking	−	Mild hypotonia with inadequate coordination; associated reactions	Facilitate muscle tone and strength to support functional movement
III. Reactivity to sensory input	Appropriate responses to tactile, visual, and auditory output	✓	Limited opportunities to observe tactile discrimination and responses to risky movement	Further evaluation to rule out specific sensory deficits
IV. Stationary play positions	Head and trunk righting appropriate in most activities	−	Equilibrium responses not fully functional	Improve control of posture and movements

302

Summary Sheet for Sensorimotor Guidelines

Name of child: _Rachel M._

Name of observer: _____

Date of birth: _July 15, 1990_

Discipline or job title: _____

Age: _2 years, 5 months_

Date: _December 15, 1992_

Observation categories	Areas of strength	Rating	Justification	Things I'm ready for
V. Mobility in play	Positions assumed alone; well-controlled position changes in sit and four point	−	Poor control of transitions in higher positions (standing)	Improve control of posture and balance
VI. Other developmental achievements	Able to perform some milestone skills, such as maneuvering a riding toy	−	Higher-level skills need refinement	Increase opportunities for advanced gross motor activities
VII. Prehension and manipulation	Good visual attention; intermittent demonstration of higher-level skills; high interest in maneuvering objects	−	Poor finger dexterity and release of objects; associated reactions	Improve coordination of arm and hand movements; improve the controlled use of two hands together
VIII. Motor planning	Good imitation of motor acts; age-appropriate management of body and space	+	Functional play and age-appropriate adaptive activities	None

303

PROGRAM PLAN: CHILD

Child's Name: Rachel M. Age: 2 years, 5 months Date: Dec. 15, 1992

Desired Outcomes	Services Needed	Method	Frequency	Initiation Date	Projected Duration
1. Rachel will spontaneously initiate conversations and maintain the topic through three turns.	1. Consultation to father and babysitter on wait-time and turn-taking.	Home visits, observation of tapes	1 time/week	January 1	Re-evaluate in 1 month
2. Rachel will spontaneously use 2–3 word utterances 75% of the time.	2. Rachel would benefit from a pre-school with normal language peers.	Referral to Early Learning School	Daily ½ day	January 1	Year
3. Rachel will begin using higher-level semantic structures.	3. Speech-language therapist provides stimulation suggestions to preschool teacher, father, and babysitter.	Consultation to Early Learning Center and family	Weekly	January 1	Re-evaluate in 1 month
4. Rachel will spontaneously sequence 5–6 steps in dramatic play while in interaction with a peer.	4. Speech-language therapist (with input from teacher) will provide suggestions to preschool teacher, father, and babysitter.	Consultation to Early Learning Center and family	Weekly	January 1	Re-evaluate in 1 month
5. Rachel will initiate play interactions with her father or babysitter and maintain interactions through three turns.	5. Father and babysitter need assistance in facilitating Rachel's interaction skills in play.	Home visit, consultation, observation of tapes and modeling	Weekly	January 1	Re-evaluate in 1 month
6. Rachel will be able to attend individual and group activities within her classroom for ten minutes.	6. Teacher will need consultation on modeling and reinforcing attention and social interaction.	Psychologist consultation to Early Learning Pre-school teacher	Weekly	January 1	Re-evaluate in 1 month
7. Rachel will express happiness, anger, and sadness concepts both verbally and in actions, in appropriate context.	7. Teacher will need consultation from psychologist relating to incorporating emotional themes into books and dramatic play.	Psychologist consultation to Early Learning Pre-school teacher	Weekly	January 1	Re-evaluate in 1 month

#	Goal	Services		Frequency	Start Date	Re-evaluation
8.	Rachel would benefit from physical/occupational therapy. Individual handling sessions will be needed to develop foundational automatic reactions and muscle control needed to acquire age-appropriate coordination. Consultation with the educational team will be needed to simplify and modify gross and fine motor activities. Suggestions will include how to couple movement with verbalizations and exaggerated expressions.		Physical/occupational therapist consultation with early learning preschool team	Weekly	January 1	Re-evaluate in 1 month
					Immediately	Ongoing evaluation during treatment
9.	During individual therapy, the physical/occupational therapist will work on equilibrium responses using a variety of positions and movements. The teacher will need consultation from the therapist regarding appropriate seating arrangements in class (e.g., table and chair height/size).		(a) Physical/occupational therapist consultation with Early Learning Preschool team	Weekly	January 1	Re-evaluate in 1 month
			(b) Individual physical/occupational therapy	Once weekly for 45 minutes	Immediately	Ongoing evaluation during treatment
10.	The teacher, father, and babysitter will need consultation regarding appropriate gross motor activities.		(a) Demonstration of desired postures and explanation of potential compensations when activity is too stressful	Once; follow-up as needed	Immediately	As needed; re-evaluate in 1 month
			(b) Physical/occupational therapist will accompany father and babysitter to local park	Weekly initially; then every 4–6 weeks		Re-evaluate in 4 months

Goals (restated):

8. Rachel will demonstrate improved ability to push, pull lift, and carry large objects (e.g., push open front door, pull peer in wagon, carry sand pail).

9. While seated in a chair, Rachel will demonstrate improved equilibrium responses by reaching for a toy and returning without falling or compensating 75% of the time.

10. Rachel will demonstrate improved stability and equilibrium responses by:
(a) manipulating a toy in standing without leaning against a support.
(b) squatting and retrieving an object from the floor without falling.

(continued)

Desired Outcomes	Services Needed	Method	Frequency	Initiation Date	Projected Duration
10. (c) coming to a "bear-stand" by planting one foot forward.		(c) Integrated group obstacle course; demonstration of techniques to assist Rachel	Monthly		Re-evaluate in 6 months
11. Rachel will demonstrate improved bilateral manipulation skills by consistently assisting with the non-active hand during a two-handed activity.	Rachel would benefit from a wide variety of activities that provide a high level of kinesthetic and tactile input.	Physical/occupational therapy consultations to Early Learning Preschool staff	Weekly	January 1	Re-evaluate in 1 month
12. Rachel will develop more mature control of arm and hand movements by: (a) approaching objects with the thumb appropriately oriented up or to the side, using less of a general overhand approach on objects. (b) demonstrating increased differentiation of arm and hand movements, as measured by the occurrence of movement at the elbow and forearm with the shoulder remaining still in neutral alignment during fine motor activities.	(a) The teacher, father, and babysitter will need consultation regarding appropriate toys. (b) The teacher will need consultation regarding modification of art activities, types/positioning of materials, and techniques of facilitating motor control without stressing Rachel. (c) Individual therapy sessions will incorporate the use of resistive materials, fine motor activities in prone-on-elbows, tactile experiences, and handling to stabilize the shoulders.	(a) Arrangements will be made for Early Learning Center to borrow age-appropriate gross and fine motor materials/manipulatives (b) Toy lending library for families (c) Physical/occupational therapist will provide demonstration to early learning staff (d) Integrated group art activity; demonstration of techniques to assist Rachel (e) Individual physical/occupational therapy	Every 2 weeks · Every 2 weeks · Weekly · Monthly · 45 minutes weekly	January 1 · Immediately · January 1 · January 1 · Immediately	As needed · As desired by family · Re-evaluate in 1 month · Re-evaluate in 6 months · Ongoing evaluation during treatment
13. Rachel will demonstrate decreased associated reactions by efficiently stabilizing age-appropriate toys with her non-active hand.	Father, babysitter, and teacher will need to learn what Rachel's associated reactions look like, how to avoid eliciting these reactions, and how to redirect activities when they occur.	Physical/occupational therapist will provide in-service assistance	One time	January 1	Re-evaluate in May 1992

PROGRAM PLAN: FAMILY

Service Coordinator: _____Mr. M._____

Agency Representatives or other: _____

Position or Relationship: _____

Child's Name: _____Rachel M._____

Age: _____2 years, 5 months_____

Date: _____Dec. 15, 1992_____

Family Strengths	Family Needs in Relation to Child	Outcomes	Resources	How Measured	When Measured
1. Strong commitment to Rachel	1. To increase Rachel's initiations of interactions	1. Rachel will initiate interactions approximately 50% of the time.	Speech-language therapist and psychologist	Observation	Weekly, then monthly
2. Time and desire to work with Rachel	2. To increase wait-time and facilitation of turn-taking	2. Rachel will be able to sustain a conversation with father and babysitter through three turns.	Speech-language therapist	Observation	Weekly, then monthly
3. Willingness to learn about interactions with Rachel	3. To increase Rachel's play sequences and turn-taking in play	3. Rachel will be able to take turns with father and babysitter through three turns.	Speech-language therapist and psychologist	Observation	Weekly, then monthly
	4. To provide social interactions with peers	4. Rachel will play with a neighbor child or at the park two times a week.	Local park, three neighborhood children	Discussion with case manager	Weekly, then monthly
	5. To increase Rachel's functional, spontaneous use of language	5. Rachel will comment on objects, people, or events without being asked a question.	Speech-language therapist	Discussion with case manager	Weekly, then monthly
	6. To increase Mr. M's knowledge of community resources for children	6. Mr. M. will take Rachel to two children's activities with the community.	Service coordinator	Discussion with case manager	Weekly, then monthly
	7. To increase opportunities for advanced gross motor skills	7. Dad will take Rachel to the park two times a week; Rachel will play on the see-saw, climb the ladder, play in squat in the sandbox, and carry a pail filled with sand.	Physical therapist, local park	Observation	Weekly, then monthly

307

Cumulative Summary Sheet

Name: _____Rachel M._____   Date: ____December 15, 1992____

Address: _____50 Beehive Lane_____

_____Denver, Colorado_____

_____

Areas of strength

Cognitive: Rachel's play skills are at age level. Her attention span when playing with an adult is good. She imitates a variety of play behaviors and is persistent in problem-solving. Symbolic skills in play and in drawing are good. Understanding of numbers is above age level.

Social-emotional: Rachel engages in purposeful activity and enjoys interaction with adults. Her play relates to meaningful themes. She is beginning to be interested in peers.

Communication and language: Rachel uses words to communicate. She initiates interaction and indicates her wants and needs. She imitates new structures and uses a variety of types of words to communicate meaning. Her communication is 80%–90% understandable.

Sensorimotor: Rachel functions well in her environment. She walks and uses a variety of positions in sitting and standing. She is capable of moving from one position to another. Rachel has a desire to master gross and fine motor skills.

Primary things I'm ready for: *Motor:* Rachel's movements are awkward due to lack of smooth control of her body, including her trunk, arms, legs, and hands. This is partially due to low tone, lack of strength, and immature balance reactions. Specific skills or tasks are less important at this time than to help Rachel acquire the foundations of automatic balance and alignment mechanisms. Her fine motor incoordination is thought to be related to the same underlying deficits as the gross motor delays.

Secondary things I'm ready for: *Social:* Rachel is ready to increase her ability to take turns through a sequence of activities. She is also ready to begin to play next to peers and to initiate conversations with peers.

Language: Rachel's language is within the normal range, but the teacher and her father and grandmother could work on expanding her utterances by one word. Taking turns in conversations is also a goal for Rachel.

Identified intervention team members: Mr. M.   Physical therapist from the Center
Teacher from the Early Learning Center   Psychologist from the Center
Speech-language pathologist from the Center   Service Coordinator

Signatures of persons present at the meeting:

Name	Title	Agency
_____	_____	_____
_____	_____	_____
_____	_____	_____
_____	_____	_____
_____	_____	_____

Persons not in attendance to whom a report will be sent:

_____   _____   _____

_____   _____   _____

_____   _____   _____

Parental consent:

I have been informed of my rights, and I am in agreement with the assessment findings and the program plan for my child and my family.

Signature: _____   Date: _____

Signature: _____   Date: _____

11

Parent Involvement in the Assessment Process

HISTORICAL ROLE OF PARENTS IN ASSESSMENT

Those who work with young children recognize the need to involve parents in their child's program. The role of the parents in early intervention programs in the 1990s, however, will be far different from their role in the 1980s. Historically, two federal programs have influenced the roles that parents currently assume. IDEA mandates parent involvement in the staffing and development of the individualized education program (IEP) process for school-age children, and programs funded under HCEEP (Handicapped Children's Early Education Program) require an active parent involvement component. As non–federally funded programs evolved, they incorporated the same aspects of due process found in programs for school-age children and the same type of parent involvement activities found in the HCEEP model programs.

Infant and preschool programs have traditionally invited parents to meetings and asked for their input on goals and objectives for their child. Depending on the program, a variety of other options have also been offered (Robinson, Rosenberg, & Beckman, 1988). For example, some parents receive home visits where they are taught how to work with their child who has disabilities (parent-mediated instruction). Other programs offer instructional classes for parents on topics concerning their child with disabilities. Still others give parents instructional readings, offer support groups, have parents volunteer in the classroom, develop parent resource rooms, have parent coffees and family recreational activities, and offer numerous other activities (Bailey et al., 1986; Karnes & Stayton, 1988; Turnbull & Turnbull, 1986). These activities are encompassed in the six components or services identified by Welsh and Odom (1981) as frequently offered in early intervention programs:

1. Social-emotional support
2. Advocacy
3. Decision-making
4. Family education/training
5. Teaching by family members
6. Communication

Will these activities change? Probably not. There is value in all of the above, as has been shown by program evaluations (Guralnick & Bennett, 1987).

THE CHANGING ROLE OF PARENTS

With the arrival of the Education of the Handicapped Act Amendments of 1986 (PL 99-457), and subsequently the Individuals with Disabilities Education Act Amendments of

1991 (PL 102-119), emphasis has been placed on the inclusion of families in a more meaningful way. With infants, in particular, the idea of *family-centered* (Bailey, Buysse, Edmondson, & Smith, 1992) versus child-focused programs is being emphasized. The new requirement for individualized family service plans (IFSPs) for families of infants with disabilities from birth through 2 years of age means that programs must now assess the needs of families in relation to their child with disabilities. Programs must then coordinate the provision of services to meet the identified resource needs, and family priorities and concerns.

Although this new requirement for an IFSP is only mandated for programs serving children through the age of 2, many programs, especially those serving children from birth to 5 years of age, will decide to make the IFSP a total program policy. To maintain philosophical consistency and ethical standards, the family orientation will need to be continued at least through the preschool years.

On the surface, the IFSP appears similar to an IEP, but the inclusion of the *family* service plan result in major changes in most programs (Robinson et al., 1988). The eight elements that each IFSP must include are discussed in Chapter 5.

These elements will make early intervention programs more family-centered. Recent intervention models are therefore focusing on the family system and the network of services needed to maximally affect the child and family (Bailey & Simeonsson, 1984; Bronfenbrenner, 1977; Gallagher, Beckman, & Cross, 1983; Turnbull & Winton, 1984). Emphasis is placed on supporting parents in their interactions with their child, other family members, and agencies within the service delivery system.

Many infant and preschool programs may begin to offer additional services to families to meet their needs. All programs will need to refer families to other community resources that offer services not provided through the programs. Many questions remain unanswered with regard to the IFSP and family services. What constitutes a family need that is a legitimate focus of early intervention? What assessment process will be used to identify family needs? Who is responsible for identifying family needs? How will information about families, which is relevant to the enhancement of the child's development, be obtained without being intrusive? And what information is pertinent? These questions are causing quite a furor among service providers and families. These issues are being debated and policies are being developed at both local program and state levels.

Some programs are examining factors such as family composition and structure, roles and responsibilities, emotional and material resources, stresses, critical life events, coping strategies, parent–child interaction, and numerous other aspects of the family functioning (Robinson et al., 1988). It is difficult to see how this process can be accomplished without being intrusive.

Developers of these procedures need to keep in mind that only information that is relevant to the child's developmental progress need be gathered, and only after the parents understand how the information will be used. Parents always have a right to refuse to provide information; they also have the right to help interpret information and determine what their needs are (or are not). They also have a right to decide which services, if any, they wish to use.

The purpose of this chapter is not to examine all of the aspects of assessment and involvement of families in early intervention programs. However, there are two particular areas of parent involvement in the assessment process that deserve attention: 1) the involvement of the parents in the assessment of the child; and 2) the observation of the child's interactions with the parent, which can be viewed as both child assessment and family assessment. Both are relevant to the TPBA process.

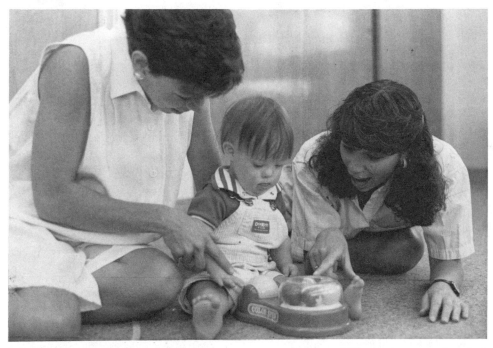

Involvement of the parent in the assessment process and observation of parent–child interactions are two important aspects of transdisciplinary play-based assessment.

PARENT INVOLVEMENT IN CHILD ASSESSMENT

Although IDEA mandates parent participation in the IEP process, studies show that parents are not active participants or equal decision-makers with school personnel (Lynch & Stein, 1982; Soufer, 1982; Turnbull, Turnbull, & Wheat, 1982). School personnel frequently have negative attitudes about the IEP process (Morgan & Rhode, 1983) and about parents' ability to make appropriate decisions about their child (Vincent, Laten, Salisbury, Brown, & Baumgart, 1981). Parents are seldom included as the actual "partners" professionals have named them. The parents' role in the assessment and IEP process is often a perfunctory one, where parents attend, are informed of the results of testing, and are presented with IEPs that were developed prior to the meeting by the school staff. Parents are then asked to concur with the findings, recommendations for placement, and programming, and to sign the IEP form (Brinkerhoff & Vincent, 1986; Robinson et al., 1988). This does not reflect a positive approach to parent involvement.

Due to Part H, the emphasis on parent involvement in the child's program is even greater. The parents are to be included in the decision-making at all levels. Parents need to be involved from the very beginning in the assessment of the child and the determination of appropriate goals and priorities for intervention. Information about the child's development should be obtained prior to the assessment of the child, if possible. Knowledge about the child's skills and parents' concerns makes planning a functional, relevant IFSP easier.

How can parents best assume a meaningful role in this process? Two ways can be identified. One is to include parents in the actual data-gathering process, by having them record the skills they observe in their child at home. The other is to include parents in the team assessment process itself. The inclusion of the parents in the actual assessment is demonstrated by, and has been reflected in, the earlier chapters of this book. The former approach is explored in more detail in the following discussion.

Parents as Evaluators

Parents are accurate evaluators of their child's current level of functioning (Beckman, 1984; Ireton & Thwing, 1972; Vincent et al., 1981), because they usually spend the most time with their child. They observe the child at all times of the day, in various situations, and with different people. They understand the variability in the child's performance, and how the child reacts and adapts to different types of stimuli. Parents have information about how the child behaves in his or her natural environments, in his or her home and neighborhood, in stores, in the park, and in church.

Calhoun and Newson (1984) found parents to be competent evaluators and an integral part of the ongoing assessment process for children who are difficult to test. Thomas, Chess, and Birch (1968) used parents as the source of information on their child's temperament characteristics. Subsequent researchers have continued to use parents as the evaluators of temperament (Carey & McDevitt, 1978; Keogh, Pullis, & Cadwell, 1980; Persson-Blennow & McNeil, 1979). Mastery motivation is also reliably assessed by parents (Morgan, Harmon, Pipp, & Jennings, 1983).

Parent Report Instruments

Questionnaires are frequently given to parents to determine behavioral or emotional problems (Garrison & Earls, 1985). Adaptive behavior scales, such as the Adaptive Behavior Scale for Infants and Early Childhood (Leland, Shoace, McElwain, & Christie, 1980), may also be parent-administered. Many such scales allow the parents to identify the child's level of performance in all areas of development. The Vineland Adaptive Behavior Scales (Sparrow, Balla, & Cicchetti, 1984) is one such scale. The Battelle Developmental Inventory (Newborg, Stock, Wnek, Guidubaldi, & Svinicki, 1984), another assessment instrument, also has parent-administered components.

These instruments provide valuable input to the assessment process. The assessment team determines the developmental level of the child and the specific skills that the child is able to perform. However, the parents know if, when, and how the child actually uses these skills. Tapping into the parents' knowledge about the child is helpful to the team who will be conducting the play-based assessment; this allows the team to prepare an environment that is developmentally appropriate, with toys, materials, and activities that will promote the child's optimal capabilities.

Assessment tools that delineate functional skills that the parents observe the child doing at home are also available. Information so gathered can be combined with data from the team assessment to yield a more accurate and complete picture of the child's abilities. The parents also find it easier to contribute to the IEP or IFSP process if, like the professionals, they have actual data to which they can refer in discussions about the child. Parents become active members of the assessment team, and equal partners in the program planning process (Brinkerhoff & Vincent, 1986).

Requesting that parents document skills is also helpful to the team in another way. It helps the professionals to translate their test information into terms that are understandable to the parents. The psychologist, on the one hand, may refer to the child's level of understanding of object permanence. The parents, on the other hand, may have noted that the child does not look for toys once they have disappeared from sight. The team can learn to use the parents' information to explain the importance of this skill for the child's long-term development (in language development, for instance).

The Minnesota Child Development Index (MCDI) (Ireton & Thwing, 1972) is a parent-completed inventory of the child's skills in the major domains of development. It has been found to be a reliable source of information concerning the child's abilities. Another such instrument is the Parent Inventory of Child Development in Nonschool Environments (Vincent et al., 1986). This is a parent-administered assessment of typical milestones and critical adaptive skills for children under 6 years of age, and enables parents to:

1. Match the information school staff use to develop IEPs
2. Pinpoint the child's strengths and needs
3. Identify which skills the child should work on next
4. Choose which skills to target as educational goals

The Parent Inventory is divided into four developmental age ranges, with skills divided into five subsections:

1. Interactions (fine motor, gross motor, communication, cognition, and social skills)
2. Communication (understanding and using language)
3. Self-help (feeding and toileting)
4. Things we like children to do (adaptive behaviors)
5. Things we wish children did not do (maladaptive behaviors)

The scoring in the inventory gives parents the option of determining the level to which a child is capable of performing a skill. They can also check whether or not they want a skill targeted as a goal for their child, and whether or not they want a further explanation of why a skill is important for their child.

Vincent and her colleagues have developed another tool, a Daily Routine Recording Form, to be used in tandem with the Parent Inventory (Vincent, Davis, Brown, Teicher, & Weynand, 1983). This instrument is a systematic means for recording daily activities for each half hour of the day. For each time segment, the parents indicate: 1) the participants in the activity occurring at that time, 2) the level of assistance the child needs for the activity, and 3) the parent's perception of the quality of the interaction for each participant in the activity (whether it is a "good" or a "bad" time for each participant). This allows the intervention team, along with the parents, to examine aspects of the day that are particularly difficult or rewarding for the parent, caregiver, siblings, and child. Use of such an instrument can lead to the identification of priorities for intervention that will ease the stress on the family. Helping the family to focus on the pleasurable times of interaction is another positive outcome.

Instruments such as the ones just reviewed give professionals an opportunity to see what life with the child is like and to see what goals are important to the parents. The goals identified by the parent may not be the same as those targeted by the staff. In this event, discussion and negotiation need to take place to ensure that both parents and staff are satisfied with the direction that the intervention is taking. An example of the usefulness of such an approach follows.

Assessing Amanda

Amanda, identified as environmentally at risk, has been referred to a team of professionals for developmental evaluation. She was born 1 month premature, to a 20-year-old mother with developmental delays. Amanda's 30-year-old father, who is presently living in the home, is an alcoholic.

Abuse and neglect are suspected, and Amanda is therefore being followed by Social Services. Amanda is 13 months old.

Initially, a traditional team evaluation was completed on Amanda. Several items from the cognitive section of the report illustrate the findings of the team. On the Bayley Scales of Infant Development (Bayley, 1969), Amanda was found to have a Mental Development Index (MDI) of 89 (+/− 6.7). (The mean on the Bayley is 100 and the standard deviation is 16, placing Amanda within the average range.) Item analysis showed her to have relative strengths in motor imitation (patting the doll, dangling the ring), expressive language (she "jabbered" expressively), and object permanence (she uncovered the blue box to discover its contents). Her relative weaknesses were in fine motor skills, manipulation, release, and eye-hand coordination (she was unable to put cubes in a cup, turn pages of a book, put beads in a box, place pegs in a peg board). Cause-and-effect understanding (pushing a car, turning the bottle to remove a pellet) and receptive language skills (following directions) were also relative weaknesses. Recommendations in the cognitive area related to increasing imitation skills, cause-and-effect understanding, fine motor problem-solving, and ability to follow directions.

Prior to the team's assessment, the Daily Routine Recording Form and the Parent Inventory of Child Development in Nonschool Environments were completed through an interview with Amanda's mother. Results of the Daily Routine Recording Form revealed that Amanda's mother spends most of her day in the apartment with Amanda. She and Amanda directly interact around maintenance activities, such as feeding, bathing, and diaper changing. Amanda's mother reports that the best time for them is their playtime, after Amanda's nap. She stated that the most difficult times occur during feeding, bathing, and diaper changing, because Amanda does not hold still and will not cooperate.

On the Parent Inventory of Child Development in Nonschool Environments Amanda's mother indicated that she wanted Amanda to be able to look at books, get toys for herself, walk and run, play nicely with other children, talk, and stop having temper tantrums. She identified walking, talking, and being able to play by herself without tantrums as priorities.

Clearly, the two sources of information, formal testing and parent report, agreed on several points. Differences are also evident that are critical for the intervention program with this child. Behavior, for instance, was not identified as a problem by the assessment team, who focused more on cognitive and fine motor weaknesses. Amanda is only slightly delayed. The areas identified by the intervention team are relevant, but not critical, for her further development.

Amanda is environmentally at risk, particularly with regard to appropriate parenting. Amanda's mother has expectations for her development (particularly with regard to the tantrums) that may be unrealistic for Amanda; however, her desire for Amanda to walk and talk are realistic expectations. By looking at the parent's input, other members of the team could see that Amanda's mother needed to be supported in her observations of Amanda and given assistance with the areas that were causing her frustration.

The fact that most direct interaction times revolved around maintenance activities, and that these interaction times were not of a positive nature, indicated that Amanda's mother needed support to learn to make these times less stressful. Amanda's mother agreed that she would like these activities to be easier. She also stated that she didn't like getting angry with Amanda, and would like assistance in how to deal with her child's tantrums. The professional team members offered to visit her at home and observe the interactions that took place. Data from these observations could then be used to improve the parent–child interactions, especially during the most stressful times. The other team members could also support the mother in the positive aspects of her give-and-take with Amanda, enabling her to more fully participate in the ongoing assessment of Amanda.

As the vignette above demonstrates, by examining the parent assessment data along with the team assessment data, the team was able to focus on a broader range of issues concerning Amanda's development. The parent's input, obtained in this case through interviews, was helpful for identifying priorities for intervention for Amanda, and recognizing areas for supporting her mother in developing parenting skills. This is just one brief excerpt from a total evaluation that included much more information and many recommendations for the family. This example, however, does illustrate how input from the parent can provide valuable information for the development of the IFSP or the IEP, whether using a traditional or a transdisciplinary play-based assessment model.

While visiting Amanda in her home and observing the parent–child interaction, the professional team members also conducted a transdisciplinary play-based assessment. The parents thus had the additional benefit of seeing an assessment during which Amanda's activities were similar to those seen daily in the home. The parent's prior evaluation was used during the assessment to point out parallel observations, to explain the rationale for including certain items, and to identify discrepancies. For example, Amanda's mother pointed out that Amanda usually made more vocalizations while she was playing. In addition, the parent facilitator was able to explain how the play facilitator was eliciting higher level skills than Amanda's mother had noted in the pre-evaluation. In both instances, communication about Amanda was setting the stage for a partnership in intervention.

PARENT–CHILD INTERACTION

Amanda's story also illustrates the second significant area of parent involvement in the assessment process: the child's social or interaction abilities. Parent–child interaction is an important component of the child's larger social interaction abilities. The primary persons with whom a child interacts are naturally his or her parents. An analysis of a child's interactions with parents can provide useful information for determining intervention targets for the child, and for supporting the parents in their efforts to facilitate their child's development. The TPBA model not only encourages this area of involvement, but specifically addresses parent–child and other interaction skills within the social-emotional development guidelines (Chapter 7).

Research in the 1980s on parent–child interaction (mothers, in particular) between children without disabilities and their parents and between children with disabilities and their parents has led us to re-examine our previous assumptions about how parents can best be involved in intervention programs. The literature reviewed below has led us to alter our philosophy and approach to parents and children. The "teaching parents to teach model," which a great many early intervention programs have espoused, may in fact be detrimental to the interaction patterns between the parents and the child (Affleck, McGrade, McQueeney, & Allen, 1982).

Parent–child interaction has been shown to have an impact on the child's later communication and language skills, social development, and cognitive development (Bricker, 1985; Holdgrafer & Dunst, 1986; Johnson, 1983). Parent–child interaction is also related to the development of healthy attachment between the parent and child. Securely attached children have been shown to acquire some cognitive milestones earlier, to develop nurturing behavior and prosocial behavior earlier, and to explore the environment and interact with others more freely (Bricker, 1985).

Characteristics of both the child and the parent contribute to the development of interaction patterns. Children with disabilities and their parents may be at greater risk for developing interaction patterns that put the attachment process at risk. Research on children who have disabilities, are medically at risk, and are environmentally at risk has offered some insight into some of the potential problems on both sides of the parent–child dyad; these characteristics and problems become areas of potential concern in assessment.

Child Characteristics that Affect Parent–Child Interactions

Numerous characteristics of the child with developmental or medical problems contribute to the child demonstrating atypical interaction patterns. High-risk and developmentally delayed children show fewer communicative signals to parents early in life, and interaction later in infancy is described as less reciprocal. Many studies have been conducted with babies with Down syndrome, because they are an easily identified population. These studies show that babies with Down syndrome differ in critical interaction variables, showing less smiling, laughter, vocal activity, and motor development (Rothbart & Hanson, 1983). Babies with Down syndrome also have more difficulty with state regulation (Cicchetti & Sroufe, 1983), and the child's state is harder to "read."

Focused gaze in the baby with Down syndrome takes longer to develop (Rothbart, 1984), and the development of referential gaze from adults to objects is delayed (Gunn, Barry, & Andrews, 1979). Referential gaze is important because it tells the parent what the baby is interested in or wants. These babies also pay more visual attention to objects than to adults (Krakow & Kopp, 1983). However, with babies who do not have disabilities, increased attention is first paid to the human face, and only later to objects. This attention is important to the parent, who so desperately wants to be the focus of attention for the young infant.

In addition, Emde, Katz, and Thorpe (1982) found that the babies with Down syndrome demonstrate less activity in their arms and legs, probably due to their low muscle tone. Motor movement is, however, a form of gestural communication in the young child; so decreased motor activity implies decreased nonverbal communication with the parent.

Other researchers have discovered delayed development of other coordinated communicative acts, including gestures, gaze, and vocalization in babies with Down syndrome (Bricker & Carlson, 1981; Holdgrafer & Dunst, 1986). The development of vocalizations such as crying, cooing, babbling, and prespeech vocalizations are all affected (Smith & Oller, 1981). Consequently, there are fewer vocalizations in social interactions with the parent (Stevenson, Leavitt, & Silverberg, 1985).

Overall, the babies with Down syndrome have less eye contact with their parents, initiate fewer interactions with the parent, and are less likely to give the parent an opportunity to participate in an interchange. The baby with Down syndrome does not provide the same signals as the baby who does not have disabilities, and if he or she does provide normal cues, it is later than expected. These seemingly minor differences can have profound effects upon parent–child interactions, and therefore can affect the child's development. Identifying these differences in an assessment can help the parents to understand why they may feel frustrated in their interactions with their child. Parents' feelings of guilt associated with the lack of plea surable interactions may also be ameliorated, once they understand why they feel frustrated.

Several studies on early interactions of high-risk infants have reported that these infants also exhibit less attentiveness (Field, 1979a), less smiling and positive affect (Field, 1979b), and greater fussiness (DiVitto & Goldberg, 1979). Infants with physiological, sensory, or cognitive impairments may not provide signals that clearly indicate their needs, or they may give inconsistent signals (Thoman, Becker, & Freese, 1978). Other infants may be hypersensitive to environmental or internal stimuli, making it difficult for the parents to understand the source of the child's distress.

Attractiveness and cuddliness have also been shown to affect parents' response to the infant (Brazelton, 1973). Infants with disabilities frequently look different from infants who do not have disabilities and motor problems may influence the child's ability to cuddle. These qualities may make the child less appealing to the parent, having subtle negative affect on the parent–child relationship.

Many parents of children with disabilities have reported other characteristics in their children that make play and other interactions less rewarding. Parents have expressed concerns about a lack of sustained attention on the part of the child, rough or inappropriate use of objects, and apathy and lack of pleasurable interactions (Cicchetti & Sroufe, 1976; Field, 1983; Linder, 1982). Other research has demonstrated that infants and children with disabilities may exhibit narrow and inflexible methods of exploration, that they may "perform" rather than respond, or that they lack the ability to initiate behaviors (Mogford, 1977). Children with disabilities may also provide their parents with fewer opportunities to praise or reward their behavior or accomplishments (Jones, 1977). These characteristics are important to identify in the assessment process.

Researchers who work with children with cerebral palsy have found these children to be more difficult to engage. Infants with physical disabilities play less than infants who do not have disabilities or those with mental retardation (Hewett, 1970), and engage more in simple looking behavior (Field, 1983). Blind infants have also been shown to demonstrate disturbed interaction patterns (Fraiberg, 1974).

These atypical characteristics are relevant not just in infancy but may also affect later development. Follow-up studies have shown that interaction disturbances demonstrated by preterm infants in early infancy seem to persist in later childhood (Bakeman & Brown, 1980; Sigman, Cohen, & Forsythe, 1981). Similar trends have been reported for children with Down syndrome (Jones, 1977) and infants with cerebral palsy (Kogan, 1980). As Field (1983) reports, "there is some disconcerting evidence for continuity between early interaction disturbances and later developmental delays" (p. 80).

How do these differences affect the parents? The seemingly higher threshold for stimulation noted in preterm infants (Field, Dempsky, Ting, Hatch, & Clifton, 1979), children with Down syndrome (Cicchetti & Sroufe, 1976), and infants with mental retardation (Kogan, 1980) often results in the parent making aggressive attempts to engage the child in interaction (Field, 1983; Jones, 1977). However, these children are also easily overstimulated, and are difficult to console once their thresholds have been exceeded, exhibiting gaze avoidance, fussing, and crying. A major problem, then, for a parent of an infant with a disability is knowing when and how to interact with the child. As Mogford (1977) has stated:

> For the handicapped child whose disability delays his independent exploration, and who through failure and frustration, may learn to be passive, much effort and skill are required of the mother or caretaker to encourage and help the child structure his experience. (p. 172)

The parent must become adept at reading the unusual "cues" from the child in order to facilitate interactions. Without realizing exactly what they are doing or why they are doing it, parents do tend to modify their behaviors in response to the child with disabilities. Brooks-Gunn and Lewis (1982) also showed that mothers of infants with disabilities tend to engage in play with toys (primarily demonstrating and giving) more frequently than mothers of typical infants. This concentration on play with objects may represent their increased efforts to engage their child in play. The emphasis on toy play, however, persists as the child gets older. When children who do not have disabilities switch to more social interactive play, the children with disabilities tend to persist in solitary toy play. Interactive social skills do not develop. These studies all have implications for assessment and intervention.

Parent Characteristics that Affect Parent—Child Interaction

The parent may also contribute characteristics that can positively or negatively affect interaction patterns with the child.

Parents who themselves have developmental disabilities or are depressed, psychologically disturbed, abusive, or otherwise emotionally unavailable may not be able to respond to and initiate appropriate interaction patterns. They may be unable to send the infant necessary cues and signals concerning how they feel or what they want from the child (Musick, Clark, & Cohler, 1981). Such a parent may not look at or touch the infant while the infant is gazing at them. Messages, such as vocalizations or bodily excitement, that are sent by the child to the parent in hopes of continuing the touching, talking, or "game" that has just occurred may be ignored. In addition, the parent may not imitate the child's behaviors or initiate play interactions with the child. He or she may be unable to engage in turn-taking behaviors or to sustain play interactions. The parent's behavioral expectations may be inappropriate for the developmental age of the child.

The consequences of poor parental cueing and responsiveness may be devastating to the attachment process, to parent—child interaction, and to the course of the child's development. Many different degrees of interaction difficulty are possible. A parent may exhibit a range of interaction difficulties, only a few, or none. More research is needed to ascertain the differential outcomes associated with various interaction patterns.

Parent Child Interaction as a Variable in Intervention

Previously, early interventionists have taught the parents about the child's disabilities, helped them to follow through on therapy, and suggested techniques to foster the child's development and meet program objectives. The research just discussed is now pointing to the need to also focus on the relationship between the parent and child as an important aspect of intervention (Affleck et al., 1982; Brooks-Gunn & Lewis, 1982; Field, 1983; Kelly, 1982).

As noted in the literature, the child with disabilities and his or her parent may have greater difficulty forming a strong attachment. Their interactions may be less pleasurable, less reciprocal, and shorter in duration (Field, 1983). Helping the parent to improve these interactions should, therefore, have long-term benefits for parent and child. Traditional intervention approaches that teach the parent to "teach" their child or provide "therapy" time may actually be detrimental to the parent—child relationship. Intervention should make the parent—child relationship more positive and pleasurable for everyone. New skills and therapy need not be experienced in a directive, work-oriented approach that is demanding of both the parents and the child.

Research has shown that children with disabilities do not initiate or maintain interactive behaviors as frequently as children who do not have disabilities (Cunningham, Rueler, Blackwell, & Deck, 1981; Field, 1983; Hanson, 1984; Jones, 1978). They may also need a longer response time. The result may be that parents, teachers, therapists, and others may become more directive in order to elicit responses. They may not allow the time necessary for the child to process environmental cues and organize a response without prompting. At the infant level, it is important to help parents learn to read their child's cues and initiations, to extend wait time, and become less directive. At the preschool level, it is important to incorporate the same processes into the classroom as well as into the home.

Programs such as the Transactional Intervention Program, developed by Mahoney and Powell (1986), are designed to improve the quality of interactions between the parent and child. A variety of other programs are making similar efforts in working with parents and children to develop optimal interaction patterns (Beckman, Robinson, Jackson, & Rosenberg, 1986). The research that has accompanied these efforts is demonstrating that significant changes can be made. Kelly (1982) found that videotaping parents for 10 minutes at a time and providing feedback to parents over eight sessions was helpful in changing interaction patterns, in terms of increasing positive initiating and positive responding on the part of the child. Overall infant behaviors were more positive, while parental controlling behaviors decreased.

Affleck et al. (1982) also examined the effect of relationship-focused intervention. After 9 months of treatment, experimental parents: 1) showed greater responsiveness to their infants; 2) participated more frequently in reciprocal activities; 3) showed more organized involvement with the child (e.g., structuring play activities); and 4) tended to identify positive evidence of the infant's differential responsiveness to them. The developmental quotient of treatment infants also increased compared to infants in the control group.

These results and others are leading to an increased interest in including a focus on parent–child interaction in early intervention programs. Numerous assessment procedures have been devised to identify targets for intervention. The Maternal Behavior Rating Scale (Mahoney et al., 1986) is a tool developed to be used with a relationship-focused program. The Attachment-Separation-Individuation Scale (A-S-I) (Foley & Hobin, 1987) can be used for both clinical and educational purposes. Based on the theories of Margaret Mahler (Mahler, Pine, & Bergman, 1975), the A-S-I identifies the level of interaction of the parent and infant ages birth to 36 months and serves as a basis for making recommendations for intervention. The Parent Behavior Progression (PBP) Form I (Bromwich et al., 1981) for infants ages birth to 9 months, and Form II (Bromwich, Kass, Khokha, Baxter, Burge, & Fust, 1981) for infants between 9 and 36 months, are two scales developed by the staff at the UCLA (University of California–Los Angeles) Intervention Program. These tools look at both parent–child interaction and parent provision of experiences to foster growth and development. The Human Interaction Scale (White & Watts, 1973) codes and analyzes mother–child, child-child, child-peer, and child-adult (nonparent) interactions across five dimensions, and can be used with children up to 6 years of age. Other approaches to assessing parent–child interaction are reviewed by Rosenberg (1986) and Fewell (1986).

The previously mentioned instruments are in-depth measures that can be used to identify interaction strengths and weaknesses. TPBA serves as another method for looking at the child in the context of interaction with the parent. Interaction patterns that are recurring between parent and child can be seen. The parent is involved in the play-based assessment in both informal play interactions and in a more structured "teaching" task. Specific observations were discussed earlier in Chapter 7, where the social-emotional development guidelines offer a brief look at parent–child interaction and can be used to determine whether a more in-depth measure, such as those discussed in this chapter, may be appropriate.

TPBA also offers the team and the parents an opportunity to compare the child's interactions with various people—the play facilitator, the parents, a peer, and possibly other adults. The benefits of differential observations are many. First, the parent usually has established effective means of communicating with the child, and the team can learn much about establishing successful interactions with the child through observation of the parent's techniques. Second, if there are concerns about interaction on the part of the child, the parent, or both, this can be noted and discussed with the parent after the session. A more in-depth observation or analysis is then scheduled. The availability of a videotape also allows the team and parents to watch interactions together and identify examples of behaviors that are facilitating or hindering pleasurable interactions.

Interaction Between Amanda and Her Mother

Returning to the home observation of Amanda, observation of Amanda and her mother during the TPBA play session revealed important clues to the problems Amanda's mother was experiencing. As the vignette below clarifies, Amanda's mother was trying to direct Amanda's play, which Amanda resisted. Amanda was at a lower developmental level than her mother expected.

The other professionals on the team asked Amanda and her mother to play together both with familiar and unfamiliar toys. Amanda and her mother appeared to have different "agendas." The mother was trying to get Amanda to attend to and perform certain skills with a cause-and-effect toy. Amanda was interested in a doll, and was not paying any attention to her mother. These differences in attention recurred repeatedly.

Amanda's mother was also not allowing enough time for Amanda to respond to her. She asked one question after another: "Can you put this here? What color is the truck?" Many of her questions were too developmentally challenging for Amanda to comprehend. Amanda, for her part, demonstrated limited positive affect. She became impatient and frustrated very quickly. She was also difficult to calm once she became agitated.

Overall, both parties were less than satisfied with their interactions. Amanda's mother felt unrewarded for her efforts to engage her child in play. Her difficulties interpreting the cues that Amanda was giving were leading to stressful times. It was important for the other team members to identify with Amanda's mother points for intervention.

The team was able to further analyze the interaction patterns on the videotape and discuss their impressions with Amanda's mother. Recommendations included working with Amanda's mother to help her follow Amanda's lead, take turns with Amanda, and increase her wait time. The team planned appropriate language and play for Amanda's mother, to show her how to incorporate games into bathtime, and they worked with her to understand Amanda's temperament characteristics, so that her mother was not interpreting Amanda's behaviors as "not liking her." They also were able to offer suggestions for dealing with Amanda's behavior when Amanda became frustrated or short-tempered. Goals were established with Amanda's mother, and included in the IFSP.

As Amanda's example demonstrates, transdisciplinary play-based assessment offers an informal means of gaining an initial impression of the interaction patterns of the child with the facilitator, the parents, and a peer. Comparisons across persons provides a reference point for parents as well as professionals. By observing and participating in the assessment process, the parents have an opportunity to integrate the information they have seen in the play session with the information they have previously provided regarding their child's functional skills at home. The team and parents can then work together to determine the relationship between the home-based assessment and the play-based assessment. When combined with additional assessment data on the child and the needs assessment data acquired from the family, the play-based data can lay the foundation for the development of a functional, family-centered intervention program. Transdisciplinary play-based intervention (Linder, 1993) can then be used to plan pleasurable interactions between the family members and the child.

FAMILIES AND TPBA

Since passage of the Education of the Handicapped Act Amendments (PL 99-457), the need for *timely, comprehensive, multidisciplinary* evaluation of infants and preschoolers and of the needs of their families (in relation to the children's development) has been recognized in the law of the land. IFSPs are becoming central to early intervention services.

As noted in the work of the many researchers cited in this chapter, one area of identified need for families may be the parent–child relationship. Strengths and patterns that are less effective can be seen in either or both partners in the dyad, and with one or both parents. Sibling–child relationships may also demonstrate difficult interaction patterns. By examining interrelationships, points of concern as well as specific strengths can be noted, and goals and objectives may be determined. Appropriate stategies for supporting and strengthening parent–child interactions, and thus families themselves, can then be planned.

As programs become more family-centered, numerous new ways to assess the needs of families in relation to the development of their child will undoubtedly emerge. Addressing these needs in ways that are the least intrusive and most meaningful to the family is critical. The suggestions offered in this chapter for incorporating parents' information about their child and responding to observations of parent–child interactions during the assessment process are meant to respond to these dimensions. (See, for example, the chapter on involving families in the *Teacher's Guide* of *Read, Play, and Learn!* [Linder, 1999].) It is hoped that the TPBA model as a whole can be used flexibly, in a way that is both natural and purposeful, to provide better assessment of and intervention for children and their families.

SUMMARY

Recent legislation recognizes the importance of identifying and serving young children with disabilities as early as possible. Part H provides an ideological basis for programs serving infants and young children with disabilities, with broad guidelines for programs to allow flexibility in services for children and families. The law recognizes the importance of families in the child's development, and the need to support families in their attempts to meet their child's needs. Assessment alternatives that are appropriate for young children are encouraged, and families are to be involved in all aspects of the child's program. The use of a transdisciplinary play-based assessment process that involves parents is consistent with the intent of this legislation.

Transdisciplinary play-based assessment plays an important role in family intervention. Comfortable rapport and communication are established from the onset of the process. Parents contribute the initial assessment data on the child's developmental skills and desired goals; and as a result of their involvement in the TPBA, the family gains a greater understanding of how their knowledge of the child relates to the team's determination of the strengths of and priorities for their child. They also have an opportunity to observe facilitative interaction techniques during the play session. This provides the foundation for supporting parents in play-based, functional intervention approaches. The transdisciplinary team process, the involvement of the parents, and the use of play as a medium for assessment are three vital components that serve as the philosophical core and vital link to child and family-focused intervention programs.

REFERENCES

Affleck, G., McGrade, B.J., McQueeney, A.D., & Allen, D. (1982). Relationships-focused early intervention in developmental disabilities. *Exceptional Children, 3,* 259–261.

Bailey, D.B., Buysse, V., Edmondson, R., & Smith, T.M. (1992). Creating family-centered services in early intervention: Perceptions of professionals in four states. *Exceptional Parent, 58*(4), 298–310.

Bailey, D.B., Jr., & Simeonsson, R.J. (1984). Critical issues underlying research and intervention with families of young handicapped children. *Journal for the Division of Early Childhood, 9*(1), 38–48.

Bailey, D.B., & Wolery, M. (1984). *Teaching infants and preschoolers with handicaps.* Columbus, OH: Charles E. Merrill.

Bailey, D.B., Simeonsson, R.J., Winton, P.J., Huntington, G.S., Comfort, M., Isbell, P., O'Donnell, K.J.,

& Helm, J.M. (1986). Family-focused intervention: A functional model for planning, implementing, and evaluating individualized family service in intervention. *Journal for the Division of Early Childhood, 102*, 156–171.

Bayley, N. (1969). *Bayley Scales of Infant Development.* New York: Psychological Corporation.

Bakeman, R., & Brown, J. (1980). Early intervention: Consequences for social and mental development at three years. *Child Development, 51*, 437–447.

Beckman, P.J. (1984). Perceptions of young children with handicaps: A comparison of mothers and program staff. *Mental Retardation, 22*(4), 176–181.

Beckman, P.J., Robinson, C.C., Jackson, B., & Rosenburg, S.A. (1986). Translating developmental findings into teaching strategies for young handicapped children. *Journal for the Division of Early Childhood, 10*(1) 45–52.

Brazelton, T.B. (1973). Neonatal Behavioral Assessment Scale. *National Spastics Society Monographs.* London: William Heinemann & Sons.

Bricker, D.D. (1985). *Intervention with at-risk and handicapped infants: From research to application.* Baltimore: University Park Press.

Bricker, D., & Carlson, L. (1981). Issues in language intervention. In R.L. Schiefelbusch & D. Bricker (Eds.), *Early language intervention* (pp. 477–515). Baltimore: University Park Press.

Brinkerhoff, J.L., & Vincent, L.J. (1986). Increasing parental decisionmaking at their child's individualized educational program meeting. *Journal of the Division for Early Childhood, II*(1), 46–58.

Bromwich, R.M., Kass, E.W., Khokha, E., Barter, E., Burge, D., & Fust, L. (1981). Parent behavior progression (PBP) Form II. In R. Bromwich (Ed.), *Working with parents and infants: An interactional approach.* Austin, TX: PRO-ED.

Bromwich, R.M., Khokha, E., Fust, L., Baxter, E., Burge, D., & Kass, E.W. (1981). Parent Behavior Progression (PBP) Form I. In R. Bromwich (Ed.), *Working with parents and infants: An interactional approach* (pp. 341–352). Austin, TX: PRO-ED.

Bronfenbrenner, U. (1977). Toward an experimental ecology of human development. *American Psychologist, 32*, 513–531.

Brooks-Gunn, J., & Lewis, M. (1982). Assessing young handicapped children: Issues and solutions. *Journal of the Division for Early Childhood, 2*, 84–85.

Calhoun, M.L., & Newson, E. (1984). Parents as experts: An assessment approach for hard-to-test children. *Diagnostique. 9*(4), 239–244.

Carey, W.B., & McDevitt, S.C. (1978). *Infant Temperament Questionnaire (ITQ).* Media, PA: Carey Associates.

Cicchetti, D., & Sroufe, L.A. (1983). The relationship between affective and cognitive development in Down's Syndrome infants. *Child Development, 46*, 920–929.

Cicchetti, D., & Sroufe, L.A. (1976). An organizational view of affect: Illustration from the study of Down syndrome infants. In M. Lewis & L.A. Rosenblum (Eds.), *The development of affect* (pp. 309–349). New York: Plenum.

Cunningham, C.E., Rueler, E., Blackwell, J., & Deck, J. (1981). Behavioral and linguistic developments in the interactions of normal and retarded children with their mothers. *Child Development, 52*, 62–70.

DiVitto, B., & Goldberg, S. (1979). The effect of newborn medical status on early parent–infant interactions. In T. Field, A. Sostek, D. Goldberg, & H.H. Shuman (Eds.), *Infants born at-risk.* New York: Spectrum.

Emde, R.N., Katz, E.L., & Thorpe, J.K. (1982). Emotional expression in infancy: II Early deviations in Down's Syndrome. In M. Lewis & L. Rosenblum (Eds.), *The development of affect.* NY: Plenum.

Fewell, R.R. (1986). The measurement of family functioning. In L. Bickman & D.L. Weatherford (Eds.), *Evaluating early intervention programs for severely handicapped children and their families* (pp. 253–307). Austin, TX: PRO-ED.

Field, T. (1979a). Interaction patterns of high-risk and normal infants. In T. Field, A. Sostek, S. Goldberg, & H.H. Shuman (Eds.), *Infants born at-risk* (pp. 317–335). New York: Spectrum.

Field, T. (1979b). Games parents play with normal and high-risk infants. *Child Psychiatry and Human Development. 10*, 41–49.

Field, T. (1983). High-risk infants "have less fun" during early interactions. *Topics in Early Childhood Special Education, 3*, 77–87.

Field, T., Dempsey, J., Ting, G., Hatch, J., & Clifton, R. (1979). Cardiac and behavioral responses to repeated tactile and auditory stimulation by preterm and full term infants during the neonatal period. *Developmental Psychology, 15*, 406–416.

Foley, G.M., & Hobin, M.S. (1987). *The attachment-separation-individuation (A-S-I) scale.* Reading, PA: Family Centered Resource Project.

Fraiberg, S. (1974). Blind infants and their mothers: An examination of the sign system. In M. Lewis & L.A. Rosenblum (Eds.), *The effect of the infant on its caregiver.* New York: John Wiley & Sons.

Gallagher, J.J., Beckman, P., & Cross, A.H. (1983). Families of handicapped children: Sources of stress and its amelioration. *Exceptional Children, 50*, 10–19.

Garrison, W.T., & Earls, F. (1985). The Child Behavior Checklist as a screening for young children. *Journal of the American Academy of Child Psychiatry, 24*(1), 76–80.

Gunn, P., Barry, P., & Andrews, R. (1979). Vocalizations and looking behavior of Down's Syndrome infants. *British Journal of Psychology, 70*, 259–263.

Guralnick, M.J., & Bennett, F.C. (1987). *The effectiveness of early intervention for at-risk and handicapped children.* Orlando, FL: Academic Press.

Hanson, M.J. (1984). Parent–infant interaction. In M.J. Hanson (Ed.), *Atypical infant development* (pp. 179–206). Baltimore: University Park Press.

Hewett, S. (1970). *The family and the handicapped child.* London: Allen & Unwin.

Holdgrafer, G., & Dunst, C. (1986). Communicative competence: From research to practice. *Topics in Early Childhood Special Education, 6*(3), 1–22.

Ireton, T.W., Hall, S., Dickson, K. (1986). *The Minnesota Child Development Inventory.* Minneapolis, MN: Behavioral Science Systems, Inc.

Ireton, H., & Thwing, E. (1972). *The Minnesota Child Development Inventory.* Minneapolis, MN: Behavioral Science System, Inc.

Johnson, N.M. (1983). Assessment pardigms and atypical infants: An intervention perspective. In D.D. Bricker (Ed.), *Intervention with at-risk and handicapped infants* (pp. 129–138). Baltimore: University Park Press.

Jones, O.H.M. (1977). Mother–child communication with prelinguistic Down syndrome and normal infants. In H.R. Schaffer (Ed.), *Studies in mother–infant interaction* (pp. 379–401). London: Academic Press.

Jones, O. (1978). A comparative study of mother-child communication with Down's Syndrome and normal infants. In H. Schaffer & J. Dunn (Eds.), *The first year of life: Psychological and medical implications of early experience* (pp. 175–195). New York: John Wiley & Sons.

Karnes, M.B., & Stayton, V.D. (1988). Model programs for infants and toddlers with handicaps. In J.B. Jordan, J.J. Gallagher, P.L. Hutinger, & M.B. Karnes (Eds.), *Early childhood special education-Birth to three.* Reston, VA: Council for Exceptional Children.

Kelly, J.F. (1982). Effects of intervention on caregiver-infant interaction when the infant is handicapped. *Journal of Early Childhood Special Education, 5*, 53–63.

Keogh, B.K., Pullis, M.E., & Cadwell, J. (1980). *Revised Parent Temperament Questionnaire.* Unpublished report, Project REACH, University of California, Los Angeles.

Kogan, K.L. (1980). Interaction systems between preschool aged handicapped or developmentally delayed children and their parents. In T. Field, S. Goldberg, D. Stern, & A. Soster (Eds.), *High-risk infants and children: Adult and peer interactions* (pp. 227–247). New York: Academic Press.

Krakow, J., & Kopp, C. (1983). The effects of developmental delay on sustained attention in young children. *Child Development, 54*, 1143–1155.

Leland, H., Shoace, M., McElwain, D., & Christie, R. (1980). *Adaptive behavior scale for infants and early childhood.* ABSI, manual. Columbus, OH: Nisonger Center, Ohio State University.

Linder, T. (1982). Pleasurable play: Its value to handicapped children and their parents. *Journal for Special Educators, 19*(1), 59–68.

Linder, T.W. (1993). *Transdisciplinary play-based intervention: Guidelines for developing a meaningful curriculum for young children.* Baltimore: Paul H. Brookes Publishing Co.

Linder, T.W. (1999). *Read, Play, and Learn!: Storybook activities for young children. Teacher's guide.* Baltimore: Paul H. Brookes Publishing Co.

Lynch, W.E., & Stein, R. (1982). Perspectives on parent participation in special education. *Exceptional Education Quarterly, 3*(2), 56–63.

Mahler, M., Pine, F., & Bergman, A. (1975). *The psychological birth of the infant.* New York: Random House.

Mahoney, G., & Powell, A. (1986). *The transactional intervention program: A child-centered approach to developmental intervention with young handicapped children.* Farmington, CT: Pediatric Research and Training Center.

Mahoney, G., Powell, A., & Finger, I. (1986). The maternal behavior rating scale. *Topics in Early Childhood Special Education, 6*(2), 44–55.

Mogford, K. (1977). The play of handicapped children. In B. Tizard & D. Harvey (Eds.), *Biology of play.* Philadelphia: J.B. Lippincott.

Morgan, D.P., & Rhode, G. (1983). Teacher attitudes toward IEP's: A two year follow-up. *Exceptional Children, 50*(1), 64–67.

Morgan, G.A., Harmon, R.J., Pipp, S., & Jennings, K.D. (1983). *Assessing infants perception of mastery motivation: Utility of momm questionnaire.* Unpublished manuscript. Colorado State University, Fort Collins.

Musick, J.S., Clark, R., & Cohler, B. (1981). The mother's project: A program for mentally ill mothers of very young children. In B. Weissbaurd & J. Musick (Eds.), *Infants and their social environment* (pp. 111–128). Washington, D.C.: National Association for the Education of Young Children.

Newborg, J., Stock, J., Wnek, L., Guidubaldi, J., & Svinicki, J. (1984). *Battelle Developmental Inventory.* Allen, TX: DLM Teaching Resources.

Persson-Blennow, I., & McNeil, T.F. (1979). A questionnaire for measurement of temperament in six-month old infants: Development and standardization. *Journal of Child Psychology and Psychiatry, 20,* 1–13.

Robinson, C.C., Rosenberg, S.A., & Beckman, P.V. (1988). Parent involvement in early childhood special education. In J.B. Jordan, J.J. Gallagher, P.L. Hutinger, & M.B. Karnes (Eds.), *Early childhood special education: Birth to three* (pp. 109–127). Reston, VA: Council for Exceptional Children.

Rosenberg, S.A. (1986). Measures of parent-infant interaction: An overview. *Topics in Early Childhood Special Education, 6*(2), 32–43.

Rothbart, M.K. (1984). Social Development. In M. Hanson (Ed.), *Atypical infant development* (pp. 207–236). Austin, TX: PRO-ED.

Rothbart, M.K., & Hanson, M. (1983). A care-giver report comparison of temperament characteristics of Down syndrome and normal infants. *Developmental Psychology, 19,* 766–769.

Sigman, M., Cohen, S.E., & Forsythe, A.B. (1981). The relations of early infant measures to later development. In S.L. Friedman & M. Sigman (Eds.), *Preterm birth and psychological development.* New York: Academic Press.

Smith, B.L., & Oller, D.K. (1981). A comparative study of pre-meaningful vocalizations produced by normally developing Down's Syndrome infants. *Journal of Speech and Hearing Disorders. 46,* 46–51.

Soufer, R.M. (1982). IEP decisions in which parents desire greater participation. *Education & Training of the Mentally Retarded, 17*(2) 67–70.

Sparrow, S.S., Balla, D.A., & Cicchetti, D.V. (1984). *Vineland adaptive behavior scales.* Circle Pines, MN: American Guidance Service.

Stevenson, M.B., Leavitt, L.A., & Silverberg, S.B. (1985). Mother–infant interaction: Down syndrome case studies. In S. Harel & N.J. Anastasiow (Eds.), *The at-risk infant: Psycho/socio/medical aspects* (pp. 389–395). Baltimore: Paul H. Brookes Publishing Co.

Thoman, E.B., Becker, P.T., & Freese, M.P. (1978). Individual patterns of mother–infant interaction. In G. Sackett (Ed.), *Observing behavior, Vol. 1: Theory and application in mental retardation, 1,* Baltimore: University Park Press.

Thomas, A., Chess, S., & Birch, H.G. (1968). *Temperament and behavior disorders in children.* New York: New York University Press.

Thomas, A., Chess, S., Birch, H.G., Herzig, M.E., & Korn, S. (1963). *Behavioral individuality in early childhood.* New York: New York University Press.

Turnbull, A.P., & Turnbull, H.R. (Eds.). (1986). *Families, professionals and exceptionality: A special partnership.* Columbus, OH: Charles E. Merrill.

Turnbull, A.P., & Winton, P.S. (1984). Parent involvement in policy and practice: Current research for families of young severely handicapped children. In J. Blacher (Ed.), *Severely handicapped young children and their families: Research in review* (pp. 377–397). Orlando, FL: Academic Press.

Turnbull, H.R., Turnbull, A.P., & Wheat, M.J. (1982). Assumptions about parental participation: A legislative history. *Exceptional Education Quarterly, 3*(2), 1–8.

Vincent, L., Davis, J., Brown, P., Broome, K., Funkhouser, K., Miller, J., & Grunewald, L. (1986). *The Parent Inventory of Child Development in Nonschool Environments.* Madison, WI: Department of Rehabilitation Psychology and Special Education.

Vincent, L., Davis, J., Brown, P., Teicher, J., & Weynand, P. (1983). *Daily Routine Recording Form,* Unpublished paper. University of Wisconsin, Dept. of Rehabilitation Psychology and Special Education, Madison, WI.

Vincent, L., Laten, S., Salisbury, C., Brown, P., & Baumgart, D. (1981). Family involvement in the educational processes of severely handicapped students: State of the art and directions for the future. In B. Wilcox & R. York (Eds.), *Quality education for the severely handicapped: The federal investment.* Washington, DC: U.S. Dept. of Education.

Welsh, M.A., & Odom, C.S. (1981). Parental involvement in the education of the handicapped child: A review of the literature. *Journal of the Division of Early Childhood, 3,* 15–25.

White, B., & Watts, J. (1973). *Experience and environment: Major influence on the development of the young child.* Englewood Cliffs, NJ: Prentice-Hall.

Index